Christ Crucified

CHRIST CRUCIFIED

K. SCHILDER, Ph. D.

A Sequel to
CHRIST IN HIS SUFFERING
and
CHRIST ON TRIAL

Translated from the Dutch
by
HENRY ZYLSTRA

THIRD EDITION

WM. B. EERDMANS PUBLISHING CO.
Grand Rapids, Michigan
1948

Many of the merits and none of the defects of this translation are owing to Dr. Henry Beets, who carefully read and edited the manuscript.

—The Translator.

FOREWORD

THIS volume completes Dr. Schilder's Trilogy on the Passion of our blessed Lord.

"And I, if I be lifted up from the earth, will draw all men unto myself."

All manner of men.

All kinds of people.

In many different lands.

This statement of our Lord still rings through time with ever increasing force.

It is proclaimed by tongue, by pen and by brush of all those who love Him, and who look for His appearing.

Professor Schilder as an orator lifts up the Christ and draws men unto Him.

As a pen-artist he pictures the Lord as One altogether lovely and much to be desired.

This particular volume has to do with Christ in the deepest agony of His suffering. He went into the valley of death, but came out as the Victor over Satan and his hosts, leading a great company of sons and daughters to the glory of salvation here, and everlasting life hereafter. *Christ in His Suffering*, and *Christ on Trial*, the two volumes already published, enjoyed a fine welcome. The publishers now offer the last volume in this trilogy to the English speaking world.

In our day the forces of darkness and light are pitted against each other in more definite battle array than ever before. But, strange to say, the brotherhood of believers, the ecumenic character of Christendom, looms larger than ever before.

Men and women of all lands cling closer to the Cross and to the wounded side of the Crucified One than in days of national quietude and material prosperity.

There is an inner conviction and a strong faith that after all Jesus is THE PILOT of the vessel which carries His chosen ones.

Dr. Schilder, in this monumental trilogy, has rendered a real service to the Christian Church.

HENRY BEETS, LL.D.

Grand Rapids, Mich.

CONTENTS

CONTENTS—Continued

Christ Being Cast Outside of the Gates

CHAPTER ONE

Christ Being Cast Outside of the Gates

● *And they took Jesus, and led him away. And he bearing his cross went forth into a place called the place of a skull, which is called in the Hebrew Golgotha.*

JOHN 19:16b-17.

CHRIST is sinking deeper, ever deeper, into His passion. We saw Him made an exlex:[1] that is, one whom men have thrust outside of the sphere of law. Thereupon He was sentenced to death: He was condemned. But now He plunges even deeper into the shaft of humiliation. He is about to be *accursed*. For He goes now to be put to death on the cross, and "accursed is everyone, that hangeth on the tree." We shall be compelled to return to that curse, and to the meaning of the word itself, several times during the course of this book. Much of its significance must for the time being be postponed.

The thing we want to discuss now, as Jesus Christ goes out to the place of curse, is the awful weight of the justice of God which puts upon Christ a burden which to our mind is a superhuman one. This burden God places upon Him in order that He may reach out from this maze of sin, from this knot of human falsehood, from these skeins of arbitrariness and injustice, in which He has become entangled and been taken captive thus far — may reach out, we say, to the firm hand of His God in order to submit to His justice, painful as it may be. He must submit to His justice now, to the one justice of God. That, and nothing else, He must do.

For we can truly say that from the human side there is nothing but injustice here. We have seen that before,[1] and shall say noth-

---

1. In the several chapters of *Christ on Trial*, the preceding (second) volume of this trilogy.

ing about it now. However, there is a difference between one kind of injustice and another. The world knows of a kind of injustice which, terrible though it may be, nevertheless is characterized by a certain consistency and pattern; obstinately it draws up its own program and never lets itself be deflected from the logic it has first chosen. But there is also an injustice which can hardly be said to be characterized by any consistency or pattern. In this kind of injustice logic is quite lacking; it gives no one an opportunity to know what it is all about.

It is this second kind of injustice which accrued to Jesus. Must we take time to prove that? Surely not, for that has become obvious again and again as we followed the pathetic maze of the trial. But there is one thing which we want to emphasize particularly now. This one thing is precisely a question of pattern, of consistency, of inherent logic. We mean the sequence of the several states of justice in which the people placed Christ on public display, or are still to place Him.

This is that sequence of events: first, Christ the *exlex*. Thereupon, Christ *condemned*. Finally, Christ *accursed*. Now this sequence of events in the trial of Christ is essentially and even from a purely human point of view sheer nonsense. We use the word seriously — we mean that the logic of this course of events is outright nonsense. There is no logic in it, and, observed precisely from the human point of view, there is neither rhyme nor reason in it.

That conclusion comes very naturally. For, after all, it is only after a person has been condemned first, and accursed afterwards, that he can, at the end of his trial, be placed outside of the sphere of the law, outside of the "gates" of justice. Plainly, a person can be an exlex only when the law has exhausted itself in reference to him. This is a person's right, for everyone is born in a context of law. And this is also the prerogative of law. It need not give up its task before it has exhausted itself; until then it need not give its province, its status, its prerogative of meting out punishment and of concluding cases to any other. Obviously, then, the exlex cannot be proclaimed that until the end of the trial. That is as plain as day.

Condemnation, then, legal *condemnation* is quite impossible except in a context of *law*. In order to condemn anyone all the machinery of the legal structure must be set in motion against a person. Condemnation can indeed be defined as a mobilization of the machinery of law against a guilty party. And if the curse is to be added to the condemnation, if, considered negatively, even the least privileges which the law still gives its worst enemies are denied, and if, considered positively, the condemned person is to be made the victim of every method of perdition which the law can possibly heap upon one, then, and then only, can the guilty one be constituted a curse and regarded as standing outside of the province of law. The law has nothing further to add to an accursed party who has been condemned first of all by the powerful but pure pressure of the law. All that the law can add after that is the confirmation and the complete execution of its final statement, as well by negative as by positive means. The law which as the exacting principle and as the exacting force has pronounced its judgment is satisfied then; the thirst of the law is quenched then by the condemned blood.

This would as a matter of fact be the course of all condemned people in the world, and this would be the end of the whole matter, if all the laws which obtain in human society did not in a certain sense contain an element of grace. Does that statement, possibly, surprise anyone? If so, we do well to remember that it is a Biblical idea, which we sometimes pass over too rapidly. On the whole we are thoroughly convinced that the law is *opposed* to us, that it condemns, and curses, and protests against us; but we too often forget that the law nevertheless is characterized by an element of grace.

Indeed, the law has a twofold grace in it: a negative grace inasmuch as it does not place the full burden of its wrath upon us while we are here below; and a positive grace to the extent that it never, here on earth, isolates anyone from the dispensation and purpose of the grace of God.

Those are two separate concepts. We must study each one of them more specifically.

In the first place, the law which God gives men, puts in the language of men, writes with a human pen into a human book, can never in its expression completely embody or exhaust the unmixed concept of the wrath of God. Moreover, it cannot in its execution completely administer the whole wrath of God. Now as far as the expression of the law is concerned it can never, being phrased in human language as it is, be as powerful as God Himself. What is true of the law is also true of God's written Word, and of all forms of revelation. Revelation is true and genuine, but it is not complete, is not exhaustive; it cannot express everything contained in the depths of God's being. Just as all Scripture is *revelation* but God Himself always remains richer than His spoken Word, just so the word of the law, which, as we know, also belongs to God's revelation, merely approximates and never reaches the completeness of the essence of God Himself. God's wrath is more terrible than the law can define. What holds true of the Gospel terms of redemption also holds true of the legal terms of condemnation: they say a great deal, they tell the truth, but they do not tell the whole truth. So much for the *word* of the law. What now in reference to the *deed* of the law. The law, we know, also determines the penalty, assigns the punishment, and, even here on earth, administers the penalty. But all the penalty which the law can effect here below, terrible as it may be, is never so terrible as it can be. It can be as terrible as it is in hell. But hell is not realized on the earth. The chasms which the wrath of God will some day open there are deeper and darker than any into which the law can plunge us while we are on earth. Therefore the law in this world is always limited, limited by itself, in its threats and also in the active administration of God's wrath.

That is the first point which bears on the situation with which we are dealing here. There is a second point. We said that the law in this dispensation is never independent of the dispensing and the purpose of grace. The proclaiming of the law is an act of grace. Yes, it is an act of judgment, but it is first of all an act of grace. The fact that the law makes its threatenings heard is an expression of grace. Indeed, it is also an expression of judgment, but it is first of all an expression of grace.[1] For the law comes into a world which, even where special grace has not achieved a domain for itself, nevertheless lives by common grace. No single, practical execution of a penalty taking place in the world by human agency, human words, and human instruments can ever isolate itself from the common grace which is active in the world. If it should ever happen that someone in some far corner of the world

---

1. Think of "the vicious circle," *Christ on Trial*, pp. 58 ff., 126 ff., 153 ff., 514 ff.

should be annihilated by the full energy of wrath inherent in the Lawgiver, an exhaustive effluence of the vengeance dwelling in the heart of God, we would find that the world would burst, would fly apart in that particular corner. At that point the world would begin to be rent in twain. For wherever the waves of the wrath of God beat against the head of a sinner on earth, that wave meets with the resistance of common grace. True, the wave of wrath will overcome the grace. That is natural. For who could hope to thwart God's wrath and who could think that the weaker element — the common grace — could resist the stronger and definitive element — the eternal power and love of justice. Yes, indeed, the wave of wrath will break through the resistance of common grace. But it is also true that the wave of wrath is tempered by it. It was God's own will that this should be so. Perhaps we can make the matter clearer to each other by the use of a figure. You have seen the sun. You know that its rays are weakened by the atmosphere. Light is mitigated by it and loses some of its radiance because of it; moreover, shadows are also tempered by it and lose something of their undesirable darkness because of it. Or, to make it more vivid, think of the heavenly bodies which are not surrounded by an atmosphere. You know that worlds not surrounded by an atmosphere send out untempered rays, and that there, consequently, the rays which are dispatched are far more penetrating and the shadows much darker than they are on earth. From this, now, you can glean some sense of the difference between *hell* and *earth*. Here we are surrounded by the atmosphere of common grace; here, therefore, the rays of God's love are tempered, and the waves of God's wrath are mitigated also. There is not a single form of execution on earth which gives full expression to the exacting hunger of the justice of the chief Author of the law. For example, Christ could not punish the Antichrist in this world and at this time as He could the sinner who is to be beaten with the fewest stripes in hell.[1] Accordingly, we do well to keep these two thoughts in mind. First, the law, as the Word of God, can never give complete expression to its legal will. Second, this world, as the stage and workroom of common grace, can never satisfy the hunger of God's exacting justice completely, nor perfectly execute the justice of His will. Remembering those two

---

1. Luke 12: 47, 48.

things, you will catch a faint glimpse of the terrible significance of
the word *curse*. And then you will also understand why the justice
which God has proclaimed among the people of *special revelation*
can make someone an exlex even on this earth.

That we must consider now. Readers of *Christ on Trial* will
perhaps feel inclined to say: But now you are contradicting what
you said in the other book. For there we did indeed say that God
does not acknowledge, He does not recognize, He does not know,
the exlex. Yes, we said that. And we insist that it is so.[1] There
is no conflict whatever between these two contentions. God does
not recognize the exlex, and the law of God in Israel shows us the
exlex. The first thesis — God does not know the exlex — is one
which speaks of God Himself. If we study the justice of God,
as it exists in Him, as He knows and experiences it in the depths
of His being, as it cries out aloud for satisfaction from His profound abysses and as it is carried out in hell, we must say: There
is not a single thing, there is not a single person, there is not a
single phenomenon which from God's point of view is not connected with the law of God. Hell, we know, is the place where
God exercises His justice to the fullest extent and where not the
slightest remnant of common grace resists the penetrating rays of
His wrath.

But the situation changes when we look upon it as it is *here on
earth*. In this world, as we stated above, the law and the wrath of
God cannot express themselves fully nor find those forms which
completely embody God's most exacting wrath. Here on earth,
consequently, there is a certain unconsumable, a certain inexpres-
sible and unadministrable, remnant of wrath. The thunders of
wrath which cause us to tremble now, or of which we dream in
our boldest probings or dogmatic speculations must always be such
as to leave room for a more awful thunder which has never yet
been heard in earthly sounds; there is, to the apprehension of
faith, always a wrath which cannot be executed by the instruments
of punishment and of torture which this world has been able to
forge and set in motion.

This unconsumed remnant of wrath it is which is acknowledged
in Israel by the concept of curse, and by the concept of the exlex
which is its corollary. Hence the curse operates in the realm of

---

1. See *Christ on Trial*, pp. 185 f., 421.

special grace; precisely there, in the realm of special revelation. Therefore the curse is operative in *Israel*. O sublime majesty of God, O majesty of the God of the Word, terrible art Thou. Who can stand before Thee? When men, when the judges, when the priests of Israel pronounce the curse, then the curse is their strongest gesture. But it is also the weakest thing they can do. For those who curse and make the criminal an exlex are saying: Lord, we can go no farther; we have reached the limits of our law. No profounder judgment is possible to us and yet we know, O God, that we have not gone far enough, that Thou canst see and say things more profoundly, that Thou wouldst punish further. Lord, here is the candidate for the torment of hell; we can go no farther . . . Surely, it is a sad day for the ministers of justice in God's theocratic country when they must utter such things to God and man.

Hence when someone in Israel is first of all condemned, then accursed, and finally made an exlex, nothing is being done in conflict with the austere proclamation of hell according to which, as we said, the exlex is not known. For the exlex in Israel, who has been made exlex after having been condemned and accursed, embodies in his dumb death this very preaching of hell. We can say that He is being pushed in hell's direction, but that the hands of the judge do not reach quite far enough. The people, the judges, and those who maintain the laws among the people of revelation, all cry out to God: We can do no more to this object of wrath. Nothing that can be conceived by the human mind and carried out by human instruments can now be done to Him. Therefore we say that He is an exlex. We transfer Him to the Lord. Let the birds feed on Him, the children play with His tattered clothing, and the wolves feed on His corpse, for He that hangeth on a tree is a curse to the Lord.

Therefore the exlex in Israel — that is as long as Israel is faithful to itself and to its Lawgiver — is not an invention of the judges who, like Pilate and the others, overlook the law, but it is an acknowledgment of the judges, an acknowledgment of the fact that their appreciation of the law and their execution of the law is imperfect; it is an acknowledgment of the fact that God's thunders are sublimer and His punishments more perfect in the other world. There, in that other world, the law is expressed not in human phraseology but by an unrestrained effluence of God's wrath, without a hint of the restraint of common grace.

We can understand, therefore, why the concept of the exlex was introduced into the law in Israel; in the law, that is, that they first had to put a condemned man to death and after that hang him upon the tree. The hanging on the tree embodied a curse, the curse of Jahweh. In Israel, consequently, a course was followed which was diametrically opposed to the one pursued in the presence of Pilate, of Herod, of Caiaphas, and Annas. God's word took a different course. In the presence of the judges the sequence of events was such that each of the four first made Christ an exlex, then a condemned man (by agreeing with Pilate), and then an accursed man, when they proceeded to hang Him on the cross. For these all do indeed curse Him. That becomes apparent from a correspondence between the narrative of John and the synoptic gospels. The synoptic gospels tell us that the military leaders of Rome led Jesus to the place of curse which was Golgotha, but John emphasizes the fact that it was the high priests who led Jesus away.[1] They did the supervising and pointed out the way: "We have a law and according to our law He must be put to death." And Pilate had held them to that word.

Those are the stages followed by the judges: exlex, condemnation, and curse. That is what Pilate, and Herod, and the Sanhedrin, all of whom have abandoned God's Word and no longer tremble before the concept of the exlex,[2] wish. Now this course of events is in diametrical opposition to the Word of God and the Law as these were entrusted to Israel. Had the course of the law which God had given by revelation been followed, the sequence of events would have been different: first the condemnation, then the curse (the deed), and finally the proclamation of the exlex. The second is the course things should have taken — that is what God would have wished in every case from every human being. Note the adjectives: *every* case and *every* human being.

Learn to tremble, O man, before the great day of Golgotha. We return to our point of departure. We say: now the Christ must be very careful to keep the legal action of God carefully dis-

---

1. The chief priests are discussed in John 19:15, and the 16th verse also mentions them. Compare Nebe, *op. cit.*, p. 166.
2. See *Christ in His Suffering*, pp. 169 ff., 173 ff.

tinguished from the crooked activity of the people, even of His own people. And what distinction does He make? Pay close attention. He sees very clearly that what God would forbid and prevent in any other case, for any other human being, God is Himself now doing to Him. The sequence of events which God would characterize as a violation of the law if followed in the case of the meanest slave, of Achan the thief, of the sons of Rizpah, of Korah and his band, or anyone, God Himself approves of in the trial of the Saviour. Exlex first, then condemnation, and finally the curse. He was an exlex already. His doom has been sealed. Now He goes to the cross — and accursed is every one that hangs upon the tree, that is cast "outside of the gate."

This is a sad day. God's sequence of events is always different from that of Jesus' judges, but today He appropriates and accepts their own program of activity. Why did these judges of Jesus begin with the idea of the exlex? Because they had themselves as judges first of all abandoned the law. Now God accompanies them. The least among the accursed of Abraham's lost children has more right than Jesus to be legally condemned in terms of the law and in virtue of the voice of the law and not until then to be condemned and hanged as a curse. God grants His Son less than that. Even the sons of Saul, whom Rizpah wanted to keep from becoming exlex, were treated genuinely, that is, according to the logic of the Word of God. Put to death first, and then made a curse. Mary, afflicted mother, is God less concerned about your Son than about the sons of Rizpah? Who will help us out of this bewildering maze? Who will give us the key to the explanation? Judge of Israel, must not Christ Jesus be treated as the least of earth's disgraced ones are treated: condemnation first, the curse next, the exlex only then — abandoned to the God vengeance only then? Lord, this world is a topsy-turvy world; the whole of the legal structure is turned upside down in dealing with Thy Son. He became an exlex at His *first* entrance into the courthouse, and was that at every stage which followed. Of course, on the part of Pilate and of Herod and of Caiaphas and of them all, this was a sin. But can we say that God imitates this wickedness? Is such evil compatible with God's holy justice? Can the God of truth triumph through such crooked transactions?

Yes, God answers. These things must take place thus in this unique hour, in reference to this unique defendant. God's justice was poured out through the funnel of men's crooked dealings. The key to the explanation lies contained in a single word. That word is Suretyship. All these things must happen thus because the Christ, who is suffering here as the Surety, had to suffer the sorrow of being an exlex *not after but before His death.*

Be very cautious now, be very careful, for the place on which you are standing is holy ground. However, do not be silent about what the *Scriptures* teach you. And the Scriptures teach us that Christ is taking up His cross here *as the Surety,* and that as the Surety He goes to the place of curse as a condemned man. As the *Surety* Christ now comes to pay the debt which His people have made. The chastisement of our peace was upon Him. Now a part of that chastisement which brings our peace was that we in *this* world, overagainst this earth, and overagainst common grace become exlex. Every sinner must *know* that the punishment which he has earned is always more terrible than the modes of penalty and the words of punishment that obtain on earth. And after that the pain and penalty of hell awaits him. After that — that is, after his death. But if the Christ also were to suffer the pain of hell after His bodily death, *He could not be our Mediator.* For the mediatorship must not only repay God but it must completely settle for God's wrath. The indebtedness must be completely stricken. There must be an end, there must be finality, when the Mediator pays God, in the stead of His own. Without that there could be no *It is finished.*

Therefore the torment of hell, the penalty of hell, the infinite, the incomparable pain which comes to all others who die outside of God *after* death, must accrue to Christ *before* He dies. The whole mystery of the descent into hell, as it is regarded, among others, by the Heidelberg Catechism, is based on that thought; and the same concept is emphasized in the fifth and sixth Lord's Days of this Catechism. There, too, we confess that the Mediator who is to truly redeem us must consciously experience in His earthly life, before His death, before His departure from the world and from the circumference of time, that which the lost human being will suffer after his death and on the other side of this bourne. Before the Mediator can say "It is finished," the eternal punish-

ment, the eternal, perfect expression of an unrestrained and un-
bounded wrath of God must be endured and left behind. Not after
His death, understand, but before His death. Not in the other
world, but in this world. Not when He has been hurled from this
earth, outside of "our" domain — the domain of the vicious circle, and of common grace — but here in our world, in our life, in
our earthly home of common grace and of "common" wrath.

We expect to say more of these things later in this book when
we reach the dark chapter of Christ's suffering in hell and of His
fourth utterance on the cross: "My God, My God, why hast
Thou *forsaken* me?"

But if we may be allowed to anticipate a little of that now we
shall do so simply to free Christ exlex from the caricatured versions of Israel's and of Pilate's vitiation of law, and to teach our
soul that both the idea and its realization finds its rightful place
only in the true course of justice in which God — our God —
punishes the Surety — our Surety — and makes Him to be sin
for us.

Rejoice, O my soul! What man had intended for evil, God
turned into good. In all other trials it may, from God's point of
view, be an atrocity if anyone becomes an exlex before he is condemned and accursed, but in this hour of the Surety that very
thing happened in accordance with God's holy logic. "What is
truth?" This is truth. "What is justice?" This is justice. The
lawgiver opens and closes the doors of law according to His good
pleasure and that in the last analysis is simply the end of the
matter.

You ask what the chief Lawgiver would teach us at this time?
He teaches us the obligation of the Surety to be the exlex, fully
conscious of its implications while here in His human life. Just
as Christ suffered the pain of hell before His bodily death, fully
conscious the while of all of it, so also He suffered the pain of the
exlex, the misery of which had always been depicted by the Word
in Israel as the beginning, the first phase of the transition to the
condemnation of hell. This, too, He must suffer during His life,
before His death, and with a full consciousness of all of its import.

Praise the Lord, O my soul, with all thy strength. Out of the
chaos of the illogical ideas of those who vitiate the law He builds
the cosmos of the ideas of the Logos according to His justice. In

this the greatness of Christ is preached to us. Our second volume[1] is really explained by the third, even though the third lay contained in the second. For now it appears that Christ's descent into hell — which must be taken to mean His suffering of the pain of hell — did not impinge upon Jesus suddenly, mechanically, without a gradual transition, when, on the cross, He had the assured feeling that He has been forsaken of God. No, that descent into hell was a gradual, an "organic" — alas, our pathetically inadequate language — development, growing out of the day of His death. The passion of hell therefore was a slow but certain process. The descent into hell? That begins in the presence of Annas, when Jesus is struck on the cheek. Then Christ had already been made the exlex. Then He knew that these people could go no farther. He knew that they had done their utmost to Him. A servant struck Him: He felt His cheeks being struck by God. He knew with perfect certainty that He was a child of hell. For now He was the exlex who — you will remember — was thrust outside of the door of the domain of thought and activity in Israel, and was in God's name pushed into the no man's land of hell and condemnation. He was the exlex — the sheer outcast . . . Jesus is caught between two worlds: the world of human law and human punishment can do nothing further about him; and the world in which God exhausts His laws and perfectly satisfies them has not yet consumed Him. He is brought to no man's land — between two fronts: the front of men and the front of God, the front of this world and that of the other. And no man's land is also every man's land — anyone may do to the exlex what he wishes.

Christ, then, knew He was the exlex already at the time of the preliminary hearing. That was at the very beginning. That is saying nothing about what follows. In all that followed Christ remained the exlex. He felt the same cruel pain of being an outcast as He stood before the Sanhedrin, before Herod, and also before Pilate. And now Christ is being led to the workshop of the curse. They press the cross upon His shoulders; He had better carry that Himself. Each step which He takes now is taken with a full consciousness that He is condemned, that He is condemned

---

1. *Christ on Trial.*

of God, that God has already forsaken Him, that God is awaiting Him with the untempered pains of hell.

To go on, however, God's program, God's sequence of events, has not yet been announced. As we ponder that, we get a better insight into the necessity of the fact that Christ has to accomplish His departure in *Jerusalem*. Faith is willing to acknowledge also the *place* in which Jesus dies. He gives up His life in Jerusalem, the city which was entrusted with the Word of *revelation*. This, too, is not a mere accident, not a disconnected particular. He could die in no other place, because in no other place could he recognize in the crooked transactions of people who are making Him an exlex the holy sequence, the sacred program, of the God who is making Him an exlex.

We must consider that fact now. First of all we note the city of *Jerusalem*. Even though the Saviour was condemned by Pilate, and even though the law of Rome cast Him out of center and suburb of the *world*, Jesus may not forget for a single instant that He must stand and fall in the country, the city, of *Israel*. He must reduce the wicked dealings of the *heathen* in reference to Himself to the straight ways of the God of Israel.

But how is He to find His *God* in these, and how is He to understand *God's* language, if He does not read the Word and live by it, if He does not always keep the law of Israel clearly before His spirit? He may not allow the roll of the book of Israel, the Scriptures, to recede from His awareness. For Israel is still the people of revelation; Jerusalem is still the "holy city." This city, and this road, and the *via dolorosa* also are still subsidiary parts of the sacred inheritance in which special revelation makes itself known. The plan of Jerusalem is something more than a mere topographical thing; it is the plan of the ecclesiastical city. It will be that until God sends out the apostles by means of the Spirit to preach and to baptize in front of the rent veil of the temple.

Obviously, now, if Christ separates the disorganization of this human legal process from Jerusalem, and from the sacred roll of law, He is lost. For — as we said — the people are putting the concept of His being the exlex in the wrong place. They have wrenched the proper sequence of events apart. That which had to come last, the exlex, they placed at the very beginning. The heathen did this, yes, but also the Jews who have abandoned the word of God. Observed from the human point of view, therefore, the carrying out of the concept of Christ-exlex, precisely because it was placed at the very beginning, was an act of superficiality. In such an act one can detect only the flippancy of men, and none of the seriousness of God. And if Christ should explain the people in terms of the people now, without reference to the Word of Jahweh, His status as the exlex will not be able to depress Him. On the contrary, He will then simply be able, overagainst God, to appeal to this fact, saying: I caused them no difficulty, no hard work. Lord, my God, I am therefore not affected by it in the least. The indigestible food of the laws of Thy kingdom they have converted into easily digested bread. They began with the concept of the exlex, and they should have ended with it. Then the fact that he had been made an exlex prematurely, an untimely exlex, would have been the apology of the accused overagainst His judges. Then God would not have been acknowledged in the present, in the naked facts of this historical day.

But Christ *did not say that*. He was not allowed to find an excuse for Himself in the crookedness of the human procedure. He who would be the Surety may not look for excuses. He who must descend into hell today must not appeal to the higher court of the morrow. Nor was He allowed to explain the people in terms of the people nor the particular day in terms of the particular day. Had he not fiercely protested against that very thing Himself? No, let the Christ Himself first of all bear the burdens which He places upon the shoulders of others. Let Him look at everything which overtakes Him in the holy city in the light of the sacred Word of Revelation which still lies exposed in that city and still awaits *Him* only. For the Word of Revelation is indeed still in Jerusalem, and it is presenting one request: Keep me clearly in mind. Am I still an integral part of your experience? Am I? And if Christ does *this,* two things become clear to Him, become fixed in His spirit, draw the blood out of Him, very terrible, but in righteousness. Those two things are these: first, that the passion of the exlex is the beginning of the descent into hell; and, second, that He must die *outside* of the city gates *within* which He has been declared an exlex.

This in reference to the first consideration. Only among the people of revelation is the exlex one who has been surrendered to

hell. Wherever else the concept is used, the exlex is a foolish fig-
ment of the human imagination, an act of robbery committed
against the law and against its awful tension. Everywhere else
— save in the legal system of Israel's God. There to the extent
that the Word is being faithfully followed, the exlex first experienced what the law had in it to inflict, and only after that was
humiliated beyond the point which human language can express
and the deed which human beings can execute. Everywhere in
the world the placing in pillory of the exlex by human beings is
an evasive attempt to escape from the law, and a closing the ears
to the thunder of the law. But in Israel the Word of Revelation
says this: When our ears are tingling with the thunder of the law,
and man can go no farther, then the condemned person is the exlex. In Israel, consequently, the exlex has not been segregated
from the pressure of law, but has been subjected to a more than
human tension.

That is why Jesus dies in *the city of the Word*. True, His
judges have freed themselves from the pressure, but He personally, as the accused, must feel that extra-human tension. Jerusalem, Jerusalem, you are still necessary. They cannot get along
without you. You are the only city in which Christ can stand
under the pressure of the Word. You are the only city in which
He as the accused can overcome the sin of the judges. You are
the only city in which He — the Author of the sermon on the
mount! — cannot derive an excuse before God from the sins of
men in an effort to escape from the awful pressure of hell upon
Him.

You are the only city in which He cannot *today* appeal to tomorrow, before the higher Judge. For the *highest Judge was
present in the room*. Here Christ is directly bound to the Word,
here He softly whispers to Himself: Away with all self-defense
by means of an appeal to their superficiality, for thus it is meet
for me to fulfill all righteousness.

So much for the first consideration. Now the second. Jesus
sees Himself being rejected and thrown outside of the gates of
Jerusalem. This circumstance, too, He must relate to the laws
of the people of Israel. Again the consideration holds true that
Jerusalem does not just happen to be the city in which the history
of the passion takes place. It is the only place in which the Lamb

of God could die outside of the gates, in which He could die as one unclean and accursed before the Lord God.

We mentioned the *Lamb* of God. That is a name which Christ puts into relationship with the law of sacrifice of — Israel. That law of sacrifice, that Word of God, which declares that Christ is the exlex, is also the only law which can proclaim that He is the sacrificial Lamb. The sacrificial Lamb — are there any priests in the neighborhood? Yes, indeed. We have pointed out already[1] that, as John tells us, it is the high priests who take the lead in the matter of this day's execution. After all, they have cast Christ outside of the city gates. We said just a moment ago that we could not do without Jerusalem. Well, we cannot do without the priests either.

We cannot do without the priests. Now for the first time Christ's being taken out, Christ's being led away, becomes a sharply delineated, separate moment in the passion of Christ. All of the gospels tell us that He went forth, that He was led out of doors, that He was thrust outside of the city gates. Now if Christ places this act of rejection into relationship with the place where it happened, He will say to Himself: I am being thrust outside of the domain of sacred words and works. Exlex, yes, and exile also. Outside of the law and outside of the country! No, no one may segregate the gospel narrative of their leading Jesus outside of the gate from the dogmatic statement: "For the bodies of those beasts, whose blood is brought into the sanctuary by the high priest for sin, are burned without the camp. Wherefore Jesus also, that he might sanctify the people with his own blood, suffered without the gate" (*Hebrews* 13:11-12). The writer of these words is recalling a regulation stipulated in *Leviticus* 16:27. There we are told that the flesh and skins of the bullocks and goats offered for a sin offering had to be brought without the camp. Obviously, the body of these beasts which were slain for a sacrifice is "done away with as unclean, and there is no more fellowship between the people in the camp and the sin laden sacrificial animal."[2] Now this stipulation of law centuries ago fixed in the minds of all,

---

1. *Christ on Trial*, p. 540 f. and p. 546; also this volume, p. 22.
2. Grosheide, *De Brief aan de Hebreeuwen en de Brief van Jakobus*, A'dam, Bottenburg, 1927, p. 381.

— and in reference to Christ — that that which was brought without the gates, without the camp, might no longer be regarded as clean. Because it is unclean it does not belong in the fellowship of the clean.

Can you feel now how grievously Jesus is being humiliated here? So often we human beings think: well, presently the pain and humiliation will begin, presently — when the nails are driven through His hands. We like to make everything very gory at once, and nothing but the shedding of blood can excite our interest. But for Christ Jesus the moment in which He had to pass through the gate, His back to the temple, was the equivalent of a scourging from heaven. And all those "mean" things which we said on purpose in *Christ on Trial* about the Jews who were too "sensitive" to enter a pagan house, well — we need not retract them here but we ought to remember now that God is fully agreeing with those Jews today. We must understand very well that both God and Satan are whispering this message into Jesus' ear: "They were quite right, however; you do not belong in the city which is holy. They were quite right, for God Himself is casting you outside of it. He preserves Jerusalem as the domain of holiness, and adds that you are not worthy of the city." Let your thoughts pause here for a moment; otherwise they will hurry on — on the *via dolorosa*. Thinking is very dangerous here. Close your eyes for a moment, and repeat the words of Paul: *He is made sin.* Then go on. Then you will appreciate that it is not heresy to say that God and the devil are together whispering into Jesus' ear. Then you will believe that God drives Jesus outside of the gates, the very gates which He had entered not so long ago, exalted, riding on the foal of an ass. Now you will believe that even that Jewish pride which hit upon the idea of an Akeldama (in which, as we observed, their passion for distinctiveness was carried out to the limit) is being employed against Christ by God Himself in His legal action at this time. God will punish the Jews for it; but meanwhile He will put Jesus to death by it. Yes, indeed He is *made sin* for us. Hence He is cut off and cast out.

What we have here is a sin-offering. Now please do not begin singing a Latin aria just now: *agnus Dei, qui tollis peccata mundi.* Latin is a kind of distant thing, and rather unreal for those who attend Roman Catholic churches as well as for those who, for aesthetic reasons, avoid churches. No, first go to the priests, look at the blood and filth; look upon the entrails which have been burned. The Scriptures would take you to that point. Sin offerings are after all as ugly as death itself. They are instinct with the curse. One must not sing the word "curse" in a strange language, but must say it in one's own. God wants us to do that; if we do not, it does not affect us. Accordingly, we say again: This is the sin-offering. Please step out of the neighborhood, for He is unclean. *He has been made sin.*

Now let Him carry His cross, for who is to help the utmost exlex. *Via dolorosa* — people pronounce that beautiful word — Latin again — with a quivering voice. But the angels say: There is a stench here. No wonder, for the road leads *outside of the gate.* And Christ is now being cast into fellowship with that which is unclean. That which is unclean and is thrown outside of the camp — why hesitate to say it — that is thrown on the dung hill. Do you start at the word? That does not matter; we ought to be startled today. Dare anyone think the word is unbiblical, unbecoming, or irreverent? Then he does not know his Bible. For the Bible itself teaches that the dunghill is a symbol of *hell,* and that the place where men throw filthy and unclean things, when seen in a prophetic light, is a symbol of the darkness of hell. In the days of Judah's faithful kings, Josiah appointed the dale of Hinnom, a place which had first been used by the idolatrous worship of Moloch as a dung-hill. This he did intentionally. And the spirit of prophecy made a symbol of this place, a symbol of uncleanness first and of hell afterwards (*Jeremiah* 7:31, 32; *Isaiah* 66:24).[1]

Hence we are following a Biblical course by placing things in the connections we have outlined. The dunghill and the Latin aria are unlike each other, but the dogma of Christ's suretyship cannot get along without the vernacular which Scripture uses to point the sin-offering outside the gate. Therefore we conclude that the descent into hell would not have been possible to the spirit of Christ, which responds genuinely to all things, *inside* of the walls of Jerusalem. Nothing comes by chance. Golgotha had to be located outside of the city walls. Only by going forth outside of the gate, only by being accompanied by the fugue of the wrath of the Judge of heaven, who expressed His vengeance in Israel's

---

1. See my *Wat is de Hel?*, Kampen, J. H. Kok, 2nd ed., p. 29 ff.

law, could Jesus perfectly regard Himself as descending into hell, as experiencing the curse, as consciously being the exlex. Only in that way can He really know that He is the scapegoat who, laden with sins, died, and washed away our uncleanness in His blood. Day of atonement—Good Friday.

Accordingly, we are compelled by heaven itself to sing *psalms* on the way which leads upward, or downward—how shall we put it today?—to the dunghill of the world and the galleries of hell. Does anyone feel like saying, I cannot do that; or another, It seems to me that it is not fitting? The latter sins worse than the former. Be that as it may. Our noble thoughts and our good taste and our humane feeling and even our self-respect, must pause to consider the blunt description: Let us go forth therefore unto him without the camp, bearing his reproach (*Hebrews* 13). Every system of dogmatics which refuses to accept the satisfaction of Christ is doing injustice to this text. It refuses to go outside of the gate. It pulls up its nose at the dunghill of God's universe, and consequently it can never get itself to see that God's angels are today turning away from the filth of *our sin*. However, the disciple of Calvin, apprehended by the Scriptures, knows that the phrase "without the gates" is related to the concepts of hell, and is permeated with the stench of hell. He refuses to have the foulness of his sins blown away from him by the gust of humanism. He wants to discover himself at the dunghill of the world. *Without the gate, without the gate.* He will rest in Christ who suffered all this for him, and endured it all for him. And accordingly he does not want to forget that this was the dunghill of filth, or that the path thitherward was his own path. Now this has become a strange history. We paused to observe the human chaos, and found that everything was out of its place. Consequently only the cursing word of God kept Jesus standing erect and brought Him back to the straight course. The chaos of men which had turned the program topsy-turvy did not perturb His thinking. He saw the cosmos of God's justice rising, and He stumbled on, a hero. He went to Golgotha and courageously strode outside of the gates. He knew that men had thrust Him outside of the sphere of Mosaic law, but in spite of them this was the way by which He returned to it.

We can say that a beautiful irony characterizes the moment in which Pilate uses the key of Rome to open the gate of Jerusalem in order to bring something which stank to the dunghill of the world. Did the pilfering devils probably hurry to the scene? If so, their game was lost from the very beginning, for He who was chased from the inheritance of Moses was explained only in the light of Moses' own law. He who was prematurely made an exlex was now according to right and justice made an exlex overagainst His God at God's own perfect time. All that men turned upside down God again turned right side up.

And in saying that we are saying nothing yet of what we called the "forgotten chapter."[1] At the time we observed that the forgotten chapter was the priesthood of Christ. Now note the beautiful irony again. The high priests cast Jesus outside of the gate and thereby in spite of themselves minister the preparation of God's last sacrifice. The sacrifice for sin. O Noah, you have seen them hammering on the ark they scorned. O Jesus, you have seen them working on the despised offer. They test the Lamb, and find it wanting. They say it is not a Lamb which can serve as the sacrifice. But in spite of themselves they must perform upon Him all that they ever did to the scapegoat. And inasmuch as He is willing to enter upon His death, and to take the cross upon Himself, He is, besides being the scapegoat, also the Passover Lamb in meekness.

Now the Saviour goes outside of the gate humiliated, degraded. But whoever has seen God, as He saw God, will raise a hymn of thanksgiving to Him: Lift up your heads, O ye gates, and be ye lifted up ye everlasting doors, that the sacrifice may go out. And every oppressed soul who sees no exit within the gates and no entrance outside of the gates, should pause here and read a marvelous truth about suretyship and satisfaction and atonement. Until he has done that he should not go farther on the way—the way of Christ as He emerges from His suffering.

---

1. *Christ on Trial*, pp. 427 f., 432 ff.

Christ's Right of Requisition Completely Denied

CHAPTER TWO

Christ's Right of Requisition Completely Denied

● *And as they came out, they found a man of*
Cyrene, Simon by name: him they compelled
to bear his cross.

MATTHEW 27:32.

I N the Heidelberg Catechism the church confesses it to be the
will of God that His Christians "be instructed not by dumb
images but by the living preaching of His Word."

If ever the emphasis of this statement is to impress our conscience it must be now as Christ takes the way to Golgotha, the
via dolorosa. The Roman Catholic church against which the statement of the Catechism was directed in the first place has, so to
speak, placed a row of images along both sides of the *via dolorosa.*
Some of these are dumb images and some of them are speaking
images, some are fixed and some are moveable, some are such as
are found regularly in all Roman Catholic churches—the well-
known "stations" of the cross—and some of them are more or
less legendary in character. And Romish poets and parish preachers, each in their own manner, thereupon proceed to give the commentary or illustration of these. So it goes: illustration upon
illustration, commentary upon commentary.

Now it would certainly be arrogance in us if we were to maintain that the basic fault, the characteristic fault in Christian thinking which has conceived and drawn up all these images had entirely been kept out of the domain of Protestantism. On the
contrary, the Protestant spirit also, even the orthodox spirit, has
never completely emancipated itself from this characteristically
human tendency towards concrete representation. The longing to
give external shape and form to spiritual things which accounts

for all these images moves every human spirit. But the incentive which causes these to arise is not one conceived entirely by the Spirit, the Spirit of God, and it is one which "gives expression only to that which it has heard."

Therefore we must take special pains *beforehand* to arm ourselves against this danger, and to set ourselves against it. We must be on guard also as we study Simon of Cyrene on the road which leads from the gate of Jerusalem to the hill of the cross. We must be on guard against this yearning for concrete representation as we pause to consider Simon, who had to meet Jesus of Nazareth, and who bore the cross for Him. Simon of Cyrene — after that dark Friday he has always been included in that rather long, time-honored procession which the "edifying imagination"—the author of those images just referred to—likes to present as walking behind the cross-bearing Christ. In that procession there are others who accompany Him; there are the women of whom the Bible itself speaks, and who are therefore in no sense legendary; but there is also that long series of persons created by fiction among whom Veronica is especially prominent. All these according to the Christian, or better, according to the erstwhile Christian narratives of the memorabilia of the Great Friday, formed a part of the procession that followed Jesus. For it has long been the custom to surround the somewhat colorless picture of Christ in isolation with a rather dazzling frame. Veronica is the one who with her kerchief dried the bleeding and perspiring face of Christ —and as a sad reward always preserved in that kerchief an impression of the bleeding face.

But that is but a legend, someone says. Pass on to a more beneficial message. But—and that is why we mention it here—that very remark indicates the direction which the old Christian fantasy wanted to pursue (or it did have a purpose in mind). It wanted to put Christ, our cross-bearer, in a congenial setting of warm and solacing sympathy. Erring Christian feeling wanted to burn incense for the Jesus who was thought unworthy of a sweet smelling offering by the priests of His own people. This took place some time after the reading of Paul's letters, and in this way Simon of Cyrene was also given a place in that congenial surrounding of sympathy which was created for Jesus. He became involved in it, and he did not know himself how this happened to take place. See how good, how amiable it is that sons of the same Christian house dwell in unity with Jesus, there where the ardor of love is never extinguished. The fragrance of love cannot but influence everyone, just as the oil which dripped from Simon's head saturated his beard and workman's clothes. Blessed be Simon: he bore the cross of Jesus.

You see that they want to explain Simon's bearing of the cross in two ways; or, better, they wish to derive a double conclusion from it. First, that the piteous Jesus certainly was in a most miserable situation. You can see that: He could not even carry His cross any farther. Second, that just at the right time a few sweet drops of consolation were poured into Jesus' bitter cup of passion, solacing drops prepared by the love of Simon of Cyrene, and by those others whom history or imagination has placed in His retinue. All these others came after him. *After him* — if you stumble over that detail, we will do something to change it. You should not make such trivial criticisms.

What these people want to do is to see in the assumed or protested love of Simon of Cyrene a kind of continuation of the anointing with which Mary served Christ in the beginning of the passion week as a preparation for His burial. Broken alabaster boxes are well worth preserving; you can always squeeze a little more out of them. Besides, Judas is dead; he cannot spoil such ministrations with his calculating criticism. Musicians and poets and preachers consequently whisper soft words of comfort into the ears of the suffering Christ Jesus. They would indeed have helped Him in the anxiousness of His death if they had not been born too late. They tell Him: Have a little patience, Jesus, for the same love which gave you the foal of an ass on the basis of your own right of requisition when you came to ride triumphantly into the city, still surrounds you. The same willingness to serve which on the basis of your own right of requisition prepared a room in which you might eat the Passover and prepare the first holy supper is still here and would serve you again. Look, look yonder, the father of two Christian sons is putting his shoulder to your cross.

Nevertheless, we would posit certain other ideas overagainst these. In the first place we would turn that very carefully developed picture of the "service" of Simon of Cyrene and the drift of the narrative of the other incidents surrounding him in a different direction, by the matter-of-fact remark that we know preciously little about the man, and about the service he performed. And to that we would add that the appearance of Simon of Cyrene in no sense constitutes a hiatus, a pause, in the suffering of Christ. On the contrary, that which the Saviour experienced because of Simon of Cyrene *aggravated* His suffering, and made His humiliation more conspicuous to the eyes of men.

Yes, we know very little about the person of Simon of Cyrene. The Bible tells us that as the sad procession proceeded on the way of death, it did not take very long before the cross of Jesus, and that by the compulsion of the Roman soldiers, was laid upon a man who just happened to step out of the field, a man called Simon of Cyrene. We are told in old books that there was a regulation which had it that a man who was condemned to be crucified, as a general rule, had to carry his own cross. Whether this regulation stipulated that the whole, heavy cross had to be carried by the condemned person, or only the crossbeam, or possibly only the vertical beam, we cannot say. As a matter of fact, the exact shape of the cross is unknown. Three opinions are defended. The one opinion has it that the cross formed the figure X; the other maintains that it had the shape of a T, the third defends the position usually taken — and the one which seems the most plausible — namely, that the cross had the form of the figure †. But we shall say nothing further about this particular. It becomes apparent that Christ could no longer support the cross. If we remember the physical and spiritual exhaustion which must have been His as a result not only of the night which had just passed, but also of the preliminary scourging, and of the whole of the fatiguing and exhausting suffering which ravaged His body in those last hours, we can easily understand that He could not support the burden. And we remember the condition of His physical exhaustion again as we think of the fact that the Saviour is the one who died first of the three crucified together.

There are some who think of a further particular in this connection. They suggest that for a definite reason the high priests thought it unwise to have Jesus bear His own cross. These drove their legal formalism so far that they took exception to having a son of Abraham supporting a burden on a day of the feast, for

CHRIST'S RIGHT OF REQUISITION COMPLETELY DENIED   41

the law of the Sabbath, which also applied to feast days, forbade
the bearing of burdens at such times. To this hypothesis another
is generally added : namely, that the murderers crucified with Jesus
did not bear their own crosses. It is possible, they say, that the
vertical pillar had already been placed in the ground for them beforehand. After all, their execution was not an unexpected one.
But that of Jesus was an unexpected one, and the cross of Jesus,
because of the haste which had characterized the trial throughout,
still had to be specially brought to the place of execution. What
shall we say of these things? The other possibility might also
hold : namely, that the execution of the others was advanced somewhat now that Jesus was to be executed. We have not the necessary information to decide definitely which construction is correct.
It seems to us that the explanation just presented is a highly unlikely one. Be these things as they may, the fact is that Simon,
who was just returning from the field, is coerced by the soldiers
to carry the cross of Jesus. It may be that this took place very
close to the gate of the city.

The Bible tells us that this man came out of Cyrene. Cyrene is
one of the most prominent places in Lybia, of the so-called Lybia
Cyrenaica which lay off the north coast of Africa. We know that
the city of Cyrene maintained all kinds of relations with Jerusalem. Business relations were maintained between Cyrene and the
Jews. Besides, we know that for some time a large number of
Jews had been living in Cyrene. Many Jews had emigrated to
Lybia during the reign of Ptolomy I ; in addition, many Jews had
gone there from Alexandria. To some extent these Jews in the
alien land had remained faithful to the religion of their forefath-
ers ; but, on the other hand, many were absorbed by the heathen
culture.

Who, now, was Simon? Was he a Jew who had come to Jerusalem with the special intent of celebrating the Passover? We remember, for instance, that on the day of Pentecost many religious
Jews had come from Lybia also. Or was he one of those many
farmers who after they had made a neat little sum in the foreign
country, had come to spend their last days in the shadow of David's grave, and of the temple of the fathers? That is possible, but
such comfortably retired folk as a general rule are well advanced
in years, and who would constrain an old man to carry the heavy

cross? Can it be that the man was neither a Jew, nor a relative of the Jews, but an out and out heathen, who had unwittingly strayed into the company of all those celebrating Jews, but who had nothing to do with the celebration, the temple, or the Jewish customs?

You see that there are several possibilities. All of these have their defenders. But there is another question. What did Simon intend to *do*? One says that he was a Jew, living in Jerusalem, and just returning from his labor in the field in order to buy or sell something in the city. No, another scornfully replies, he was coming from his work this early in the morning, because he wanted to celebrate the feast; and he still had to make all kinds of preparations for the Passover meal. True, protests a third, but the man does not give you an impression of such piety, for he was coming from the field, and must have been working on that field. And that on the feast day—Sabbath desecrater! Now, now, interrupts a fourth, you must not take that so seriously. It may be that he had not even worked in the field. It is possible that the word translated *field* should be translated *estate*. He had not been working, but had simply gone on this off-day to see how things were getting along on his "villa." And this opinion, in turn, is supported by a fifth contender who maintains that even clothes, on which the earmarks of field work were plainly perceptible, are not convincing evidence of the fact that he had desecrated the law of the Sabbath on the feast day. For in the case of many a well-circumscribed instance the work of the Sabbath day or the feast day might still be so extensive that one could not possibly appear in his "Sunday-best," if you will forgive us for the anachronism.[1]

Thus the opinions differ. However, there are many who think they have a rather good reason for thinking that Simon of Cyrene was indeed a pagan. "If the supposition to the effect that of all those people in that neighborhood at the time Simon was selected because he was a stranger, as was very likely obvious from his color — a stranger, lest the people be offended — we can deduce from it that Simon was not a Jew, but an alien, very likely a Moor."[2]

---

1. See Strack-Billerbeck, *Kommentaar*, II, pp. 828, 829.
2. Grosheide, *Kommentaar op Mattheus*, p. 348.

How little, how very little, therefore, we know of Simon's past. The same is true of his future. The same erstwhile Christian legends to which we referred a while ago probably account for the rumor that he later became a Christian. We do, however, have to acknowledge that this notion is more than an edifying guess. The Bible tells us that Simon was the father of Alexander and Rufus. Now the special mention of these two names points to the fact that these persons were well known and were men of good repute in the circle of the Christians. Of good repute, we say, for there is not a single reason to identify this Alexander with the heretic named in *Acts* 19:33, or in I *Timothy* 1:20, or in II *Timothy* 4:14. And Rufus is doubtless the same man whom Paul names in *Romans* 16:13 and whom he graciously greets. According to this interpretation, then, the two sons of Simon must have occupied a place of honor in the Christian church. And that makes the supposition that Simon embraced the faith or, at least, that he was not antagonistic to it, a plausible one.

Nevertheless we must not blink at the fact that the person of Simon, even though we regard him as the father of those two well known Christians, remains hidden in obscurity. He is shrouded in the same kind of darkness as are those two others whose services were claimed during the passion week of Christ. We pointed those out before. In the first volume of this work[1] we have seen that a request came to a man to let the Saviour use his colt in order that He might ride into the city on it, and that a similar requisitory request came to the family who had to prepare the room of the Passover for Jesus. Of these people, too, we knew very little. We were not even sure that they were friends of Jesus; it might also have been that they were just in a general sense sympathetic to Christ and His disciples. Very often the Bible lets the people who surround Christ stand in semi-obscurity in order to keep the limelight full on Christ Himself. Indeed, it is even their duty to stay in the dark. For His sake. And is ours the right, then, because of our avid longing for a treasury of Christian legend, to give a greater amount of credence to things which God has intentionally left unrevealed than these things actually deserve? Surely, that is just another way of "kicking against the pricks." No, let us be on guard against soiling and

---

1. *Christ in His Suffering*, pp. 106 and 150.

defiling the way of Christ's worst and most extreme necessity with our vain fantasies. Good Friday is too good for guess work.

Yes, there is a great difference between the Christian imagination of old times, as it worked out its ideas in directions suggested above, on the one hand, and the astonishing fantasies of the so-called religio-historical school, on the other.[1] At bottom all of those fantasies, let them differ from each other as much as they may, are a sinful activity, for they oppose an erotic or esthetic[2] emphasis to the account of the most bloody *reality*.

We do not know Simon, and we will never know him. Whether he lived on a "villa," was a farmer or a peasant, was of the black race or of the brown, whether he lived in Jerusalem or merely tarried there, whether he took the cross upon his shoulders willingly or resisted the coercion of the soldiers—these are all things we do not know, and we do not wish to act as though we knew them.

What, then, *do we know with certainty?* We can answer that question the moment we fasten our thoughts again upon the main thing; that is, upon Christ, the Man of sorrows Himself. In this matter our thoughts have a resting place in the Greek word which is used in the text of the gospel by way of indicating that the soldiers *compelled* Simon to bear the cross of Jesus. The word which the gospel uses in this connection is found only twice in the New Testament. In both cases it can be translated as a coercive demand made upon a subordinate by an authority of the government or at least by someone who regards himself as a superior. The Greek word used comes from the Persian. It is derived from the renowned postal service of the earlier Persians. In the interest of a speedy disposition of the mails these Persians demanded that men and horses be claimed at any time for carrying the post from one stage to another. From that origin the word began to be used for broader activities. Later it is used for all kinds of requisitory activity by the government such as even we know it in connection with the mobilization of troops and the requisition of property in time of war. It can also refer to the stat-

---

1. These have made Simon of Cyrene the image of Kurenaios. This is the Greek name for Bostes, who is a charioteer, who bears a sickle in his hand, and, accordingly, is supposed to be returning from the field. This, as you see at once, is a figure borrowed from the astronomical world.

2 There are still others who think of Simon of Cyrene as a symbol of the Greek Hercules.

ute labor of feudal times. Christ Himself uses the word in a related sense when in *St. Matthew* 5:41 He speaks of people who
compel another to go a mile with them. And it is in this sense that
Simon of Cyrene is required by the military hand of Rome to give
his services.

That is about as much as we know with certainty. It may be
that this strongly suggestive word points to the fact that Simon
was an alien. Especially if we remember that the chief priests, as
we observed, were a part of the procession, and were partly in
command of it. It is very likely that this coercion upon which
they insist would not apply to a Jew but to a colored man. He
would be good enough for that. Be that as it may, the element of
a coercive request, of requisition on the part of the government,
is definitely connoted by the word used. And if we cling to that
it will become evident to us how deeply this humiliation cuts into
the passion of Christ Jesus.

Requisition, we know, is a demand by the government, a demand made upon a person's property, upon his time, upon his will,
or upon his person. And we remember that the account of Jesus'
passion began with the phenomenon of requisition. We have already recalled that fact. In passing we mentioned that Christ, in
the full consciousness of the fact that He was the King of the city
and the absolute owner of everything in it, exercised the right of
laying claim—no milder phrase will do—to the foal of an ass first,
and a room in which to keep the Passover next. Yes, in Jerusalem.
That was the place of the great king who came to you in the name
of the Lord, and who knew that. There, Jerusalem, your King
came, and He knew that He was the King before God. There
your King came; and also as a prophet He troubled Himself by
that public requisition of the foal of an ass to vividly demonstrate
the prerogatives of a king. Those of you who recall what we said
before[1] about the "necessary circumlocution" which Christ described by way of impressing His prerogative of requisition upon
the consciousness of the people and by way of demanding an un-
conditional acknowledgment of that right, will feel at once that
this particular is of great significance in the passion story. For
now a stark contrast is set up between the beginning of the passion week and its tragic conclusion. The very gate out of which

1. *Christ in His Suffering*, especially p. 100.

Jesus is being thrown at present is the same through which, not very long ago, He triumphantly entered into the city on the foal of an ass which He had claimed. Jerusalem—the song echoed in His soul—thy King cometh. The same city which no longer thinks Him worthy of a place within its walls once had to offer Him a room in which He could institute His holy supper. It had to offer Him the place which was to be the birthplace of His world-vanquishing work, of the formation of the church, of the conquest of the pseudo-religion and pseudo-culture of paganism and Judaism. For that is what the place would become by means of the liturgy of the Christian supper. Jerusalem—the song echoed in His soul—thy Priest cometh. Judas found the room very small, and altogether too peaceful. But He heard storms in the offing: storms of Pentecost, reformations, thunderings, trumpetings, and the sound of many instruments. Yes, those were His two acts of requisition. They had presented themselves to Him. At the time He had felt very strong. These acts of requisition were functions of His Messianic consciousness. In the first of them Christ asserted Himself as the king (remember the foal of the ass) ; but in the second the message of His kingship was developed in a priestly direction. As the High Priest of the confession which gives everything it has to give, He demanded the room of the Passover, in order that in it He might give away the holy supper for all of God's defeated people.

Draw the threads together now. Here are two acts of requisition, the one kingly, the other priestly. The conclusion of both was that by means of them He displayed Himself to His people as the Priest-King, as the fulfillment of that Joshua who, according to the word of Zechariah, was the type of Christ Himself.

Joshua, the Priest-King,—do you remember that still? We paused not long ago[1] to study the fact that Christ knew Himself to be the fulfillment of the prophecy of *Zechariah* 6. In the prophetic vision the faithful Joshua stood as a priest and king at the same time, and as such the type of the Christ of God. Now this Christ, whose last labor of passion again and again was determined by the prophecy of Zechariah,[2] saw and recognized Himself

---

1. *Christ on Trial*, p. 428 ff.
2. We referred to that prophecy repeatedly in *Christ in His Suffering*, and also in *Christ on Trial*.

as the Priest-King, and saw Himself as such before His name was coupled with that of Barabbas on one and the same ballot. Moreover, in the full consciousness that He was the true and the complete Priest-King Christ made His demands during the last week of His passion. He did this fully aware of the fact that as such He was being completely faithful to the trend of prophecy. He did not make His requisitions according to the cruel law of Saul, who made his demands for purposes of personal aggrandizement. Nor did He insist upon His requests according to the wicked notions of David, who thought himself a sultan as he passionately proceeded to count the people. Nor did Christ make His demands according to the display of power characteristic of Solomon whose taxing of the people displeased them greatly. Nor, for the matter of that, were His requests made according to the tyranny of Zedekiah, David's last king, who tyrannized slaves and made his requisitions without any tempering of mercy. For Jesus knew that His royal requisitions demanded much, but that His priestly love first of all gave much. Jerusalem, what more could you demand? He made His first request in order to be the master of all as a king. He made His second request by way of asking for a place in which He might wash His disciples' feet. Was there ever such harmonious requisition? Is this not a paradoxical requisition? Is this something different, O Jerusalem, from what Zechariah wanted: king, commander, priest, chief servant of all, and all these united in one person? True, He made His demands and insisted upon them, but He also gave His life, gave His blood, gave His soul, and gave Himself as a ransom for many. He felt free to make His demands upon His people, but He also endured the demands which God makes upon His people, shouldered the burden of them Himself, and as the Surety and Mediator of all bore their myriad burdens.

Such is the account of His harmonious requisition. What remnant remains of that royal, of that priestly, glory? Look, the long fingers of priests are pointing, and the strong arms of soldiers are seizing a man upon whose day and body they laid claim in order that he might bear the cross of Jesus.

The king of the whole world, He who is the peculiar and the unique Priest is here, but the paganism (of the soldiers), and the Judaism (of the priests), make their demands on Him, over His head, and without Him. The royal sun is rising sluggishly in the distance. Caesar "Augustus" lays claim upon the whole world, and the Son of David, the Joshua of Zechariah's nightly vision, can only look on. Such is the vision of the day and such is the judgment of the night and day. Caesar Augustus makes his demands, makes them very brutally, and right in the presence of the king of righteousness. The priests of Aaron are a part of the procession and they say: Just lay claim upon the time and energy of that man. Caesar demands; hence they call him Lord and God.[1] He demands his royal services. Demands are violently made on the way of the cross; but the whole demand proceeds from the idea that Jesus Christ may make no demand, that He is not a Lord, that He is a condemned slave. No royal services for Him, and no honorary services for Him, and that is the end of it. Never did human aid ever humiliate so profoundly as did the help given by Simon of Cyrene. Claudia—do you still remember?[2]—is a very friendly woman, but she does Him an injustice. Simon is the last aide, but he humiliates Him. The whole of His display of peace between a priesthood and a king's authority, the whole of His perfect reconciliation of the antithesis of giving and taking all, as these were preached in His two acts of requisition, are covered up and are swallowed up in this procession. Hardened soldiers curse and pedantic priests make pedantic gestures. They have rings on their fingers, helmets on their heads. And the Joshua of prophecy holds His peace.

This is another instance of negation. Not one drop of myrrh falls on Jesus' cloak, the cloak of shame. Just let those fragments of Mary's alabaster box lie where they fell. Humiliation here, sheer humiliation! Only the curse operates here. The Priest-King of *Zechariah* 6 is now being negated in the presence of the devils. One cannot do a king a greater injustice than by making the subject of all concepts of requisition the object of need.

Now we greet Thee, Son of David, in Thy terrible shame. When David by reason of his fleshly longing for requisition—that denial of his theocratic office—turned away from the oppressive pestilential wind which moved over his densely populated country—a fragment of the world then, but it had to become the

---

1. *Christ in His Suffering*, p. 220; *Christ on Trial*, pp. 331-332.
2. *Christ on Trial*, chapter 25, especially p. 481 ff.

church again — he, with the extreme fastidiousness of an Ornan, did not want to demand but wanted to pay for the place where the sacrifice was to be offered up, as well as for the flesh of the animal to be sacrificed. In this also—for repentance makes one very sensitive—the repentance of his heart becomes manifest. He knew again that the theocratic prince might never *take* unless he also *gave*. But here, O great Son of David, Thy remunerating offer, which Thou with Thine own blood art compensating for and presenting to Thy God and to His people, is being totally forgotten. For Thou art a slave in the eyes of men. Thou art a pauper, a pariah, who cannot even accomplish His empty death in the ordinary manner of slaves. How could such a death ever be adequate to a task designed to bless? That is what Thy sensitive ear can hear them asking. Pagans are making demands upon those whose royal services Thou as a king mightest demand. And that is part of being *in the form of a slave.*

Moreover, who does not think in this connection of the name which Christ would have, the name of *Kurios*. He wants to be called the Kurios, the Lord, the Owner of His own, the Chief-Requisitioner. Well, Simon of Cyrene will bite his lips to pieces before He can say to such a Jesus: My Kurios, my God. Simon of Cyrene—was he a pagan? Was he a Jew or a relative of a Jew come from a foreign land? I do not know, but I do know that he was either one or the other. And therefore we can say that the requisition of this man in this manner for this work was a molesting of the Spirit by Satan.

Only a few more weeks will pass, and the Holy Spirit will on the day of Pentecost demand the life and soul and spirit of Jews, of the relatives of Jews, and of the most outlying pagans for Christ Jesus. Then He will deliberately fetch His Jews, His pious men, and will bring them to the stage of Pentecost. He will even fetch His own from Lybia and God will call those living on the most distant shores of far away seas. Simon of Cyrene, together with all Lybians and all the pious men of Cyrene. But before the Holy Spirit proclaims Christ Jesus' right of requisition over Simon of Cyrene on the feast of Pentecost, Satan brings him next to Jesus' bloody and repulsive nakedness. It is necessary that a pagan be present here, or someone standing afar off, to see with his eyes and at close range the deplorable state of Christ the exlex. This is Satan's way of attempting to put a dead fly in the ointment of Pentecost prepared by the spirit of Christ, in order that the feast of Christ might be spoiled by that one man who could not acclimate himself to the repulsive experience which he has had and which he has felt in his own flesh. If you or I had had to take upon ourselves the cross of a slave, wounded to the point of bleeding and that on a hot, summer mid-afternoon, would we then, several weeks later have announced to all the devils and to all the angels and to all men: This is my Lord and my God. Alas, what a sacrifice Jesus must give for His royal and priestly right of requisition, for that right which He exercised at the beginning of this same week. Accordingly, we shall not inquire—as so many do—what reward Simon of Cyrene was given. We shall not ask whether Simon's reward in heaven was very great because he bore the cross of Jesus. No, we shall not even ask whether his grace-given remuneration was the conquest of his heart by the Crucified One who looked upon him, and with His eyes probably penetrated deeply into Simon's soul. We do not know, and we do not want to know. Of what concern is Simon to us unless our most poverty-stricken One some day greet him in the eternal tabernacles. It is not ours to judge.

But this we would still say to ourselves. If we are to bear Jesus' cross today, we will have to do it in a way different from Simon's when he was compelled to bear it. There is but one who may exercise the privilege of requisition, and make it binding upon us. He is the Saviour, the Crucified Himself. It was a part of His humiliation that He might not make demands, that the double-edged sword of God's sublime mockery was exerted against Simon before his own eyes, bidding him to help Jesus for a moment. No, we shall not thank Simon who bore the cross for Jesus; we shall thank only Christ Jesus who endured the suffering caused by Simon. Without resistance He bore this act of usurpation on the part of His cruel enemy. Not Simon, who bears the cross, but Jesus, who gives it up, is our Lamb, standing dumb over-against him who demands it. All of Jesus' official right is being denied to His very face, and thus He endured. Great will be His reward in heaven.

As for Simon, and you, and I? Great will be our reward in heaven, great will be the reward of grace if only we will open our eyes and acknowledge Jesus as the One person in heaven who has the right of requisition. Losing this right, He achieved it for Himself for all time and eternity. There are those, we read in the Scripture, who have entertained angels unawares. Thus did Simon of Cyrene on this day unwittingly entertain the great Angel of Jahweh, thus did he accompany the faithful Messenger of God on His way to the cross.

Hence we see the clouds breaking behind this spectacle of sheer affliction. He who bears the cross today, and who even had to be released from this task, will soon be establishing His throne and His chair upon the stars. To His own He will say: You have clothed and fed me, given me to drink, visited me, and you have borne my cross. And they all will answer: Lord, when did we clothe and feed Thee, when give Thee to drink, visit Thee, and bear Thy cross? We know nothing about that. By our sins we placed the cross upon Thee, merely placed it upon Thee. But, looking around Him, He will say: These who have done the will of my Father, these have visited and fed me, and these have borne my cross.

May I therefore on this day fulfill the remnants of the suffering of Jesus with a holy reverence and with simplicity of heart. My name may not be Simon, but I am the spiritual father of Alexander and of Rufus. And on the *via dolorosa* where my sweat mocks all the kerchiefs of Veronica, He will be my Surety, great in concealment. He demanded everything of me today, because He first gave everything to me.

But say no more now, for I dare not utter a word about my work for Him. O God, I must first go and see. Thou dost demand my days, my nights, and my eyes, so that I may go and see what it is that Thou dost first require of Him. Father, Thy requisition presses upon Him. Thou dost oppress Him sorely, but as Thou doest so, Thine eye is fixed upon me. I hear Thy threat: Thou, miserable one, thou hast done this to Him.

The soldiers of Rome, and the priests of the Jews are very saints as compared with me when I think of this. They constrained Simon—a Moor, some say. By means of my sins I constrained my Lord and my God to bear my cross. He bears it, I bear it, yet not I, but Christ bears it for me. I have not the foal of an ass to offer Him, I cannot give Him a room in which to keep the Passover, but He lays claim on my heart: He would keep the Holy Supper. "Now Joshua had filthy garments." He came from Simon's field, and had drawn the furrows deeply. But be still. I know very well that filth can be of various kinds.

Christ's Last Ministration of the Word

CHAPTER THREE

Christ's Last Ministration of the Word

> *And there followed him a great company of people, and of women, which also bewailed and lamented him. But Jesus turning unto them said, Daughters of Jerusalem, weep not for me but weep for yourselves, and for your children. For, behold, the days are coming, in the which they shall say, Blessed are the barren, and the wombs that never bare, and the paps which never gave suck. Then shall they begin to say to the mountains, Fall on us; and to the hills, Cover us, For if they do these things in a green tree, what shall be done in the dry.*
> LUKE 23:27-31.

NOW we are to study Christ's last and final ministration of the Word. Some would call it His *ultima ratio*. It was a strange hour, and the place was most inappropriate for a service of the Word. Hence the discourse was very short. Nevertheless it was a ministration of the Word. He who was speaking always made His short addresses count heavily; as heavily as the ministry of the Word. Besides, the Word He spoke was public. Moreover, He spoke from the Scriptures.

The procession moved on farther along the road. Suddenly Jesus saw a commotion among the people. He heard terse words. A soldier snapped at another: Go to it: have at him. A priest spoke in a tempered and modulated voice. The cross was suddenly taken from His shoulder, and placed upon another man. You know his name; it was Simon of Cyrene.

Even if we have appreciated only the smallest part of the truth in our preceding chapter, we can feel free now to say that Jesus felt a piercing pain. He heard Himself defied. Yes, I am referring to what happened to Simon. I say that He was being defied. By whom? By men? But, from all outward appearances, these were not unfriendly to Him. Besides, He heard the sobbing of women; and Simon of Cyrene did accept the burden of the cross. Well, then, by whom was He defied? What is it that makes Him dare to speak of defiance now?

Be still, for He hears Himself being defied in the presence of God. But let us keep things from running together, and not mistake our words. He heard Himself being *mocked* by God.[1] For if Christ related the right of requisition which the Roman soldiers and the priests of Aaron had usurped to His own privileges as a King and to His own right of requisition, we can be sure that everything we mentioned in our preceding chapter not only pained Him far more grievously than we can state but also that He referred all those things to God Himself. Aha, God says to Him, Thou art the very one who rode into the city on a requisitioned colt, saying: Here am I, the owner of beasts of burden, of houses, of the clothes of citizens, and after a while, of the clothes of the priests also. Art Thou the same who established a memorial for Thyself at the Holy Supper in a requisitioned room? But I, saith the Lord, am making Thee to be sin; I take away from Thee all Thy rights of requisition. Thou must pay me, Thy God, for Thy requisitioned colt, and for Thy requisitioned room. Pay me the last cent. Give me my wages.

Then Jesus felt Himself repulsed. God pushed Him aside. A cross had just been taken from His shoulder. O God, put another in its place at once, a cross as heavy as—as heavy as—the Word. Yes, Christ, Thou art outside of the gate here, Thou art enroute to the dunghill of the world.[2] Do not let this seem strange to Thee. Do not think it odd that the Lord is giving Thy honor to another, for, in the last analysis, there is but One to whom all toll must be paid. He is the Chief Requisitioner. His name is Lord of Lords.

Indeed, this was very tragic. It excited a greater and a more painful astonishment than the soldiers' mockery of Him as a frustrated king. This suffering was worse than that of the crown of thorns, of the gorgeous robe, and of the reed. This was worse, for now it was God who mocked Him.

---

1. For the difference between mockery and defiance, see *Christ on Trial*, p. 182 ff.
2. See page 32.

Did Jesus succumb? Did He fall back from God's presence? Did He lose His Messianic consciousness, which, in God, had confirmed Him in His requisition? Did He say: Father, Judge, I am indeed the dry wood which will never again in all eternity bear any fruit. Did He Himself prove to be the accursed fig tree?

No, no, He did not recede, He did not fall back. Listen to Him, as He praises Himself: I am the *green* tree; I am the *green* tree; praise is becoming to me. "Not he that commendeth himself is approved, but he whom the Lord commendeth." Would anyone chide Him with those words? But, remember that He is talking in the face of this fundamental statement: I am the green wood of Israel; I have not lost my right as a king. If the green wood is to be hewn down in the garden of Israel today that garden will undergo the same experience which is undergone in any garden where huge trees, which first stood in their "Eden," are made to fall. My fall will be the fall of everyone. If they abuse Me Who am the green wood, the dry wood will be destroyed with Me in my fall. They will quickly gather it up, and burn it in an oven. Accordingly, Christ knows Himself to be the green tree, the tree of life in the Paradise of Eden. Perhaps you wonder why we refer to Eden here. We do so because we are thinking of the prophet Ezekiel in connection with this statement of Christ. Ezekiel sees the "mighty" of the earth; he compares these crown-bearers of the nations with trees that have been planted in a Paradise of "God," the Father of creation.[1] Proud, imposing trees they are, things of beauty in the garden of God, they have been planted in Eden, the Eden of God. Common grace[2] and the culture which issues from it have given these beautiful trees a rich soil in which to flourish. The healthful waters on which the trees must feed have been hidden deep in the ground. Hence, when such trees are chopped down, the whole of Lebanon laments the fact. Then God spreads a curtain of crepe over the world. The fall of such trees means the same to God as the devastation of the natural Eden.[3] And this is being said only of the Eden of common grace, the beautiful parks which have been meted out according to the architecture of our natural life.

---

1. Ezekiel 31; see chapter 28.
2. "God," not "Lord" (Jahweh).
3. Ezekiel 31: 15, 16.

Today, however, Christ—even on the way which leads Him outside of the gate, and leads Him up to the boundary line of the dunghill of the whole world—is still, as He Himself sees it, standing on *holy* ground. He is walking within the confines of *special* grace. He is the green tree in Eden, the beautiful park which has been meted out by the architecture of the God of all *grace* and of all *comfort*. The soil of this holy ground has not yet been given up to devastation. This is not an "Eden" of nature, but is still an "Eden" of grace. Jerusalem, Jerusalem, as the holy city, as the institute, you are the headquarters of all the chariots of Israel, and of all their horsemen. And as the holy garden, as "Eden," as the *organism,* you are the beautiful park, the forest of God's magnificent trees. Your name is "the garden of Eden." That is your name not in terms of nature, but in terms of grace and of the Word. It happens, however, that the great, the one, the flourishing, the *green* tree of that "garden of Eden," is being hewn down today. That tree is the tree of life. It is the *green* tree. Hence God will spread a curtain of mourning over the mountain of Zion. Lebanon will weep because of the fall of this one tree. The fastnesses of the earth will tremble at its impact with the ground. The architects of the city (the institute) will say to themselves: We are removing an *obstacle*. As a matter of fact they are taking the cornerstone away. Hence their building will crumble to ruins. The keepers of God's garden, of the Eden of God's people of revelation (the organism) will say: We are taking the parasite out of our beautiful park; now all the trees can flourish again. But their trees are dead already; never will life reanimate them. Now that the one tree whose beauty induced the Owner to preserve the garden from destruction has been felled, only the dry and rotted wood is left. What can the Lord of the garden do with all these stumps? He will abandon the garden, and cast the dead pieces into the oven. The judgment will begin at the place of this one, green, uprooted tree. The judgment! The days are coming in which they shall say: Blessed are the barren, and the wombs that never bare, and blessed be the garden which is fruitful no longer, blessed be Eden, also the Eden of nature, to which God has locked the door. For what we, Christ's murderers bear, is but the generation of vipers, and does not deserve to live. Even if the stump could live, there would be no fruit, for that on which it feeds has disappeared. God withdraws the nutritious waters that flowed beneath our barren soil. We have only the dry trees left, the bare branches: just so much kindling for the oven. That which our garden still produces is but the hot-house plants of Asmodeus,[1] the poisonous plants of hell. Jerusalem is blessed not because of her children, but because of her barrenness, for she has put her great Child to death.

Frankly now, this statement sounds like foolishness, coming at *this* hour and spoken by *this* mouth, does it not? Yes, indeed, "foolishness and offense" Gamaliel would say, and his pupil, a certain Saul, will repeat it until his death. The statement is sheer foolishness and offense. For Jesus Christ never fears great folly. He cannot do without it; with it Paul would have nothing to say. On the other hand, however, can you say that the statement contains anything but Messianic self-consciousness? God mocks Him. God has the devils tear His requisition-papers to pieces; the fragments twirl about His cloak of mockery. Nevertheless Christ knows that the God who mocks Him will take Him seriously; He knows that this day is not a *ludus angelicus,* a game of the angels bent on pleasure, but the drama of all the worlds. He is so convinced of this that He lays claim to the whole world, saying: Here is the one important thing.

How did this all happen? Whence this astonishing word, spoken from this dull procession. This is how it happened. As Jesus went on the way to the cross, the "daughters of Jerusalem" accompanied Him. Now these were not the well known Galilean women, for they, prompted by their love, had constantly followed Jesus and we see them standing at a distance later. They brought up the rear, or, if you will, fetched a large compass around the master. Nor were these "daughters of Jerusalem," as some suppose, women from Judea or Galilee in general. The name "Jerusalem" does not designate the whole of Israel. No, these are the women of *Jerusalem,* the ladies of the "great city."

Now we know that women of the big city know how to resort to tears. They know what is meant by weeping, and especially what is meant by sentimental love. They have read the beautiful statement in the Bible which says that the daughters of Jerusalem

---

1. The Hebrew name for the chief of the demons; see Tobit 3:18 and 6:14.

must be told that there is a bride who is sick with love. This message does not escape them. The theme of "the sick with love" grips them. However, even though they are fond of discussing this theme without asking whether they can excite a genuine love, they cannot evaluate these things correctly. Just when people are sick with love and just where the energies of love—in its sublime manner—can flourish wholesomely they cannot exactly say. Love seems to them to be a beautiful adventure and, accordingly, being sick with love also charms them. For the rest everything is rather vague. But who in matters of love looks for learned definitions? These women have heard it said, and that by very interesting men, that definitions have no place here. And with that they can heartily agree.

Consequently, there is much work to be done by these ladies of the big city. There is a *great* prophet. No one can deny that He is aflame with love. That He is sick today is also obvious enough. This moves the women to follow Him. Many prophets of the inner chamber[1] have comforted them. Everything is vague here. That is just the point. There is a love, and it is sick. Just what *health* is . . . well, that is a different matter . . . Come, sisters, let us weep. Someone with a vague love is sick. Who would not weep!

They weep. Such weeping always causes a commotion in the world. Thus the day has brought to pass the sorrows of the daughters of Jerusalem.

We suggest that you do not busy yourself too much about those learned dissertations which try to find out whether their sorrow was genuine or not. Roman Catholics even ask whether it was "natural" or "supernatural." Other Christians evaluate these tears by consulting their list of the "marks of grace" and then—as is their way—still grope in the dark. Do not emulate them. The daughters of Jerusalem are many. Among them are those whom God has predestined for the joy of His Pentecost. Who can say what preparatory grace is accomplishing in their soul at this time? There are also among them those who will not hold out against the fire of Pentecost, and *these* "daughters" will be sick, will continue, that is, to live in death. But Christ, as He ministers His word, addresses them *all* as daughters of the holy city. He still calls the

---

1. *Christ in His Suffering,* p. 339; *Christ on Trial,* p. 33.

city by its own name; He faithfully administers God's Word to
it; He points it to the connection between this day and the great
day of days, and also to the connection between His own fruitful
death-travail, and their fruitless labor.

Daughters of Jerusalem, ye who have no future, who are the
last children of a barren city, weep not for me. Such is Christ's
pure reaction. It is a reaction which is good for *all*. For everyone.

The true and the false is mingled in the weeping of these women.
Among them are those who pour out their hearts as though they
were in the presence of God. But there are also falsetto voices
among them. Jesus hears their lamenting. Now the word "lamenting" has nothing repulsive in it. Lamentation is a technical
term: it was the gesture of mourning which, together with all of
its ceremonies, was the custom with the Jews whenever death cast
its shadows upon them. The Jews had mourning women; they
even hired them. These knew how to weep, and had the time to
weep. The Jews liked to use people who had the time to do things.
For the synagogue they hired ten visitors, whose *duty* it was to
visit the synagogue; ten of them, the required minimum, and
these ten are people who "have time for such things"; they
are the *opus operatum*. Just so the Jewish rulers proceed to
hire mourners, people who understand the art of weeping, and
who have time to do it, the *opus operatum*.[1] Jesus, who
had always opposed the idea of the *opus operatum*, now also opposes these mercenary, insincere mourners. When they caused a
tumult in this or that house, Jesus more than once drove them out.
He who would purge temples, must go on from the temples into
the houses.

Today, however, He does not have to drive people out any
longer; nor does He have to distinguish between the true and the
false. He has the same message for all. What else has He, but
the ministry of the Word?

He gives what He has. He presents God's Word. But, in order
to minister the Word, He must first purge Himself of their tears.
For their weeping is not what it should be. It seems to us that the
meaning of those who would relate this episode to the Talmud is

---

1. A piece of work, generally religious, which is sufficient to itself, which, once
done, has no further purpose. It satisfies those who would save themselves by
works mechanically dispatched.

too far-fetched. These interpreters point to the fact that the Talmud forbade the mourning of the death of someone who had been condemned by the Sanhedrin. Consequently, they regard the weeping of the women as a protest against the government. This is altogether incredible. Even if the sound of mourning was intended as a note of protest, would that have justified it and made it pleasing to God? Whoever does not put the death of Jesus into relationship with the crises of his own life has lost himself, though he weep never so much. Hence Jesus—looking neither to the right nor to the left—turns abruptly around and says to the women: *Weep not for me, but weep for yourselves and for your children.*

To these words He adds a discourse. The discourse is long enough for one whose back has been scourged, whose every step brings Him nearer His death; and it is brief enough for One who has so comprehensive a view of all things of time and of eternity as He has.

We can discover the true meaning of this statement of Christ only if we find its place in the history of the passion. We have already mentioned the fact that this statement is a public statement; it is a public ministration of the Word. The day of Pentecost has not yet come; hence that is not the reason for which He must address Himself to the people of the city. After He pronounced this short discourse, He never again made any public address. He did not speak to the public from the cross, for His seven utterances from Golgotha were not directed to the people in general. After His resurrection, too, Christ never once used His human tongue to direct a public address to the people at large. The discourses of Jesus, the Son of David, have an end. Does that not make you tremble? If this is the last public discourse which Christ Jesus pronounced on earth, we may be sure that this statement was for God (to whom a thousand years are as one day) immediately bound up with the forthcoming public discourse which Christ will address to the community which is in the world. You ask what the scene of that forthcoming public address will be? That will be on the last day, when the world will quake, and when everything that is said here will be completely fulfilled. Then the sound of lamentation will be addressed to the mountains demanding that these fall on them, and to the hills asking that they cover them. That will be when man will desire to live no more, nor any womb to give birth.

This public statement of Christ was a threatening one, and He who pronounced it was a broken Man. Nevertheless He was highly exalted. The full expression of the Messianic consciousness, the full strength of Jesus' sinless soul is in it. Is He harmed by it? He is harmed by everything. And yet by *nothing*. He is very sound; the simplest word is the best here. God and Satan are here, inciting these women to tears. The Lord incites them; such is the Biblical language. Satan incites them also; that, too, is Biblical language. God compels them to follow Jesus; He makes them weep their tears. God wants to *try* His Son. Satan constrains them to follow Jesus; he makes them weep their tears; he wants to *tempt* the Son. He would wrench the steadfast Soul loose from its steadfastness. Well, nothing human is strange to Jesus. We may as well admit that it is not easy for any human being to be unaffected by tears which another human being sheds for him. It is not easy, when tears begin to fall, to give expression boldly and emphatically to that well-known, dignified statement of office-bearers, to that stately first and final predication of the ministration of the word, to the effect that the people must look beyond the minister, and beyond the speaker who is at the same time the complainant. Tears of the audience and spectators are a temptation to the office-bearer of God. Let everyone weep for himself. Let him not stop at the speaker who excites the tears, but let him look beyond the speaker. That is easy to say, but is it as easy to mean? Those of us who know ourselves will immediately say that it is not. But Christ, who is our Surety, never lets Himself be thrust outside of the official sphere, from which alone He may acknowledge His God. We see Him as *Prophet,* as *King,* and as *Priest.* Let us not tire of seeing Him again as He is in this three-fold office. For whoever thinks this spectacle tiresome is one whose "knowledge" is not prompted by "love." In other words, he becomes puffed up. And nowhere does such pride express itself as foolishly as on the *via dolorosa*.

We said that Christ is a *Prophet* here. Hardly dismissed by the judge, He addresses a discourse to the crowd. The transition from the second volume to the third volume of this work really is an astonishing one. The note of silence was very prominent in our second volume. As a matter of fact, the whole of it was dominated by this motive: But Jesus held His peace. At times He made a statement, but for the most part His speaking was subordinated to His silence. But now, as soon as we have been allowed to penetrate the third part of Christ's passion, something else impresses us forcibly. The dominant motive now is not "Jesus held His peace." Now He speaks. He speaks in the ministration of the Word. He speaks His seven utterances from the cross. He cries aloud. He cries with a loud voice. Crying with a loud voice He gives up the ghost. Who can say that this is not prophecy? We must give this fact even more careful attention when we observe again that Christ does His speaking out of the Scripture. "You and your children"; that is the language of the Bible. From the days of Abraham the phrase has been repeated again and again. You and your children. Thereupon, Christ speaks of that distant, near-by day in which they shall say to the mountains, "Fall on us," and to the hills, "Cover us." Who is there that does not recognize in this Hosea 10:8: "And they shall go into the holes of the rocks, and into the caves of the earth, for fear of the Lord, and for the glory of His majesty." And who could fail, when he hears the words "daughters of Jerusalem" to remember the cadences of the Song of Solomon.[1] Certainly, then, if Christ during His last hours still speaks from the Scriptures, He remains the Prophet. Then He is being obedient to His prophetic office as a man also. If ever a Prophet of God was tempted to keep the *moment* which he was experiencing before his own mind and before the minds of others, and to accentuate that *moment* at the expense of God's one continuous work, it was He, the Prophet of our confession, Christ Jesus. All of His humanity, His nerves, His heart, His scourged back, cries aloud: It is good to weep for me. The moment is a horrible one; in this broken flesh the world is breaking. Listen, you can hear it breaking, you can hear it cracking in God's universe. Weep for me, for by my fall God causes the heathen to tremble. No, His prophetic spirit masters His flesh, puts it into service; His prophetic spirit makes the flesh subservient to the laws of the eternal Spirit. In this way He immediately links His own specific *moment* with the chain of the "times and seasons" of God. Al-

---

1. We do not mean to say that Christ is intentionally quoting from the Song of Solomon.

though His tongue cleaves to the roof of His mouth because of the thirst He suffers, it immediately gives voice to the whole of the Scriptures again. His discourse includes the whole of prophecy, and in this He is being God's official minister.

We can say, then, that a great compassion characterizes Christ's prophecy at this time. We can put the truth this way: The announcement of the devastation, of the conquest of the vicious circle, the circle of natural life, concerning which we heard Christ speak in our second volume,[1] is now being transferred from the "intimate" judgment hall to the public domain of the *via dolorosa*. If Jesus Christ had uttered His royal word, His word of life, in the judgment hall alone, it would never have reached the people to whom He was sent. True, He had, before this time, repeatedly testified to that people that He was the Messiah whom they, whom "this generation," would see as He came in glory. But today He relates His coming in glory to this particular moment. "This generation" now witnesses the day of His final dissolution. But this generation will also see that in His dissolution He also dissolves. "From now on ye shall see"—with that statement He admonishes the Sanhedrin and with that statement He now addresses the masses. He is taking His final prophecy out of seclusion and making it a worldwide proclamation. Now He lets the people, the many, see that He is breaking the cycle of natural life on this day.

As He does so He thrusts—Jews, do you see how terribly logical He is?—the mourning women away from His own death bed. For we must know that these women of the great city are pushing Jesus into the circle, the daily circle of life's funeral march; they weep for Him just as they weep for "a" son of man. But Jesus manifests Himself as "the" Son of man. He shows that His day is the day of the whole world. From now on, from this hour on, judgment will break over the heads of all. He reveals Himself now, not as a man who can be compared with any other, but as the One, who has His own peculiar essence, as the one green tree in a forest of dry trees. He shows them how He is loosing judgment upon them, how condemnation is breaking overhead. All because of Him. He laughs about that foolish pairing of names

---

1. *Christ on Trial*, chapter 7, especially p. 139.

which had been drawn up some time ago,[1] even though a trio[2] of names now defies Him in His spirit. Judgment now comes upon Him. What judgment? Is it the wrath of Rome, which will devastate the city of David after a while? No, it is not that; or, better, it is not that alone. Christ shows us (see Matthew 24), that "the day of the Lord" is one day; therefore He organically relates the wailing and weeping for the downfall of Jerusalem to the last judgment day. Thus Christ speaks to His people, administering God's word. He speaks to those who are still His own[3] in a plain, adequate way. There is not the hint of a maschil[4] in His discourse. The manifest character of revelation characterizes the whole of His final ministering of God's word. He raises His head high above the disdain of men. He sees Himself and His cross as a power sufficient to darken the sun. Thus He enters into communion with the swarm of grasshoppers of whom Joel, the prophet, spoke. Just as Joel—how nervous that prophet was—saw the beginning of the judgment day in the plague of grasshoppers of his time—the insects darkened the sun—and just as Joel saw the fiery chariots of Jahweh at the head of the cloud of grasshoppers, so Christ now announces: The God of the grasshoppers darkens the sun before Me now; soon darkness will impinge upon the city and upon the temple. God's fiery chariots are drawing Me to Golgotha. He hastens to set up my cross as a stumbling block to the Jews. Simon, I can go on; the Lord is with Me, Him will I fear. Did you want to help me, O man? But who can hope to move the heavy wheels of God's chariots when they are standing still? And who can put his hand to the spokes if the chariots are hastening on?

This is beautiful prophecy, is it not? Satan, thou hast sent the women in pursuit of Jesus; Thou wantedst to see whether He would remain true to Himself. It is true, is it not, that He very frequently drove the mourners away when He had to fight death, and had to make of a death-bed the work-room of His life? Thou wouldst like to know whether He will let them weep for Him today. This is His answer, Satan. He drove the women away again.

---

1. Jesus-Barabbus. See *Christ on Trial*, p. 455 ff.
2. His, and those of the two murderers.
3. John 1:11.
4. See *Christ on Trial*, p. 81 ff.

He remained true to Himself. For this Jesus has now seen the way of the cross as the work-room of His life. The way of the cross is a work-room rather than the death-bed of Jairus' daughter. He purged the atmosphere which was contaminated by the women. He did not thank them, not even now when they gave Him their tears.[1] Alas for Him if He had done that!

Then His prophecy would have been lost with Him in that shedding of tears which has drowned so many good words. The women weep; and tears always dim the eyes of men. But Jesus' eye is not dimmed, neither by blood, nor by sweat, nor by tears. He knows that these women are weeping only for "Jesus." The masses have no eyes with which to weep for "Christ." And "Jesus" does not wish tears which are wept for a "Jesus" who has been separated from the "Christ." He does not because of pity for Himself wrench Himself apart. For Himself He has no pity. His person is one person; it is undivided. That one person governs His two natures. His will is one. The pity of men cannot harm or wound Him. He is conscious of Himself, but He never stops there as human pity does. And now it is my turn. And yours. For He has driven the women away. It is our turn. This His prophecy is sounded everywhere. As Jesus, He does not want to be lamented; He wants to be believed as Jesus Christ. We listen to Bach's *Passion of St. Matthew,* and to its closing chorus: "Wir setzen uns mit Tränen nieder." As often as that chorus is being sung, as often as the singers run through the piece, and the ladies of "the great city" have their ermines handed to them, Jesus stands at the rear of the hall and says: Weep not for me, but weep for yourselves and your children; for the days will come in which those who have not wept because of me shall call upon the mountains and the hills to take away the sight of God and to protect them from the wrath of God. What shall we say to these women? We may as well be honest: Jesus also stands in many a church. He stands in many an orthodox church, in which the preacher by a "beautiful" sermon has caused tears to fall here and there. He has described rather than prophesied; his is a church in which "Jesus" was pictured, and Christ was not proclaimed.

---

1. This interpretation is not at all like that of P. G. Groenen, *op. cit.,* p. 445, who says: "The Saviour, consequently, recognizes the noble disposition (of the weeping women), and as a reward He speaks to them lovingly." Surely this is a typical Roman Catholic attitude of mind.

We may also honor the Saviour-Messiah as *King* on this occasion. The word which Jesus directs to the people on this day is a reference to what the people themselves have said. We remember that Pilate once asked: Shall I crucify your King? Shall his blood be upon you? Then the people had replied: *His blood be upon us and our children.*

This King is here now, and He says: My blood shall be upon you and upon your children. Time will come when you cannot endure your children because you will pronounce the name "lost son" proleptically (very different from prophetically) in referring to your child. The travail of My death will never still the travail of your birth-pangs. The day of My death will make your maternity chambers a funeral grotto. You will know this, and will say this, and will sigh because of it. You are taking the true Life out of your midst. Hence you will be unable to live after a while, unless you repent. In that day you will seek out death, and will not be able to find him. Your delight will be a burden to you, and each new child a brutal martyrdom. You want to be a community. And as a community you said: We shall purge ourselves of the blood of the Nazarene; we shall cut this piece of Jesus' flesh out of our common body; we shall safeguard ourselves and our children against this accursed individualist. But now you will not have the strength for a community life, for you will be unable to bear children. You will praise the barren as the blessed among you, because you cannot achieve a community of fellowship any longer, nor build a community any farther. Your sin will divide every man against every other after a while, the father against the child, the man against the woman. Your sin will be the disintegrating influence which will break up the form of the community and will make it an impossible conglomeration of antipodes, a concussion of reciprocally repulsive elements. And this basic denial of life, this piercing scream accompanying the sundered community will culminate in your absolute death. Judgment, dread, the fear of the Lord — in those forms My royal blood will be upon you and upon your children.

The King knows Himself; that much you can hear. Not for one moment is He dependent upon His subordinates. He does not use the tears of men to justify Himself in the eyes of others. He even wrenches the crown of the martyrs off His own head. He does not wish the tears in which the impotent opponents protest against the overbearing vindicators of the right of revolution. He does not use their complaints to divide His judges from their subordinates, and to assert Himself overagainst the people. *This* King asks for no *Totenklage,* neither before nor after His death.

No muted trump, no mourning weeds,
No funeral dirge His body needs.

For His kingdom is not dependent upon men. His royal majesty remains purely itself in its self-manifestation.

Consequently He is also able to discriminate nicely between the true and the false weeping of men. When His mother begins to weep later, He dries her tears; her sadness is in conformity with God. But these tears are impersonal, and He sends the weeping crowd only to the temple, and to the Word of prophecy. This message is good for all: it is a last admonition. When love and faith weep together, He gives the mother a son, a son whom she has not borne. For the spiritual fellowship which is born of the Spirit of Christ dominates nature. By sheer Spirit it binds mother and son together, even though the same blood does not course in their veins: Woman, see thy son; son, see thy mother. But where faith is lacking, and love is not active, Christ tells the mothers: Woman, thou art no longer able to see thy son; son, never again wilt thou find thy mother. Woman, thou wilt not even bear a son in thy thoughts, for thou regardest thyself as very blessed when thou no longer needest to bear Abraham's children, because he will certainly refuse to acknowledge them, now that thou hast refused this, his great, Child.

Thus the Spirit of Christ governs the bonds of flesh and blood also. That Spirit governs blood and nature, the synthetic and the antithetic, binding and loosing. But always the Spirit will govern. He ties new fetters: Woman, see thy son. That is synthesis, a joining together. He tears old fetters apart: Woman, thou hast no son, thou dost not want him, thou dost even reject him in thy thoughts. That is antithesis.

Thus does Christ as a king break the vicious circle of life: from now on they shall see Him as the life-giving Spirit and not as the living soul. They shall see Him positive and negative, binding together and loosing, organizing and disrupting. As the life-giving Spirit He will become manifest to all nations. For His Spirit constrains the blood, and constrains His posterity. His Spirit robs Abraham's oppressed but impenitent mothers of their fleshly children, and by His will calls into life children who are full-grown men. These He calls into life in Abraham's oppressed and yet, in Him, comforted widows. Woman, lose thy son. Woman, see thy son. Son, leave thy mother. Son, see thy mother. Spirit, constrain the dust, for he who would weep in Jesus' presence must weep in spirit and in truth. The old covenant will not perpetuate itself in the superficial tears of women, but in the powerful sermon of a fisher of men. The son and the mother whom the Spirit of Jesus has brought together will not be lacking at the banquet which sanctifies all tears and which makes sacrifices of thanksgiving of them (Acts 1 :13, 14).

O second Adam, life-giving Spirit, come, preach in our fellowship. We will suppress the tears, O Lord.

We hear women weeping out of doors, we hear them sobbing; they say, and their saying it disturbs Thy preaching: Alack, where is His poor mother? Pitiable the breast that nourished Him in Nazareth. We hear the sobs, O Lord, and they are very human. But Thou lookest around Thee and dost say: They are looking for My mother. They want to press her hand and offer her condolences. Such is the custom of a great city. Who is My mother save he that doeth the will of My Father? Other than she I have no mother. Mother, do not accept their hand: Because Thou hast become My mother according to the Spirit, and doest My Father's will, they will crucify thee with Me. Didst Thou say these words, here in our company, O Lord? Then look around the room again, convert us to the will of the Father. Teach us to keep our sins near the baptismal font on which are written about each of thy brothers in particular these words: Lord, unite us in the will of the Father. It might be that at some time we will not love each other any more, that we will be jealous of each other, even as Thou hast seen jealousy in genteel women. When our eyes, as we move along the *via dolorosa,* look out in two directions — toward Jesus and also toward the priests — or even if our eyes, looking in one direction only, see the humanity of "Jesus" without penetrating through that humanity to the divinity of the Son and to the office of Christ, then our delicate weeping is the beginning of the jealousy of our own flesh.

Listen, He says to me: I am the king, but My kingdom is not of the earth. All kings who are not of the earth can use temporary faith very effectively for their purposes. Excitement, enthusiasm, and bursting tears reinforce their power. But I am the King of Zechariah 6; My kingship is united with the office of the priest. I do not like those tears, for in themselves these tears are but an expression of temporary faith. Woe is me if I do not wrestle with God for a saving faith, O weeping daughters of Jerusalem. Here is the Bridegroom, a king's crown, a priest's soul, and He does justice to the daughters of Jerusalem. He struggles for their preservation. He is not faithless to the law of marriage: He does not despise the tears, but only evaluates them, in order that the faithless bride of the Lord, the Maker, who was her Husband, might still honor Him.

In the third place, we consider the *Priest* of our confession. He knows that He is the Priest. Hence He is not satisfied with being the object of pity. He wants to suffer in His own strength, and in His own strength be a sacrifice for many. Now Claudia has her answer; now Pilate with his "ecce homo" also has his. Satan may tempt Him, the devil may try by means of the sadness of the women to make Him forget His own program of work, to distract Him from the demands of God's holiness, to make Him flee from the wrath of God. But Satan will not succeed in this. Christ did not desire the superficial sentiment of the women of Jerusalem for Himself in order to withhold from faith His determined will to be a sacrifice. The tears of Delilah have not kept Samson from his work today. True, He is put into the prison of the Philistines, but not because of those tears. It was a part of His task to enter the prison. He derives His reasons for doing things from Himself even on the day of His death. There were women here who wanted to detain Him when He wished to pay the dowry of the true bride of His heart. He struggled through their thronging; He had to pay, and He would. He does not know what concubines are; the true bride can see Him and pay and buy in haste. In haste. He does not stumble, O bride, over the impediment of the strange eroticism of strange women who do not recognize a buyer in Him. Tears have always detained those who were running in the race course. But He went steadily on, quite undetained, on the way of genuine obedience. And thus He becomes the "chief leader and fulfiller of faith," who will presently remove every burden from us, including the burden of tears wept by erotic women. The tear stricken face showing itself to the left and then to the right of Him, as He wiped the sweat from His eyes and could again see for a moment, that tear stricken face of a woman which longed for a glance from His marvellously deep eyes did not hinder Him from seeing the face of God. For God's face demanded but one thing from Him: absolute condemnation. Justice had so arranged it.

The women did not mention it to each other in the evening, but they had admitted it to themselves for a second. After all, He had been less interesting than they had thought. But that precisely is the case: He curses all interesting people, the peddlers of the spirit, and their organizers.

This is the Priest who is meet for us. Once He Himself wept when He approached the city and said that she did not acknowledge her sins nor that which could work her peace for her. God is now evaluating the tears which Christ wept then. For all tears which man weeps now and then are not evaluated until they maintain themselves genuine and uncontaminated overagainst those of *another*. If Christ's tears had fallen upon Jerusalem solely as tears of weakness — He could do no miracles because of unbelief! — these would have manifested that weakness now in an avid acceptance of the sadness of these women. If this soul — the *anima sensitiva* — accepts the tears of others as a sacrifice of incense today, if He accepts them as they are, separated from the spirit which is in Him, then He as a Mediator will be disrupted. Precisely that is what constitutes the temptation of Satan by means of the women. Satan wishes to disturb and move Christ's human soul; he would segregate it from the direction of His spirit. But now that He is maintaining Himself according to soul and spirit overagainst this extensive and yet limited sadness, He remains the strong. We know now that the tears which He wept yesterday are not to be separated from the blood which He sheds today. The tears of another have frequently hindered a person in offering his own deed; but Jesus was not hindered by them. Now that He has maintained His tears in their own pure strength they have remained united with His dear blood.

Now it is our turn to weep in His presence. We must weep with Him, through Him, and for Him. Whoever has seen Jesus' tears and blood fall upon the road which He travelled as Surety, will not weep because of the weakness of "Jesus," but will find himself weeping in the strength of "Christ." As a priest Christ reveals Himself, and lets Himself be seen.

Listen to what He tells the women. This is His priestly address: My death is not My natural fate but My supernatural deed. It is not My natural destiny, for I am not a dry tree, but a green and flourishing one. It is going against nature to hew down a green tree. Only dry and dead trees are justly cut down. A green tree when felled receives what it really has not deserved; such a tree is taking upon itself that which should have overcome the dry tree. Dry wood and dead branches are indeed fit for the fire. Such wood is but getting its deserts when it is cast into the oven. Well, every branch of the tree of Israel which acknowledges Me no longer is dead wood; it must be destroyed, for that is its destiny. But when I, the green tree, allow Myself to be despised and put to death today, I am assuming the fate of the dead branches. I am taking your lot upon Myself, O daughters of Jerusalem. I shall let Myself approve of your fate even in My death. Come to Me, all ye who labor and are heavy laden. Alas, if only you would acknowledge in this hour what it is that makes for your peace. Did Simon of Cyrene hear the sound of a dry sob? He could not be sure, for he could not look up, he could not look up into the eyes of the people.

Priest, High Priest, incomparable in grace. When, after a while, the people shall cry out, Mountains, fall on us, they will be trying to escape from God and the Word and from Thy priestly face. They sought to protect themselves from Moses' dazzling face by asking that a veil separate his from theirs. That veil must become a mountain presently; as thick and solid as a mountain it will have to be. Mountains, cover us! For who can withstand the eyes of the Lamb? But this priest draws God and the Word toward Himself: He can withstand the eyes of God. He can look straight into them. He does His work consciously always.

Do not call Him Mara; do not call Him the most unfortunate of men; for that is the name given Him by the women of Jerusalem. That name spells defiance for Him. He who calls Jesus the most unfortunate of men is pronouncing His name in the same breath and placing Him in the same category with all those other "unfortunate" ones of this world, is failing to discriminate between the green wood and the dry, dead wood. But Christ has expressly distinguished Himself from all those others. He is the green tree in the decayed forest. He is not the most unfortunate of men, daughters of Jerusalem; He is the Mediator of all the condemned of God, of all those who reach out to Him, of all those who would live by His death. Say no more, "Lo there goes the most unfortunate of men. *Ecce homo. Les miserables* of Jerusalem are the women and the priests. With whom then would you compare Him? I hear someone say that He died of His own pity, but this hour has proved the falsity of that. My Priest, who in the distress of His death could still turn pity away can never die because of pity. He can only govern all. From a distance we already hear the Spirit praising Him by means of the Word, praising Him who can have a true sympathy for our weaknesses, and who teaches us that the sorrow of the world does indeed work death in us, but that the sorrow of God, the sadness which is in conformity with God, works a repentance unto salvation never to be regretted.

Give me my children. They were born in Jerusalem; it is late; the ends of the ages have converged upon us. Give me the children of the Jerusalem of the latter day. Otherwise they might escape from me. *Fin de siecle.* And unite me with my unborn child, with the child of my mind, unite me with him before the cross of Jesus Christ. And teach us as we are together here a Passover song.

But do not teach it to me too quickly. I mean, do not teach it to me prematurely. I may overlook nothing today. Jesus has preached destruction, and has preached it to the children within her walls: *ceterum censeo Iesum esse delendum.*[1] God will punish me if I dare not make this terrible statement, dare not make it on His authority. This is a wonderful day. Tears and tears —

---

1. For the rest I mean that Jesus must be destroyed (a play on the familiar reference in classical literature).

but God makes but one statement: namely, there is such a thing as authority. He makes it very difficult; for I hate authority, especially when it makes itself binding upon my tears. I found those tears so pleasing. Yes, yes, *ceterum censeo Iesum esse delendum*: Lord, do not destroy me.

> Open my eyes that I may see,
> Open my lips that I speak truth.
> Oh keep me from all spurious ruth,
> From sentimental sympathy;
> For that would stain Thy majesty.[1]

---

1. Adapted from Albert Verwey's *Christus-sonnetten*.

Christ on Golgotha

CHAPTER FOUR

Christ on Golgotha

> *And they bring him unto the place Golgotha,*
> *which is, being interpreted, The place of a skull.*
> MARK 15:22.

THEN the procession arrived at the hill of Golgotha. That is where the sacrifice which is to take away the sin of the world was brought. Men's imaginations throughout the centuries have, in spite of the fact that God did not want to point out the place specifically, nevertheless persisted in trying to designate it exactly. They found it too terrible to believe that the statement of Psalm 103 could be applicable to the Christ: *And the place thereof shall know it no more.*

In this respect, too, however, we shall have to be guided by the will of God. The fact is that no one has ever been able to designate exactly where Golgotha was, and that he who would look for the soul of his Lord among the dead, and among the tombs of the dead, will have to walk around in the old Jerusalem without arriving at any certainty.

It is not surprising that a legend-weaving tendency should have busied itself with Golgotha. Some say — we shall only allude to a few of the guesses — that it was the very place in which Abraham offered up Isaac. It is said that Golgotha is the exact center of the world; that the skull of Adam was buried there; and that the blood of Zechariah as well as the blood of Jesus left its indelible stain there. There are many legends besides. In recent times the so-called religion-historical school has also presented its opinion about Golgotha. These maintain that the name "Golgotha" is derived from a root which means "roundness," and was a reference to the point at which the sun stands still. You see that

79

this is again relating a Biblical reference to mythological data derived from astronomy.

We prefer to abandon these considerations at once. Those who cling to the strictly historical interpretation as well as those who look only for symbolical significance in the historical data must feel ashamed by these attempts to cover the grave of Jesus and the death-scene of Christ with the poetic creations of human fancy. We shall not judge those Christians of the ancient day who, we are told, would at given times come together upon the hill of Golgotha to weep. "Even as the Jews still weep and wail at the wall of the temple, so the first Christians wept at the foot of the rock on which the cross stood. In the fourth century, and afterwards also, the congregation would stand there from twelve o'clock until the hour of Jesus' death, that is, until three o'clock, and would listen to the accounts of the gospel concerning the death of the Saviour, and to the prophetic utterances of the Old Testament."[1] No, we repeat, we shall not judge these people, for as long as the place of the hill of Golgotha was definitely known, people could stand there and could weep there prompted by the Spirit of Christ. The childish piety which would seek out the place of Golgotha could become a hampering demand on God only after God Himself had covered it with the grass, and sods, and dust, of many centuries.

Unfortunately, that is just what happened. God Himself has in the succeeding centuries removed the traces of Christ's way of the cross. We must bow to the counsel of God, and must give the hint narrated in Psalm 77 its appropriate meaning. In that psalm we read (the reference is to the Red Sea): *Thy footsteps are not known.* The water has completely removed the traces of the advance of God Himself, of His camp, and of Moses. In the same sense, we now say to the Lord God, who leads His people in the person of a Greater than Moses, but this time in reference to Golgotha: *Thy footsteps are not known.* The dust has removed every trace of Thy steps. Shall we lament this fact? To do so is to identify ourselves with the poet of legends to whom we have just alluded, who from this negative attitude passed over quickly

---

1. Nathan Soderblom, *Het lijden en sterven van onzen Heere Jesus Christus.* Translated into the Dutch from the Swedish by J. Henzel, N.V. G.J.A. Roys' U. M. Zeist, 1930, p. 291.

to the positive one: Thou leddest Thy people like a flock. He who sings that of Golgotha, who sings it in sincerity of heart, can be said to have been upon the hill of Golgotha in spirit.

We shall not burden the reader with a summary of what has been said about the hill of Golgotha as such. We wish to say simply that an identification of the hill of Golgotha with the hill of Goat, which in the opinions of some is called the hill-of-dying, is unwarranted. Those who so identify the two argue that the word "Goat" can in one way or another be derived from a root which means "to die." This fantasy must give way to the plain statement of the Bible itself, which says that the word "Golgotha" is related in one way or another to the concept of a skull. The connection between the Aramaic word for "skull" and the name "Golgotha" does not consist of the fact that according to custom the skulls of those condemned there were buried there also — a custom which some wrongly suppose is indisputable. The connection can very likely be ascribed to the fact that the hill resembles the formation of a skull. This interpretation also makes it highly probable that the hill must not be regarded as a mountain proper. On the contrary, we must think of it as a small rise of the ground, small, but large enough to make it easy for those who passed the spectacle to see plainly. This is in agreement with the custom of that day to choose for purposes of execution a place which was near a prominent thoroughfare, and one which because of its conspicuousness attracted the attention of all those who came along the highway. To this extent, therefore, the name "skull," or "place of a skull," suggests the Biblical thought that Christ had to be publicly lifted up. Golgotha was not a secluded spot, but a public place near the city. There the Lamb of God (according to the law of God) had to be brought. This consideration leads our thoughts to what Jesus Himself once said when He referred to His dying as a "being lifted up." Such considerations lead us in the right direction. Golgotha to us is not this or that place of topographical significance, but it is the stage and the work-room of the power and of the Word of the Lord.

Our only duty, consequently, is to determine the significance of Golgotha by means of the Word of the Lord. For Golgotha, which was Jerusalem's place of execution, responded fully to the needs of Christ's own prophecy.

In our previous volume we mentioned the fact that, according to Christ's own word, His crucifixion definitely had to be an exaltation.[1] Before this time He had consciously and periodically and purposely avoided the threatening death which He now willingly assumes. Again and again we read the line: "His hour was not yet come." By way of analogy that statement might also read: His place had not yet been reached. Now His place, the place of Christ, the place of His death, is not a secluded one; it is not found in the inner chamber; it cannot be seen in the desert. Neither is the place distinguished by earmarks very different from those which characterize other places in the world. Like Himself in His revelation, the place of Jesus is very ordinary. If the cross had been erected upon Mount Gerizim or Ebal, or over the Forum of Rome, say, or the Acropolis of Athens, then the determination of the place of Jesus' death would have occurred by means of a different logic from that which characterized the whole of Jesus' life on earth. Everything which Christ as a human being living on earth has, and wants, and finds, and takes as His own, is serviceable only to the purpose of revelation. We noticed before[2] that the Son of God took the given name of Joshua — a very ordinary name. He lived in a city which was typically human. In all of His life and His work He never established a memorial for Himself unless everything which should remind men of Jesus in the future would send their thought up to His God and serve as a remembrance of Him.[3] Now, according to that same law of revelation, the hill of Golgotha was not placed where men might place their monasteries or Colosseum or monuments. The choice of this hill — and was it really a "hill"? — was determined simply by these two considerations: first, the place is public, and all who pass may see that Christ is being lifted up on the cross; second, the place is ordinary, so ordinary that He who looks for it or finds it, will not even see it nor understand it if he does not believe. And on the other hand, all who do believe cannot fail, in spite of all the particulars of the place, to ponder the great significance of what happened there.

---

1. *Christ on Trial*, chapter 15, especially p. 297.
2. *Christ on Trial*, p. 464 f.
3. *Christ in His Suffering*, p. 231 ff.

These two requisites Golgotha fully satisfied. It is a part of the Old Testament that large, or at least conspicuous mountains, such as Zion, Horeb, Moriah, and Carmel, should attract the attention, and that historical events are given definite places which are conspicuously marked by monuments of one kind or another. In the Old Testament each new essence tries to attract attention to itself by a new form, by that which is obvious to the eye, by that which appeals to the senses. But in the New Testament the external form gradually is given less emphasis, the sensuous presentation is abandoned more and more, and the direct thought which God writes upon the hearts of men by His Spirit moves them so convincingly that the spiritual eye can see it, even though the physical eye is given no tower or promontory to assist it in discovery. Golgotha is but a very ordinary mound, a slight incline; it is no more than that. And this is in keeping with the incarnate Son of God. No rock offering itself to Him for an inscription; the Word, that is His epitaph. He does not plant His cross on an Acropolis; the whole thing is quickly achieved in the presence of the people on a very ordinary rise of the ground, the very same mound that was used for all executions. This sufficed for God. That which He plants on the Acropolis is the banner of the Word. He affixes no monumental tablet to the Forum of Rome, but, traveling along the many ways of the Spirit, He earns the rent for a room in which Paul can speak with the Jews of Rome unhampered. Thus the topography of Golgotha fully satisfies the law of divine ideas as these were manifested throughout the course of special revelation. It was this law of revelation which more and more separated and abstracted the inner essence, the spiritual life, the Word-content, from the forms of the external things, in order that the church of the future might not be *bound* to those places, nor have to say some time: The Antichrist has cut off access to our monuments, and now *we cannot remember the death of the Lord any longer*. For the church can remember the death of Jesus through the Spirit — if necessary without a linen cloth — and with bread, a cup, and a prayerful heart. If necessary, the church can remember the death of the Lord solely through the Word. Yes, if necessary, even without the preaching of the Word, but then by the universal, regenerating Spirit of God. He who has celebrated the Holy Supper no longer requires

the conduct of a guide to direct him to Golgotha. He *has* climbed
Zion, has seen Gehenna, and has embraced the cross on Golgotha;
he has been in the garden of the Passover — and has been seated
in the heavenly places. "From thence He shall come to judge the
living and the dead," to a place at which He is not expected.

Hence it was not a loss which we can ascribe to heaven, or
heaven to our apathy, that Golgotha was not more plainly marked.
The old Christian church, and even the earliest church has not
done anything by way of pointing the holy place out to its children
or grandchildren. As we see it, that was better than what was
done later when the church became corrupt and began to look for
material out of which to build a Biblical geography.

This was a geography to which Saracens might also have contributed if they had wanted to; a geography which had no need of
faith. God designated no wailing wall for the Jews, and no hill
of lamentation for the Christians. The wailing wall of the Jews
is a silent protest against Jesus Christ, quite in the manner, we
might say, of the emphasis of Akeldama.[1] It is a camouflaging
of the one great accusation which God has against the wailing
Jews; accordingly the Jews, so far from wailing too much, wail
far too little. At the wailing wall, they do not lament because of
their sin but they weep in order to conceal the death of Jesus.
Now a hill of lamentation would have been a similar protest on
the part of Christendom against the resurrection and the ascension, and a suppression of the need of the prayer with which the
Bible ends: *Come, Lord Jesus; yea come quickly.* When I read
that prayer, I can understand why Golgotha is such a very common place, and why God did not give it any prominent earmarks
by which it might be noticed in the future. The Spirit and the
Bride say, Come — and they sing no special prelude for those
living in the neighborhood of Jerusalem.

Accordingly we must not look upon the topography of Jerusalem and its vicinity as a restriction upon the Spirit, for it is precisely the Spirit which limits nature, also the nature represented
by this city and its neighborhood. These the Spirit limits by
means of the Word and the mind of God. Dust does not control
the Spirit, but the Spirit controls the dust. True, the Spirit im-

---

1. *Christ on Trial*, chapter 13, especially p. 267 ff.

presses its traces upon the ground, molds nature in the shape of its well-selected symbolism, but the Spirit never allows itself to be bound or restricted by it.

Therefore we can say that in the last analysis there is a *symbolism* here which we may embrace. There are *three* well known places in Jerusalem: Mount Zion, the Dale of Hinnom (Ge-hinnom), and — Golgotha.

Zion is the place of fellowship with God, the mount upon which He makes His dazzling appearances. This is the place of the descent from heaven, and the starting point of that union by which God wishes to unite Himself with His people in all eternity. *Ge-hinnom* is situated on the other side of Zion. It is the dunghill, the place of filth, a symbol of hell, and typical of the place of outer darkness.[1] Zion also represents a *fellowship;* Ge-hinnom a thrusting away. Zion means union, Ge-hinnom schism. Zion sends out its fragrant sacrifices, and Ge-hinnom gives us a taste of what Isaiah 66 states in conclusion: The abhorrent stench of carcasses, the vapors which are an unquenchable fire.

Golgotha is situated between these two. Bear in mind that the word "between" is not a geographical designation. We are looking for the topography of the Spirit. We know that the Spirit as it goes about the classification and arranging of the various places in the city of Jerusalem follows the course outlined in the Word of God.

This work of arranging, the Spirit does very quietly, very unobtrusively today. The Spirit raised some clamor in connection with Zion and with Ge-hinnom: remember the "necessary circumlocution." But He has told us nothing further about Golgotha. From that place He has gradually enticed all His good Christians with Him into the abundant life. He said: There you must worship the Crucified One in spirit and in truth. Let the Samaritans have their church — the motley people their Gerizim, but do you pray *here*.

Golgotha, the unknown place. Paul does not use the word. You cannot find it in the letters. The Revelation of St. John mentions Zion, Jerusalem, the court of the heathen, the seven hills of Rome, the cities of Asia Minor, and the temple of Aesculapius,

1. **Page 32.**

but never once mentions Golgotha. Not a word is breathed about Golgotha *as a place,* because as a place it is, on the one hand, the culmination of God's long course of altars, and, on the other hand, it is the starting point of Christ's return to judgment. Now God, who is ever hasting, did not adorn that place with a monument. He did not put a marker at the place on the red highway where the blood of sacrifices and of altars ceased to flow, but hastened on and impelled His letter-writers, as well as St. John, His great writer of the apocalypse, not to look for a particular spot, but to spread their hands abroad, and to point in two directions: the way of the Old, and the way of the New Covenant. God points out directions, not specific points. The God of the Word does not mark the point at which the vicious circle was broken, but establishes and commemorates *the fact that it was broken.* God is great in making us remember. He is just as great in making us forget. His footsteps cannot be found; but the meek can learn *the way* of Him.

Now that I know this, *now* I return to Golgotha. I see it lying "between Zion and Ge-hinnom." Yes, in very fact, there is a road which reaches from *Zion* to Golgotha, *and* a road which reaches from Golgotha to *Ge-hinnom.*

For Golgotha brings *both* curse and blessing, union and schism. It has given us the adoption of children through the sovereign good pleasure of God, and it will supply a deeper and profounder basis for judgment, inasmuch as from this time on that *grace* entered in which will not ever recede again. Golgotha represents blessing and curse alike; represents both election and reprobation. The restless soul which is being driven to and fro between Zion and Gehinnom, and which cannot find Golgotha, can find the Word, the Holy Scriptures of God, written by the Spirit. That word outlines its own topography, a science unknown to Samaritans and Saracens. It presents its own symbols, geographical symbols, too, but it warns us against an accentuation of these at the expense of the Word. The Word lays down a spiritual bond which unites our souls with Golgotha — Golgotha, a little hill. The Spirit of God teaches us to ask the mountains, mighty in size, why they exalt themselves against this tiny mound, this ripple in the earth, this insignificant place of which no one can say: There it is; see, over there! Why do the mountains proudly leap? God Himself desired this place, not for a dwelling place, no, for Golgotha points to Zion and to all other points as dwelling places. But God desired this place as a place of conquest, in order that He, being honored here, might from this point forth manifest His glory. The Lord who keeps His faith eternally would dwell in us forever.

Golgotha, the forgotten place. One can hardly find it any more. Pompeii is laid bare, but Golgotha has gradually been thickly overgrown. No, it is not God's fault if my thoughts wander. Golgotha and the "forgetting grass" belong together.

> The water goes up and goes down,
> the water goes in and goes out;
> a child throws a stone in the water,
> and the water goes in and goes out.
>
> The earth went up and went down,
> the earth went open and shut;
> when, higher than other men's graves,
> they made *Him* a grave, saying, *There.*
>
> The earth sank gradually down,
> the earth subsided again;
> and groping fingers of grass reached out,
> of grass forgetting and growing.
>
> And the earth went up and went down,
> the earth went open and shut;
> till soon it was all as level and green
> as level as all things alive.[1]

We thank Thee, Lord. Grass has grown over Golgotha. Hallelujah ! Thou hearest prayer. All flesh can come to Thee. Thou dost not lead us into erotic temptation. Grass grew over Golgotha, but now a voice can be heard above the place that can be found no more. It is the voice of the Word:

> Oh *voice* of the bare wooden Cross,
> Oh *voice* of the plain wooden Cross,
> I pleaded so often, so often, and prayed
> And . . . the *answer* was always: the Cross.

The place of His dying is known no more; *but* the *Word* of the Lord endureth forever.

---

1. Freely translated from Guido Gezelle.

Christ Not Repelling
His Judge

CHAPTER FIVE

Christ Not Repelling His Judge

> *They gave him vinegar to drink mingled with gall: and when he had tasted thereof, he would not drink.*
>
> MATTHEW 27:34.

> *And they gave him to drink wine mingled with myrrh: but he received it not.*
>
> MARK 15:23.

WE SOMETIMES hear the phrase: A man is what he eats. We do not believe that this is true. Not that there is no connection at all between the food and the heart, between what is taken into the mouth and what the heart expresses. For there is such a connection. Christ Himself has taught us that. The meal a person takes is also a confession. Even the rim of the cup discloses what is in the inner heart. That is why we prefer to turn the saying just cited around. Rather than to maintain that a man is what he eats, we would say he eats according to what he is. It may be true that food and drink affect the body not only, but influence the soul also, and that to this extent food is a kind of education; nevertheless the deepest essence of our life remains inaccessible to the effects of bread and water, of food and drink. Food does not explain the soul, but the soul explains the food. Tell me the kind of bread your soul feeds on and I will tell you the kind of food your body uses.

There is only one person in whom this connection between the heart and the food proved to be complete. He was Jesus Christ. In Him the external and the visible is always a faithful expression of the internal and the invisible. He is the highest truth; He is what He seems to be; He seems to be what He is. You can recognize Him in everything He does; in everything He does you can see Him as He really is, if you look at Him with the eyes of faith. Observe His mouth, and you will know the attitude of His heart. Pay attention to what He eats and drinks, and to what food and what drink He refuses, and you will know the food of His soul, and the drink of His heart. His food is to do the will of His Father; it is to drink the cup of His Father. But all cups of devils are repulsive to Him.

That is why He is our Mediator in everything, in His eating and His drinking also. Yes, even in His drinking. His drinking quenches thirst. His thirsting also quenches ours. Faith can find nothing in the whole of that awful passion night at Golgotha in which it does not recognize the tense will of the Redeemer for feeding His people. The law of His death was the same as the rule of His life: "Whether ye eat, or whether ye drink, or whether ye refuse to eat or to drink, do it all to the glory of God." Would He not drink the cup which the Father gave Him? Would He not drink it to the dregs? Would He not drink it unadulterated? Throughout all these years, from the manger to the cross, He has been drinking that cup, and He never allowed anyone to add a different drop to it; that which the Father had put into the cup, that only He drank. Now He has reached the dregs; a few more hours, and the cup will be empty. Could it be possible for Satan now to introduce a different ingredient into the cup of the Lord, an ingredient which God had not prepared for the Servant of the Lord? No, to the very last Christ keeps the bitter drink in its pure condition; He leaves it as His Father had poured and given it to Him; He leaves it quite unmixed. Let us consider the significance of that.

When the procession had reached Golgotha the preparations for the crucifixion were begun. One of these was that the crucified persons be given a sedative drink. This is also given to Christ. The drink consisted of wine mixed with gall. St. Mark tells us that the wine was mingled with myrrh. Some observers think that St. Matthew, who speaks of gall, is contradicted by Mark, who mentions myrrh. However, there is no conflict here. The word "gall," as we find it in the Greek language, can, just as the Hebrew word "marah," be used in the broad sense of something which is bitter. Whoever follows the meaning of the word in the Greek translation of the Old Testament will find convincing evidence of the fact that this is true. Consequently the myrrh which was mingled with Jesus' wine was the same bitter substance as that which Matthew called gall.

Who prepared this drink for Jesus? Opinions differ about this also. Some think that the women who followed behind Jesus, weeping, brought this drink with them. "Nowhere do we read that the Romans knew of this custom. Hence the drink very likely was prepared and brought along by the friends of Jesus, most likely by the women of Jerusalem who followed Jesus on His way to the cross. These, then, must have seen to it that this drink was handed to Jesus by the soldiers."[1]

That, however, is no more than a hypothesis. A more plausible explanation is that the offer of a sedative drink was a fixed custom in connection with executions, a custom used by the Jews, permitted by the Romans, or probably even known to the Romans themselves. The pain of a crucifixion was so gruesome, that, moved by their "philanthropy," they would give a person condemned to crucifixion such a sedative. Not that it would immediately remove all pain — how could that be, when nails are being driven through hands and feet? — but it did at least gradually put the consciousness to sleep, and make a more or less easy dying possible.

We are not going to try to determine the origin of this custom. It is true that this use of a bitter sedative at crucifixions is compatible with Jewish usage. Various Jewish writings contain references which suggest that felons condemned to die were to be given a reed dipped in wine and so to induce a gradual deadening of consciousness. In order to explain the custom, commentators sometimes appeal to Proverbs 31:6: "Give strong drink unto him that is ready to perish, and wine unto the bitter of soul."[2] These considerations are not very significant but there is one point which has some worth for us. These same Jewish writings also tell us that the custom was designed, besides serving as a sedative, to draw a confession from the condemned. Not that they wished to forego the death sentence in that case, but — think, for instance, of the persistent pressure brought to bear upon martyrs at the stake by dignitaries of the Roman Catholic Church by way of

1. Groenen, *op. cit.*, p. 447.
2. Strack-Billerbeck, *Op Mattheus*, p. 1037.

eliciting a confession from these — but the intent was partly theological. They supposed that a confession made at the eleventh hour might at least serve to gain him access to the next world, even though the condemned person was denied a life in this one.

We should be imposing unwarranted fantasies upon the account of the most bloody reality the world ever witnessed if we were to insist that this last purpose also governed the Jews when they, by means of the Roman soldiers, extended a cup of wine mingled with myrrh to Christ. The supposition is not entirely untenable: church officials of a degraded kind have been known before to whisper weakly into the ears of a man whose blood was being demanded by the church: My son, give God the honor and make a confession before it is eternally too late. We do not know.

But we should not like to overlook the possibilities. We know, for instance, that Pilate mitigated his rigid justice by extending a sedative drink. Just so it is very likely that the Jews are perfectly willing with one of their hands to support Jesus a little, even though the other is ready to push Him into hell. Church officials have been known to be willing to help a person on the way to his death and the other world if only they were sure of being rid of him in this one.

Be that as it may, it is, even though the Jews themselves never once thought of eliciting an eleventh hour confession from Jesus, for Christ Himself indeed the important question. He must indeed make the good confession. For He does not want to drink the sedative, precisely because of the good confession, because of the good deed, which He would fulfill in its completed sense, and while He is fully conscious of what He is doing. The Jews perhaps would have welcomed a constrained confession, because an *opus operatum* fits beautifully into their perverted procedure. But if they want such a confession, they can be sure that they will never get it from Christ. He will never confess that He acknowledges the evil that they ascribe to Him. Moreover, in addition to this negative attitude there is another one which in the highest sense of the word is a positive point of view. Christ must make the good confession to His heavenly Father; He must confess truth, justice, life, love, grace, curse, time and eternity. Now this confession which as an office-bearer He must make before angels and men in the hour of being forsaken of God and of being compelled to meet God demands His whole soul. It requires the whole spirit of Jesus Christ, our Lord.

Hence a sedative drink, which would have dulled the sensitivity of His human feelings, would have rendered Him useless as the Mediator and as the second Adam. We are not putting it too sweepingly if we say that the offer of this drink was a Satanic temptation.

However, again we see Christ as genuine man, as true man; we see Him as the Mediator of God and man.

We said that we see the Saviour here as genuine, as true man. In this connection we think of that detail in the account which tells us that Christ tasted the wine just for a second. He did not prepare for this circumstance beforehand; His human nature, like ours in all respects, met with an unexpected experience here. Accordingly, Christ tastes of the wine which is extended to Him. What else could be expected? His exhausted body is crying aloud for water, and, in our compassion, we would like to call out to Him: Drink now! Drink now, Thou scourged mock-king; for these mercies of the ungodly are brutal indeed, but who would shun the last gesture of sympathy on the part of cruel bullies? Drink, empty the cup, take what they give Thee; it will dull the senses, take the world away for a second; the burning sun cannot reach Thee then, the tears of Thy mother will not wrench Thy heart in two . . . yes, drink. In this dumb cry of Jesus' torn flesh we detect a faint resemblance of the parable which He Himself once spoke about the lost rich man who in his pain called for a drop of water. No, the resemblance is not far fetched, for this is *the descent into hell*. But that is precisely why Jesus is not like a laborer who calmly works out his schedule because he has beforehand figured out every reaction to every circumstance which would confront Him. Jesus responds immediately as a true man to the offer of the drink. He is very eager to drink something. Learn of Him, for He is meek and lowly of heart. Is not that your experience also? Even though He has perfect insight into the scandal of this crooked, legal procedure, He in no sense resembles the man who, while biting his teeth, stoically asserts: I shall insist upon my pride. I shall spurn their drink. Christ does taste of it. The soldiers need not think for a moment that He is not in a condition to pray for them. He will do so very soon. But God

before all things, God first of all. This sinless soul responds immediately and genuinely to every stimulus coming to it from without.
Genuinely, that is, according to the law. It is a spontaneous response — but it fits perfectly into the framework of obedience.
The moment Christ but smells the myrrh, and knows that it will
deaden His senses, He refuses to drink.

And why does He refuse?

Because He is the *Mediator,* the Mediator of God and men. If
in this most momentous hour He should deaden His spirit, then
He, overagainst God as well as overagainst His people, would be
doing wrong. Then He could not have represented God overagainst the people and could not have represented the people overagainst God. Then He would not have been the minister of the
Word who in what He says and what He does not say, rightly proclaims the truth and justice of God to men. Then He would not
have been the intercessor for His people, even though the hour
now demands that He be that. Then we would have lost the seven
utterances on the cross, voicing as they do a great love and a great
passion. Then He would have been ashamed in the presence of
Gabriel and Michael, and of all the angels, who are ever alert to
God, and who also are always looking upon the face of His Father,
whenever they do something good to the least of God's people.
What think ye — could the least of God's angels be a greater than
He? The angels are ministering spirits sent out to minister to
those who are heirs of salvation. Christ Himself taught us that
they come to the little ones who can hardly manage to sustain
their lives. They are around Him here, they support Mary, they
sustain John, they save Nicodemus from suicide. They labor
with the *gratia praeparans* — the preparing grace — in the souls
of the darklings who are still shouting themselves hoarse, but who
will after a few weeks and after the sermon of Peter be saying:
Men and brethren, what shall we do? What shall we do? Legions
of angels are present here and the spirit of God, praying in unspeakable groanings, is here, and is also there in the souls of men.
The devils are here; the whole company of them is here. The
spiritual world, good and bad spirits alike, is here.

Now suppose for a moment that of all those spirits the One
who is called the Logos had fixed a separation and an antithesis
between the perfect activity of His alert *Spirit* and the quailing

activity of His human *soul*. In this we are touching on the extremity of the possible; and we all know that the idea is folly, the idea of a deadened Son of man among all those weaker, waking spirits.

We mentioned just now that we are standing on the border line of the possibilities which are in Christ. We referred to the problem of the relationship between His human and His divine nature. This is a mystery which no one can ever fathom, and no one can ever put the relationship between Christ's divine consciousness, between the self-awareness of the eternal Word of God, on the one hand, and His human activity, the activity of His human soul and spirit, on the other hand, into a human concept, into a human formulation.

But there are some things which we do know. First we know that the divine nature can never let its alertness and activity be lessened or even changed. Second, we know that the sensitivity, the susceptibility, precisely because He is true man, is always finite, and therefore changeable, mutable, in process of becoming, and bound to everything which in this colorful life is subject to the sensuous apperception and vacillating movements of the soul, and the tensions of the spirit. Third, that this soul-activity of Christ is ever free from sin, and that consequently the effect of the outside world upon Him can never contaminate Him. Now the corollary of those considerations is that the divine knowledge of the Logos and the human knowledge and awareness of the soul and spirit of Christ, distinct from each other as they may be, never can be separated from each other, and never can be said to be antithetical to each other. True, His human soul works differently than His divine consciousness; His human soul engages in different inquiries of the heart from those which are the inquiries of the Logos and of the Spirit. But, precisely in this characteristic of the man Jesus inheres the possibility of that man to work in God's direction all of the time and to conform the motivations of His soul to the conscious activity of the Logos of God.

That is why the problem of the apparently innocent drink is so very important. At this time Satan is abusing the discord which is active in Jesus' human life because of the curse of our sin. Satan would, by breaking down Jesus' body, cause Him to cry so loudly for drink that the sublime activity of Jesus' soul may give its attention to an accident rather than to the main issue. Satan would induce Him to transpose the emphasis from the soul to the body, from the spirit to the soul and body, from God to man, from duty to pain, from eternity to time, from the history of God's revelation to Jesus' own experience at the moment. A change of emphasis, that is all. But that is enough, in His case, to break the world in two. Change the emphasis? That would mean that the man Jesus had chosen to stand overagainst God; for God always puts the emphasis upon the right place. Ah, a scattering of attention, a desire, a single act of the will designed to repel the judge who is driving the cold sword of His perfect wrath through Jesus' soul and body, *and all is lost*. Then the Mediator is broken.

Therefore we can say that all eternity, that the whole of theology, and that the whole of God's revelation in the incarnate Word lies *between the rim of the cup and the lips of Jesus Christ*. We are standing on the border line between two worlds, and we shudder. Soldiers bite their teeth and others curse, muttering under their breath because of this obstinate Jew.[1] But the angels are aware of the fact that there is a quaking in the Kingdom of Heaven. They know that all science and all philosophy will be given the unending task of thinking about what is happening here.

Let my soul ponder it also. The human soul of Jesus is, even in the most pronounced temptation, immediately ready to conform itself to God and the Logos. He at once senses the folly of this intoxicating image: a deadened Son of God and man among the waking sons of God, among the angels. Never did Christ have to fasten His attention upon the body so closely, and upon the tortured body presently, as He did at this time. Alas, that body can be so agonizingly big at times. It can cover the soul, it can darken the clouds, it can stand in the way of God. But Jesus sees His God even through His own clouds, and ever seeks Him out with a wise, a singing, a lamenting, and a longing attention. He seeks and finds God. No, God need not go out to ask a secretive Adam: Where art thou? A hoarse cry issues from the inner soul of Jesus, and that cry is seeking God. Where art thou, where art thou? I see Thee, I shall not let Thee go, even though Thou shouldst con-

---

1. From the Greek text we gather that the soldiers persisted when Jesus refused; that Jesus was compelled several times to spurn what was offered Him. This drama was enacted before the eyes of the people (a prophetic drama!).

demn me a thousand times. Never did the danger of a break between a whole series of the years of His life and this one moment of driven spikes and grinning faces threaten as overwhelmingly as it did now. Christ's attention is being demanded for only this moment, but if He gives it, it will be at the expense of that period of thirty-three years of obedience. The life-work accomplished in thirty-three years is now in danger of drowning in a single cup of myrrh. But the human soul of Christ did not accentuate this moment at the cost of introducing discord into the logic of His whole life. The cup of myrrh did not interfere with the course of His obedience to God. He is the faithful worker of God: He builds His temple, laying stone upon stone. In this moment Satan incites Him, lures Him, to temptation, asks Him to bite His teeth, to lay this one stone somewhat crookedly in the way, and to give it a smart rap expressive of repressed animosity. But this is not the way it took place. Moses may strike the rock in a fit of anger, the rock out of which the miraculous water freely flows. But the greater-than-Moses does not strike the rock out of which His own blood must, as the drink of life, necessarily flow. God will not be able to say to Him: "Thou hast not hallowed me." When Moses strikes the rock He spurns the service of the Word. This, accordingly, was his sin as an office bearer. Now Jesus must at once be both the Moses who breaks the rock by means of the Word as well as the miracle-working rock itself which must provide the water. And as He proceeds to be that He remains faithful to Himself, never once fixing a schism between the service of the Word and the service of blood.

No, you must not haughtily say that it was impossible for Jesus to be dulled or deadened. Do not say that, for that is not the issue here. True, from God's point of view it was impossible. Jesus' death presently is a different death from that of the other two. Christ presently will bear the pain of hell, and will endure the curse of the descent into hell. It would be folly to suppose that Jesus could be dulled; the terror of hell suffices to keep anyone awake. The attempt to deaden the senses of Him who must meet God and Satan in the extremities of death and curse is as ridiculous as the proposal Simon Peter suggested on the Mount of Transfiguration when he tried to cage the fluid sunlight of heaven in an insignificant hut.

But, once more, the point at issue here is not what is and is not *possible*. The point is whether the human nature of Jesus not only spontaneously and consciously spurns the evil choice, but also makes the good choice by a complete activity. This choice He made. He was not thrust into hell; He *descended* into hell.

Consequently Christ is susceptible to suffering the curse of sin. The curse will break Him. It will be His portion to endure the catastrophes of that curse in all their vehemence. For this He willed to do.

We have just referred to the catastrophes of the curse. By that we mean this. The curse which impinges upon life because of sin does not begin catastrophically but it does end catastrophically.[1] As soon as sin had entered the world, the curse also entered. It spread out, penetrated farther; even though in varying gradations of intensity, it spread out through the entire world of created things. But this is important. At the first entering in of sin, the curse came very imperceptibly. It came, if we may be allowed to express it that way, on stockinged feet. The power to unbind, to loosen, which we call the curse, a power which disrupts the organic unity of creation so that the parts in relationship to each other and to the whole have lost their proper places, comes creeping into the world very surreptitiously and quietly after the first sin. The sun continued to shine, the streams of Paradise rippled on, the birds still sang. It seemed as though nothing were wrong. The flood, centuries later, came with far more obtrusiveness than the disruption of nature at the first advent of sin.

Nevertheless, the curse was present. Although it does not begin with a catastrophe it will end in catastrophe on the last day. Christ knew this. He saw the curse which follows close upon the sin of the world; He saw it simmering for thirty-three years. He saw it in the foliage of the trees. He saw the curse lowering in the sun. As children laugh while looking at the sun, and as the poets sing their sentimental songs about the moon and stars, Jesus says: The sun shall be darkened, the moon shall be turned into blood, and the stars shall come thundering down. He felt the curse in His own flesh; His thirst was a problem to Him and His hunger a theological difficulty. A person suffering from fever presents the problem

---

1. We shall return to the subject in the next chapter.

of the disruption of the temple to Him, and the problem of a rift in the clouds.

Now return to the cup of myrrh. Can you believe that Jesus had become used to the "phenomenon" of the curse? Can you suppose that He no longer had an eye for that terrible conductor of our lives, after He had seen him throughout these years? We get used to things, but He did not. He always related the hovering of the curse over nature and life to the first and the last things that are to be in the world. In the last analysis He saw no fundamental difference between a toothache and the day of judgment. He knew very well that the grim persistence, the mad perseverance of the curse in this world, had begun in Paradise and had to culminate in the last or judgment day. That day would witness a catastrophe: moving mountains, a torn world, a devasted temple, and a sea of fire. The pain of these catastrophes He must bear today. His flesh must be torn; that which is tremendous is meet for His death. Presently He will live through the day of judgment in His own person.

Now pay close attention to His Word. He did not want to repel this tremendous judgment of God. His ears might not begin to hum, His eyes might not begin to blink, and His spirit might not subside within Him. Had He wanted that, the judgment day, which is the world-catastrophe of the final curse, would not have had a place in His soul. He may not repel, He may not thrust aside, He may not spurn the judge. "Whosoever lookest on a woman to lust after her hath committed adultery with her already in his heart." He who does not look God straight in the eyes to perfectly desire Him has already committed the great denial against Him.

However, He preserved Himself, He refused the cup. He refused it spontaneously; He understood it all in a moment. This is the second Adam; not even the most rapid invasion of Satan can harm Him. Man can cut His body to pieces, but no one will succeed in driving a wedge between His soul and spirit in order that Satan may enter in.

Now suppose that this Priest had actually permitted Himself to be dulled and deadened by the cup. Then He would have been dismissed from the priesthood. The priest may never be drunk in the house of God. The sacrifice needs the prayer of the minister;

he who offers the sacrifice may not become inattentive. As for the sacrifice itself, it may not mitigate the pain of death which justice demands. As for the temple, it can brook no stench of decay; hence the incense of pure prayer may not become mingled with the humid vapor of souls who seek something other than God. Whom have I in heaven above to compare with Thee? What is there on earth for me to desire, for me to yearn for, as adequate and pleasing as Thou? In Thee I can rest. No, Father, in Thy house there is nothing besides Thee. Hence the Son cannot want to be deadened or dulled. He is too full of Thee; He who is full of God cannot suppress Him; for God, in such a person, occupies the whole space.

O Priest, O High Priest. This Priest of our confession faithfully fulfilled His priestly service. Some say that the word "priest" is related to the root "stand": and the work of priests is designated in the Scriptures by means of the technical term, "Come near." We know that a drunken man cannot stand; he sinks down. Nor can a dazed man "come near"; he stumbles, he gropes. But Jesus who refuses the myrrh both stands and comes near. Now He ascends to the altars of God, to God, to His God, the source of suffering. Now He descends into hell and yearns for the commandments. God is striking Him — hence He *must* feel the pain.

Jesus feels that the heavenly pronouncement of justice differs from that which is pronounced on earth. When God punishes He punishes completely. His verdict is not characterized by that inner contradiction which characterizes the verdict of a Pilate who wounds the victim with a nail while he soothes him with myrrh. When God in His flaming wrath begins to punish, He does not administer one stroke too many, nor one stroke too brutally. Hence every stroke He gives must be felt. God is not playing a game. The world may hold a sword in one hand and a soothing cup in the other but God holds a sword in the one hand and a sword in the other. God is wholly love or He is wholly wrath. Therefore that cup of myrrh could not be given Him by God.

Our soul must not overlook these things in passing by. The refusal of the cup of myrrh is just as important as the shedding of Jesus' blood. Any fantasy of a holy grail or of a vessel which caught up the blood of Jesus must stand or fall with His refusal to accept the soothing wine.

Priest, High Priest. And, second Adam. Let us, as He Himself did, go back to the very beginning. When the first Adam had suppressed his God as a Father and Judge from his attention under the shadow of the tree of knowledge of good and of evil there must have been a moment in which this suppression of God, and this inattention, and this removal of the emphasis from the center to the periphery, was consciously *willed* by Adam. Otherwise his sin would have been *weakness,* not wilfulness. If so, the contrast now is complete.

The first Adam consciously did the deed which thrust God out of his soul and his spirit. It was the deed of enmity. Now the second Adam must *refuse* such thrusting aside and must refuse it consciously. Actively, consciously, with the whole force of His human constitution fixed upon it, He must refuse the cup.

No heart can go beyond this. I see God standing here among the murderers. I know that Paradise is returning here, and also know that God is trying the second Adam more severely than the first. God prepared the first Adam for the coming test. Adam was told: Lo, there is a tree; stay away from it; do not eat of it. It was the tree of knowledge by which he might know whether he was to thrust God out of His place or leave Him in the place He should occupy. But the second Adam was given no preparation. He does not know, He does not notice. He even tasted of it, because the cup had been set before Him in a very common and ordinary way, and He was thirsty. But the moment He noticed the stench of Satan's hot breath still clinging to the cup, He knew everything, and He refused it. He saw His mother standing there, and He knew that she wanted Him to have a drink. She could not bear the spasms of His death. Mary means more to Jesus than "the woman" meant for Adam in the hour of temptation. He would rather send His mother away than mitigate the dire tragedy of His death, and drink from a cup which justice and the commandments had not given Him.

Now we greet Thee, O King of the earth, who in the Holy Supper of the Lamb will pour out wine in glory. Thy lips crushed death to pieces, just as the teeth of the first Adam ground life to pieces. Your lips, O second Adam, parched with thirst, tasted of the problem of time and eternity, for Thy heart, although sorely tested, can taste only according to the law of God. Thy lips re-

fused the food of the dead and the drink of devils. Now serve the
wine of Thy love and . . . may He kiss me with the lips of His
mouth, for I have not perished. Whoever has seen Him in that
way will possess a Christ Whose love was in no sense drunk with
wine, but Who is a glorious wonder of love known to no mortal.
The beautiful wine of love beams out to Him from the rejected
cup of devilish wine. This wine of love Christ Himself prepared
here. The cross of weakness will become the throne of Christ's
might.

Christ Under the
Catastrophic Curse

CHAPTER SIX

Christ Under the Catastrophic Curse

● *And it was the third hour, and they crucified him.*

MARK 15:25.

THE hour has now come in which the Son of man is to be crucified. Come, ye Jews, feel free to break down the temple, as He Himself has said. Come, Romans, break down the temple; you have done it before and you will do it again. For Christ the moment has come. He has refused the sedative drink, and it may be that the refusal caused the soldiers to drive the nails somewhat more forcefully through the body of the Son of man. Someone was hissing between his teeth: obstinate fool, he refuses the sedative, does he? Come then, we will show him.

We must say at once that there is no unanimity of opinion about the manner in which the crucifixion took place. One commentator supposes that, according to the usual method, the cross was first laid upon the ground, and that the person to be crucified was nailed upon it as it lay in that position. Others think that they may infer from historical records that the cross was first set up vertically in the ground and that the condemned person was then nailed upon it. Even then, however, opinions differ about the further details. Some maintain that the soldiers lifted the one to be crucified up and that one or two others then stood on a ladder in a position to drive the nails through the hands. Others again entertain the notion that the condemned man was compelled to jump up on a stile prepared for the purpose, in order to place his body in the desired position. A third group hold that they tied him to the crossbeam with ropes, that they also tied his trunk and legs, and that then the nails were driven through the flesh of the hands. Whether the feet also were impaled is another question about which opinion differs. Some think that the feet were allowed to dangle freely but others assert that these as well as the hands were nailed to the beam, both feet together or each foot separately. And again there is a difference of opinion about the position of the feet. According to some the sole of the foot was pressed against the beam. If this were true the knees would first have to be bent into a position which allowed for that; but others believe that the legs were stretched out to their full length and that the nails were driven through at the bottom of the foot. It would be to profane reverence if we were to make any attempt to choose one or another of these possibilities. The choice has been made innumerable times, both in classic art and in the written and the spoken word. But we shall not commit ourselves to any one position, for we lack certainty. We do believe that we are justified in inferring from Luke 24:39 that the feet of the Saviour also were impaled. But for the rest we lack an accurate designation of the particulars concerning the crucifixion of Jesus.

Let us honestly admit at once that we do not regret this fact. We believe that God Himself threw a veil over the naked body of His lost Son. Ours is not the prerogative to remove this veil. At this point we return to the thought we entertained before, when we pointed out the fact that the place of the crucifixion cannot be exactly pointed out. We revere the will of God Who does not allow us to fix our thoughts upon unrevealed, historical particulars, but Who wants us to fasten them upon the idea, upon the prophecy, upon the revelation-concept which comes to us in the martyr's death of Jesus Christ. We can say, of course, that the crucifixion itself, however it may have taken place, was a terrible punishment. All kinds of enthusiastic and arbitrary spiritualization of the event, all kinds of falsely mystical imaginations or bloodless symbolism have, it is true, attempted even to take the sting out of this worst of terrors. But Scripture points us in a different direction. It forbids us to follow that method of argumentation, common in ancient representations of the event, which sees in the extended arms of Moses, as he prays in the battle against Amalek, the sign of the cross; or that which sees in the bisection of the vertical beam by the crossbeam the bisection of the "horizontal line" by the "vertical line," the bisection of the eastern-western line, the horizontal line, by the northern-southern line, the vertical line. The cross of Jesus and its unknown form does not lend itself to a game of words. It does not want to be a symbol but a reality which concerns us directly.

That reality, we may be sure, was very terrible.

"The extent of the physical suffering has been described by a physician in the following terms: The unnatural, constrained position of the body with its arms spread outwards for so long a time must have been a torture which cannot be described in words. This is especially true because not the slightest movement could be made without causing unbearable pain to the whole body but particularly to the impaled hands and feet and to the back, made raw as it had been by the scourging. The nails had been driven through the body at precisely the places were numerous sensitive nerves ran together. Some of these were excited, and others suppressed, a situation causing the severest pain, and one which must gradually have increased. The irritated parts of the body, gradually exposed to the influence of the air, must slowly have become swollen and bruised. The same result must have taken place in other parts where the liquids of the body were held back by the tremendous tension and consequently were frustrated. Now the pain of the inflammation in these parts could only increase from moment to moment. The blood which is carried to all parts of the body through the arteries by the left auricle could not find room enough in these badly inflamed and swollen parts, and consequently would have to flow to the head in greater proportions than usual, would have to distend and press hard on the arteries there, and thus cause ever increasing headache. However, because of this hindrance in the circulation of the blood the left auricle would be unable to send out all of its blood, and consequently would be unable to receive all of the blood coming to it from the right auricle. There was, therefore, no free circulation of the blood in the lungs. This would cause the heart itself to be oppressed; all the arteries would necessarily feel the added pressure; and an unspeakable sense of oppression had to result.

"Add to these considerations the fact that the person could never turn or adjust himself amid all his pain, inasmuch as the head alone was free. The body was persistently in an unnatural position. This meant that a gradual stiffening of nerves, arteries, and muscles had to result. Nor must we forget that a burning oriental sun beat down upon the condemned man. There was not a blade of grass to cast its shadow upon the cross. Fiendishly annoying insects hummed around him, and settled upon the open wounds, aggravating the pains."[1]

Pardon the long quotation. We insert it because of an attempt to restrict the matter to what is definitely known.

It is terrible enough.

We must look upon these things in the light of our faith. The cross takes on significance for us when it is regarded not as a symbol, but as a bloody reality, which was inevitable for Jesus Christ because the great Judge wanted to minister the curse of sin to Christ solely through the cross. The crossbeam was not an accident, a circumstance which gives a sort of perspective to Golgotha, but which might also have been lacking. It is not a "tragic feature," or coincidence, for nothing in the trial of Christ deserves that name. True, the cross of Jesus Christ, just as the whole of that fatiguing trial, does arise very gradually and naturally out of the life of His time and out of the usages of that time, and, to this extent, it is completely human. But from God's point of view the cross of Christ is the form by which we human beings were instructed in the ministration of curse to the Surety and Mediator. Of all possible *operata* of curse and death, God chose this particular *operatus* for the Surety.

The question, consequently, arises: Just why the cross, and why no other form of punishment?

We have previously indicated that the cross, inasmuch as it was a Roman and not a Jewish mode of execution, gave expression to a definite idea of God. The Christ had to be *lifted up*, we said. By means of that exaltation He had to be raised above the particular sphere of the forms of Moses' religion and law. Consequently Christ had to die according to the verdict of the world empire which was then extant. This is one consideration: the cross is international in scope. But this is not the only consideration. The form, the manner of the crucifixion, is also the particular one which God chose to express the idea that the Mediator had to be *publicly exhibited*. This public display is indeed a Biblical idea, and that is something which cannot be said about the too facile

---

1. See P. Biesterveld, *Van Bethanie naar Golgotha*, pp. 357-358.

and hardly poetic expression which talks about "swaying between heaven and earth." Heaven does not want the crucified One, and the earth can endure Him no longer. But all these notions, and others similar to them, are the products of a false imagination. Let us be very cautious here at the border line of hell, and let us listen to the Bible. God chose the form of crucifixion which required that the condemned person be raised above the common lay of the land: the emphasis had to fall on the *public exhibition*.

These, then, are the two perspectives given us. First, God willed the crucifixion because He wanted to lift Christ up before the world. Second, the crucifixion was willed by God because by that means Christ could be publicly displayed before men. The first perspective deserves the amplification that not alone did Christ have to be raised before the *world*, but that He also had to be *lifted up* before the world. Again we think of the analogy between the brazen serpent and the Son of man both of which were lifted up, in order that anyone whose eye looked forward to what could redeem his life, might look upon this life-giving wonder. To these two considerations we must add a third.

In the death by crucifixion the curse achieves its confirmation. We want to point out the fact that hanging on a tree is a form of punishment which must also be seen in the light of the law of Israel. The form of the cross speaks a language known to all men. The legal definition of the cross is laid down by Rome, and the theological exegesis of it is contained in the law of Israel. Nothing is accidental, neither the form of the cross, nor Roman power, nor the law of Israel, to which Christ was still conscience-bound. He was not permitted to separate His cross, not even His cross, from the law of Moses; He was not allowed to look upon it solely in the light of Rome, for then He would have been unfaithful to the law which He was not to break down but to fulfill. No, He might not break down that law, even though it was breaking Him. All of those Romans together were not permitted to keep Jesus from seeing the ghost of Moses, for Jesus was dying within the domain of special grace. This, too, God had willed. Moses' book of law could not be pushed aside by Roman law in the consciousness of Jesus. Just as the law book of Rome was being read to Him by devils, and angels, so the law of Moses is being recited in His soul by the eternal Spirit. Moses says: The *curse,* it is the *curse* which is expressed by crucifixion. *Cursed is everyone that hangeth on the tree.*

The curse . . . yes, the curse. We have spoken of that before.[1] We saw then that the curse which ordinarily came to the condemned man *after his death,* had to be consciously assumed by Jesus before His death. We saw that for this reason He had to be hanged upon the tree *not after* but *before* His death.

In this circumstance we see a wonderful confluence of the streams of the providence of God. We see that the God of history has given Israel its law book throughout the centuries by means of inspiration and theophany, thus arriving at the Christ. But we also see that the same God for the sake of the coming Christ had already pointed the Roman book of laws, and the Roman jurisprudence and the Roman history throughout the centuries in that direction which would enable it to realize this curse in Jesus. General history exists for the sake of Christ. Roman antiquity had to meet Mosaic antiquity at noon of the Lord's day of revelation. Both of these have their task and function. *Roman* law had to determine the time of Christ's hanging upon the tree; Roman law had to see to it that He was hanged before and not after His death. In this God permits the law of Rome to impinge upon the ordinance of Moses in order that the Surety bear the curse before His death. But Rome cannot suppress or push aside the spirit and the exegesis of Israel's theocratic law. Hence Jesus can find the exegesis of His own hanging upon the tree only in the law of Israel. He knows that law; He knows very well that to *hang upon the tree* means to be *accursed.* Thus the God of the centuries, the Potentate of Potentates, lets the legislative avenues of His Spirit which come to Christ through the Holy Scriptures of Israel meet with the legislative ways and avenues of the existing world empire, in order that the cross might stand at the place of their bisection. This makes the cross the result of the foregoing century. The cross arises out of the fruition of the realms of culture and of grace. These *two,* the unbound word of Israel's inspired law book and the binding words of Rome's unsanctified tyranny are both taken into God's service today. They must bring Jesus as the Surety and Mediator to the place where He is to suffer the

---

1. Chapter 1, pp. 20 ff.

curse, and to suffer it *before* His death. As we see the ways of Rome's military power and of Israel's Word-power crossing each other here in order to enable Jesus to suffer the curse in the right way and at the right time, we get a new glimpse of the almighty, and ever-present power of God which we call His providence. The God of the world not only descends to the earth from the Mount of Horeb but also from the seven hills of Rome. We are given a new motif for the preaching of God's providence. This is a new knot in our confused, but also unravelled thinking of faith. We will be profoundly awestruck in the presence of the crucified One, for God will be coming to us from all directions. The world will be full of God and full of the ludicrous. The world will be full of God and full of scandal, full of God and full of folly and arrogance. Alas, to think that the Saviour can understand the cross only in this way. His thinking is far superior to that of all poets. His thinking is genuine and is true.

But does this exhaust the content of the Biblical thoughts contained in the crucifixion? He is foolish who supposes that it does. If what was said above is true, we may not say: Well, it was very tragic; now let us stop thinking about it. Instead we say to ourselves: Now it begins. If Christ sees God coming down upon Him from all sides, the God of history, the God of Horeb and of the seven hills of Rome, then it is God Himself who is hanging Him upon the tree. It is God, the God who buried Moses, Who slays the Lamb.

There is another matter which attracts our attention in the cross. This is the *violence* of the breaking down of the body. Hands and feet were torn apart by nails; hammers wrenched the flesh asunder. This too deserves notice. To ignore this particular would make us poorer than the poets and painters and musicians who have been fascinated by this terrible, tortuous death, and would keep us from attaining to the overwhelming riches of thought contained in the Scriptures and the Church. For the Scriptures emphatically point us to the nailing on the cross, to the drawing of the blood, to the breaking of the body. And the Church, accordingly, has in her liturgical forms preserved the memory of the breaking of Christ's body in the breaking of the bread at the Holy Supper, and of the pouring out of the blood in the pouring out of the wine. Obedience to the Scriptures and fidel-

ity to the Church consequently teaches us emphatically to ask for
the significance of revelation in the violent treatment inflicted
upon the body of Christ by the crucifixion. We have observed[1]
that Christ more than once concealed a maschil in the word which
spoke of the breaking down of His temple. By that maschil He
wanted to present His body as a temple of the Spirit. This should
suffice to induce a heart given to reading the Bible to say: A cry
issuing from the highest temple is, if seen in a prophetic light, as
awful as is the falling of a star. Precisely the fact that the body
of Christ is a temple gives so profound a significance to the violence with which the nails are driven through His flesh and to the
vehemence with which the temple in which God's spirit lived unreservedly is broken down. Just as the narrative of the creation
of the first Adam out of the dust of the earth, and the breathing
upon it of the Almighty, definitely affects all basic problems of
philosophy and theology, so the violent breaking down of the
body of the second Adam, as it is recorded in the Bible, directly
affects Christian philosophy and theology. In the last analysis,
the life-and-world view of thinkers who are faithful to the
Scriptures must reverently bow to it.

Accordingly, we must attempt to appreciate the theological
significance of the cries issuing from Christ's broken flesh, from
His torn body, from His driven blood, from the gruesomely and
tortuously constrained limbs. Doing that we feel we must say
that Christ in the moment of His crucifixion felt Himself being
cast into *the catastrophic curse!*[2]

What do we mean by the catastrophic curse? Let us attempt
to define it. In our preceding chapter we observed that the curse
is *one* curse, but that in its manner of expression it may and always does adopt *two* forms. In its beginning the curse, as well as
the blessing, is "merely" a principle. But observe the use of the
little word "merely" — for we are using that word in a human
sense; from God's point of view, the word is *nonsense*.

The curse, then, is a principle. Now principles are realized
gradually, perhaps, but certainly. They work to the inside of

---

1. *Christ on Trial*, pp. 80 ff., 102 ff., 363 ff., and 403 ff.
2. The scourging was a different thing; it was an interlude, (see *Christ on Trial*,
pp. 508 f., 519 f.) and besides, it was not until after the scourging that Christ was
thrown "without the gate," a step which must be regarded again as a separate
one in Jesus' way of suffering (chapter 1, this vol.).

things first; there we call them energy. Afterwards they work to the outside; there we call them explosion. At first principles become effective slowly, causing neither break nor schism, neither violence nor explosion; they move gradually and slowly along certain lines. Principles must be believed before one can see them in their expression, but if, after the preliminary influence, the expression begins to realize itself, when the principle, in other words, attains to its "par-ousia," then that par-ousia is something sudden, something mighty, something explosive, something overwhelming. Now the curse, just as the blessing, begins very unobtrusively. It comes into the world unperceived. It is a power of death which seems hardly alive. But the curse ends in violence. It ends with cloudburst, with tornado, with earthquake, with stars falling from their courses — in short, with catastrophic things. A well-known paper once wrote an article about "the apparatus of the last judgment."[1] The terminology of the caption was inexact to the extent that the person using the words thought that the last judgment was something introducing a new element into the world, an element not there before. And the terminology was inexact also to the extent that the person who wrote it thought that something new was being introduced into the world by a means of abrupt acts of mechanical violence. Behind every explosion of wrath in the last day lies a persistent energy of forces which have been gradually growing throughout the centuries. These forces and this energy give expression to death in its function of disintegration. These are forces which unobtrusively but persistently exert themselves in the world. The Scripture tells us that wrath is being reserved. To this extent the language which refers to the *"apparatus* of the last judgment" is not Biblical. But it contains an element of truth inasmuch as it suggests that judgment will come with catastrophies, with quakes, with mighty phenomena.

These considerations will become more concrete to our imagination, and will become more vivid and vital to us, if we ponder once more what we said about the so-called vicious circle. We shall not repeat what we said about that before,[2] but for the sake of clarity we want to summarize it in order to find room in this

---

1. The *Nieuwe Rott. Courant.*
2. *Christ on Trial*, p. 52 ff.

scheme for what we have to say about the curse of the crucified Saviour.

Originally — we observed — the whole world, the world before the fall, seemed destined to a gradual development, to an evolution, an unfolding of the life which had its origin in creation. This evolution which God first had in mind and which He ordered, would have brought the first man and the world created around him gradually to a state of perfection in which not only the energies of nature would have attained their extreme fruition, but also all faculties and potentialities of the human spirit, of body and personality, would have reached full and perfect development.

Now if sin had not disturbed the scene, that evolution of life would have been reached without any new intervention, without any return to the beginning, without any "new" creature, without any invasion of new forces. This evolution would not have placed the crown upon Adam's head from above, but would have allowed it to issue out of His own flourishing, "organic" life. An imposed crown, a super-added crown is suitable to a fallen world, but in a world undisturbed by sin that crown comes naturally, just as the crown of a flower or a tree grows out of a tender shoot "of its own accord."[1] However, when sin invaded God's created world, things changed. Then the world had deserved the curse, had deserved absolute death; and this absolute death would have annihilated the world and that catastrophically and at once, if God had not introduced a hiatus, a moratorium, by which the curse was tempered, and a state was introduced in which God — according to the plan He had conceived before — made it possible for a new life-principle to flourish, a principle known as re-creation. Thus God introduced into the world that circle of human life which to a certain extent kept the life of creation from developing gradually along the courses of evolution upon which it had originally been placed, but which also tempered the activity of the curse until the day of Jesus Christ. Now the corollary of this, naturally, is that the new life of re-creation which thrusts its foundations under the life of creation can reach its purpose only through Christ.

Therefore we can say that since that time the world has been placed — if we may use the term — "in the sign of" the *new*

---

1. The factor of God's providence (sustenance and maintenance) is not being neglected here, but is not the issue in these contrasts.

creation. "The Lord hath created a new thing on the earth." Such, from this time on, is the peculiar language of prophecy. No longer is there that gradual evolution, but there is a spasmodic eruption of the "new" day and of the "new" creation and of constantly "new" redemptive events. This series of spasmodic eruptions from now on characterizes the course of history. Something "new" is introduced into the earth, and this new thing constantly comes in the form of an *invasion.* It is the invasion, the constantly new invasion of God's irresistible power which spasmodically and not gradually brings the life of re-creation to fulfillment in Christ. It is along this line of activity that such a miracle as personal regeneration (the new creation, the quickening of the dead, the laying of a new life principle, without any "cooperation" on our part, in each one of God's elect) has its place. Along this line also the sudden, instantaneously effected, perfect sanctification — spasmodic also! — of the soul in the dying hour (immediately taken up to Christ its Head); thus also the — catastrophic — renewal of the earth, the instantaneous mutation, the resurrection of the body from the dead, in short the "restoration of all things."

On the other hand, however, the *curse* also is realized in the same catastrophic manner, for now the curse also comes spasmodically. This could not be otherwise: the ways of the curse are dependent on the ways of the blessing and of life. The curse may again and again be restrained in the world, but such postponement for those who do not share in the life of re-creation does not mean a dismissal. Even though the sun continues to shine in its friendly way, even though the course of life may roll smoothly on, even though the heart of man may be full of inclination to evil because judgment does not come at once upon the evil deed, nevertheless the curse will eventually break through in the form of an explosion of the power of death, a sudden and violent invasion of the essence of death. And there are a number of things which are appropriate to this line of activity also. These are found in those who remain outside of God. The outright hardening of a human life, sometimes in a sharply delineated crisis of life (think of the blasphemy against the Holy Spirit); the complete sinking away into a state of unrestrained sin and ungodliness (think of the dying hour in which even the "decent" impenitent immediately[1] sinks away into the demonic) ; and also the change "in the twinkling of an eye," the coming before judgment, the casting of men and of devils into hell and of the Antichrist into the pool of fire and of sulphur; the acute, catastrophic annihilation of the sin-erected "Babylonian" tower, the ejection of the children of Babel from their own palace, the last day, and the thunder of the last judgment. These all again denote the invasion, this time the invasion of death, of the curse. This is the explosion, the catastrophe.

This acute, spasmodic, abrupt breaking through of life (the blessing) as well as of death (the curse) again and again is a dominating moment in the "day of the Lord." He comes in woes, He comes in the pains of travail, it is true, but in pains nevertheless. They are the pains of death also. "The first woe is passed? But the second comes apace." Such is the law of catastrophic things. And the last catastrophe is the eschatological culmination of them all. Whether it be in personal life, or in social life, or in the life of the whole world, the circle of time, of today and tomorrow, will be broken, and this disruption will be the conclusive triumph of the newly created life, a life which transcends the restraint and tempering of common grace and the common judgment. But overagainst this triumph of the new life there is the equally conclusive and catastrophic breaking through of the forces of perdition which are to annihilate the world.

Think now, after this necessary digression, of the Christ of God. As Mediator and Surety He is the second Adam. As such He has been placed under the law of the catastrophic curse unto death, and under the law of the spasmodic evolution unto life.

Yes, He must endure the catastrophic curse, for that curse must break through today in perfect righteousness. The curse must be *satisfied* now. If the Mediator is really going to *redeem,* He must now endure the very same curse which would without Him have plunged the lost souls in an infinite duration of misery, and of the ministration of punishment. He must exhaust this immeasurable curse in a given point of time. Hence the curse must break through Him today with the portentousness of the last judgment, that most catastrophic of days. It is a part of our faith in the God of

---

1. Compare the "immediately" with the words Christ assumed; see above, and compare the Heidelberg Catechism, Lord's Day 22.

revelation and the history of redemption to believe that *if,* say, the eighteenth day of March, 1939,[1] was the dying day, the curse day, the death day of our incarnate God in the humanity of our second Adam, then on the eighteenth of March, 1939, the powers, the catastrophic powers of the last day, broke out upon Golgotha against the incarnate God. On that day Christ Jesus, not as apocalypticus, but in concrete experience felt the reality of the seven seals, of the seven trumpets, of the seven souls, of the seven thunderings, of the storming horses which drew the chariots of death, of the four winds which are loosed, of a breaking world and a devastated temple. In short, in this historical and actual moment of time He experienced the judgment and the woes of — catastrophies. That is why He can later have John write about these things on Patmos. The Primary Author of the Revelation of St. John is the Spirit of the Christ, and that Christ knows, has experienced, and can never forget what He felt upon Golgotha. All this has been stated in the Book of the Revelation written by John. Behind the Apocalypse lies an *experienced* Golgotha.[2]

Here, then, is Golgotha. The curse comes and takes with it its deeds of violence. It comes with its convulsions. True, the curse has accompanied Jesus Christ throughout His whole life. Christ heard God's voice in the form of the curse always. But He also knew — and this makes Him *weak* and *strong* at the same time — that until His hour had come, the curse had been tempered because it had been introduced into human life such as that life was being lived in His days. That life was organized on the basis of certain laws of existence, of certain potentialities for development, was organized on the basis of common grace. But in agreement with this knowledge which He had, He now assumes the necessity of experiencing the catastrophes, the quakes of the irresistible judgment. For now He has come to the end. That judgment must *explode* into His life now. Today He must experience the impact of the last judgment. His soul admonishes itself: *Dies irae, dies illa.* O my soul, do thou bow low; why art thou disquieted within me? This is the catastrophic curse; this is acute death.

---

1. *Christ on Trial,* p. 545.

2. In fact, Golgotha as experienced by Christ was far more terrible than the word of revelation as given in the last book of the Bible. This last book was written in language *we* can comprehend, and consequently reveals less of reality than He Himself *experienced.*

By this means He is able for the first time to take the blessing upon Himself acutely. Now the feast of the Passover will become the invasion of the new power which places His life in the firm frame-work of eternal youth, a new power which will make the life of His body thirty-fold, sixty-fold, a thousand-fold — spasmodically, you see, — more glorious than it is on earth. This is a power which suddenly, abruptly, spasmodically again, places Him in heaven, and thus glorifies Him. This is also the breaking through of His life. It follows its course. This comes spasmodically. This much the Church has understood, for the Church speaks of "steps" of exaltation. The Passover is much, the ascension is more, the exaltation at God's right hand is an even greater fruition, and the influence of His might over the world afterwards will cause Him to flourish more and more. Finally the evolution of His life will be perfected in his *par-ousia,* His abrupt appearance before our eyes on the Last Day.

All this God has in mind for Him, for Him who is called the second Adam. If Christ is to earn that right of the breaking through of His life, He must first submit Himself to the law of the breaking down of His life in His death. If ever He is to reach the high-water mark of the "day of the Lord" He must go down to the low-water mark of that day of the Lord on this occasion. *Steps* of exaltation? Then *steps* of humiliation also. Leaps, spasmodic leaps into life? But leaps down into death also. Leaps these are. He is not being *shoved.* He cannot push Himself gradually into death, because He cannot push Himself gradually up to life. If the Passover is to be an invasion, a sudden breaking in, a leap, an acute manifestation, a violent bursting forth of life, then His death now must also be a leap into death. He must be driven in, acutely, catastrophically, with all the violence of the excited madness of the last judgment. The catastrophe belongs to these things; the vicious circle of human life simply has to be broken through by the Christ. The work of breaking up, of tearing into pieces, is catastrophic work.

The harmony here is a perfect harmony. The order is a holy order. Now we see one of the reasons for Christ's crucifixion on the cross. The cross, and the breaking to pieces represented by the cross, makes the chronic suffering of Christ acute. Suffering and death were chronic with Him at first. He tasted of them throughout the years of His life, even though He knew that the curse was tempered. But in His last days the curse comes in leaps and bounds. Gethsemane, grief, the tortures of hell, the judges, the scourgings, the cross, the beams and the nails. The nails are lances of God, the wedges of the day of judgment. The nails represent the catastrophe. They represent the breaking in two, the splitting. Oh God, my bowels are severed, and catastrophe has come. God has come. God has torn the clouds in two, and caused the mountains to melt. Dogs and bulls and the whole catastrophic series cited in Psalm 22 are here. Must this be, my God? The nails, the hammer and the world passes away; but it passes away in my person. Soldiers and whores remain erect, but I, I am the world, and I am destroyed. I have been given up to devastation. The chronic breaking to pieces has become acute now. My tongue cleaves to the roof of my mouth. David spoke of broken fragments and of bulls and of dogs. But how mild were the words He used. He said, "Thou hast brought me into the dust of death." But today God is breaking me into fragments, is casting me into the deep abysses of death and perdition.

Now shudder, O son of man. The catastrophe was inevitable. The last judgment has struck in the body and the soul of the second Adam. This is the breaking through of the vicious circle. This is great joy, immeasurable grief. This is disorder — chaos.

Nevertheless there is an order and a harmony in the thought of this: God "thinks His thoughts." And we can detect the order and the harmony. For us, too, every historical particular given here has its appropriate place in the ensemble of Biblical ideas. It is possible to look upon the crucifixion of Jesus simply as a more or less accidental execution by the Romans, an execution which Pharisees happened to witness. We can stand alongside the cross and say: Alas, this must have caused grievous pain. And when we go to our homes again, we go there without having understood anything. But if the extended arms of the soldiers become the eternal arms of God as we see them with our mind's eye, and if the nails of the Romans become the lances of the day of judgment, and if the flickering eyes of perspiring soldiers become filled with the threat of the angels of wrath whom God will some day send out, then we can hear the thunders rumbling, then we will read to our brethren at church the chapters which tell of the seven seals, of the seven trumpets, of the seven thunderings, and the seven vials; then we will read to them the chapter about the pit of hell which burst, and say: Now the curse of the vicious circle has broken out and is having its effect; it is taking the form of its catastrophe; now common grace no longer exists for the second Adam.

Indeed, common grace no longer exists for Him. The robe of Christ will presently be raffled away. God's sun will presently disappear. Now these things assume their proper places for us, for in this way we can see God who is withdrawing His common grace from the second Adam. In this the curse attains its catastrophe.

Jesus Christ, now it is necessary for Thee to make amends for Thy exalted statement. Thou dost remember Thy proud, Thy exalted statement in the presence of the Sanhedrin a moment ago; *Hereafter . . . hereafter.* That was the word which represented the catastrophic power; that was the word by means of which the Almighty introduced His "chedasjah," His ever "new" creation. From now on — those were the words of Thy paean of victory, by means of which Thou didst announce that Thou hadst broken through, that Thou hadst penetrated all. This day is the day of breaking through, and here, O Prophet of Nazareth, here is the breaking through, for here are the nails, the thundering storm, the whirlwind, the explosion, the being hurtled into death. All Thy temple walls are tumbling down; ha, ha, break down this temple. Hereafter — thus He Himself has said.

Accordingly the hour of the crucifixion of Christ, of the violence with which He was afflicted is indispensable to the history of the world. It is indispensable because it fulfills the sacrifice. Sacrifices and offers are catastrophes. The knives of the priests come to rest in the spikes and the nails. Every sacrifice of blood throughout the centuries had been an act of violence. Today this violence is being fulfilled before our eyes. Throughout these centuries the sacrifice exhibited Christ, and Christ throughout the centuries to come will represent the last judgment. His nails and hammers are an anticipation of the judgment of the last day. Thus the cross of Christ comes to explain and to fulfill the sacrifice and the offer.

However, no one will see the offer in this event unless he sees it by faith. The knife of the sacrifice had always been manipulated by the hand of a priest. These spikes, however, are being driven through His flesh by the firm hand of the accomplices of Cain. Nevertheless, this is the offer. The whole of Christ's own work lies behind the act of the soldiers. He Himself led the process of events to this point; He Himself arranged His feet upon the accursed wood; in the last analysis He Himself manipulated the nails and the hammer. He is the priest, therefore; He has nailed Himself to the cross. He has slain Himself. That is why the Lamb, after a while, can "stand as the slain," hallelujah!

God's hand, therefore, strikes most terribly at the Son of man. God breaks Him into pieces. God alone can make and break. Fear Him who cannot fail to kill the body when He must kill the soul, the soul of Him Who has been made sin. Fear Him in this portentous hour Who up to this time has withheld all His nails and lightnings in order that they might strike the Son of man now. God can only despise Jesus; God must turn His ear and eye aside from His supplication. God sees very plainly that it is I who am hanging there: God must despise me, and must turn His ear and eye from all my supplications.

I have been to Golgotha. I saw Adam in exile, and immediately afterwards a cloudburst. I saw a flood, I saw a stroke of lightning. Men said: How firmly He strikes the nails, how steadily the spikes go in! The world quakes; there was the day of judgment. And all these things constitute a single thing; they are all the day of the Lord.

Spikes, and hammers, and a distorted mouth. I have reference to the soldier. And God nods at me, and says: Watch this. But I cannot see it; I can only read epistles and gospels. Lord, I thank Thee for having thrown a veil over the nakedness of the second Adam, who has quickened me to life, and that Thou art willing to teach me of Him through the Word. Lord, I know no particulars, I know only that there is such a thing as sin, as the curse, as the catastrophe, and I pray that I may not in all eternity become a Shem, one who lifts the veil, when he should lay it down, or leave it lie.

My language is a frail language, and I believe that Thou wilt regard me as a lost man if I fabricate words on this occasion. The generation of Shem also knows the art of articulating sounds together, but judgment is proclaimed upon the children of Abraham. And who can stand in this day!

The nails, the hammer . . . but every spike is but the apparatus of an eschatological judgment. Judgment begins in the house of God: break down this temple!

This is the judgment; this is the judgment upon Israel; this is the judgment upon man and nature.

This is the judgment upon Israel. Jesus says: My flesh is a temple. He means that His flesh, His body, inasmuch as it is the temple of the Spirit, is the temple of Jahweh. His flesh is the flesh of Abraham. Hence He who breaks down Abraham's richest temple is letting the Spirit of God recede from the people of Abraham. Thus does the communion of Israel as a fleshly people place the wedge of disruption into the temple of Abraham. Thus the spirit is driven from Abraham's natural posterity. Praise Him, all ye heathen.

But dare the heathen praise God? Alas, they immediately grow quiet again. They are shocked; they fear, because they remember that Abraham was of Adam and lo — Adam is also being broken. When Jesus Christ says that He is a temple, that His body is a house of God, He does not mean only the broader but also the narrower implications of the figure. Hence He is not only the temple of Jahweh in Israel but also the temple of God in man and nature. His body came from Adam, and in that sense also God dwelt in Him. That temple of His humanity is also being broken down. The whole world witnesses the breaking and says: Clap your hands and rejoice and thank God with rejoicing. Yes, nature does not hide her face before Him. Hence the Spirit is being withdrawn from the whole of the human race and from the whole of nature.

This my God does by means of a hammer and a few spikes. For the rest, we have the Spirit and also the Word. This is the way they treat the Temple. And where shall the ungodly and the sinner appear? All that is dust and nature and man and Israel is consumed by the curse. The wedge which Adam drove into the world, Golgotha drove farther. This is the catastrophe. The sun stands still, the moon goes no farther, the world whirls about in space. And all flesh must see and acknowledge that only on the other side of the broken vicious circle of life is there the straight line which leads to the life everlasting. Beyond the vicious circle lies the life which is in Christ. For nature there is this life. The whole creation groans, expecting the day of His perfect evolution, an evolution catastrophically achieved and continued perpetually. For man and for humanity there is this life: the Christ whom the vanity of the world broke in two by means of the nails exhibited the true man to us once more. And for Israel there is this life. Abraham again recognizes all the children who have been born of this one Son . . .

I hear the hammer's stroke again. And I despise myself because I am able only with the greatest difficulty to hear something of the thunder of the last judgment in the falling strokes of that hammer.

Christ Isolating Himself in the Catastrophic Curse

CHAPTER SEVEN

Christ Isolating Himself in the Catastrophic Curse

● *Then said Jesus, Father, forgive them; for they know not what they do.*

LUKE 23:34a.

THE words of Christ Jesus constitute a deep abyss. This is true also, and that not in the least, of the seven utterances on the cross. These are well known, and have made a deeper impression on many souls than have the other words of Christ. Who would dare to deny that this fact represents a weakness in Christian thinking? But those were the words of a dying man, I hear someone say, in explanation of his attitude. We reply that this is not true; they are the words of *the* dying man. Yes, he adds, but nevertheless they are the words spoken by Him when He was dying. To which we answer: He told Paul beforehand: I die *daily*. Who, therefore, can dare to think more highly of one of His utterances than of another?

Nevertheless it is a fact that the words of the Dying One have been better remembered than the words of the Living One. Children learn them by heart; the teacher numbers them. Moreover, think of the literature. The seven words on the cross have been included in the literature of the middle ages and of later times as well as in the critical commentaries of all times at the expense of the other statements of Christ. The detrimental effects of such a disruption of the words of Christ soon became apparent. Men forgot themselves and forgot Him in such exegesis. Human fantasy was fond of weaving a cover which it might throw over the light shed by Jesus' seven last lamps, inasmuch as obscurity pleases the human heart. And, again, the words which He spoke from the cross were segregated from the momentary condition in which the second Adam then found Himself.

It is unnecessary to assert that the Scriptures themselves do not wish to take this direction. True, the seven words on the cross spoken by the Saviour constitute an architectural whole, but that is just another reason for which we should not consider them without actual and unintermittent reference to everything He is thinking and experiencing and doing on this day. Besides, these same seven utterances are much more than a natural and immediate "reaction" to what He is experiencing at the moment. They are at the same time a genuine revelation of the heavenly reality, of the divine depths of His spirit.

This holds true also of the seven words as a unit. Even the sequence in which they were uttered pleads for the truth of that predication.[1] Whoever pays close attention to the order in which the utterances were spoken will see that Christ was gradually isolating Himself on the cross, and that the seven words which He uttered plainly delineate and circumscribe the several phases of that process of isolation.

Just follow the process for yourself. First the large, inclusive circle of the whole of human life still enjoys His attention. The first utterance on the cross mentions the soldiers and the Jews who are urging them on. To both of these He says, Father, forgive them. The second word on the cross circumscribes a narrower bourne. It is addressed to a murderer who has come to the faith. In this statement Christ is entering the domain of His church. In the third word on the cross He addresses Himself to His family and to the intimate friend, to His mother, and to His disciple, to that disciple "whom He loved." In other words, this is not the church, but the intimate group within the church. Mark the marvellous unity of the sequence. First, man in general, then the man of the church in particular, and finally the ones inside the communion of the church who, both according to the law of blood

---

1. We are sometimes, and that quite rightly, pointed to the fact that the sequence of the seven words on the cross cannot be determined with absolute accuracy on an exegetical basis. We grant the truth of this. If we, in spite of this fact, assume that the sequence ordinarily accepted is the right one, we do this—very frankly—because of a certain predilection, a certain assumption, which is also enjoined upon us by the Scriptures. It is the assumption that Christ always has a harmonious plan in His discourses, and that even His spontaneously uttered speeches manifest the general logic and style of the whole of His genuine being. Christ's spontaneous responses are just as artistically and authentically constructed as our artistic mosaics.

and according to the law of the spirit, were most intimately related to Him. Only then, after the circumference of attention on the part of His active and alert life had gradually narrowed itself — the scope of attention of any dying person gradually narrows itself in this way, and such is also the case in the last judgment — only then, we say, is the fourth word on the cross uttered. In this fourth statement Christ calls Himself forsaken of God, and thus He relates the stress of the moment to the spiritual world, the fact and actuality of which He had known before but had not experienced completely until now. When He utters that statement, therefore, He is alone with God, and it is inside the circle of those two, of God and Himself, that His last three statements are made.

Christ's seven words on the cross, consequently, do constitute an architectural whole. Moreover, we discover with astonishment the process of isolation to which we alluded a moment ago. We discover it with astonishment, but also with gratitude. We do not want to get along without that word any longer. Our first volume[1] ended with the isolated Christ. Our second volume[2] continued the discussion of the isolated Christ. And the isolated Christ must also have a place in our third volume.

But with God the sequel is always richer than the precursor; therefore our third volume can relate greater wonders than could our first and second. Now, for the first time, we can plainly and sharply see that the isolation into which the Son is hurled by men and God and Satan is not only a fate which makes Him suffer and before which He bows, inasmuch as it is inevitable now, but it is also a circumstance in which He rises up to His own full strength, girds up His loins to do His own deed, to carry out His own isolation. He does it Himself. He isolates Himself. He Himself prays fervently for His isolation.

Yes, He prays for it. We shall see presently that Christ's first utterance on the cross is a prayer by means of which He isolates Himself. As we notice that, we shall also see that precisely by means of this prayer He by His own deed appropriates the great fact of the day: namely, that Christ is to be alone, absolutely alone overagainst the universe. He is to be alone in the catastrophic curse. There will not be so much as a voice asking Him:

---

1. *Christ in His Suffering.*
2. *Christ on Trial.*

What art thou doing here, Elijah? There is no whirlwind, there is no earthquake, no fire, no terrible calm. But the prophet Elijah nevertheless has found a Greater than he here. Elijah complained about his isolation but Christ prays for it. And Moses, also, has found a Greater. He was allowed to climb the mount of His death, knowing that God was awaiting Him in love. But Christ knows that God as His Judge is isolating Him in the curse, and Christ nevertheless prays for that isolation. Moses and Elias, He is reversing the roles. Now He is coming to *you* to tell you of His departure, of His decease, at Jerusalem.

Our task now is to point out that all these considerations are warranted by the Scriptures. Let us follow our text carefully. The sound of the words we are considering now has a familiar ring: Father, forgive them, for they know not what they do. The words are no less than a prayer of Christ. This prayer issues from His lips as the hammers fall and the soldiers swear. Horror and anxiety make every spirit captive on this hill of death and suppress every voice. But there is one voice which gives forth a clear sound, a sound full of confidence. It is the voice of Jesus, it is the prayer. He asks the Father to forgive His murderers because they do not know what they are doing.

Just who are those for whom the Saviour is praying? Who are to share the blessing for which He now prays the Father? The Romans? The Jews? Both of these? Are they those who are of the elect, and over whom the sun of Pentecost will presently arise? This question has often been asked, and some think it is absolutely necessary to assert that Christ is praying for no one not included in election. They arrive at this conclusion by dogmatic rather than exegetical routes. They think it strange that Christ should ask a good thing for those whom He would have to call enemies and haters of God. They know that grace is particular, and that intercession also is that. Others, however, who proceed along exegetical rather than dogmatic ways, say to themselves that the obvious and the simple sense of the words is that Christ is praying for that group of people there, for the group as it is and as it led Him to His death.

Everyone will have to admit the truth of the last remark. For those who would read what is written, it is plainly stated that Jesus was praying for the people who stood there and who were nailing Him to the cross. The sense of the statement is not that Jesus was praying only for the soldiers because they were being used as the passive instruments of the government. For His words refer to the entire group of those who are responsible for this sinister business The Saviour meant the Jews as well as the Romans. The Romans are carrying out the sentence, but the high priests are in command. Now Christ asks that His Father forgive all these, because they do not know what they are doing. They cannot fathom the implications of His act nor see the extent of its consequences.

And, indeed, there is good reason for asking whether Christ, our High Priest, is praying for a mass of people. Grace is particular in character. And Christ, as a human being, cannot desire that which would be opposed to the being, to the will, and to the work of the God of election. Now if the high priestly prayer of Christ is sent up to God for the benefit of a mass, for the benefit of a crowd of people, who give no evidence at all of wishing such grace, it does seem that He is opposing the God of election.

We appreciate this consideration, but we would add to it another difficulty. If the word "forgive" as used in this prayer of Christ has reference to the same tremendous benefit of grace which Christ as High Priest has achieved for all the elect of God, and by means of which the sinner is justified freely, how could we harmonize this word with what we read at other places in the account. How could we do that if the will of Christ should here be reaching itself out to the highest possible priestly function, a function which gives redemption and which saves the sinner from the condemnation of His sin for all eternity. How, then, can we understand Him in His other statements? Had not Christ shortly before hurled His word of condemnation into the throng? Had He not Himself announced to the daughters of Jerusalem that condemnation would overtake them, and not them alone but also the community of the city and of the people? The announcement was an instance of the extreme service of the Word, and it had threatened, had threatened. And would Jesus' first reaction to the last service of His Word be unfaithful now to His preached word? Would His last preaching issue sounds of thunder, and His first preaching after that be a playing on a mellow shepherd's lute? Is Christ one who can jump down from the thundering cloud to the soft moss where the children are playing with justice and truth, not knowing what they are doing? Can it be true that the first word which Christ spoke on the cross conflicts with what He Himself told the Sanhedrin when He said: Hereafter ye shall see the son of man in his glory? By that statement He had raised Himself up above all, and had said, My blood cannot be darkened in the world. And would He write the sentence of His death in sand today, suggesting that His red blood may also be buried and covered in it? There are questions enough, you see, and just as many improbabilities.

Nevertheless the solution is easy. Again in this connection we must, in order to find the solution, read the passage very carefully. The word used in the original and translated "forgive" in our version, gives us the key to the solution. We know that the forgiveness of sins is described in the Bible by varying words. The Greek language of the New Testament uses various shades of connotation in speaking of it. It will be unnecessary here to name all those Greek words individually and to give the meanings of each. Suffice it to say that the word "forgive" as it is used here in our text can mean: to release someone, not to put the charge or sentence against a person into execution at once, not yet to effect the penalty which the transgression according to reason and right probably deserves.

Hence there are two kinds of forgiveness. There is a forgiveness which, on the basis of law, says to someone: I shall cancel that which you have done amiss. The legal issue has been carefully considered, the verdict of the court has in no sense been postponed, nor its effect mitigated; but we have found a legal basis according to which the letter and spirit of the law sets you free forever from the persecution of the law. Such forgiveness has a place, among other things, in the justification of the sinner. But there is also a forgiveness which consists solely of a temporary suspension of the charge or of the sentence. With or without a legal sentence someone whose breach of law has been alleged or proved can temporarily be freed from the persecution of law. Two possibilities for the future arise from such a temporary dismissal of action: later the man who was temporarily dismissed from the course of law can be arrested and condemned anew; or, in the interim which ensues, a legal basis may be found by means of which he definitively and strictly according to the requirements of law is forever acquitted.

It was such a detention of the execution of law, preliminary and incidental, which Jesus had in mind. This detention is not a plea for the justification of the sinner, and is not a plea against justification; it simply desires that God will temporarily withhold the terrible punishment, the catastrophic annihilation which must necessarily follow the condemnation and cursing of the Prince of life by this generation of vipers. May it please God not immediately to let the powers of the last judgment break through against these. May it please God to wait and not to send the storms of the last judgment into this scene. May it please God, "not to make any work of it," today, not to make any work of what is being done by human hands, by Adam and his generation today. In this prayer Christ manifests a very strong Messianic self-consciousness. And He makes the implications of that consciousness relevant to God. The Saviour is, also as a human being, so thoroughly permeated by the thought of His own universal significance and of His Messianic righteousness before God, that He, even when He must raise His head up to the storm clouds of absolute condemnation, associates the most terrible of judgments with the sin of His murderers. If the Judge is to do what these deserved, the flood will be but a shadow in comparison with what will take place here. Then the abysses will at once have to open and swallow up these people.

Surely, this is a pronounced self-disclosure of a Messianic spirit which is very conscious of itself. No, indeed, this statement is not a denial of what Jesus said in the presence of the Sanhedrin or of what He said in the last service of the Word, as it seemed to be a moment ago, but it is a confirmation of these things. He knows He is the Messiah, and He knows that the righteousness of His "case" is perfect before God.

But as the Messiah He also wants to make Himself effective in His prayer. He knows very well that God is much concerned with the Messiah whom He has sent out. Hence the condemnation which must accrue to the murderers of the Saviour cannot be meted out unless He Himself acquaints the Father with His will in the matter. This is a strange contrast. He who is accursed, and who knows that God has cursed Him, nevertheless knocks at

God's door and says: I have a desire, and I shall not put aside my feeling of freedom to make My desire known to Thee. I pray Thee, Father — My prayer rests in a confident sense of My own worth — that Thou suspend the judgment for a time. I ask forgiveness for these sinners. I would leave some room, some room for the future. I would leave room for the justification by faith of all those who are present here, and are included in the election. And I would also leave room for my living Word to become effective, so effective and so persistent, that the measure will presently be full and the judgment can come.

We can deduce from this that Christ by no means in His thinking is opposed to the good pleasure of God. He is not pleading for acquittal where the sovereign good pleasure did not choose to grant it. No, there is another element here. Christ adds to His plea: They know not what they do.

But what further? There is a saying which has it that ignorance of the law is no excuse. And ignorance, certainly, is no excuse for sin. The failure to appreciate all of the consequences and implications of one's evil does not take away the guilt of sin. We would reply that this is quite true. But we would add that Christ is not asking for forgiveness in the narrower sense. The fact that these people do not know what they are doing is not an argument for their eternal salvation, but a basis for suspending the judgment. Time must come when they must know what they are doing. Golgotha must be explained by the Word; and may God grant the time necessary for those fisher-folk, who will be apostles later, to preach that word to the world. The world must know what is happening here, in order that the hearing of the preached word may bring the one to true repentance and faith, and may aggravate the responsibility of the other, if he does not subject himself sincerely to Him who speaks on Golgotha.

Hence Christ is not praying for a cancellation of the execution, not even for a postponement of execution, but for the suspension of the judgment of wrath which is sure to come in any case. Christ is praying for a period of time in order that, on the one hand, all those souls who would seek acquittal in the execution of Christ might seize on grace to that end, and in order that, on the other hand, an even profounder legal basis may be placed under the condemnation of those who are here condemning their God in

Christ. Father, the Mediator's voice cries out, The world must pass away, but keep back Thy catastrophes for a period, and let Me stand alone in My catastrophic curse. Father, there are many branches on Israel's tree. According to right and reason all these dead branches must be broken off by the storm of the last judgment at once, and the whole tree be cast into the fire. But do Thou withhold Thy four winds for a time, Father; let the tree of Israel stand today in order that there may be occasion for grafting new shoots to the old trunk, and in order that thereafter the dead branches may by a more conclusive gesture be thrust into the oven.

Accordingly, it would be a vain task if someone should attempt to "play off" this New Testament word of Christ against the Old Testament imprecatory psalms. These psalms, surely, cannot be in conflict with the spirit of Christ, the crucified Intercessor. For those imprecatory psalms were also given us by the Logos. They can be explained only by the Logos which has been made flesh. No, but on the contrary, Christ is uniting Himself with these psalms of Israel. Christ's soul is becoming one with them. At the same time, however, His soul is very eager to have the wrath consumed by love. Christ's mellow statement which asks forgiveness for His murderers here may not be placed overagainst the imprecatory psalms of the Old Testament.

For the New Testament carries these psalms straight into heaven. You remember the prayer of the "souls under the altar," who asked God, who cried with a loud voice, saying, How long, O Lord, dost thou not judge and avenge our blood on them? Now the link which unites the Old Testament with the New Testament prayer of vengeance is this first utterance from the cross. For Christ would also have time enough for Himself in which to let His work ripen, to avenge His blood, and to provide the service of atonement in His blood. He does not curse the furious horses of the last judgment, He does not restrain them; He merely prays that the Father may withhold them for the present, in order that His hand may presently take the reins. Father, let them go today, for the whole of judgment must be made the prerogative of the Son. Do not dismiss Him, Father, before the time has come.

Christ, accordingly, appears here in His full length. As the Messiah He asks that the privilege be given Him to lay His own hand on the wheel of the world. Thus He fastens His cross to the last, to the final day. Thus the cross becomes a link.

But there is more to say. He also reaches back to the first day. This is the second link. As the Son of God, who continuously remains identified with the man Jesus, even though He is cast into the catastrophic curse which brings the last and final judgment very near Him, He nevertheless is doing the work of God as that work was done on the first day of the advent of sin into the world.

The first day? The very beginning? Yes, indeed. We shall not repeat here what has been said before about the will of God who interjected history between the first advent of sin into the world and the realization of that sin in the form of the curse. We shall not repeat here what was said then about the circle of earthly life. We have said more than once that God interjects history between the moment of the first sin and the final and absolute curse, in order to make room for the Christ who would make both the blessing and the curse effective in the world. We shall not allude to that again.

We recall it here for a moment simply because it must point out the direction which we must take in pondering Christ's first utterance on the cross. Remembering that, we can go farther. Now we can say with reverence, as we look upon the cross: Behold, He is doing perfectly that which God did in Paradise. At the first advent of sin, when the "day of the Lord" dawned, when the sun of grace arose, God said to Himself: I "forgive" them their sins, for they know not what they do. Even that was not the complete justification of Man and Woman, but it was an expression of the strong, divine will, which restrained the curse, and which kept the thunder of God shut up in its treasure-rooms, by way of restraining the explosion of hell.

Then it had been morning: the beginning of the "day of the Lord." Now it is high noon of that same day of the Lord. The clock of the "day of the Lord," the "jôm Jahweh," is at the moment pointing to twelve o'clock. And again the voice is heard: Forgive them, they do not know what they do. This was said twice, therefore. The first time in Paradise, the second time on the cross. The first time the Logos pronounced these words before the incarnation; now He announces them in and by means of the incarnation. The first time He spoke them as the eternal God, who, however, stood ready to be the servant; and now He speaks them as the servant of the Lord but as one who in the form of a servant perfectly preserves and vindicates the will of God which is also His own will. Tremble, O Pilate; and shudder all ye facile caricaturists. He remains faithful to all His ideas.[1] He is God and man in one person.

We also must tremble here. For, the first time the Logos prayed that the Father forgive them, He wrought the possibility of general history, He wrested that possibility from the abyss of God's justice and truth. Now He prays a second time — it is midday — but now He is struggling for the preservation, for the maintenance, for the continuation of general history, in order that special history whose incipient triumphs had been achieved in the Old Testament, might flourish in the full energy of the New Testament, by means of the feast of Pentecost and of the formation of the church. Christ is praying that God give His chosen vessel, a certain Paul, his opportunities; He prays for that commander-in-chief of the Roman soldiers, whose name is to be Constantine the Great. He prays for Luther and for Calvin. He prays for us. He was as universal as possible; Father, forgive "them," — this perverted crowd. But it is His sublime, blessed, and exacting manner of prayer never to let a general statement fall without causing it to have a most special effect.

Listen: Jesus Christ is praying. Praise God, for He indeed is praiseworthy. He manifests His strength in the skies and above the clouds. No matter how profound the need, God sends out His Son in order that He may slay the enemy. He is given all power in heaven and on earth.

What more can we do now? We must try to find the connection between these things. We must bind into a synthesis the main idea of our preceding chapter with this chapter, with this first word on the cross. In our preceding chapter we said that Christ was living under the tension, under the pressure, and in the oppressive atmosphere of the last day. We pointed out how He is experiencing on the cross the suffering of the night of the day of judgment, the night of the "jôm Jahweh." To His ears the

---

1. *Christ on Trial*, pp. 519-522.

strokes of the hammer came with the sound of thunder. The nails and the hammers of the soldiers were as the lances of God to Him. Too sweeping, you say? By no means, for His eye never once "armed" itself with a magnifying glass.

Now it is high noon. He has the evening and the night in His thoughts. And He has just returned to His morning prayers. Therefore our soul must testify of this Worker of God's one day, this Worker of the "day of the Lord," that again He has suppressed nothing. This Servant of God, my Lord and God, experiences in every successive moment the organic interrelationship of the whole season of God. This is the hour of Golgotha: this is high noon. He is referring for the moment, however, to the morning and is experiencing the catastrophes of late evening. Thus He vindicates all prophets. The prophets also saw the day of the Lord as one great, unbroken, single day, though as comprising many centuries. Christ's first word on the cross is the apology of all prophets. Take Golgotha out of the picture, and these all are psychopathic cases, overwrought personalities. But Golgotha is their apology. They made no mistake; the "jôm Jahweh," the day of Golgotha, is the turning day of the centuries. Christ experiences this in the vehement pulsing of His own blood as it is poured out, and also in His passionate yearning for His spoken word. The Word has become flesh. This is its sublime message. In His flesh He is suffering the pangs and the woes of the one "day of the Lord," but also as the Word of God, as the uncreated Logos, He shares in all the hours of the one "day of the Lord." Thus does God enter into our distress. The first word on the cross looks like a mellow prayer, innocent and meek as the wafted fragrance of a blossoming flower-garden. But in the presence of this first word spoken from the cross we also say with profound reverence: In all our afflictions He was afflicted. For He experienced the "jôm Jahweh." And it happened that at the end of the day (the catastrophe) it was noon (the struggle for the continuation for the world); yes, and also morning (the affirmation of His prayer of Paradise: Father forgive them).

Consequently that which Christ is praying here must always be distinguished from the prayers of others, even though they use the very same words. True, there was Stephen (Acts 7:60), and he also said later: Lord, lay not this sin to their charge. And there is Paul, who said: Being persecuted we suffer it, being reviled we bless (I Corinthians 4:12); and again: All men forsook me; I pray God it may not be laid to their charge (II Timothy 4:16). But can you believe that these and other persecuted followers of Jesus Christ were standing on the same sublime heights as Jesus was? That which they asked was but the fruit of His prayer. Because of that prayer Stephen could say in His terrible death: I see Jesus standing. And Paul could say that Christ's Spirit itself made intercession for him with groanings that could not be uttered. When other people address God by means of the words, Father forgive them this sin, there are only two possibilities. If they use these words prompted by the Spirit of Christ, their prayer is the fruit of Jesus' praying. And if they segregate their will to love from the love and justice of Christ, then their petition for mercy is in the last analysis a praying against Christ. For the prayer of Christ is not expressive of rebellion against the justice of God, but it is a struggle to give both God's justice and His love their fruition in a world which presently will have become ripe. Christ who, after His final and personal service of the Word in the state of humiliation, pronounces this first word from the cross by way of application to it, was asking God for the *permanent* service of the word, in order that He might thus cause the world to ripen, the world and its "clusters of the vine of the earth" (Revelation 14:18).

In other words, Christ as God and as man is busy asking for a continuation of what we called "the vicious circle." Not that, in doing this, He is recalling what had been His glory in the presence of the Sanhedrin: namely, to indicate that He Himself was vanquishing the vicious circle.[1] It is precisely because He has conquered the vicious circle, that He takes the reins of the world's cyclical movement into His own hand from now on. All power is given Him in this hour. The word spoken before the ascension, "All power is given to me in heaven and earth," is a powerful paean of rejoicing in which the Conqueror stretches out His arms, fills His lungs, and exclaims: God be praised, My first prayer on the cross has been heard. The Father could not but hear.

---

1. *Christ on Trial*, chapter 7, especially pp. 143-144.

And for that reason, O man, this word spoken on the cross has a direct significance for you. For if it is true that this petition uttered on the cross is a prayer for the prolongation of the vicious circle of world history, we cannot but think of the Ecclesiast of the Old Testament again, for it was he who spoke of the vicious circle. Well, he also observed how the people, slaves as they are of the passion of their own sin, and foolish in spirit, seem to build their life upon the cyclical movements of nature. Hear what the Preacher says: Because sentence against an evil work is not executed speedily, therefore the heart of the sons of men is fully set in them to do evil (Ecclesiastes 8:11). He is saying that because the catastrophe of the judgment has not yet exploded, because Good Friday does not strike the planes of our life with lightning. Therefore the world is willing to settle down comfortably even at the scene of Golgotha. Even at the cross, men play at roulette and never dream of condemnation. Soldiers raffling garments next to the cross — such is the keynote struck for the following ages. Because Jesus' first petition on the cross was heard, the heart of the children of men is fully set in them to do evil. So we may translate Ecclesiastes 8:11. Christ's cross breaks the circle of the history of the world only for those who have faith. It was His will that this should be so. He prayed that the merry-go-round of this life might continue to whirl, and that the merry-go-rounds of God continue to turn as slowly as they had before. Hence the course of sin was prolonged, and the struggle of faith and unbelief was continued also. May the church tremble, for the church has named the mystery of God's relationship to sin by means of the designation: *active permission*.[1] But in this petition on the cross the active permission becomes human as well as divine: here it is not only a secret of God but also of Christ Jesus our Mediator. He let the world go on; that is permission. He prays that it may continue: that is activity. In the one, the first petition on the cross, He heals the ears of all the Malchuses of the world. He guarantees Cain and Malchus that they will have a place on the earth until the last day. At noon His voice said to God: Father, do not let the evening come earlier than usual; let the afternoon gradually move towards the night. Therefore the heart of the world is still full of the desire to do evil. Christ will presently and

---

1. *Christ in His Suffering*, p. 436 f.

throughout His days fall into the skeins He Himself has woven, because those who mock at the foot of His cross continue their reviling. Why? Because His prayer has been heard. Satan can still battle against "the remnant of the seed of the woman" (Revelation 12).

But this does not take away your heavy responsibility, O son of man. Precisely because Jesus at mid-day of the "jôm Jahweh" acknowledged and in the last analysis asked for the justice of God to make its appearance in the evening, therefore His mid-day prayer naturally becomes weaker in sound, less audible in tone, as evening approaches. Remember, His great argument is this one: They know not what they do. But each new day, each new dawning and sunset spreads further the knowledge of God in Christ through the world. Gradually people will learn to know what they are doing. The word of the cross is preached: the crisis is made a conscious one. The Antichrist will know perfectly what he is doing. And the more the world runs to the end of its course, the nearer the Antichrist comes with his false prophet, the better will men know what they are doing.

As soon, therefore, as the day will have come in which, according to the Biblical statement, "the earth shall be full of the knowledge of the Lord, as the waters cover the sea," Christ's mid-day prayer will no longer be heard. This will be the end; then evening will come; evening and a silent Christ who can find no more words in which to couch His first petition on the cross. The moment He closes His mouth and no longer assumes responsibility for the content of His uttered prayer on the cross, it will be evening, the evening of the "jôm Jahweh." Then the catastrophe will break loose, the same catastrophe in which He is now isolated according to His own will. Then all the sluice-gates of God's floods of vengeance will be flung wide. Consequently every service of the word, and every deepening of theological thinking, is an eschatological thing: it makes more blunt the sharpness of the modifying clause in the first petition from the cross. For, so much is plain, "They know now, what they have done."[1] Judgment comes, and the

---

1. Therefore the church which makes dogmatic thinking as broad and as deep as possible is the Maranatha-church. An institution which presents the Maranatha-message but ignores or does not plumb the depths of dogma is less eschatological than a church which is faithful to dogma. The church which makes the deepest and broadest confession is always busy eschatologically.

innocent voice which seemed to whisper the words *Father forgive them,* grows into a veritable tornado:

> Day of Judgment, day of wonders,
> Hark! the trumpet's awful sound
> Louder than a thousand thunders
> Shakes the vast creation round!
> How the summons
> Will the sinner's heart confound!
>
> But to those who have confessed,
> Loved and served the Lord below,
> He will say: Come near, ye blessed,
> See the Kingdom I bestow,
> You forever
> Shall my love and glory know.

The last thought provides a resting place for our poor heart. We should want the courage to wait for the judgment if we could not at the same time confidently speak of His priestly love. But be of good cheer: He is our Priest. Simon, you isolated Him, and you still remember that, you remember the curses and oaths which you swore. But be of good cheer, disciple, weeping bitterly, for today He is isolating Himself. Father, He says, I am stepping into the dark, but give them the full light of the sun until the last day. I want to be in the catastrophe alone. Father, the seed of the woman is being *wrenched away today;* the word has a catastrophic connotation. But give the remnant of the seed of the woman a further place in the world. Reserve, prepare, a place for them in the wilderness;[1] I want to be alone in the catastrophe. Thus Christ wrests the catastrophe, into which He Himself has been thrown, from the soldiers, and from the priests, and from the temple, and from Caesar. And the Batavians on the west coast of Europe can divide their loot in the evening, and wait for Boniface because Christ prayed this prayer. Be of good cheer, ye disciples, and you also, you who flee anonymously.[2] All of you have isolated Him but a short time ago; but now He isolates Himself. He is not the object but the subject of His own isolation.

This is a miraculous thing: He is isolating Himself. Note carefully the fact that He did this by means of a prayer. The prayer must not be regarded as an accidental particular which we may with impunity overlook. For prayer, being divine, means to

1. Revelation 12.
2. *Christ in His Suffering,* chapter 27, especially p. 460.

make the will of God our will. In prayer the commandments become our food and drink. The person who prays is uniting himself with the will of the Lord by his own deed. Prayer is not an unconscious expression of life, is not a naive self-expression, but is a deed done by the spirit of man, which unites itself with the familiar commandments and burdens of its God.

And Christ prayed "Father forgive them." He prayed, and by His prayer, by the strongest assertion of His deed, He isolated Himself in catastrophic death. Thus His priestly soul by means of its active obedience completely acquiesced in the destiny pointed out to Him: namely, to be isolated from the whole world. By praying He completely embraced the command of isolation which God had given. He suffered alone, He stood in the thunder and lightning of the last day alone. Not only because He had to, but also because He wanted to. Yes, He had to. Fellowship, company, is a concept appropriate to planes. The vicious circle is a plane. Social life is possible on a plane. But the breaking through of a circular plane can take place only at a certain *point;* it creates a kind of vacuum. Now one is always alone at a point of bisection; a vacuum can offer nothing but a descent into isolation. What, therefore, is more natural than the isolation of Christ in the moment of the breaking through of the circular plane of life. Indeed, He could not but be isolated. But God be praised: He *wanted* to be isolated also. He prayed that He might be alone in the catastrophic curse; He prayed for His isolation at the time of His descent into hell. He prayed: that is, He attracted the isolation to Himself. His name be praised; but give the praise very cautiously. He *had* to and He *wanted* to.

These two may never be separated. He is being isolated, yes, but not only because He wanted to. Had that been the case, He would have been guilty of suicide, of forsaking God and the Church. Again He is isolated not only because He had to be. Had that been the case, His isolation would have been His fate, and His abandonment would then have lacked redemptive power. But now that He must do what He wants to do, and wants to do what He must, everything is right.

No, we may not overlook this prayer contained in the first utterance from the cross. The specific prayer-form into which this word of isolation comes to us fulfills the preaching of isolation as pointed out in our first and second volumes; it amplifies God's message, and imparts a new depth to our own praying. For the true humanity of the Son of man as He was even in His catastrophe gives our prayers body and depth and genuine humanity which, at the same time, through Him is compatible with the true essence of God.

Now this day is a miracle to me. The sun arose this morning and I looked upon my day. It came from Him; He did not hinder me from doing my work because I had crucified Him. Christ, great in mercies. *Pia anima.* O holy heart of Jesus.

Christ, the catastrophe is upon Thee. Thy heart is beating wildly because of it. Thou sawest that the world was oppressed by the heavy burden which God sent upon it because of Thee, and Thou Thyself didst say that He would forsake Thee. Those were two truths, and they supported each other. Thou sawest both of them in Thy spirit, and Thou didst profess both of them without reservation. The harmony of the two is a melting together of paradoxical reality. What have I left but the Word, but Thy authority? But let me know, Lord, that Thou by reason of Thy own will didst descend into the curse which is catastrophic in character alone. A Christ who has isolated Himself in the curse by His own deed teaches me to number my days. Moses also asked that we learn to number our days,[1] but he could not recite the text while standing beside the cross. The pagans teach me the phrase, "Carpe diem," in vain; they cannot translate the first utterance on the cross from the inside. I can do that if I believe, for if I believe, I have myself been present at the cross. Lord, teach me to number my days at the cross of Golgotha in order that I may become wise at heart, and realize Thy own work in Thy servants. Father, forgive us, for only at the last day shall we be fully able to see what we have done here . . . Brother, mark the day. Have you noticed how His voice has weakened already? Each day He speaks less loudly of the people who know not what they do. A speaking Jesus is terrible: a silent Jesus far more terrible. I dare not sleep. As I turn the leaf on the calendar I know that His voice speaks more softly than it did yesterday. He knows how much I know. This is the dogma of the Church — and He Him-

---

1. Psalm 90.

self taught it, for He greatly desires His judgment day. He calls
the counsel together in Nicea, He is present at Wittenberg, in
Geneva, and in Dordrecht, for He is eager that we should know.
Could you suppose that His judgment day has been infinitely post-
poned? He spoke the prayer from the cross, you say. Yes, but
postponement is not cancellation. He hastens to the fulfillment of
His judgment day, provided that it come in the right manner.
Jesus' mild prayers are prayers of steel. Only if I am *in* Him can
I fall safely asleep beside my dear Lord. On Patmos He summoned me by His Spirit to amplify His first word from the cross
— amplify, mark you, not contradict — by that final prayer:
Come, Lord Jesus, yea, come quickly. The first word on the cross
certainly must be one of those things which is sweet in the mouth
— the first contact — but bitter in the belly — the further amplification and fulfillment.

Go where it is quiet now. It was morning, and it was noon:
the first day. Sun, never stand still over Gibeon, and thou Moon,
over the vale of Ajalon. It seems that the second Joshua prayed
the prayer of the first Joshua together with him. But in reality the
prayer of Jesus Christ transcended that of Joshua. This was His
privilege, His right. Come, Thou great Joshua, come quickly.
And for the rest — the *grace* of our Lord Jesus Christ be with us
all, amen. Otherwise . . . no, let me be still at last in His presence.

Christ Among the Bandits

CHAPTER EIGHT

Christ Among the Bandits

● *Where they crucified him, and two others with him, on either side one, and Jesus in the midst.*
JOHN 19:18.

WHEN Christ came into the world He lay amidst the magi and the bringers of gifts, amidst the shepherds who were also men of prayer, and amidst venerable guests of the temple. When He seemed to be passing out of the world, He was in the company of bandits.[1] The gospel tells us that when Jesus was brought to the place of crucifixion, two other malefactors were simultaneously taken there. We cannot say who these two others were. It is true that their names have been mentioned; the apocryphal imagination of men has dared to pronounce them. Thus we have been told that one of them was called Zoathan and the other Chammata. And others claim that the two had definite names, that the one was called Dysmas (or Dismas), and the other Gestes (or Gestas). And there is even a third version of the matter which has it that the two were called, respectively, Titus and Dumachus. That this tradition, which, as you see, contradicts itself, is unworthy of acceptance needs no contention. Just so we know little about how it happened that these malefactors were put to the tortuous death of the cross on the same day Jesus was executed. It may be that the execution had already been fixed for this day beforehand; it may also be that Pilate decided, once Jesus had been assigned to His death anyhow, that these other two could very well be put to death at the same time. We do not know. We may accept with certainty the fact that Pilate wanted to mock the Jews by his action in this matter. He thought it rather a

1. This word was selected in agreement with Grosheide, *Kommentaar op Mattheus*, p. 351.

happy idea: the king of the Jews: the sentimental Jesus ought to have the escort of two bandits. We cannot accept the fact that Pilate in the first place wanted to revile Jesus by placing Him on a par with the scum of this nation. His repeated affirmation of Christ's innocence was too formidable to allow us to think so. He simply had in mind to mock the Jews. They had been such a nuisance to him all day long that now he wanted to avenge himself. How could he do that more strikingly and "proudly" than by sending two varlets along with the self-vaunted king of the Jews to serve as His subjects. Once before Pilate had put all his pride and disdain, mingled with regret, into his ironical statement: Behold, your king.[1] A little later the same disdain, not unmixed with bitterness and sarcasm, was written into the superscription placed over the cross: Jesus the Nazarene, the king of the Jews. Those, then, were two ways in which he had reviled the Jews. They had been prompted by grimness and the boredom of exhaustion. Now we can better fit this sombre procession into this background of the two former acts of Pilate than in any other kind of context. Pilate did indeed want to mock the Jews as a people. Aha! Look! that king of the Jews was nailed to the cross in the company of two "subjects" of the lowest kind. This by way of a delicate and delicious mockery of the poisonous generation of Jews.

Thus, however, Jesus as the King of the Jews was being reincorporated into the body which had rejected Him before. The Jewish people are being mocked by the same judge to whom they have catered in their effort to have him carry out their will against Jesus Christ.

However, the important thing is not what Pilate does, but what *God* does through Pilate. The Gospel according to Mark indicates that this levelling process, this degrading of Jesus, was a fulfillment of the old prophecy which had been made about the suffering Servant of the Lord: He was numbered with the transgressors (Isaiah 53:12). Some think that this reference to Isaiah, as it appears in the gospel of Mark, was not written by Mark himself, inasmuch as there are other manuscripts which give a different version. Personally, we do not believe that this con-

---

1. *Christ on Trial*, p. 547.

tention is necessarily sound. In any case, however, the citation of Isaiah 53:12 is completely appropriate to the historical narrative of the gospel. Christ Himself also stated at the Passover supper: For I say unto you, that this that is written must yet be accomplished in me, And he was reckoned among transgressors (Luke 22:37). This plainly is a statement springing directly from Christ's own Messianic consciousness, and this statement provides the link between what Isaiah wrote concerning the servant of the Lord and what Jesus of Nazareth experienced in the day of His suffering.

It provides the link, but it does more than that. Not only is there unity and correspondence between Isaiah and Jesus, but there is also a fulfillment of the word of Isaiah in the reality of Jesus. For Christ had been reckoned with transgressors before. What still needed doing was the actual fulfillment. The levelling of Christ, I mean of God, with the scum of the street and the outcasts of society still had to be actualized in experience. For Satan still has in mind a nice question, which he means to put to the church. Throughout the centuries he will ask the church: Can it be that God said, He *resembles* my Son? That question is being prepared today.[1]

For Prophecy is active again; the Word is moving on. Hence it is by no means merely Pilate's fit of anger or his delicately woven network of sarcasm which is the cause of the fact that Christ in the moment in which He is being lifted up and advertised,[2] is publicly placed on a par with two varlets. No, this was caused by Christ's own direction, by God's government, and by Satan's evil desire. It represents not only the control of God but also a deed of Jesus Himself. He allowed Himself to be numbered with transgressors, "He allowed it to please Him that His people regarded Him as one punished by God for His sin, and as one sent to His death as a malefactor." He allowed Satan to classify Him with the rabble, for He personally dares to ask whether God has ever said: He *resembles* the Son of God. Presently He will Himself raise the question: homo-ousios or homoiousios: the equal of God, or merely one who resembles God. Hence He must be placed on a par with the rabble and there bring the greatest sacrifice in

1. Homo (i) ousios.
2. See *Christ on Trial*, chapter 15, especially p. 297 ff.

order that seeing they might not see, and hearing might not understand.

Again you see the imperious style and the pure will of God interjecting itself into the chaotic transaction of Pilate. Christ had to be numbered with the malefactors. This fact gives expression, from our side, to the wickedness of the world, and from His side, to the severity of His struggle and to the depth of His self-humiliation.

Yes, the caprice of sin is expressing itself through the escort which was assigned to Jesus. Christ continues to be treated by Pilate in the way in which Pilate has abused Him all day. Pilate wants to mock the Jews and the Jewish nation by hanging the scum of the streets next to Him. Three unfortunates, all next to each other, and their pathetic king in the middle — by arranging it so Pilate persists in the attitude which has been his throughout the day. The judge avenges himself upon the *Jews* but he does so at the expense of the Nazarene. The Jews put Pilate into a bad temper, but Christ has to suffer the effects. God lets the scourging fall upon the back of Christ, and Pilate draws an ugly Jew upon it, a caricature. The man who asked, "What is truth?" persists in ignoring the *ethical* problem. First of all he sins by placing Jesus on a par with those who have neither any might nor any right. But his second and greatest sin is that he places Jesus on a par with *malefactors,* and he does that notwithstanding the fact that he himself is willing to acknowledge that a great gulf is fixed between the varlets and the Nazarene.

However, it is not for us to single Pilate out for criticism. His sin is but a recurrence of the old root-evil: the world places Christ in its *own* light. That is the beginning. Having begun that way, it soon dares to degrade Him to the level of the least of men, to the plane of the misbegotten of civilization, as the world *itself* describes them in its books. The phenomenon occurs again and again: like Pilate, the world has Christ move around its own arrogant ego.

Accordingly, we can safely say that the caricature which the soldiers had given of Jesus' kingship continued to be displayed before the eyes of men on the cross. This caricature of the soldiers Pilate pasted on the cross-beam, on the same little placard which bore the "title" of Jesus.[1] But this is remarkable: the two murderers were also subjected to caricature. These poor fellows — they too must suffer because of the Nazarene, just as Barabbas had to suffer.[2] For they would not have had a place in the caricaturing if it had not been for Jesus. Alas, now everyone must be put to shame because of Jesus Christ. Yes, even the Jews are mocked together with Him. He takes them all with Him into His degradation. There are three crosses: that of a self-vaunted king, and those of two other "pretty replicas" of father Abraham. Pilate insists that this three-fold chain must by no means be broken, for it serves beautifully as a caricature of the whole Jewish people. Two dead branches and a thicker one which can serve as a trunk. That is the best way to make the tree of Abraham ludicrous. Thus Pilate subjects all the dry branches of Abraham to mockery. He does injustice to the green tree, but a voice sounded from this bush also: if they do this in the green tree, what shall be done in the dry? Almost at once that voice was fulfilled.

Painful as this caricature was to Christ, He nevertheless had to remain faithful to His labor. He may not despise the people that despise Him. Paul's great question, Hath God cast off His people? — a question asked when He let them struggle on without grace and the covenant — that question today for the first time lives in Jesus' soul.

Therefore, we must again speak of a temptation of the Saviour at this point. We know that His own people despise Him. According to the standards of justice, therefore, this people has lost its right to a place under the sun. As a carnal community it is in very fact deserving of death. Now Pilate is mocking this weak and twice-dead people, and is publicly exhibiting its pathetic frailty. Nevertheless as the Son of man, Christ must in His spirit take just as keen an exception to this blunt characterization as He did when He Himself was made the subject of world-caricature by means of the crown of thorns, the reed, and the gorgeous robe. Unless Jesus Christ, even in His severest passion — no, precisely in His severest

1. See chapter X of this volume, especially p. 192.
2. See *Christ on Trial*, p. 459.

passion — is just as active about the problem of Israel as His servant Paul under the inspiration of Christ's Spirit is later on (Romans 9 to 11), the soul of Jesus, according to the standards of divine justice, will be delighting itself in the sinful manifestations of Pilate's mockery. Then His approbation will make Abraham's seed an exlex,[1] precisely as Pilate made Abraham's great Son that. Then Christ will be degrading Himself to the level of Pilate. Then, indeed, these varlets will be the escort most becoming to Him, for then He will become one of them. Then He will be returning evil for evil; then that part of the sermon on the mount which says, Pray for them that persecute you, will return to Him like a boomerang. For, in this connection the petition means, "Force your way back into the sphere of law from which you have been cast out." Then Jesus Christ is not being infinitely busy in righteousness with the question Paul is asking, "Hath God cast off His people?" Then the inspiration of the Scripture by Christ's own Spirit will be lost. Then indeed everything is futile.

Alas, the Man who is like us in all things. Woe to Him if He does take exception to the Pilate who mocks those that mock Jesus. Yes, indeed, now again everything hangs suspended before our frightened gaze by a silken thread. At the same time, of course, everything is anchored in the pure soul of the Son. If Jesus Christ had delighted in, or if He simply had not opposed,[2] the mockery heaped upon the seed of Abraham by Pilate, Christ would have been unfaithful to His Messianic office. Then His own evil soul would have driven the seed of Abraham away from Him in a spiritual sense. Then He, delighting in Pilate, who delights to tread upon the dead branches of the tree of Abraham, would Himself have been chopping that tree down.

This He may not do because God still has a future for the tree of Abraham's seed. God cannot chop down a single tree which He has planted, says Paul. When He plants new shoots He simply grafts these shoots into the old trunk. Woe to Christ if He does not live by this law. God never destroys the old trunk. Woe to Him if He does not live by this law, and if He

---

1. Concerning this concept see this volume, chapter 1, and various chapters of *Christ on Trial.*
2. By active obedience just as well as by passive obedience.

cannot through the *Spirit* be the Father of the inspired writer of Romans 9 to 11.

However, our soul believes in Him and through faith our soul acknowledges that inwardly He wept for the Jews who were being mocked by Pilate. When He had approached the city, He had wept because of it. But that was in the past. When He is being cast out of the city, He still weeps because of it, and says to God: It is not true, my Father, it is not true; the seed of Abraham has not been rejected! I say then: Hath God cast off His people? No, God hath not cast off His people which He foreknew.[1] Father, Father, protect these varlets; put them in their place. That man Pilate, O Father, is taking everything out of its place. My people, O Father, is not what this caricaturist chooses to make them. Father, protect the rights of all varlets. Thou hast never yet created an alms-taking people, heavenly Father, even though Pilate says so a thousand times. I praise Thee, Father, and I praise Abraham, here among the varlets.

Then the angels said to each other: Blessed are the peacemakers for they shall be allowed to build up middle walls of partition. Indeed, He was a peace-maker, essentially He was that. He confessed the miserable congregation of Abraham in the presence of Pilate. He who is still willing to confess Abraham's varlets before the Father, Him will God confess to Himself.

Consequently, *I believe.* I believe that this pathetic escort of two malefactors was a temptation to Jesus. I believe that He was conscious of this. The mockery of Pilate comes back upon the head of the Jews, but I, second Adam, may not rejoice in that. I believe that His spirit struggled between the malefactors and Father Abraham to whom God once showed a thousand stars and then, doubling them, said: Thus shall thy seed be, and I the Lord shall *not* cast them off in all eternity. I believe He upheld Abraham overagainst Pilate, the Beast of Rome. I have no certainty other than the certainty of this *faith.*

This certainty suffices: faith will not be put to shame. Faith will presently see Him laboring so long, so hard, with such

---

1. See the beginning of Romans 11.

concentration of His spirit that of these two men, who with Him were brought into the caricature of the world, who shared with Him a place on this print of mockery, He will save one for eternal life. Jesus' sustained struggle for the preservation of that murderer is evidence for us which proves that He did not acquiesce in the ways of Pilate's sin and in the ways of "all flesh." When He Himself was made the exlex, He did not multiply the number of those who bore that title. Presently He raised the sound of rejoicing by way of taking exception to Pilate's mockery. Exuberantly, He shouted: Exlex, my brother in caricature, *today thou shalt be with me in Paradise.*[1] This second statement from the cross certainly is an acknowledgment of Abraham. By this statement He is refusing to chop down the tree of Abraham. From this point on the victory of the Spirit which inspires Paul begins. Here He purified Himself overagainst all Jews and indicated that He did not desire that meager comfort of hell which consists of laughing at the destruction of another.

Isaiah, and Ezekiel too, tell us in reference to this comfort of hell that the condemned in Hades mock and disdain *each other;* that the one delights in the misfortunes of the other. We have the very opposite of that in the Man of sorrows. The great Exlex can derive no comfort from an exlex. The mock-*king* gets no comfort from the mockery of His *subjects,* but He labors to save a man who is faltering to death. He struggles to receive a child of Abraham, who like Him, will presently lack everything, into the eternal tabernacles.

This is the Saviour of our heart. We thank Him for the fact that His pathetic escort, so far from being able to tempt Him, could only give Him an opportunity to manifest His true majesty. Fall down and worship Him: He makes friends out of the unjust comedy in order that, when all semblance of truth will be lacking to Him — on the cross — they may recognize Him in the eternal tabernacles.[2]

The Father praised the cautious, dialectical Master: He had not been fooled by the caricatures. The angels sang of reality and truth. The world did not fall to pieces simply because He

1. For further consideration, see the next chapter.
2. See Luke 16:9.

CHRIST AMONG THE BANDITS 159

could not endure Pilate when he chose bandits as models for a malicious caricature of the Jewish nation.[1]

The labor of Jesus' spirit to look upon the mockery of the seed of Abraham theocentrically at this time naturally spelled *suffering* for Him. Always there is this attention on His part, an attention which may never for a moment subside. And there is always the official obligation to give even though everyone is taking. And there is that severe struggle of the soul to save the seed of Abraham, which does not protect Him against Pilate, — to save it from Pilate in His own soul. And then that levelling process. Lo, this is the hour in which Christ is not only to be the Head of the covenant of Grace, that is, the Head of the lost varlets whom God in Him regards as the "congregation of just men made perfect." In this same hour Christ is made "common," is degraded. False appearance, of course! Not only is He placed on a par with the malefactors (negation of His holiness) but He is even denied beforehand the power to make from what is disgraceful and despised a masterpiece of the Spirit of regeneration. For the caricature of Pilate — like all caricature — can only be understood in such a way that the main person in it — in this case the king — who is being gorgeously decked out, is the most deeply mocked and humiliated.

But we do not lament any longer. God still gave His Son a task to do. Before He completely descended to hell He had the heavy task to accomplish for a lost person His great, messianic, world-mission.

If we look upon the matter in this light, we see that the company of bandits in which Jesus was placed was willed by God. From Jesus' point of view, this company was absolutely inevitable for Him. Not the slightest hint of accident this; the full justice of God places Christ here in the position assigned to Him. This is the true relationship: Jesus among the worthless ones. These are not political prisoners, these are not Barabbases, these are not the sons of eminent rabbis, are not people of whom we know that they have been put in prison for reasons of a political character — no, these are simon-pure bandits. These are the least of the least; they are despised of everyone. And

---

1. Material for a sermon on Jewish missions.

these had to accompany Jesus. God purposely reaches into the lowest layers of that to which sin gave birth — the world of malefactors — seizes two of them, and places them in Jesus' path, the one to the right, and the other to the left of Him.

Why does He do that? To humble your pride and mine, for we always think we are better than these two malefactors. Nevertheless, according to heavenly prophecy, He is here in the presence of those who are His appropriate company, His fit subjects. Yes, we may say so reverently: this is an instance of the right Man in the right place. Christ among the bandits. God reaches down into the lowest possible layers by way of pointing out that Jesus when He Himself, in this company, answers the question put by Paul and thus labors for life, does not work through culture but through grace, does not ask men to be civilized, but to be penitent. God does this by way of showing that He does not build up on what is still present in man but on what can give you and me life only in a new creature. He says to the women who weep for Him: What is your glory: are ye Abraham's seed? I say to you that God even out of these varlets can raise up children unto Abraham.

He says this to us also for we all come from the lowest levels. The bandits who accompanied Jesus had to disclose and exhibit to us the essence of sin precisely by the forms of their despised lives. For the essence of sin is in the last analysis the same in all those who depart from God; the same, and even worse. For even bandits are not an adequate expression of the terrible nature of sin. The *locus de peccato* is given an inadequate illustration even in their company.

Thus the whole issue is made to converge upon us, upon us "decent" people, for, the moment we have become, not the superman but the sub-bandit, we will have understood a little of it. Then we will say to Pilate: poor fool, you can engage in your levelling processes if you want to, but Jesus Christ can only make confession of the law of election and reprobation. The good pleasure, the eternal and sovereign good pleasure of God, is active here. That good pleasure will place Jesus "in the midst of them," the two bandits to the right and to the left of Him. Thereupon that good pleasure will command Jesus to reveal in the repentance of the one and the hardening of the other the wonders of election and reprobation, the segregation of Abraham's sons and bastards.

After this manifestation of naked reality it is no longer a sin to speak of the symbolism of Golgotha. We noted above[1] that the topography of Golgotha had a symbolical significance inasmuch as routes led from it to Zion (the communion), and to Gehenna (the forsaking). Just so this same symbolism is again plastically developed at this place, on this mound of death. Jesus between the murderers represents the way to fellowship and the way to abandonment. On this day there will be two people in one escort: the one shall be taken and the other left. There is no such thing as a levelling process when God has a hand in it. This is always true and is true everywhere. God makes of Golgotha, that dry and evil place on the world's surface, a cultivated field in which wheat and chaff must be made public according to His good pleasure. That which Pilate would make evil by means of His sarcastic levelling, that God would make good by perfectly realizing the ideas of God in full reality. For who can separate God from the beginning of the counsels of God? Who is to make blunt the knives sharpened by God's will? And who can avail to make the presence of true varlets such a hindrance to the attention of Jesus that He will cease to be the theocentric Theologian? God has appeared to Him in person. He Himself is God.

Thus He goes on His way laden with His curses, but in His soul He sings an idyllic hymn: Pilate would cast this people off but I, I say then: Has God cast off His people? God forbid, Pilate, I am the true Israelite of the seed of Abraham, of the seed of David. God cannot cast off the people whom He foreknew. Hence, Pilate, this escort of bandits, is, it is true, together with the whole people, an enemy as far as the gospel is concerned, but as far as the election is concerned they are the beloved for the fathers' sake. For the gifts of grace and the calling of God are not to be repented of. God has included them all among the disobedient, in order that He might be merciful to the elect. That is now their abundance, their wholeness; this is their true pleroma.

Pilate, does this sound strange and unreal to you? I shall prove it very shortly. Today this bandit here will be with me in Para-

---

1. See p. 84.

dise. As for the other? That other one is not a Jew, for His is
not the circumcision of the heart. The other is not of the seed of
Abraham, for he has not Abraham's faith. Pilate, the caricature
has failed miserably; the devil is honoring you for nothing today.
God's elective mercy is still looking for her children among the
Jews whom you despise. Mark this, Pilate: the Judge of heaven
and earth is protesting against the mockery heaped upon the seed
of Abraham. Pilate, I, Jesus Christ, I do not recognize the exlex,
not even among the bandits. My God, my God, have mercy upon
the refuse of Abraham. O depth of the riches, both of the wisdom and of the knowledge of God! How unfathomable are His
judgments, and untraceable His ways! They assert themselves
even in the reprobation of the man who engages in levelling
processes. They reveal the law of election and reprobation, they
separate the seed of Abraham from the bastards. What more
could Abraham wish? Furthermore, God has never denied
Abraham; for of Him, through Him, and unto Him are all things.
His be the glory forever, amen.[1]

Thus the Saviour walked among the bandits. Presently He
was permitted to call one man to the wedding. Well, it was not
surprising that the king should say to the servant: Call in wedding guests from among the varlets, that my house may be filled.
But it was surprising that the king stripped the servant who was
to do the inviting of his livery and placed him in a bandit-garb.
The voice of One crying; but do not regard His clothes. A *voice,*
the Word — that suffices for God.

Thus the Saviour walked among the bandits. He was on the
way to the altar. The Priest is on His way to the sacrifice but He
so perfectly embodies foolishness and offense, also as Priest, that
God gives Him as His companions on this final journey to the
altar not two common Levites, but two mean bandits. Yes, indeed;
foolishness and offense. All these words are known to God from
eternity, and therefore I see, I seek, a significance in them. I do
not find it strange to see these bandits around Him. But this
journey to the altar; I mean *the* journey to the altar in the company of bandits, is this not a strange thing? He places His altar
in an ugly spot. But never mind, it may be that I understand it

---

1. Compare Romans 11:1, 2, 28-36.

already. I think He wants to ask me emphatically once more —
the voice of One calling from among the bandits: poor fool,
whether is greater, the altar, or the gift that sanctifies the altar
(compare Matthew 23:19)?[1] Are you still as superstitious as
this? Lord, depart from me; I am a sinful man, a bandit in Thy
presence.

Thus my Saviour walked among the bandits.

When next I see the loafers, and the smugglers of liquor, and
the "scum" of society, I shall remember that Christ was among
them and that He sang His psalms from the midst of bandits.
Wist I not that He had to be active in His Judge's business? I
shall examine myself once more; I must be about my Judge's
business. And in His palace I dare not look to the right nor to the
left. In court I lose my sense of rank. I do not look for loafers.
Great grace, incomparable grace it will be, if I escape alive — I,
varlet, parasite to God.

---

1. Intentional reversal of the text. In the sacrifice of the Old Testament "the
altar makes the animal an offer" (Grosheide, *Kommentaar op Mattheus* 23:18),
but here the offer (the priest of His own offer) makes the place an altar, and
consequently the offer and the altar (the place) are necessarily related to each
other by the good pleasure of God.

Christ Disrobed

CHAPTER NINE

Christ Disrobed

● *Then the soldiers, when they had crucified Jesus, took his garments, and made four parts, to every soldier a part; and also his coat: now the coat was without seam, woven from the top throughout. They said therefore among themselves, Let us not rend it, but cast lots for it, whose it shall be: that the scripture might be fulfilled, which saith, They parted my raiment among them, and for my vesture they did cast lots. These things therefore the soldiers did.*

JOHN 19:23-24.

WE GENERALLY pay more attention to the clothes in which Christ was swaddled in the manger than to the clothes in which He went to the cross, and which were brutally taken from Him by the people. Nevertheless such an apportionment of our attention is unwarranted. The swaddling clothes were given to the babe by the providence of God, and the garment which, now that He has grown up, is taken from Him on the cross, was taken from Him by this same and most special providence of God. The clothes in which He was swaddled as He lay in the manger are less essentially a sign of His poverty than the manger itself. True, they were made a sign by which the shepherds might distinguish Him, but they were constituted a sign only in relation to the manger itself. As such only were they regarded as a symbol of His lowliness and poverty. But at Golgotha the garment alone, in relationship to no other thing, was made a sign. The disrobing of Christ was a special symbol and spoke a unique language of God. This shall be the sign unto us: we shall find the Surety, robbed of His clothes, and hanging on the cross. A merciless plundering exhibited His nakedness to the

167

eyes of the delicate priests and of the youth of the Great City of Jerusalem. Think of that. They seized on His clothes in the hour of His death upon Golgotha. And we would have been summoned to leave the place lest the penalty of Ham and Canaan come upon us, had not God Himself cried aloud that we *must* stay, inasmuch as He had made this plundering of His clothes a *sign* for all ensuing generations. Precisely this constitutes the difficulty of this day.

We want to avert our eyes, lest we should be cursed with the curse of Ham and his generation, but we may not. We *must* look on. He is greater than Noah, and consequently He is much less, for zeniths are nadirs, and robing is but a disrobing. God adjures us if we would not be unclothed, but clothed upon, to stand then and see, for thus saith the Lord: in the plundering of Christ's clothes an ancient prophecy has come to its fulfillment.

Consequently let us see, let us hear what the Spirit has to say to the churches about the naked Christ who was crucified amidst the bandits.

To all appearances the incident was a very ordinary one. Regulation had it that the property of the person condemned to death was the legitimate loot of those who executed the sentence. Accordingly, the four soldiers who were carrying out the penalty against Jesus were legally authorized to lay claim to the clothes of the bandits crucified with Jesus, as well as to those of Jesus Himself. It is not unlikely that the centurion, the "captain of a hundred," could lay official claim first of all to the property of the condemned persons. However, we have no evidence for believing that the man made good his claims on this occasion. No wonder: there was very little to take. As a matter of fact, the centurion had other things to do today besides worrying about the poor legacy left by these three crucified ones. The man concluded the day by a kind of confession of faith;[1] and that was quite a different thing. He paid very little attention to this division of the spoils. Something else was disturbing him.

---

1. There will be further discussion of this point later.

Be that as it may. In the fact and the manner of the division of Jesus' clothes we see above all a sign of His great poverty:

All rights denied,
naked, Christ died.[1]

In this connection two elements require our attention: first, that Jesus' clothes were taken from Him; and, second, that they were assigned to others, in this case to the soldiers.

Before Christ was hanged upon the accursed wood, He was disrobed. Opinion differs about whether the disrobing was partial or complete. Some think that the Saviour was allowed to retain some of His garments. Others believe that in order to make the shame of crucifixion as great as possible the crucified person was customarily robbed of all his clothes. As a matter of fact, this interpretation seems to be historically verifiable.

It is true, of course, that we would rather not look these facts in the face. Whoever has been taken captive by the majesty of Christ will say with the Baptist: I am not worthy, I am unfit to loose the latches of his shoes. Well, if the majesty of Christ is so overwhelming that we would not dare to approach Him by way of untying the laces of His sandals, how could we dare to approach Him in order to see His complete disrobing? However, we must not forget that the question is not what John the Baptist or what any other person who loves Him can bear to see at the foot of the cross. The important thing is to know what He Himself tells us. And He wants us to understand thoroughly that He in His nakedness is unfit to untie the laces of our shoes. He wants to humiliate us to the point of shame in order to exalt us, the "clothed upon," later. Accordingly, He compells us to notice Him. We must know what He allows the enemies to do to Him. Lo, without any piety whatever, they have made Him the subject of shame and have done this as absolutely as was "the *custom*" in that day. After all, He must experience all the customs, must He not? Lo, the Son of God, naked, hanging between two naked malefactors!

In this all the souls are being dis-covered. Only he who has *faith* can find his God and his Lord in this extreme shame. Such is the course which the penalty is taking. In the first place, the

---

1. Guido Gezelle.

people cannot conceive any other device to which their delight in humiliating Him can resort. But the people are not the only ones with whom we are concerned here. Besides considering what the people do to Jesus, we must also devote attention to what *God* causes the Surety of our soul to suffer.

There is but one answer. The shame of nakedness is fitted into the framework of Christ's whole Suretyship. This shame of nakedness constitutes *punishment.* Just as sin, when it had entered into the world, caused man to sense his nakedness with a feeling of pain because he knew his being lay disrupted, inasmuch as the forms of life were no longer an expression of their hidden, holy essence, but an expression also — and that an unknown one — of strange sinister influences opposed to God, so now nakedness comes in the form of pain to this place of perfectly executed punishment.

After the advent of sin to the world God gave man clothes to wear. God's special providence — thus the account of Genesis — gave man those clothes. Now the entrance of protective clothing into the world was not an accidental thing, nor a passing thing, not an alogical civilized form of a highly developed life; it was, according to the Bible, an inherent part, a definitely accompanying phenomenon, of our lives — lives in part contaminated by sin, in part protected from sin by grace. Clothing is not the product of the evolution of culture, but it is the thoughtful gift of God's grace. To go naked after God's first act of clothing us, is not to engage in a form of primitive barbarism but is to become the victim of retrogression; it is to fall from the plane of life in Paradise.

We would be going too far afield if we were to elaborate here on our notion of the function of clothes in the world. It must suffice to remark that clothes are a gift of God's common grace. We cannot understand the function which clothes have in our human life unless we again think of those marvelous indications of God to which we have alluded so often in this work — so often, in fact, as we spoke of common grace, of the vicious circle of life, and of the circulation of the blood.[1] In all of these matters we saw, in the last analysis, the same manifestation of God's

---

1. See *Christ on Trial*, pp. 53 ff., 77 ff., 137 ff., and 512 ff.

activity in the world and in its history. After sin, God introduced a *law of retardation* into the world. By this means He tempered the curse, the judgment; and by the same means He restrained the *blessing* from attaining its full fruition and its full realization. This God did in order to make room for the Christ and for the victory of the *regenerative* powers which His love and grace set into action.

This law also affects the function of clothes. Clothes are indeed on the one hand a restriction upon life and blessing; a hindrance to the perfect expression of beauty. Clothing molests the "devine theos," — the pagans say. For the body of a human being, beautiful and unblemished as God made it, gives a rich expression to the beautiful idea of God, the God of beauty — say the Christians. If sin had not disturbed the scheme, God, the supreme Artist, also in creating the human body, the final and most beautiful of His artistic creations, would not have allowed it to be covered by clothing. Consequently in the eventual elaborated state of things clothing will again have served its purpose. The riches of God's perfect artistry will then again manifest themselves to every eye in their naked form.

In another sense, or better, from another point of view, clothing is part of the activity of God's *grace*. Sin which eats its way into and out of all things makes itself manifest in everything which life offers. It devotes itself to the origins of our life also in order to defile these. Hence God gives man his clothes in order that sin might be hampered and restricted, and in order that the retrogression which sin introduced into the human body also, might be retarded and thwarted in its curse-laden, fatal work.

If we bear all these considerations in mind, we will appreciate better what God did to Christ when His hand disrobed the Son. Again the beautiful scheme of God's thoughts interjects itself into the apparently accidental and certainly customary[1] activity of men. That which we observed in the passion of Christ at every successive moment, we observe again now. Human beings are active, yes, but God especially is active. The people disrobe Christ because, well, that just happens to be part of the penalty. They did not see beyond their lugubrious disciplinary regulations.

---

1. See p. 168.

But God does the same thing by means of their activity to the Surety of the world. God lets the Surety feel the consequence of His surrender to the Suretyship. If, as was said above, clothing is a fruit of "common grace," a retardation of the curse in its relentless course, and also is a manifestation of the "common judgment," which hampers what otherwise would be the perfect fruition of beauty, then it *must* also be taken from the Christ. God could put clothing upon the *first* Adam only because he would one day take it off the *second* Adam. For clothing represented grace. But all grace — He is descending into hell — must depart from the Christ. Indeed, clothing represents judgment, but only "general" judgment. However Christ is today the subject of absolute judgment. Listen, Hosea, God is drowning out your voice: God will strip Lo-ruhamah naked (See Hosea 1 and 2). Because an unrestricted exhibition of naked reality is a proper part of an exhaustive penalty of sin, Christ must be so exhibited and despised in the world, in order that all the eloquent, illustrative expressions of the time in which the Son appeared on the earth might give as complete an expression as possible to the rejection of the Surety. He had to undergo also the humiliation of nakedness, a nakedness customary in hell (and also in heaven).

Thus the second Adam sinks to a plane below the first. The clothes which were given to the first Adam were made out of the *skins of animals*. This gift already represented great grace, a significant restoration of the condition which obtained before man fell. For from this gift it becomes apparent that the subordinate creature, the animal, is put into the service of man, even as he is after the fall.

Yes, that first piece of clothing was made of the skin of an animal. . . . Some have said that the first piece of clothing was the product of the marriage of art and worship. These argue that the clothing represented art and that the animal killed for it contained in it the idea of sacrifice. This seems unplausible to us. When first instituted, clothing did not represent *art*. It represented necessity. It was a defense, a protection. And the sacrifice of an animal for the sake of the piece of human clothing was not a cult, or a form of worship, for the element of sacrifice is lacking in the slaying of that animal. God seizes on the animal in order to make it serve man's purposes, but man does not give the animal to God. Nothing is being paid.

But, if the clothing of the first Adam did not represent the marriage of art and worship, it did represent the mastery of technique[1] over nature. It represented an intervention, the product of God's own act and later by God's active permission the product also of man's act — an intervention in what nature provides. Thus the phenomenon of technique might still serve to protect and defend the lost human being.

Therefore the first piece of clothing which God as a result of His own care gave man in Paradise, contains a beautiful if frightening lesson. It proclaims to man the whole truth of long-suffering, and at the same time entangles him in the great obsession of the law of common grace (and retardation). It still points out to man — nomad as he is upon the earth — the scope of the natural world, in order that he may still have dominion over it. And it gives the human being, brutal annexationist of heavenly gifts that he is, a certain amount of property in the world nevertheless. It guarantees the fact that technique may triumph over nature. But it adds that the triumphs will come "with fear and trembling."

Surely the gift of clothing was an instance of grace, and also an instance of judgment. Or can you believe that it was purely an accidental phenomenon? No, for this gift is conceivable only in terms of that will of God which would make human life possible in order that *Christ* could in His own time redeem life conclusively; in order, that is, that Christ could redeem life, on the one hand, by first of all *losing* the gifts of common grace — for, after all, they had been given man only on the condition of such loss — and, on the other hand, in order that the common grace, regained by His satisfying righteousness, might burgeon forth as the Lord of nature and, as the second Adam, might rise to the highest forms of kingship over the universe.

In other words, we may say that the hour of God's constricting logic has arrived. This is the very logic which He Himself preached to those who were unclothed in reference to particular

---

1. Common grace (a life which is still endurable, in which dominion is still possible) and also the "common judgment, by which is meant that there is no evolution of the basic elements of life to their pleroma without pain and suffering.

grace. Whosoever will lose his life, shall save it. Now He Himself becomes ensnared in His own net. He who is naked as far as common grace goes, must lose His garment if He is to gain it. If He cannot earn a garment, He can conquer nothing.

Accordingly, the Son must die now, naked. Fully aware of the fact that He is doing so He *must* consciously endure the shame of the nakedness which is part and parcel of existence in hell. For the *curse* is descending upon Him. Now we know that the expressions of shame, also in their bodily manifestations, await the accursed after death. This experience is called "nakedness" but the word does not do justice to what it is intended to convey. Nakedness means a frustration of the spirit. Now the one who quite consciously wanted to endure this hellish fate for us is the Christ. Hence Christ's disrobing was in no sense less oppressive and infamous to the Messianic sense of the Christ than the merciless, inevitable exhibition and ostentation of the lost life of all condemned persons in hell. What is true of all other things in Golgotha is also true of the disrobing of the Son. We must look upon them *sub specie novissimae diei.* We must see the movement of the last day in them. It is a terrible punishment for the Christ to be made a naked exhibition; for Christ is the one who would strip the authorities and powers naked and make them a public example. This to Him is the same bitter reality as that which bore down upon Him in all the other forms of His passion. The nails and hammers, we observed before, appeared to Him as catastrophic powers of the last day.[1] Well, the disrobing of the Saviour is subject to the same law; it was a part of the shame of hell.

Nothing is accidental. Clothing represents the *first* gift given to man by common grace; it is the first intentional technical creation coming after sin by way of constraining nature. Because it is just that, Christ's clothing must be taken from Him, in order that the victory of technique over nature and of the intentional and violent conquest of nature by the technique should accrue to everyone *save to the Surety Himself.* Yes, by His loss we gain. Our factories are busy, our looms, our textile mills, our technical facilities triumph over nature because the Surety first of all relinquished the benefits of the first technical triumph over nature when

---

1. See pp. 118-122.

he was on Golgotha. Golgotha, that bare and barren hill. The hill was bare, yes, but *He* was completely naked. Naked and exposed to the eyes of Him with whom He, for our sake, had to do (Hebrews 4:13).

Thus the offense and the foolishness of the cross was intensified and aggravated by the spectacle of the naked Christ. This is a thing for which all Jews and well dressed priests must either bite their lips to pieces, or laugh themselves into distortion. We have here a naked God, a naked Messiah, and hanging on the cross. Is it any wonder that even today we can find on the walls of certain old barracks of the paganism of antiquity certain caricatures in which the Saviour of the Christians was represented by this or that soldier as a crucified donkey? Such was the mockery with which their pagan colleagues chided Christian soldiers. No, it is no wonder. That would happen today again under similar circumstances. When God took the clothes from His Son, that Son no longer was allowed to move through the world, for one's clothes give one the privilege of going about. That was no false fancy but a logical insistence upon Biblical ideas which made us say a moment ago that the Baptist sighed: I am not worthy, condescending, to loosen the latches of His shoes; and that, everyone can now say of Jesus: He is not worthy, condescending, to untie the laces of my shoes. Christ has not now the right to go about freely in the world. In this the Suretyship was made perfect. Let Him hide behind the bush as He can.

But He cannot. The first Adam was able to do so! the second is still limited to His nakedness. Nails, spikes, and the heat of the catastrophic day! O God, He cannot escape, He cannot hide. Nevertheless, voices everywhere are crying: Where are Thou? Where art Thou?

On our own part, it would be to cheapen the gospel of the passion and of the story of the cross if we were to separate Christ's anxious cry, My God, why hast Thou forsaken me? from these considerations. He who knew Himself to be the Son of man did not overlook the fact that He sank to a plane below that of Adam and that He was made a public spectacle in His nakedness on the accursed cross. He could not forget that He had fewer rights than Adam. Adam's was still the right to conceal Himself. And Christ's awareness of His own shame in part prompted the plaint: My

God, why hast Thou forsaken me? He could truly lament God's forsaking Him precisely because He, unlike Adam, felt that He would never be separated from God.

But we said that there was a second consideration which required our attention. To the fact that Christ's clothing is *taken away* from Him must be added the consideration that they were *assigned to the soldiers*. A comparison of the several accounts of the gospel shows us that the soldiers in dividing Jesus' clothing separated them into two groups: first, the garments in general; and then, the coat. Of the first classification we can say that by the "garments" in general was meant the outer covering, or cloak, which served as a cover for the night among the poor. It may be that the girdle, which was commonly worn around this cloak, was also included among the garments. The sandals also, doubtless, belonged to Him. Some observers suggest that a covering for the head should also be added, but it is not likely that Jesus wore one, inasmuch as He had been taken captive at night; moreover, the brutal mockery involving the crown of thorns indicates that the covering for the head had been taken away from Him if He had had any at all.

Special mention, however, is given to the *coat,* to the so-called chiton. By this is meant the long coat which was generally worn next to the naked body and was made up of wool or linen. Sometimes the chiton was not worn over the naked skin but was used to cover a linen shirt which, in that case, was worn next to the body. We do not know the particulars; and no one has the right to act as though he did know them.

Now the soldiers divided the clothing of Jesus into two parts of equal value. The first part consisted of that first group called the "garments," and the second consisted of the chiton, which was kept separate.

Do you wonder why it was kept separate? Some believe that we must regard this indication as evidence for the fact that the chiton which Jesus wore was a very expensive garment. They point to the fact that the coat in question was seamless, that it was all of a piece. They assume that such a single piece of goods which had come in precisely that form from the loom, and was at no point sewed together, must have been especially expensive. From this assumption they derive various hypotheses. One observer, for instance, claims that Jesus' beautiful, artistically constructed under-garment goes to prove that He enjoyed a relative amount of riches; and still another commentator adds that Christ laid claim to His priestly pretensions by means of this chiton. We know that the priest also wore a garment which was woven of a single piece of cloth and was seamless. Christ, these observers maintain, by means of His seamless coat was saying: I too am a priest, and I give that fact expression by my clothes.

We need devote no argument to showing that such a play of the fancy is vain. Christ did not want to make His priestship tangible by means of a cloak, and certainly not by means of a garment, which because it was an under-garment, could not be seen anyhow. Similarly, the contention that this coat was woven of a single piece and that this goes to prove its costliness is an argument which also has nothing better than fancy as its basis. Whoever, even today, can tell us something about Oriental life will confirm the fact that woven stuffs which we regard as very expensive are worn in the East by very ordinary people. Weaving was a very common activity of the time; hence Jesus' woven chiton is in no sense to be taken as an indication of unusual wealth.

As a matter of fact, we should prefer to deduce the very opposite from the account. The soldiers divided the clothing of the Nazarene among the four of them. In doing this, they first divided the whole of it in two groups. The chiton was kept separate and formed the one group; the rest constituted the second group. The reason for this classification was self-evident. If they had done it differently, nothing valuable would have remained. If they had made a group of all the material, including the chiton, they would have had to tear it into four pieces. Then no one would have had anything worth while, for the rest was worth preciously little. Girdle, sandals, and under-garment were hardly a prize. Their decision to cast lots for the chiton goes to show that this was the only piece which "amounted to anything," and which was still worth rescuing from the meager legacy.

Hence we can say that Jesus left very little behind Him in the world. He was poor when He came into the world, and poor when He went out of it. At several times in His life He had had money in abundance; many women served Him with their goods. But by the end of His life everything seemed to have been put into the service of the Kingdom of heaven. Jesus Himself wore no more than was necessary.

Just because of that fact the raffling of His clothes was a difficult problem in Jesus' consciousness. Perhaps the easiest way for us to appreciate the significance of this will be for us to give our attention to two things: first, to His right of requisition; and, second, in connection with that right, to His self-awareness as the Son of God, a self consciousness which also asserted itself in His property-concerns. We shall consider each of these two matters.

We have previously mentioned that Christ made requisitions; Christ made His demands, by the grace of God. In this way, we said, He laid claim to His beast of burden, and to His passover room. He laid claim to His beast of burden as a King, upon His "triumphal" entry into the city. He demanded His room as a Priest, preparing the Holy Supper for His people. He did this fully aware that He was the Son of David and the priest-king of Zechariah's vision. Thereupon we observed that this right of requisition was completely denied Him. This occurred when Simon of Cyrene was compelled to bear His cross.

Now God goes further along this same line with the Son, with the Surety. Simon of Cyrene — yes, it may be that he wounds Jesus' soul, but if so he does it in spite of himself. From the viewpoint of human beings at least, the assistance given by Simon of Cyrene has the semblance of a gesture of friendship. However, even this last suggestion of assistance and good will is now taken from Jesus. They remove His clothes. This clothing — on which His disciples had lovingly labored — is now, together with a few worthless rags which had belonged to the bandits, cast upon a heap and then divided among the soldiers by lot. Surely, this is the perfect contrast to what happened a week before when rich and eminent persons threw their clothing upon the road in order that the king of Jerusalem might arrive at his residence by passing over them.

Christ's right of requisition had merely been denied when Simon of Cyrene was constrained to bear the cross. But now God and the devil go further. That right is being mocked now. So thoughtlessly does the world throw Jesus' property about that a centurion does not even think it worth his trouble to ask whether there is anything in the heap worthy of his attention; and the soldiers, grinning because of the meager loot, agree at least to give some consideration to one useful article on the pile.

Then they took out the dice. Or it may be that they did not even use the dice. They could also cast lots by means of their fingers. Be that as it may, they cast lots. It was a game of chance and it took place on Golgotha. This is the second cut of the two-edged sword of Satan's mockery. Is not Golgotha the best and the first revelation of justice from God's point of view? What place can accident and chance possibly have here — before the eyes of the Saviour? To throw the dice, to cast lots, is to catch at the hem of the garment of chance as it dances through the world.

Such was the end of the matter. He began the week by laying claim to things, and He ended it with His eyes fixed on raffling soldiers, dividing His legacy among themselves while He, alive, looked on. Such was the end of the way which began with gold and frankincense and myrrh.

In this way we naturally reach the point we wanted to give attention. Christ's Messianic consciousness, we said, placed the problem of His property also in His own light.

When at one time they had asked that He contribute taxes for the temple, He asked Simon Peter directly, in separate conversation, whether it really was not foolishness to ask Him and His disciples for taxes. Indeed, that was a topsy-turvy world. For Christ is the Son and in the house of the Father the Son is not One who pays, He enjoys the privilege of inheritance. In the house of God, says the Saviour, the Sons are free, and if this holds true in reference to assessments for the temple, it holds true in an even larger sense for all other forms of taxation. For if Christ as the Son of God is the Heir and Receiver in the temple, He is that in an even stronger sense in the house of nature. Good, says Jesus; from Him then, who is the Son of God, the Supreme Owner of the world, nothing can be demanded. True, He paid the assessment "lest He should offend them," and in order to conceal Himself as the free Son and as the sole Heir of the whole world. Nevertheless, exactly by way of demonstrating that He was that to His disciples, He performed a sign which demonstrated His absolute right as Owner. In order to be able to pay the penny demanded of Him as an assessment, He did a miracle. He had the coin taken from the mouth of a fish which was drawn from the water just at the time. This, in His self-concealment, He placed on the table of the collector of revenues.

Now these are things we must keep in mind at the crucifixion and especially as we look upon the scene in which the soldiers are raffling off Jesus' clothes. Are we arbitrarily putting two things together here which have no relation to each other? No, but who, indeed, has the right to separate these matters from each other. The life of Christ on earth is precisely comparable to His coat: it is all of a piece, is seamless. Consequently we are not trying to establish a connection between things lying far apart from each other but are simply doing our duty when we put those things together which Christ by His Spirit brought together. We can catch only a glimpse of that which suffused His Spirit when we say that Christ, while looking upon the raffling of His clothes, did not for one moment segregate Himself from His own consciously presented doctrine about His right of inheritance, about His right of assessment, about His Sonship, as He confessed these before Simon Peter "at the occasion" of the tax bill which was given Him. As His clothes were being raffled off and given away, His inclusive spirit saw the magi of the East, who brought Him rich gifts, saw Sheba who brought her treasures with her, saw the Father in heaven who made no demands upon His Son, and He saw all these things in their direct relationship with these raffling soldiers. Yes, yes, He senses it very well. It did seem as if that apparently inattentive gesture, by means of which through an aristocratic miracle He pulled a coin out of the mouth of a fish, was being mocked by God Himself. Now, Jesus Christ, Thou hast performed a wonder. Where now is that God who can provide money-laden fish at a moment's notice? Thou hast instructed Thy disciples that Thou dost govern the property of the world. Thou didst set Thyself up as the Chief-Requisitioner overagainst all tax-payers of the world. Thy self-consciousness availed to vanquish nature, and to open the mouth of a fish. Thy hand reached into the water with a playful but serious gesture. And now, Chief-Heir, Thou must make compensations for that arrogant attitude. Soldiers are dickering over Thy coat, and are casting lots for it. In other words, miracles are receding. Heaven is silent. The gift of gold, frankincense, and myrrh from the magi of the East has its counterpart now in these raffling soldiers of the West. The Orient sends its gift-bearers; the west its plunderers. Thus Christ as the Lord of the temple and as the Prince of the world went into concealment here.

Shall we weep about it? No, for our faith finds its Surety in this. If the free Son allows His right to property to be thus profaned, He by that means also "became poor, having been rich," and naked having been clothed. He raised the taxes for us all, He who can demand the revenues. Write His monogram on the cross. It must be written in the form of a fish,[1] for the cross and the fish belong together. He caught that fish in order to demonstrate His right to property to the faith of Simon Peter and also in order to conceal His right to property to the unbelief of those in the temple who demanded the taxes. If only I draw the sign of that fish over His head, I will have understood the cross and the casting of lots. Then He Himself will say to me in His profound nakedness: This is Suretyship; this is Suretyship; for know this with absolute certainty — the Son is essentially free. Thus He again conceals all His human rights of requisition and all His divine claims of taxation behind the shame of His nakedness. All the problems of theology and revelation and of the Scriptures are revealed — to Him who believes — in the naked Saviour.

Now return to our point of departure. Look back to Paradise and to the clothes of Adam. In Paradise, God took an animal in order to clothe man. God said that man might continue to have dominion over the beasts. God placed the beasts in the service of man. And Christ demonstrated that as the Son of God, He, too, can take animals, if He wishes to, by way of making the beasts subservient to man's purposes. But He did more than that. He used that animal particularly to conceal His right to property. After the dazzling miracle He satisfied Himself with the very

---

1. Later Christians used the symbol of the fish as a sign of recognition. The Greek word for fish is *Ichthus*. These are the initial letters of I(esous) Ch(ristos) Th(eou) U(ios) S(oter), which means: Jesus Christ, Son of God, Saviour.

ordinary gesture of a tax payer, who comes in the usual manner to pay His assessment.

Now this law of utmost concealment is realized in the second Adam on the cross:

> All rights denied,
> naked, Christ died.

The animal's skin to be used by Adam, and the mouth of the fish by Jesus. All this returned on the cross. His people are clothed by His nakedness, and by His nakedness His people can and may support the temple.

We can easily understand in this scheme of ideas that the Scriptures should point out to us the relationship between that apparently ordinary intermezzo between the raffling soldiers on the one hand, and the whole of prophecy on the other. The Scriptures tell us that what is written in Psalm 22:18 was fulfilled in the disrobing of Christ, that is, was carried out in its full implications. In that well-known psalm of passion David complains that they have parted his garments and cast their lots for his vesture.

Do not ask now whether this literally happened to David, and denying that it did, do not say therefore that he exaggerated. This is neither literal record, nor hyperbole. In Psalm 22 the poet laments that the misery which robs him of the experience of fellowship with God is caused by people who are doing him wrong, by robbers and plunderers. And he gives a vivid picture of these robbers and plunderers by comparing them with such common ones as are willing to raffle off the clothes of their victim and to make him the object of shame; they let him lie on the street naked. This figurative language employed by David is now being literally fulfilled in Christ. David gave expression to the idea of a plundered, robbed king, or (if David was but a pretender to the crown by reason of the promise of God at the time he composed this poem) to the idea of a plundered crown-pretender, one who has been promised a crown, but who for the rest feels himself without any rights in the world. And this sense of despair is expressed in a cutting lamentation to the effect that God is letting the clothes of His anointed be raffled off. According to this bitter plaint, the poet is one who has "seen the promise afar off, but has not experienced the reality of it." David's lamentation is the cry of one who feels the incongruousness between what is justly his and what is being given him in actuality. Now this word of David is fulfilled in his Son today.

The form of the lamentation as well as the content of it is being fulfilled. Yes, the *form* of it also. David speaks of plundering and the Son of David is being plundered on Golgotha. Robbers tear the clothes off His body. As He watches their game and their casting of lots, He loses His claim on all His clothes and stars. His is not the privilege of walking about freely, neither on earth, nor anywhere else in the universe. But the *content* of Psalm 22 also achieves its fulfillment. The contrast could not be more terrible than it is in Christ. David was robbed, but all his property which he had had before, had been *given* him by *grace*. But the Son of David is the Owner and the Receiver of taxes, and is that not by grace but by eternal right, by the right of God and also by right of the faithful Worker in the covenant of works. Now this Son of David sees His cloak being raffled off and as He watches this the problem which grieved David is perfectly present in David's Son and Lord. It could not be more oppressive in the world than it is now. The great Clother is being stripped naked; Caesar Augustus has robbed the Child of His swaddling clothes.

May all weep because of their sin! *We* have robbed God. The preaching of the *Deus Spoliatus* proclaims our shame. Away off in the distance it uncovers the dark corners of hell, the place where all are robbed of everything which God gave them. Your clothing, O son of man, is becoming mingled with the dust of the earth; Thou mayest not take it with Thee into the realm of outer darkness. And hence the demand that we should not seek for "raiment" but for the Kingdom of heaven can never be urged more strongly than at the cross of Jesus.

Do I hear someone laughing back there in the rearguard, and is he a living person? Let everyone laugh because of Jesus' righteousness, for the Author of the sermon of the mount is dying for His own discourses — hallelujah.

For, in that sermon on the mount Christ had said three important things. He referred to the right of requisition which one man would sometimes employ against another in this crooked world. He said: If any man strike thee on thy right cheek, turn to him the other also. That insistence He Himself fully satisfied.

We observed that before.[1] Besides, He is still turning the other cheek, for He who is calling up no fish from the depth of the sea, is calling down no lightning from the height of heaven; He performs no miracle to redeem Himself; He turns the other cheek to us.

But He went further. If any man, He said, would enter into judgment with thee and would demand thy children, give him thy cloak also. Well, they have taken the chiton away from Him and He also gives them His cloak. He does not curse the gamblers, nor scold the rafflers. He leaves them all of His clothes, and He prays for the gamblers who know not what they do. He allowed the fish to go on swimming in the water, for He had to fulfill the sermon of the mount on the cross and had to vindicate it in Himself.

He went still further and said: If any man should constrain thee to go with him a mile, go with him twain. This also was fulfilled in Him now. For Simon of Cyrene bore the cross for Him. That was the first time Jesus' right of requisition was being denied Him; but He endured it; it was the first mile, and Jesus went along. Now His coat is being raffled off; again His right of requisition is being denied, is — and this is even severer — being defied and disdained. Again He goes along; He also goes the second mile. He lets the fish swim on, He calls no lightning from heaven. He does not call upon Elijah. Nor does He, like Elijah, call down fire from heaven. He endures all this and knows of what Spirit He is, and prays: Father, forgive them.

Thus Christ verified the sermon on the mount. He told us there that we should endure three requisitions made upon us: "Injury of the body, impairment of property, and infringement upon liberty."[2] And Christ Himself was completely faithful to His own threefold demand.

Now we turn aside, and around; we fasten our eyes upon Him. We do not know what we should do now; alas we do not know. Woe to us if we should see His nakedness, and not believe in God. Then our name would be Ham. No, we turn aside now, and look upon Him no longer. Our eyes hurt, shame makes us blush; this is His repulsive nakedness. But the anxiousness makes us pale;

1. *Christ on Trial*, pp. 71 f. and 123 f.
2. Grosheide, *Kommentaar op Mattheus*, p. 66.

this is our repulsive nakedness. Time was when the priests could
not stand at their ministration because of the cloud, but here was
a thick mist, and we can not bear, we can not endure it. O God,
the door of hell has gone open for the moment; blindfold my eyes,
lest I should see. Nevertheless, He says to me: Fix your eyes upon
Me, look upon Me in faith. He says: Could you believe that I had
been made naked in the world in vain? He says: Am I not the
Word, clothed with power? My nakedness is prompted by a reason known to God Himself from all eternity. Am I not the speaker and the autocrat of the sermon on the mount? There must be a
reason for My nakedness; there is a reason, and it was known to
me throughout My days. And, again, He says to me: Do not go
away now, for you must see and acknowledge that this is the
Suretyship, the conclusive payment.

Thus do we bind our eyes so that they see now, and do not see
then; thus we long for the hour in which His beauty will be revealed to us. We shall see that King in His beauty. We heard
the death-rattle of a dying animal in Paradise. God killed it. He
took the lesser for the greater, even though man said in that very
moment; Lord, I perish; I am the least of all. Observe, however,
that all this happened solely for Christ's sake.

For Christ's sake it took place. For when the animal had to
serve as clothing for man it was still the privilege of the lesser,
the animal, to serve the fallen superior, to serve man: and this is
common grace. But this paradoxical service, we must remember,
was made possible only because in a later hour at Golgotha the
greatest of all should become the least of all, and He who clothes
everything, should be unclothed. In this the divine will is operative; God Himself has disrobed God. This was the final remedy.
It was absolutely impossible for it to be any different in the world.
He who had everything, was allowed to retain nothing. To him
that hath shall be given; but he that hath not for our sake from
him shall be taken even that which he hath.

Presently I shall go and pray: Our Father, who art in heaven,
give us this day our daily bread. Now if in doing so I never once
think of Christ who lacked bread and water and shelter and clothing, I am but a proud trifler with words. The soldiers gambled on
the hill of prompt payment and I am as ridiculous as they if I
should play with wine now, and parade with clothing, and bandy

to and fro the dollars of the rich without having earned in my soul
and spirit a true appreciation of the great problem of the Suretyship. That problem alone can teach a seriousness of life; without
it all decent people are but dickerers and gamblers who thoughtlessly finger the clothing of God; they are but pitiable rafflers all.

This is a kind of world-view, but it justifies itself overagainst
the spectacle of the naked Christ. We can hear a voice coming
from the cross, and the voice has in it a dominating irony. This
voice says to all arrogant men (and Paul also appreciated some of
the irony later) :[1] Now ye are full, now ye are rich; ye have reigned
as kings without me. Even unto this present hour I hunger, and
thirst, and am naked. Mark this: so the naked Christ speaks to
all those who would pay by means of their money: You are rich
and are full, and can get along without Me; you can clothe yourselves without Me, but I suffered thirst and was naked; and you
who do not allow Me to clothe you with the cloak of my righteousness remain pitiable, naked, and miserable in all eternity, for you,
O man, are really the one who was disrobed on Golgotha.

Again, then, inscribe the figure of a fish over His head on the
cross. But think in that connection of the fish which carried a coin
in his head, and think of a miracle which shook heaven and earth,
a miracle as great as the crowing of the cock,[2] as great as all the
miracles together.

Draw the figure of a fish over His head, and say to Paul: What
I have written, that have I written.

Jesus is very tired and He says quietly and reluctantly: Have I
need of madmen? Come instead as a believing one, as a fool to the
world, but as a wise person to God. And then say that you want
to draw the figure of a fish for all time on that beam of the cross,
not as a monogram but as a sign of His wonder-working power.
Look carefully then at that beam inscribed with the figure of the
wonder-fish, and look carefully upon His naked death, upon His
essential nakedness, and you will say to those who ask about it: I
am the soldier who removed His clothes: He has taken all my
clothes from me, and has put me, naked and cold, on display before
the universe.

---

1. I Corinthians 4:8-14.
2. *Christ on Trial,* pp. 212-213.

Never before did I feel so deeply ashamed of myself. Nevertheless, blessed be His hand. He did no gambling. He was in His rights. He acted justly and mercifully. A cloak has been prepared for me, a chiton of righteousness, and white clothes and palm branches for His, for my, triumphal tour through Jerusalem.

Just wait, soldiers, the Lord Himself will presently put new clothes on the second Adam. Just wait till Sunday morning, till Easter morning. Nor will any beast have to be killed for that clothing. All animals, and the whole creation will rejoice on Easter day looking forward to the day when the children of God will be clothed.

Christ's Supreme Title

CHAPTER TEN

Christ's Supreme Title

● *And Pilate wrote a title, and put it on the cross.*
And the writing was, JESUS OF NAZARETH
THE KING OF THE JEWS. This title then
read many of the Jews: for the place where
Jesus was crucified was nigh to the city: and
it was written in Hebrew, and Greek and Latin.
Then said the chief priests of the Jews to Pilate,
Write not, The King of the Jews; but that he
said, I am King of the Jews. Pilate answered,
What I have written I have written.

JOHN 19:19-22.

CHRIST became the subject of world caricature.[1] In this
caricature He was depicted as the mock-king of the Jews.
Now God says to Him: Do not regard this as though
something strange had happened to you. Do not think it odd that
you are entitled the mock-king of the Jews in the language of the
world. And indeed Christ became so used to it that He did not
regard it as strange. In this caricature He was given what was
rightly His. First in the picture of the soldiers and afterwards in
the official language of the court He was mocked and despised.
This is the title that is given to Him: Jesus. Of Nazareth. King.
Of the Jews, you understand.

For it is in terms of defiance and mockery that you can state
the significance of the superscription which was placed over Jesus'
head on the cross. They make a public spectacle of Him as the
King of the Jews. He is proclaimed as such in the Hebrew language. And in Greek. And also in Latin.

The superscription was written in three languages, but that can
be understood, for it was at the behest of Pilate that the title was

---

1. *Christ on Trial*, p. 525 ff.

written over Christ's head. If we may trust the reports which can be gleaned from the several writers, it was a custom of the day to affix a "title" to a person condemned to death. Sometimes such a "title" was written on a white placard; on this, in red or black letters, the breach of law for which the person had been condemned was inscribed. Sometimes the "title" was carried ahead of the condemned person; at other times the placard was hung on the victim's breast. In this way he himself had to give all who cared to read a chance to learn what the verdict in his case had been.

We do not know which of these two methods was employed in the case of Jesus. Perhaps neither. We do not know just when this placard — if a placard was actually used — was prepared, and when it was affixed to the cross. According to some commentators the superscription was prepared by Pilate immediately after the verdict had been read. These maintain that he thereupon at once gave orders that the placard be prepared. Many add to this the assumption that the soldiers carried the superscription. In that case it was easily accessible to the eyes of the public. Thus we can explain that it was not till after the crucifixion, until after the "title" had been placed over Jesus' head, that the high priests noticed what was written on it. But there are others who maintain that Pilate saw the high priests coming to him at once, that is, as soon as the procession had started, to protest against this phrasing of the superscription. And these believe further, therefore, that the placard, or whatever it was, was then very likely hung upon Jesus' breast at once.

We believe that the first reading of the account is the better one. We feel, however, that the significance of such inquiries is little. The only question that matters in this connection is what the superscription meant for Him for Whom it was made.

Now it is remarkable that the superscription over Jesus' head was put as tersely as it was: Jesus the Nazarene, the king of the Jews. Doubtless Pilate's sarcasm had a part in the conception of this terse phrasing. The deep disdain which he felt towards the Jews, with all their king-and-messiah problems, moved him to seek out a subtly ironic and poignant superscription. We had a taste before this of the superciliousness with which Pilate looked down on those seething Jews. And today his disdain has a special reason for wishing to express itself, for he feels more humiliated today than at any time. He had already mocked the Jews by the statement, "Behold, your king," and also by the question, "Do you really want me to crucify your king? Obviously, Pilate's mood had not improved any as time went on. The sentence which had been elicited from him had left him in a bad mood, in an angry temper. Consequently he grimly gives expression to his sarcasm in the terse statement: Jesus of Nazareth, the Jew-king.

The high priests noticed at once that the judge had given expression to his sarcasm in these superscriptions. They had been told in plain language that Pilate personally did not believe in the legitimacy of the charges which they brought against Jesus. Hence, when he by way of officially circumscribing the breach of law, states that the quintessence of the whole trial could be summed up by the word "Jew-king," everyone felt that he had in mind to mock the Jews more than to mock the poor Galilean. Ah me, these Jews! The whole lot of them are worth no more to me than this miserable, broken, annihilated king. The Jews are precisely like that man himself: they are so many good-for-nothings; they are a people who occupy space on the earth for nothing.

Consequently the superscription over the cross was indeed a severe humiliation for Christ. It is a gruesome passion to the Bearer of God's justice to be made the dupe of Pilate's moods. Let Pilate be never so angry with the Jews, he must give Christ what is coming to Him. But that he does not want to do. He knows very well that for him to disclose the truth is also to reveal his own shame.

For that reason we can say that the superscription over the cross is an eloquent symbol of our sin. Man as he is by nature does not want to admit that he is doing Christ an injustice. Hence he calls Jesus an unfortunate king of other people. Thus he supposes that he can avoid the confession that he, the man who does the maligning, is an unfortunate subject of that king. In this state, man does just as Pilate did. He bandies Jesus Christ to and fro between himself and others. But Christ can see through such a person; he knows what is in man. He knows very well that Pilate is doing nothing "strange"; He knows very well that all "flesh" by nature does what Pilate did, and that it in the same way refuses to acknowledge and establish the charges against itself. In the last analysis, the titles which the "flesh" conceives for the Saviour are all prompted by a feeling of resentment. Man knows he has been defeated by Christ, and thus he says that Christ has been defeated by another. All unfortunate subjects say: Behold the unfortunate king.

But there is much more to say. The title "king of the Jews" is intensely satanic. Jesus wants to be the king of the *world*. His kingdom is ecumenical; He gave expression to that Himself in the presence of Pilate. Nevertheless Pilate designates Him solely as a king of the Jews. The degradation[1] of Christ relentlessly pursues its own inevitable logic; it gives expression to its envy and hatred without reservation.

In this we see a pathetic contrast: Jesus is called the king of the Jews, but the name is written out in the language of the world. He is called the king of a sect, but the language in which the mockery is couched is an ecumenical language. The superscription is written in Greek, Latin, and Hebrew. Those were the three languages in which the entire world of the time might be able to read the placard. It was written in Hebrew for all the Jews going to the feast. All the guests of the temple had to read how pathetic was the case of the king of the Jews. It had to be written in Greek, for that was the language of culture, of the world then civilized. And it had to be set down in Latin, for that was the language of Pilate's king, it was the language of law and of official jurisprudence. Hebrew, Greek, and Latin: the language of the land, the language of the world, and the language of jurisprudence.[2] Hebrew, Greek, and Latin: the language of Zion, of the Acropolis, and of the Forum. The language of Jerusalem, of Athens, and of Rome. The language of religion, culture, and of the usurpation of power. The language of the ancient Orient, of the changing West, and of the incipient, newly-formed world-empire. The whole image of the beast of which Nebuchadnezzar once dreamed is given a mouth with which to speak on Golgotha. The Beast opens its mouth in order to speak grievous words against the Spirit. For all the world empires which Nebuchadnezzar saw issued in that of Greek culture, and arrived at the point of the Roman empire. These are the kingdoms, we can say, which are represented by the head, the trunk, and the appendages of the vision which

---

1. *Christ on Trial*, p. 314 f.
2. Nebe, *op. cit.*, p. 233.

Nebuchadnezzar saw. Latin is the language spoken by that world empire represented by the feet of the image of Nebuchadnezzar. Hebrew is the language of him, who in the vision of Daniel, is called the rolling stone, the stone which causes the vision of Nebuchadnezzar to crumble. Hebrew is the language of Christ Himself, the language of Daniel's Son of man, and of Daniel himself. This precisely constitutes the humiliation, the gruesome mockery: In this superscription the Hebrew is merely a subordinate matter. Pilate uses it not because he recognizes that the Hebrew language is a world language, but because he wants to mock the Jews in their own dialect. The Hebrew, well, that is but a subsidiary part of this matter; it really does not count. The Hebrew language would, in fact, have been omitted entirely in the superscription if Pilate had not wanted his mockery to be evident to every Jew. For this reason, also, the superscription is a grievous source of suffering to Jesus. He is announced in the language of the world then known as an unsuccessful dictator to a pathetic little group of people, who have no longer a rôle to play in history. The rolling stone which Daniel saw seems to have lost its power and to be unable to harm the image of the Beast. Look at the superscription, read the title written there in three languages. Does it not seem to be mockery to believe that that rolling stone could possibly make an impression on the gigantic image of Nebuchadnezzar? Son of man — that is the title God writes in the Hebrew language. And the Greek and the Latin, that is, the cultural powers represented by those two languages, were supposed to be splintered into pieces by this power. Of that victory there is no hint or suggestion on Golgotha. The superscription on the cross again comprises all the offense and foolishness of the Gospel.

Most pathetic, indeed. Even in the language in which it is expressed, prophecy is being mocked to its very face. Offense! Foolishness! Hebrew, Greek, and Latin! But the Hebrew is merely thrown in for good measure.

The Hebrew language was the instrument by means of which the antique world, in so far as it allowed itself to be served by the true religion of Israel, moved on its way. Latin and Greek were the instruments by means of which the new world, to the extent that with its pagan culture it fought against the religion of Israel, made its progress. Latin and Greek were the two languages by means of which the beast would presently oppose the Spirit, and paganism would oppose the young world of Christendom. Hebrew was the language of revelation up to this time. Greek and Latin were the tongues spoken by the opposition.

We can say, therefore, that the little white placard is suspended between two worlds, between the ancient and the modern. It hangs suspended between two cultures, the Oriental and the Occidental. It hangs between two religions, the religion of revelation and profane religion. God Himself affixed this superscription of the cross to the line of demarcation separating those two worlds.

But is this cause for lamentation? No, for through the deep humiliation of Christ the power of His exaltation again breaks through at God's behest. The Son of man is lifted up on the cross; that is, He is made visible, He is made conspicuous to all.[1] Well, it is an appropriate part of such exaltation that it be given expression in a universal language, in the language which causes two worlds, two cultures, and two religions to clash.

Christ is, of course, called a sectarian person, but He proves to faith, nevertheless, and that in the very languages in which He is being mocked, that He is the Son of man, that He is exalted, lifted up on the cross, and that He could not be thrust aside at the crossroads of times and cultures and religions.

Exaltation! Even as Moses lifted up the serpent in the wilderness, so must the Son of man be lifted up . . . before and above the world. But this exaltation could accrue to Christ only by means of His humiliation and therefore God permits Him to be mocked by all those who speak the tongues of men. He had to be given a name of mockery by all the languages spoken at the time. That was His glory, but it was also His shame.

It was His glory. Be very careful, Pilate, lest you overlook some language on that white placard. He lays claim to at least three groups of languages. Again we say that the superscription written in three tongues is His glory. In the last analysis Jesus, and especially the Jews themselves, are being mocked and defied in three languages. Moreover, it is apparent that the Jews themselves sense this. They ask Pilate, we note, to alter the superscription, not to say that Jesus was king of the Jews, but that He

---

1. *Christ on Trial*, p 298 ff.

wanted to be known as such. But this by no means changes the fact that the superscription which was phrased in three languages was also Jesus' shame. True, the mockery which the Jews would heap upon Christ returns like a boomerang upon their own heads. This is so essentially true that several expositors believe that they must detect in John's account a delicate play on words. John tells us that Jesus was called the *king of the Jews,* and thereupon the priests are very advisedly designated as the *priests of the Jews.* These expositors think, therefore, that John wanted to say this: The king of the Jews is passing into exile together with the priests of the Jews and is being mocked together with them.[1]

But what, pray, does that subtract from the passion of Christ?

We have repeatedly pointed to the fact that the shame of the Jews cannot be the honor of Jesus, and may not be that. He is not a child of hell, deriving solace and comfort from the misery and degradation of those who hate Him. On the contrary, the disdain of the Jews grieves Him. As often as Pilate uses Jesus' despicability as an argument for what, coming as it does from His mouth, is an irreligious contention to the effect that the people of Abraham is good for nothing under the sun, so often is Christ mocked, He and the community of Abraham, for He must confess these all as long as it pleases God that He should do so. For He Himself is the great mystery of Israel. He who, in the manner of Pilate, despises Israel and all her mysteries, despises especially the Christ Himself.

Therefore we say that the superscription over the cross is a proclamation of great power for us. In this title over the cross Pilate takes over the crown of thorns, the reed, the gorgeous robe, and all the forms employed by the caricaturing soldiers beforehand. The caricature which the soldiers printed now goes through another edition, this time accompanied by a commentary which is translated into all "civilized" languages. The superscription over the cross leaves Christ in the caricature of the world. By means

---

1. This would then be a striking allusion to the chapter we have discussed at various times, the chapter of Zechariah (*Christ on Trial,* p. 430) in which the priest and the king are both represented in Joshua, and can only be affirmed or denied together. In that case, the Bible wishes to tell us: Unless the Jews are willing to honor the Priest of Zechariah 6 together with the King, the Priest and the King will be together in their humiliation.

of it the Saviour is punished for the "triumphal" entry into Jerusalem.

Above Pilate's superscription God wrote His own epigram. God speaks in and through and above Pilate. You ask what God says? Notice this. The superscription on the cross, placed as it was above the head of Jesus, is a repudiation of all the sentimental imaginings of men which have woven a halo, a nimbus, around the head of Christ. As I look at the superscription I recollect again that Christ was crucified between the bandits. Therefore I would see Him who is my Lord and God, the King of the world and the King of my heart, as One who was unsuccessful according to the flesh. Pilate, that which you write or do not write, that which you subtract or leave, does not touch Him, it does not affect Him. What thou hast written thou hast not written. God wrote and He still writes, and He only writes. And the Lord my God summons me to Him today and says to me: What I have written, I have written, I, the Lord, the Almighty. I have written over His head, not that He said that He had to be the King of your heart, but that I said it, and He, and that He is that because He is that. His name, also when He proclaims Himself to be the king of your heart, is: He is what He is. And that is the end of the matter, saith the Lord, the Just One.

Hebrew, Greek, and Latin . . . Christ in the caricature of the world. Christ in the literature of the world. Hallelujah, amen! He is preparing the day of Pentecost, the day of tongues — for what the Spirit of Pentecost has prescribed, that He Himself has done.

Christ Suffering the Mockery of Hell

CHAPTER ELEVEN

Christ Suffering the Mockery of Hell

> ● *And they that passed by reviled him, wagging their heads, and saying . . . Likewise also the chief priests mocking him, with the scribes and elders, said . . . The thieves also which were crucified with him, cast the same in his teeth. And the soldiers also mocked him . . . saying . . . And one of the malefactors . . . railed on him.*
>
> MATTHEW 27:39, 40, 41, 44;
> LUKE 23:36, 37, 39.

CHRIST being mocked again: that is the theme of the pages to follow. Now I think each will hear a voice saying to himself: Let us ignore that in this connection, or at least dispatch it very quickly. We have heard so much about the mockery which men heaped upon the Saviour. That has been repeated again and again. And must that old theme be begun anew now?

The question was asked before we had time to feel ashamed of it. And, there is something of truth in it. How difficult it is for us to be patient, and to be ever alert and attentive as we sit at a death bed, that is, at a death bed which would lay claim to a few hours of our attention, or to a single faculty of our spirit. Well, the suffering on the cross by Jesus Christ also lasts a very long time. Moreover, in speaking of it the same subjects recur again and again. Hence we tire of it very soon. If a person is to talk of each one of the "instances" of mockery, he soon begins to feel a little ashamed about the inevitable repetition of the same words and thoughts. The conclusion of that is that the speaker and the auditor, the writer and reader, begin to say to themselves: Now we can appropriately pass on to another point, to something which "we have not had yet." The fact that Jesus Christ is mocked, and defied — we *had* that long ago. We have learned enough about that as we went along. One who has treated of the base defiance which the Sanhedrin heaped upon Jesus and which Herod and the soldiers of Pilate inflicted upon Him will at first blush think it rather superfluous to devote a separate chapter to the mockery which Christ had to suffer after the crucifixion. The only thing left to say — one might surmise — is that the number of those who mock Him is gradually increasing. This and the fact that besides the dignified members of the Sanhedrin, the passersby, the soldiers, the one crucified with Him, and the priestly party now engage in the gruesome game of mockery and defiance also. But when that has been said, there is indeed little that can be added, unless, indeed, one wishes to fall into the annoying fault of repetition.

Still we must say that it is not fitting to become impatient — at the cross of Christ Jesus. That is a predication which needs no defence.

No, we must not be in too great a hurry for there is *a difference between the one moment and the other*. There is a difference between mockery and mockery. Permit us to say that rather strangely and still rather naturally. It makes a great difference whether Christ is being mocked in the morning or at noon. The reason for that difference does not inhere in the mockers themselves so much as in the soul and spirit of Him who is the passive victim of the mockery. It is not the action of the people who mocked Him, but the reaction of Christ, His different response overagainst God and the world in successive moments which must provide the explanation here. Christ relates every experience which He undergoes to the actual circumstances in which He is involved. Now the process of Christ is a richly varied one on this day, and therefore His reaction to it is equally varied. Of Him we can never say that we have "had it" already.

In this way we can appreciate the consideration that a mockery of Christ taking place *before* His legal condemnation impresses Him differently and grieves Him in another way than a mockery coming to Him *after* the condemnation, after He has been led "without the gate," after His being bruised by the catastrophic curse. Such mockery is a different thing from the mockery which went on before. For this is a different hour in the great Trial.

We can point out in various ways the difference between the mockery which He experiences now and that which He felt before. For instance, there are more mockers now than there were previously; again, the things for which they blame Christ are not the same for which He was blamed before. But those are not the important differences. The greatest difference between the then and the now is that the mockery of Christ upon Golgotha is a definite and separable moment in the short but violent process of His descent into hell, of His being accursed "without the gate."

It is this last consideration which is the new significance here. When the Sanhedrin placed Christ in the middle of its group, when He stood there as the target of their mockery, and when, later in the day, the same kind of mockery came to Him from another direction, Christ was not experiencing the extreme afflictions of the pain of hell. Then He still stood within the gate of the city; He had not yet been cast out of it.

Now every violation of law is forbidden within the gate; when such violation occurs the right of appeal exists before God. We must note this. Christ retains the right of appeal up to the time in which He is "condemned," in which He is cast outside of the gates. As He sees it, He, as the son of Abraham, and as a citizen of Moses, still can appeal up to that time. True in all the things which are actualized on the day of His death (as well as on all the days of His life), in all the facts and events, whether they take place within or without the gate, He must detect the hand of God in the mockery heaped upon Him, and seek the justice of God in the violations of justice carried out by man. But the right of appeal is, as it impresses His conscience,[1] still His own. He may persist in telling those people who are making Him an exlex that He, as long as He is inside the gates of Jerusalem, may acknowledge God there, the God who does not make Him an exlex.

For the hidden things are the Lord's and the revealed things are for us children. This is the great regulation which is written down for the human attention of Jesus Christ also.

The hidden things for the Lord. That the Servant of the Lord must carefully consider. In the last analysis He must in His hu-

---

1. Interpreted here as the ever active faculty to examine critically all His thoughts, words, and actions as being conformed to the law and will of God.

man nature and in the deliberations of His "believing" heart
(which walks "not by sight") simply perform the duty of His
office, and in this He may not ask any questions about the outcome
(as if that in reference to "salvation" could be uncertain). To ask
such questions would betray unbelief. He must simply keep in the
forefront of His consciousness the fact that perfect fidelity to
God will also be perfect service for the benefit of the people for
whom God wishes peace. Hence as a human being, the whole
night of Gethsemane and the whole day up to the moment of His
condemnation were to Him nothing short of the law according to
which He had to live. These to Him were the revealed things,
and one of these revealed things was the knowledge that God
hates sin as He enters into judgment, that he who condemns the
just is an abomination to the Lord, that God regards as an evil the
mockery, defiance, and rejection from the law of the most faithful
Son of the law. He knows that every legal transgression is regarded by God as a sin, as an evil against which the accused, be he
whom he may, can appeal to the Highest Judge himself.

Because of this revealed truth, Christ, up to the moment of His
condemnation, could in silent prayers to God, the perfect Judge,
still appeal to Him against all the mockery and defiance heaped
upon Him.[1] Perhaps someone is inclined to say that this after all
was not a great privilege, this right of appeal to God. For it was
a privilege which had no practical effect; it was one which could
be entertained only in the form of thoughts. Can we say, for instance, that Jesus in the presence of the Sanhedrin, of Herod, and
of Pilate, had a voice with which to call out to God, to angels, and
to men? Could He have rent the clouds? No, the truth was not
such. Only in His *thoughts* could He appeal to God overagainst
the judges, and that — I hear someone say — *does not amount to
much.*

Whoever says that, does not know what He is contending for.
Can you say that an appeal to God which is purely ideational in
character does not amount to much? What, in the last analysis,
has man which transcends the worth of that? The riches of our

---

1. Think, for instance, of the "hymn of praise" which Christ sings before He
enters Gethsemane. It is an instance of His self-consciousness as a just man, an
awareness which becomes evident also from His apologies, His intercession, His
"supreme service of the Word."

life do not reside in what we can hear or see. Our lives are not rich primarily in terms of what can be heard by the ear or seen by the eye. Our riches inhere in what is anchored in the *spirit*. It is in virtue of his spiritual life that man is differentiated, on the one hand, from all creatures below him, and, on the other hand, is brother to the angels and a real image of God. The deepest motivations of his joys and pains lie in this personal, spiritual basis of life. All the struggles for justice common to our human life are, in the final analysis, operative in the forum of the human spirit; there they are litigated, solved, or dismissed; there, be it along legal or illegal ways, they are brought to a close.

Therefore the spiritual element in man is the conclusive, the determinative element. We live or die, we are rich or poor, elect or lost, children of freedom or children of slavery — in terms of our spiritual existence.

If we think of that, we can appreciate that in a very important sense Christ was still rich and strong, and was God's great Fellow-Owner as long as He was permitted in the realm of His thoughts, in deliberating on the several stages of His trial by means of His human spirit, still to appeal to God overagainst men. For Him too, the law of life was binding, the creation-ordinance held true, that His riches or poverty, His rising up or His falling down, His life or His death, His possibilities for going on or the immanence of His being closed in, had to depend not on what He said or did, but on the manner in which His active spirit was related to God, to the devil, and to — Himself. Keep Him from working His way outwards if you can; He will still be able to speak and to think. Hinder Him from speaking, take the privilege of speech away from Him, and He still will be able to think, to exercise communion with God in His thoughts. As long as He knows that He can do that, He knows that He is free. If a person would touch, would affect Him essentially from within, he will have to touch His thought-life.

We shall have to consider all of these things if we are to appreciate to any extent at all how Christ in one hour of time could fall into even deeper shame, into much deeper shame than had overcome Him before. For Christ descended into the shafts of humiliation by leaps and bounds; He descended, if we may say so, spasmodically. There were mutations, there were steps, in that process of humiliation. It may be that we sometimes talk too facilely and too unwittingly about the *steps* in the state of Christ's humiliation. That is something which is very easy to say: that He passed from one step to another, that He plunged from one plane to a lower in His passion. But it is more difficult for us to appreciate the meaning of this, to get a vivid and concrete picture of its significance. For that which He experiences in one moment of His passion will in the next moment seem to have been a kind of height compared with the one to follow; this will again be a deeper level of shame, a lower rung of the ladder, than the one on which He is standing.

Nevertheless it is necessary for us to consider these things and to follow Him from step to step, from rung to rung, from stage to stage. Only in that way will we appreciate why Christ, when He was mocked by the Sanhedrin, by Herod, and by the soldiers, *before* His conclusive condemnation, was standing on a different step of humiliation than that on which He rests now, *after* the condemnation, now, hanging on the cross, and why the raillery and the lashing bitterness of hellish mockery is being heaped upon Him.

For it is quite true that in the moment of the official condemnation the course of His suffering sharply broke downwards, and plunged abruptly into a much lower stage. We have observed already that when Christ was condemned He was cast without the gate. We must accentuate that again; it is a detail which is absolutely necessary for us if we are to keep the drama of the darkest day in the history of our world vividly before our apathetic minds, if we are not to let that drama become an illogical succession of pure accidents.

We must recall just for a moment what we said in our first chapter. There we must pick up the thread which can guide us now. There we discover three moments in the course of Christ's passion, three sharply delineated transitions. First, Christ is robbed of the privilege of *acting* freely; second, He is robbed of the privilege of *speaking* freely; and, third, He is robbed of the privilege of *thinking* freely. Those are the three milestones at which we have successfully stopped to ponder.

At the end of our first volume Christ was bound; that is, the privilege of acting freely was denied Him. The fettered hands were not allowed to act at His behest. At the conclusion of our second volume, the gospel account had brought us to the point at which Christ was judged, was "condemned," by the judge. That meant, accordingly, that not only was the privilege of acting freely taken from Him, but the privilege of free speech also. The condemned man cannot say anything thereafter; He will not be heard if He does.

Now it is possible for people to deny a man the privilege of acting and speaking freely, but they can never take away the privilege of *thinking* as he wishes. The deep recesses of free thought do not lend themselves to restriction. The spirit cannot be put in bonds, at least not by fellow human beings. Hence there have always been those condemned people who went to the place of execution without saying and doing what they wanted to say and do, but with a full sense of the fact that in the freedom of their ideas they were triumphing over their enemies. A paean of victory was, well — not in their mouths, but in their hearts. They stood among tyrants as free men, and it was their thinking spirit which allowed them to retain the freedom of personal selfhood.

In the case of Christ, however, this could not be the conclusion. The privilege of thinking freely, as well as that of speaking and acting freely had to leave, had to depart from Him. Unless God took this privilege away from Him it could not be said that He descended into hell. Unless the Lord opposed the Surety, unless the Lord arrested Him in the crevices of His pure logic, of His penetrating reason, and of His ever-active thoughts, Christ could not be said to have been completely condemned. In that case, He would, in fact, not be condemned at all. If by means of His human power He could thrust His thinking spirit through the mountain-pass where Wrath is seeking Him, He would internally and essentially have escaped from the Wrath. Then the Wrath would not have bruised Him; the core, the essence of His human life would have remained unperturbed, free, and entirely unbroken. The descent into hell could not be realized until He lost the privilege of free thought as well as that of the free act and the free word. His thinking, too, had to be challenged radically and seriously. The Lord God had to challenge and oppose it. Christ's might not be the privilege of freely going about, whether it be actively with His hand, or actively with His mouth, or actively with the thoughts of His unrestrained spirit.

His thinking had to be bound. O God, arrest His progress.

And it is precisely this which now overtakes Him. His thinking is being absolutely challenged by the Lord. God is molesting His thoughts. The beginning of our third volume mentioned that. When that milestone had been reached at which we paused at the beginning of our third volume, in other words, when Christ had been cast without the gate, God Himself — the stronger, the absolutely Other-One — took from the *man* Jesus His right to think freely. The spirit of Christ could no longer unrestrictedly proceed in its own power (see pp. 27-29).

In a certain sense it would seem that the harmony, the parallelism of the passion is being destroyed here. One would have expected that, just as the right to act freely was taken away from Him at the end of our first volume,[1] and just as the right to speak freely was taken away from Him at the end of our second volume,[2] so the right to think freely will be taken from Him at the conclusion of our third volume also. And yet we have pointed out that this took place at the very beginning of this volume and not at the end.

This need not surprise us. As we pointed out previously, this ought to be so. We have observed that there was a compelling logic of justice according to which the Messiah as the second Adam had to suffer the pain of hell and to experience the curse within the space of time allotted to Him for the human struggle, within the time intervening between manger and cross.[3] This He had to experience with a full and fine awareness. Now the same constraining logic demands that before His death, and with the same fine awareness He must suffer the pangs of not feeling "right" with God, not even in His ideas. His apology must be able to find "no place," not even a point of connection. He must be absolutely miserable in His paradoxical state.

Yes, it was the inevitable consequence of the justice which condemned Christ, the justice of God, that Christ had to suffer a restriction of His created spirit, the deprivation of a free, unhampered, and penetrating mind. He will have to run into a wall precisely in the spiritual conflict of His ideas. The pain of the con-

1. *Christ in His Suffering*, p. 444 f., see also pp. 435 and 421.
2. *Christ on Trial*, pp. 544-546.
3. Page 24.

cussion Christ will suffer with a fine awareness and before His bodily death. For what, to repeat, is the descent into hell, in the final analysis, other than that — the restriction of the active spirit, the deprivation of the privilege of free thought. Must Christ truly descend into hell? Surely, this sounds like luxuriating in oratory about the most gruesome of experiences. And must this become actuality today? If so, then in the name of God let every one of His unhampered thoughts be molested. Then let every asylum in which His distressed spirit might wish to take refuge be closed to Him. No, Jesus' distressed spirit may not even take flight to the narrowest of alleys today, for He is being entirely cast without the gate. That means that He must acknowledge God's forsaking Him. And this in turn, means that, according to the discipline of the church and according to the written lawbook of Jerusalem and according to the holy ordinance of an Israel not yet forsaken by God, He who is cast without the gates is a curse to the Lord; and again, He that hangeth on a tree is a curse to the Lord. God Himself is rejecting Him and is leaving no place of refuge for Him, neither under the strength of His arms nor within the spacious folds of the cloak of Father Abraham.

Does it seem that it is taking quite a while before we return to those members of the Sanhedrin, those military men, those priests and soldiers who are railing against the Nazarene? Perhaps, but we had to take this long course in order to see clearly what the significance of this new mockery is. It was necessary for us, if we may put it that way, to place all those mocking people, those dwarfs and midgets — against a background of human convention and of "humane" sentiment. We must accept these grinning dwarfs in the way the Spirit of inspiration presents them to us; and that spirit has placed them against the background of a sinister heaven which is pouring out of its darkly lowering clouds nothing less than the Absolute Wrath and the Pang of Hell. Presently the sun will shine no longer. For we find ourselves here in the ferment of hell.

He, accordingly, who would genuinely appreciate the significance of this particular moment of the passion of Christ must not overlook the hellish character of Christ's torments.

Are we exaggerating the matter? No, if we devote sound deliberation to the passion on the cross, we cannot possibly "exaggerate." Everything in Christ's suffering on the cross weighs as heavily as infinity. Of course, it is true, that he who explains the particulars of the suffering of Christ wrongly can "exaggerate," for his thoughts and propositions have their source in himself. But he who sees the crucified Saviour of souls as the Bearer of the guilt, and as the Sufferer of incomparable penalty, of the penalty of hell itself, knows very well that, inasmuch as he is following the course of sound exegesis he can not "exaggerate." Why not, you ask? Because the truth which is revealed to him by God speaks in a language which cannot possibly be exhausted. One can never give adequate expression to the penalty of hell (and to the blessedness of heaven), unless one is in hell (or in heaven) oneself. That we shall have occasion to stress more often.

Hence we can say that our account of the suffering of Christ is not liable to the danger of exaggeration as long as we interpret it in the sense of the Spirit. We always say too little of the Man of sorrows and cannot possibly say too much as long as we remain faithful to the truth about Him.

Hence we must observe now that the Christ, who is suffering the pain of hell on the cross, recognizes that the mockery hurled against Him is the mockery of hell. We know that the nails which were driven through His flesh were not "ordinary" nails to Him, but instruments of the last judgment. We know that the rupture in His side was not a wound measuring so much in length, to His consciousness, but that it was a bruise inflicted upon "this temple" by the hand of God in what is justly called a catastrophic curse. And we also know that the consumption which His soul and spirit felt was not merely the lonesomeness of this or that suffering individual, but the eternal and profound forsakenness suffered by the Son of man because of His God. And in this same sense, we must believe that the mockery which man inflicts upon Christ at the cross in its essence is nothing less than the mockery of hell. It is the defiance of hell. It speaks a sinister, diabolical language. It is the greeting with which the demons welcome the damned. That is the way Christ senses it, and as He senses it, it is. He alone feels the objective reality of everything in His whole being, for His entire being is ever turned toward God.

Now you ask how the mockery of those passersby, the defiance of those who went to and fro along the way, could possibly become the mockery of hell for Jesus Christ. If you would understand this, open your Bible, and ask Him what He sees happening in the place of outer darkness. You will not look long for an answer. The Bible itself teaches us the nature of the mockery of hell. Not only is the greeting of hell, by which one lost soul spews out his misery and despair against another, made audible to us in the poetical language of the Bible, but it is also possible to deduce along dogmatic lines from other parts of Scriptures that the essence of the punishment of hell is defined by the sinister law: *homo homini lupus*. Being interpreted, that means that one man literally consumes another. The one lost soul fiendishly preys upon his neighbor. The one who is nearest is always the farthest away. To meet the person who is nearest one is to meet the person who is most distant. The general law of dissolution drives a wedge wherever it can find an opening. It is a law of hell that the one hates the other.

Thus it happens that Isaiah speaks of condemned persons who consume each other in the realm of darkness and of the shadow of death. Isaiah refers to the king of Babel, and to the defeated ones of the realm of the world. If these tumble into Sheol, into the realm of death and darkness, and if they tumble into it without God, the first word which greets them is as venomous as death itself. Each lost person gloats over the misery of the one who is lost with him in the eternal darkness. And this is also the way we can understand Ezekiel, who speaks in the same spirit about Asshur among the condemned.

Thus Christ also heard Himself being mocked upon the cross. He heard exactly what Isaiah and Ezekiel heard, heard it coming to Him from the realm of darkness.

For what inhabitant of hell is there that does not mock the great Lost Son as He hangs on Golgotha? Lo, He is descending into hell, and, nevertheless, He knows that He still is the bright and morning star.[1] Such is the paradoxical experience, and the paradoxical self-appraisal. Isaiah once heard awful words being addressed to the lost king of Babel but those which are hurled

---

1. Revelation 22:16.

against Christ bear a heavier accent, are spoken in a stronger tone, and spring from a profounder background of justice and of wrath than these. Nevertheless, we can the better appreciate Christ's suffering for listening to the description of Isaiah:

> All they shall speak and say unto thee,
> Art thou also become weak as we? art thou
> become like unto us?
>
> Thy pomp is brought down to the grave,
> and the noise of thy viols: the worm
> is spread under thee, and the worms cover thee.
>
> How art thou fallen from heaven, O Lucifer,
> son of the morning! how art thou cut down
> to the ground, which didst weaken the nations!
>
> For thou hast said in thine heart, I will
> ascend into heaven, I will exalt my throne
> above the stars of God; I will sit also upon the mouth
> of the congregation, in the sides of the north;
>
> I will ascend above the heights of the clouds;
> I will be like the Most High.
> Yet thou shalt be brought down to hell, to the
> sides of the pit.
>
> They that see thee shall narrowly look upon thee,
> and consider thee, saying, Is this the man that made
> the earth to tremble, that did shake kingdoms?[1]

The Christ knows and feels that the suffering which is coming upon Him now is infinitely heavier than the suffering which Ezekiel pictured when he described how the dead of Asshur, that tree which had once stood so radiantly proud in the Eden of the world's culture, were received into Sheol with a bitter mockery. They were received there by the swords and knives of that hellish community.[2]

Yes, swords and knives and the community of hell — these are the things which are present at Golgotha when all ordinary folk rail against the Passover of God.

We return now to the point of our departure. Even though the people at the foot of the cross took on the proportions of hell, the severity of Christ's humiliation is not determined by the subjective scope of their intent but by the objective scope of the word of God, and of the wrath of God. Those people are but the instruments,

---

1. Isaiah 14: 10-16.
2. Ezekiel 31. See also *Christ on Trial.* p. 193.

and the instruments come from below. But God manipulates the instruments and God is from above; He is the eternal.

Now we must know that all those people are provoking Christ to rejoinder, to defense, to apology. They goad, they spur His trembling thoughts into those narrow confines where God, the righteous Judge, had always given an audience to the oppressed and accused children of the covenant. But God does not answer. He spoke to the fathers, He heard their addresses, He gave their inmost thoughts free scope.

But Christ can find no room for His apology today. Even in His inmost thoughts, nay precisely in His inmost thoughts, He can no longer appeal to God overagainst men. He lacks the power of appeal because the right to appeal has been challenged by God. He hears Bible texts being cited against Him in the challenge. Alas, it is written that He who is hanged without the gate is a curse.[1] A person cannot appeal to God unless he feels free to do so; He must have what the Scriptures call a good conscience, and that upon objective basis. That eager yearning of faith which the Bible calls a good conscience is the absolute requisite for every appeal which man, overagainst his earthly judges and enemies, would make to God, the perfect judge. It was a comfort to Job to be able to appeal to his judge, whom he called his witness for him, He who was in heaven. And this must be the same assurance felt by every accused person who in his distress because of what men do to him desires to appeal to God. Whoever makes this appeal knows that God is with him. Or, at the very least, he should be able to feel that he is not certain to the marrow and the bone that God is against him.

Is this true of Christ Jesus? No, for Him matters are very different. He feels in the bone and marrow of His being that God is *against* Him. He is man — therefore He has to keep the revealed and not the hidden things before His consciousness. Hence the word which must be seared upon His mind is the one which says that he who is hanged is a curse to the Lord, and that there is no acceptance of him with God. A great gulf has been fixed between Jehovah and Me.

---

1. Page 24 ff.

Now all His ideas jar against this high wall of God's relentlessness. All the thoughts of the Son of man beat against it. He is without the gate — and that is more than a topographical designation. It has become the active cause and the explaining motivation of all His struggles ever since this king was led out of the gate as an exile. The word written about those who are cast out was written for Him; it suited Him and it was all too clearly designed for Him.

Now it is easy to raise as an objection against this the fact that Jesus knew very well that up to this time He had been without sin. We know that He ever kept His eye fixed upon the holy pattern of the lawgiver of the universe. Consequently He must constantly have known and believed that no eternal abysses of animosity can come between the righteous soul and the righteous God. We would not think of denying this fact. We would, in fact, go so far as to say in a positive sense that the Mediatorship of Christ depends upon the soundness of His conviction that God will not condemn the righteous soul and that His soul is indeed righteous. But there is an adequate response to the objection raised. Christ must not only and must not in the first place devote His attention to His own clear and immediate knowledge, a knowledge which is His because of His pure relationship to God. As the Servant of servants He must also pay attention to that law book written of God to whose texts and codices He is subservient. This law book has announced that he who is legitimately hanged can find no acceptance with God, but is a curse to the Lord. Therefore this revealed truth demands as much of His attention as the other revealed truth which asserts that God cannot be the antithesis to "die schöne Seele." He must give as much attention to the first of these revealed truths as to the one which maintains that the glory of God cannot take a paradoxical and critically condemnatory attitude towards any righteous spirit.

At this point we must look in *two* directions. Some commentators like to emphasize the fact that Christ was convinced of His personal righteousness with God, and, consequently, of the right of apology which He had overagainst God. To this emphasis, however, we must add another, which does not contradict it: namely, that Christ, as man, as servant, as a creature subservient to the law, had to draw the Scriptures towards Himself. That means that He had to apply the Scriptural utterances about the person hanged upon a tree without the gate to Himself also. Such a person, Christ had to feel, is in a double sense a curse, an outcast, a thing which cannot be accepted by God. Dying, He still had to keep this Scriptural statement before His eyes, and He had to pave a way in His shocked spirit for the specific, concrete, and absolute application of this revealed word to Himself. He had to fix His soul upon it. He whom we see upon the cross is not a "naive" Christ who is internally but acritically convinced of the righteousness of His cause, and who does not tire or trouble Himself about the rest. No, He who is hanging here is the fully conscious Worker in God's universe, He is the Office-bearer, the second Adam. By means of a passion for reality and an effort at sensitive awareness, He must stretch His human existence to the breaking point of active strain, in order to experience, to live through, the curse, the forsakenness, the rejection, the "hanging before the face of Jahweh."

At this point our thinking meets with difficulties. We know that Christ's progress towards death, that His self-surrender to the cross, must essentially be an act of service, a gift. For a "love" which overlooks its purpose, or which departs from a clearly perceived knowledge of its goal in distinction from its means, is not love but ecstasy, eroticism, passion, self-service, or idolatry. One side, one term of Christ's mysteries on the cross, is that the love of the priest must remain aware of the fact that the priest himself is innocent, and that he consequently is in a position to give gifts, to give away what he has earned from God. Such love must know that the sacrifice from beginning to end is an act of love, of lordly, divine, and sovereign love, a love so important, so chaste, and so blameless that the word "aristocratic" would be ludicrously inadequate to describe it.

But there is another side to this problem. There must be another side to the description which love writes of itself by way of a memorial today. For now this question arises: May the awareness of His own beauty, His own purity, of His own capacity to give gifts serve as a kind of counter-argument by means of which He as the satisfying sacrifice may mitigate the terror of God's wrath? God is entering His Great Remonstrance today, and is laying it before the Son. The principal reason stated in this remonstrance is a definition of His wrath, and of Christ's obligation to suffer punishment. Now the question arises whether Christ's own sense of being perfect, and gracious, and precious in love and in virtue can become a continuous argument for Him to be included in a human counter-remonstrance. Can He enter this apology with God, the same God who is beating Him in the presence of angels? Can anyone in God's wide world really feel that he has been made a curse, if he has all kinds of counter-arguments at his fingers' tips? To ask the question is to answer it. We are sure that all sources of comfort which Christ has must be earned at the cost of awful struggle; not one of the consolation prizes has been paid for Him beforehand; we need not believe that at twelve o'clock of the "day of Jehovah" the climax of this "day of the Lord," the day which comprises all the centuries,[1] a single prize, a single consolation prize will be given away. The day demands payment, nothing less; the prize must be purchased at the cost of awful struggle carried on before the face of Jahweh.

Yes, every consolation which He wishes to keep before His eyes, and every act of lordship which He may wish to do, and every respite which He may want to enjoy, must be *earned* by Christ. Does He want to have the power to say to a murderer beside Him: I shall reserve a place for you in Paradise? Then He must struggle for the right and the power to do so by means of a fiercely fought conflict;[2] and, since that is true, there is no other possibility for the Son of man as a temporally motivated and impressionable human being than that the unhampered control of His sources of comfort first be taken from Him. The right of apology must be taken from Him, *cum effectu civili*. He must be made conscious of the pain which this denial causes Him by means of a crowd of mockers swarming around Him, to whom He can make no rejoinder. He must be bandied to and fro between the possibilities of remonstrance and counter-remonstrance, between the poles of attraction and repulsion, of conscious sovereignty (which stands above the plane of apology), on the one hand, and a conscious sense of having no rights whatever (a sense which puts Him on a plane below apology, unless the curse has been exhausted), on the other hand.

---

1. *Christ in His Suffering*, p. 314 f.
2. See the next chapter.

In the language of men, this is called *paradoxical* — a word which probes, and gropes, but which cannot state exactly what is meant in reference to Him.

We alluded to the paradoxical in the Christ. Now we are perfectly willing to confess that we are on dangerous ground. We are touching on one of the most difficult problems which it is possible for the thinking of faith to confront. We are not merely using a word which is in vogue just now, but are using it quite seriously. As we stand at this moment before Christ's silence among all those mockers without the gate we are facing a paradox. By this we mean — for misunderstanding in this matter is dangerous — that it is not we who find ourselves in the midst of a paradox, but Christ. He is being consumed by the paradoxical plague, and it is precisely this passion which delivers us from the pang of the paradoxical.

Let us approach Him again and observe. The *paradox* . . . the moment we use that word many contemporaries prick up their ears. The one will find the word interesting because of its sound; the other — with more wisdom — because of its meaning. The one will use the word loosely and facilely, taking it upon his lips five times in as many minutes. By a paradox this person means an opinion or a reality which is or seems to be in conflict with what by the standards of common sense is obvious, even though the opinion may be true, or may correspond to reality. The other person will by no means use the word "paradox" facilely or flippantly, but will bring the thunder of God and of the Word to bear upon it. By "paradox" he means that God and God's thoughts are absolutely different from us and our thoughts, and that, therefore, everything which is genuinely divine and heavenly is vertically opposed to everything which we think or can think, everything which we feel and know, or can feel and know in our horizontal plane of apperception and orientation. In recent times there have been many who point to the fact that God is entirely different from us, that a great gulf lies between Him and us which no one can bridge. These say that God is the "wholly Other." These maintain that no one who is finite can ever by means of his own human thoughts comprehend the infinite, absolute God; and that therefore, and in this specific sense, God's truth always opposes our human thinking and feeling and expression in a paradoxical way. According to this opinion God's truth is an ever-living, ever-variable judgment upon our thinking and feeling and arrogant speaking.

This is not the place to discuss these things further nor to state our own opinion about the attitude to which we referred.[1] It suffices to say here that according to our view the word *paradox* cannot possibly be used more appropriately, and that its content was never sensed more sharply, or plumbed and experienced more fully in its capacity for oppression and judgment than by our Lord Jesus Christ at this moment. And it is also our purpose to point out that the element of truth inherent in the opinion of those who think of God as the "wholly Other," never grieved a human soul by its terrible pain so intensely, nor ever shocked or cast anyone into the abyss of judgment and of bruising as it did here in overcoming the Saviour.

Now return to the barren knoll of Golgotha, and sit down calmly and quietly at the foot of the cross. Listen attentively to what the mockers dare to say in railing against the crucified Saviour. Do you not feel, here, that Christ is being consumed by catastrophic griefs which, while being catastrophic, are at the same time permanent griefs, griefs which may be characterized as constituting a truly paradoxical suffering, paradoxical knowing, and paradoxical thinking?

Thus we must return to the word "paradoxical." It was taken to mean: proposition and counter-proposition, reality and contradictory reality. And in discussing it, we encountered two propositions. The first was that Christ had to assume the curse for Himself, and that He had to acknowledge that this curse was willed of God as a power of devastation actually arising in His life. This He had to acknowledge by applying the words of the Scriptures to Himself which said that a condemned person who was hanged without the gate upon a tree is accursed.

The second proposition, was that the man Christ Jesus also had to be convinced of His own sinlessness overagainst God. These two truths force His thoughts to oppose each other diametrically. This is the paradox in His prayers and in His sufferings. He

---

1. For my personal attitude towards this interpretation I refer you to my: "Bij Dichters en Schriftgeleerden," p. 65-147, and "Tusschen 'Ja' en 'Neen'," p. 233-359.

must consider the first truth. The text of the Scriptures states that the person condemned outside of the gate is a curse, and this truth must echo in His soul in all its power. Remembering that, He must necessarily conclude as follows: It is just that I be dumb before God and men, that my breath be cut off, that my righteous speech be taken away. This is just. It is just that Christ the exlex should be silent among these many shouting people. Jesus held His peace — this was the first time without the gate that He had laid His hand upon His mouth.

But Christ must also pursue that second train of thought. Doing this He must necessarily confess that He has not deserved the curse by Himself and for Himself. He must confess that He has indeed been plunged into the dark waters of the curse, but that these could find no point in Him at which they might cause infection to set in, at which the curse might "organically" take its effect in terms of the law according to which sin in principle is itself death and curse.

To put it humanly we can say that an epitome of the first train of thought would be this: I suffer justly. And that a summary of the second line of thought would be: I suffer unjustly.

According to the first line of thought He may with good reason cry out: I am a curse; I dare not appeal to God. But in terms of the second way of thinking there is as good a reason for crying: I am just and woe to Me if I should doubt the primary scheme of God which has said that He is not antipathetic, nor antithetic, to the "beautiful," to the just, soul.

There are these two lines of thought then; they take opposite directions; they constitute the plague of paradox.

Looking upon the first of these, at the reality of His accursed status, He can but be mute. He must even be silent about the perturbation of His thoughts. But when He thinks of the fact that He is the pure man, that He has indeed a "good conscience before God," He must, with or without words, but in any case "moved in spirit" cry out against all those mockers. Then the apology, even though He does not express it with His lips, must be present in His thoughts, and able to build up its structure in terms of a logical development.

What is this, if it is not paradox? It is the paradox which tore Christ apart, which rent Him asunder.

We can be sure that this paradoxical element in Christ's experience grieved Him terribly. On the one hand, He knows that the suffering of the curse is the inevitable way, the curse is the only way. It means the forfeit of the right to defend Himself even in His thoughts. That is the way. It is the way of payment, it is the way drawn by God for the people whom I love infinitely. The Lord told David to say to Abishai that he had to be silent overagainst Shimei, the railer. And David after a while presents the message of the Lord and says: Let Shimei curse, for the Lord hath said to Shimei: curse David.[1] And is it plausible to believe that David's great Son can escape from the message of His father David and from his having no message at all to give? Let Him be silent and constitute Himself a speaking David as well as an astonished Abishai. O spirit of God, hear Him as He confesses from the depths of His soul: the Lord hath said to all the Shimeis, to all the remnant of Saul[2] who are gathered here at the foot of the cross: Curse Jesus, curse, and defile, and mock. His curse is his way. A spirit entered heaven and said: I will be a spirit of mockery in all the epigones of Saul, in order that the Son of David may fall, in order that He may be reviled on the hill of hellish mockery. The Lord said: Thou shalt prevail: go forth and do so.[3]

On the other hand, however, all that is in Jesus rises up to sing psalms to God's glory. Or, if He does not actually sing them, He at least composes them. He did no evil at any time, and He kept His thoughts pure. This had been His task had it not? Was it not His task as the second Adam to stand in the state of obedience and was not the second Adam, even as the first, promised a future which provided an unhampered vision of God that set up a relationship between "the beautiful soul" and the right to live? As Christ thinks of that, He feels constrained to say: The glory of a "good conscience," a confident presentation of my own apology to God — that is my way as well as the curse is. The Lord spoke by David, saying: Woe be to Shimei, who curses David; the sword

---

1.   Compare II Samuel 16: 5-11.
2.   II Samuel 16:5.
3.   See I Kings 22:22.

shall find him out. "Hold Shimei not guiltless, for thou art a wise man."[1] It may be that the spirit of mockery has entered into all the sons of Saul, but it is written, and it remains written: He who condemns the just man (and mocks him) is an abomination to the Lord.

O paradoxical day of Golgotha!

This paradoxical suffering of Christ's disrupted spirit was as intense as it was because this particular moment of mockery and defiance is essentially different from all the other moments in which He was also mocked and defied. The difference arose from the fact that before this time He could, and now He cannot, exercise the right of appeal to God.

In all previous instances in which the mockery of men grieved Him, the speech of God and of the Word of God could still offer Him comfort above what human beings did to Him. The Word of God weighed heavier than the word of men. It always weighed heavier, not only when it guaranteed acceptance, but also when it threatened reprobation. Again and again God Himself stood at the end of the way overagainst those who rejected Him, overagainst the false friends.

But here at Golgotha, which is "without the gate," things are different. Now God is not standing overagainst the human, but now the divine seems to be standing overagainst the divine, the Word of Scripture overagainst the Word of Scripture, the way of the covenant overagainst the way of the covenant. The non-use of apologetics today is just as necessary according to the law of revealed things as is the maintenance of the right of apologetics. What human beings call despair (irrespective of what in their case motivates it) is not only the greatest sin here but also the primary manifestation of righteousness. Here — that is, in the case of Christ, the second Adam.

Do not misunderstand us. We are not saying that there is an essential contradiction in God or in the Scriptures or in the whole scheme of revealed things. For the unity of what seems to be contradictory here is to be found in the divine counsel, in the good pleasure which laid down the law of the Suretyship, and in the

---

1. I Kings 2:9.

words written about that law.[1] But this does not take away the fact that as a man Christ felt the concussion of those two realities of experience in Himself and felt them as a concussion. It is precisely in this moment that He in the strictest sense of the word finds Himself in the paradoxical tension, for on Golgotha the divine does not stand overagainst the human as the higher power and as the *ultima ratio* (final cause), but all that is of God, and all that is of the Scripture, and all that has been revealed, now seems to conflict with itself. In each of the terrible hours of mockery and defiance which He suffered before,[2] Christ could freely draw up His apology, in His thoughts at least, overagainst the people who accused Him. He was still inside the gate. But if He wants to ascend from the human beings who mock Him to God in His thinking today, He confronts a wall, and can go no farther. My God, why art Thou forsaking me, standing afar off from my roaring? My Rock, why dost Thou forget me?

Is it a foolish undertaking to consider these things? How can anyone ask that question now? Are we not, if we look upon matters in this way, facing the absolute impossibility of harmonizing the first and the fourth utterances from the cross?

In that first utterance Christ expressed Himself with confidence. Jesus was so firmly convinced of the justice of His cause, and so naturally persuaded by His feeling of self-confidence, that He risked being the intercessor for His murderers. Plainly an intercessor who prays in faith proceeds upon the assumption that his right to apology goes unchallenged. In fact, all the apologies and all the defences of others must appeal to Him, and be pleaded on the basis of His virtue.

Overagainst this first utterance from the cross stands the fourth. It speaks of being forsaken. It is the lamentation of One whose apology simply does not register, who no longer can be heard, who has been proclaimed unacceptable.

Now do you yourself state whether this first and this fourth utterance from the cross, both of which issued from a single human soul on the same afternoon, can be related to each other by anything except the experience of extreme paradox. We shall re-

---

1. We shall consider this point further in a later chapter.
2. *Christ on Trial*, chapters 9, 16, 21, and 28.

turn to this point[1] but just now we wish simply to point out that in the most absolute sense paradox is present here. God was indeed the "wholly Other" to Jesus. The term "without the gate" was translated in Jesus' theological dictionary by that other term, "in hell." Jesus suffered under the transcendence of God and lacked the comfort of His immanence. God refused to comfort Him against the Shimeis, even though He called out the sword for their devastation. All the angels whispered to Jesus — or were they devils? — that the Lord had charged these people to curse the Son of David. This is a paradox: mockery belongs here (for Jesus is outside of the gate) and — mockery does not belong here (for Jesus is the "beautiful soul"). The words of raillery are decent (for Jesus is hanging on the tree) and they are indecent, they are an abomination (for he who condemns the righteous is an abomination to the Lord). The first utterance from the cross is a natural matter, a very natural thing: the just may pray for the unjust; Father, forgive them, for they know not what they do. And this same first utterance from the cross also has its repudiation in heaven: Father forgive Me for asking a benefit for others; forgive[2] Me, for Thou knowest what Thou art doing to Me in binding my mouth. And thus Christ is bandied to and fro. God is very distant from Him; God is the "wholly Other."

Well, we alluded to the fact that there were steps of humiliation, steps — abrupt, spasmodic stages of descent into hell.

Recall Gethsemane and try to measure the distance between Gethsemane and Golgotha. We noticed that in Gethsemane also Christ suffered grievously. We noticed that He there also had to lay a bridge over the abyss by means of His struggling spirit, that He had to construct an arch between the one mountain top and the other mountain top of God's eternal justice. But in Gethsemane He was not without rights as He is now. First His right of requisition was completely denied, and now His right of apology, of defense, is taken away. In Gethsemane Christ solved His paradoxical problem and when He had conquered it and achieved His poise, He spoke confidently to His friends saying: Arise, let us go from here. At Golgotha, hanging on the cross, He will gain another victory. But here it will be at the expense of more tears

---

1. In the two next following chapters.
2. "Aphes": do not attach any immediately responding legal results to that.

and more blood than at Gethsemane, for now He is the exlex, the refuse of all things. He is in a state of excommunication. In Gethsemane we could say: Christ's sorrows have their own peculiar end;[1] now we must say: Christ's sorrows have their own and ever-renewed beginning. In Gethsemane, the moment the power of thinking freely was His again, He could regain His poise; but at Golgotha He must battle for the privilege of free, unhampered thought. In Gethsemane the heaviness hovering over Him was caused by trying to reach God in His thinking. At Golgotha the trouble begins the moment He lets His thoughts proceed from a God who speaks in His Word, and for the rest is silent.

Yes, indeed, there are *steps* of humiliation. Only a few hours separate Golgotha from Gethsemane, and yet the distance is immeasurably wide. And just because this distance is so great and because the descent from one to the other is so sharply marked, there is no point in saying that Christ took the words of raillery hurled against Him "too seriously" and that it is unwarranted to speak of the "mockery of hell" here. The Bible itself reveals to us that the moment Christ was driven "without the gate" was the all-prevailing moment of the passion. If that were not true we would not dare to say what we have written in this chapter. But inasmuch as the Holy Spirit Himself has said these things,[2] we dare not choose softer colors than those we have selected for painting Christ's spiritual-paradoxical destruction. For Christ the people who did the railing and reviling, common, ordinary men of the street as they were, were in very fact the poison-mongers of hell. Not less than that. In fact they — were *worse* than hellish people.

We said they were *not less* than hellish people. We have pointed out previously that the person who would appreciate what is going on in the depths of Christ's soul must not ask about the person doing the mocking but what is the action and the reaction of the person against whom the mockery is hurled. Not the subject, but the object, determines the nature of the passion. We have previously stated that men cannot destroy Christ unless God does it.[3] But the moment God begins the destruction, men are also able to destroy. The instrument becomes effective by means of him who makes

---

1. *Christ in His Suffering*, pp. 379-392.
2. See the particulars included in chapter 1 of this volume.
3. *Christ in His Suffering*, p. 373.

use of it. Now we know that God as the Judge did excommunicate (without the gate). Because that is the case, those puny people of the plains, those ordinary Jews of the street who are standing at the cross, railing against Christ, are for Jesus Christ the regular customers of hell.

No, do not weigh them in your personal balances or in mine. They might have been seated at the table with us this noon, and they might have revealed the image of our own heart to us in that case. Yes, these people also were blind; and the guilt of many generations avenged itself in them; and he who gives his attention to the mockers themselves and to nothing else is sure to exaggerate if he calls their mocking the mockery of hell.

But Christ measured them with His own rule. He did not look upon the mockers as such but saw them as instruments of the wrath of God. The spirit of the Son of David on this occasion exhausted the problem of David, Saul, and Shimei. "The author sang his own psalms" in the room of the Passover and that was but a short time ago; we heard Him sing them with joy in His heart.[1] But we must not limit ourselves to this one side of the truth; there is another side: the Author sang His own psalms of wrath and cursing. And He appreciated fully that they referred only to Him. Hence He is mute. Isaiah was inspired by Him and by His spirit when He composed those songs of the mockery of hell which were too realistic for even the spirit of Dante to employ. So also Ezekiel; we alluded to him before.[2] But He who incited the Spirit that prompted Isaiah and Ezekiel is today being shocked by the fulfilled puissance of reality lurking in His own compositions about hell. All of His works are the works of God and the Logos is familiar with all His own poems from eternity. But that which was known to the Logos throughout eternity by means of a preliminary and creative knowledge, *that* the incarnate Logos must now experience by a knowledge which is a humanly limited and humanly empirical knowledge. That is why at this point, outside of the gate, the raillery of these people wounded Him sorely. It "overpowered" Him, and pressed more heavily upon Him than when Isaiah and Ezekiel in common with all prophets cried aloud: Thou hast overwhelmed me, O God of all prophets.

---

1. *Christ in His Suffering*, pp. 269-286.
2. Pages 211-12.

Approach reverently, and see whether He can sustain His own composition. Once more, however, do not say to yourself, "But these were mere men, innocent men to a certain extent; these were not devils." As though the mockery of men did not count as heavily for Christ as that of devils! As a matter of fact, we must put it the other way: Men can grieve Him worse than devils can. In this respect also Gethsemane represents a less severe temptation than Golgotha. As the Saviour left Gethsemane, He gave utterance to that heavily-fraught statement: This is your hour and the power of darkness. He saw the demons and the devils preparing themselves for a *pompa damnatoria*. They drew themselves in the form of a black procession of mocking forces.

But he who, like Christ in this hour of Golgotha, has tarried in a hellish sphere for a time, he is troubled by others besides devils. All that is personal is aroused in the land of hell and draws itself up in a disjunctive, antithetical, damnatory power overagainst all that is personal and that was cast with it into this pool of outer darkness. In other words, next to the lost angels who are called devils, the lost men take up their places, in order to hurl the mockery of hell against the others, who in turn inflict it upon them.

We can even go farther. We know that in the kingdom of heaven, and in the state of blessedness, men occupy a position higher than that of angels, inasmuch as men are the sons of God's house but the angels are only the servants in the house of God. That is why a doxology lifted up to God or men in the heaven of God's glory has more worth when it comes from human lips than when it has its expression among the angels of God. And this we would say also but in a precisely opposite sense, of the depths of hell.

In hell also a fallen man is in the last analysis more terrible inasmuch as his nature is more important than a fallen angel. All of the destructive forces of hell taken together cannot break down the ordinances of creation. Presently man will be transplaced from this changeable period and from the process of mutation and endless "becoming" to the state of perfected, and immutable things. When that happens the least among men will be greater, and hence more terrible, more sinister, than the greatest of the fallen angels. A dwarf among men will be greater there than a giant among the devils. Just as much as a son transcends a servant in glory, so much more ominous will a fallen son be than a fallen servant in the grotto of hell. For this reason, when weighed in Christ's delicate balances, the suffering which overcame Him was far weightier when it came from men than when it came from devils. Yes, in Gethsemane Christ spoke the statement which revealed prophecy: "This is the hour and the power of devils." To that Christ now had to add as an acknowledgment to His own soul this acquired[1] confession of experience: "This is the hour and the power of the people of hell."

For this reason the attack of the devils in Gethsemane was less difficult to withstand than the attack of the judges during the trial. Hence also the attack of men during the trial which took place within the gate and before the official curse was less difficult to bear than the screech of all the raillery which took place without the gate and after the perfected act of the curse.

Were they, then, mere human beings? But the fact that they are human beings is precisely what accounts for the terribleness of the travail. The hellish triumphed in the human: hence the awfulness of the passion.

We must go further. We said a moment ago that this suffering of Christ was even more severe than the suffering of hell. Why more? Because Christ suffers differently in hell than does anyone else. He is the sinless one. Hence, in hell, He is the absolute stranger. When a lost child of man has gone into the darkness of hell, and when he is mocked there by the spirits who are bound by the same bonds which fetter him, we can say that the hatred of the one is a sharp thorn in his flesh, but the other person is in the same sin; in the other person the same sinful passions are active. But Christ suffers the pain and the mockery of hell while He Himself is the *holy* and *innocent* one. It may be a terrible thing to be black among black men, a sinner among sinners, a dead person among dead people, but Christ is the white person among the black, the holy person among sinners, the living among the dead.

Therefore His suffering of hell is always a more terrible experience than that of any other person in the realm of outer darkness. No one in all eternity will ever experience this mockery of hell so intensely nor drink of it so fully as Christ does here. No one will

1. "Yet learned he obedience by the things which he suffered" (Hebrews 5:8).

ever understand or appreciate His paradoxical distress, no one in heaven or in hell. In hell He was the stranger, the one who had no relations with any. In the place of outer darkness where each rejects the other, Christ was the One Who was as conjunctive as life and love. He thrust no one aside from His pure humanity. True, His spoken word turned many away, rejected many, condemned many — all those in fact who rejected it — but that was not the fault of the Word, but was owing to the sin of those who refused to accept it. The pure soul of Jesus could be nothing less than the great attraction to everything that can be called truly human. Christ, then, was the only one among all those mockers and railers Who as the Unique One experienced "something strange" there. That is why He suffered a hellish pain which was severer than anyone in all eternity will ever be able to feel. His first utterance from the cross had still been: Father, forgive them. But hardly had this statement, by means of which He kept the world together through all ensuing centuries,[1] been spoken, before the venomous serpent of human mockery crept up against His cross, and before the sputum of hate and rejection attached itself to His forsaken soul and spirit.

Truly this was the mockery of hell. And it was more than that.

Now faith must sing a hymn of love for Him and about Him. For it is precisely by means of this spiritual disruption and captivity that He became for those who accept Him the better Mediator, the complete Mediator, the satisfying Surety.

We said that in the suffering of the mockery of hell He was the better Mediator. The *better* . . . that seems to suggest that there was *another*. Yes, there was another Mediator in the Old Testament. The Bible itself gives him this title and calls him by name. His name was Moses.

Moses also had the idea of a substitutionary suffering in his mediator's soul, and had presented it to the God of spirits and had asked whether God would not provide a satisfactory development of it by carrying it out in his own body and soul and spirit. We are told of this in Exodus 32. When Israel had dared to undertake a service of idols with its many idolatrous forms around the "golden calf," Moses, fearing that the initial vengeance of the

---

1. Page 125.

Judge would not satisfy Him, had offered himself as a sacrifice. This people have sinned a great sin, he says to God; yet now, if Thou wilt forgive their sin — and if not, blot me, I pray Thee, out of Thy book which Thou hast written (Exodus 32:31, 32). This event reveals the mediator's soul which was in Moses. His love would exert itself for the preservation of others and stand ready to be the sacrifice itself. He is willing to be cast out into the sea of perdition by God if this substitutionary endurance of the curse will only serve to keep the ship of the others upon the sea of the promise. Yes, indeed, that is what human beings call "love" and an act of love. And this act is so great as is seldom seen in the world. It is the kind of motivation which also came to expression in Paul's writing later on in which he said that he could wish to be cursed for the sake of his brethren (Romans 9:3).

Nevertheless this does not gainsay that the mediator's love in Moses was a false love and one which was helpless to redeem. We called it a false love, for Moses' offer to satisfy God for the guilt of others was in principle unrelated to the justice of God. He wanted to and he dared to dictate to God in the form of a prayer the way in which it could be done. This he did two times (verses 11-13 and 32). This he did instead of trembling and living and thinking on the basis of God's revealed Word and Counsel and Justice. To which we must add by way of aggravating and also by way of explaining the sin, that Moses broke into pieces the two tables of stone on which the first written words ever given men were inscribed, and that He did this between the two acts of prayer. Thus the primary task of the Mediator, the transmitting of the written word,[1] was neglected. Hence there was no preservation of the bond of the law, and hence we must call his love a false love.

But the love of Moses is also helpless to redeem. Moses is not a second Adam, he is not a covenant head. He cannot by means of his own death include all others with him. He is but "one" among many. Strike Moses' name from the book and that book will simply contain one name less. More than that has not happened. In this respect the Christ is a greater than Moses. He is not merely one among many but as the Covenant Head and as the second Adam He bears all men within Him. If God strikes His

---

1. "Gave the law into the hands of the mediator" (Hebrews).

name from the book of life, from the list of those who may speak freely before the gate of heaven, all other names will simultaneously be stricken from that book and that list. "All have been crucified with Him, buried with Him, all have died with Him." And hence all were with Him in the mockery of hell.

But there is another thing which demands our attention. As Moses climbed the mountain — surely the admirable deed of a calm soul and a strong spirit! — in order to present the offer of his substitutionary sacrifice to God, there is nothing poor or pitiable in him. In fact, he has much that is humanly desirable. There was no paradoxical confusion in him, nor did he suffer the mockery of hell. On the contrary, the fragrance of love issued from him. Not a single human being was clenching his fist against him. A whole camp of miserable people was hoping for the victory of Moses. He was, in fact, the aristocrat, the dazzling, the great, the strong soul. No, he was not caught in a paradoxical conflict, for he had carefully worked out his self-conceived plans for redemption. He had no fewer than three of these plans to suggest to the Lord. The first plan was: to preserve the nation as a political unit, to overlook the sin as a sin of the whole people (verse 12). The second: to spare a definite remnant, namely, which Moses had left after a punishment he had felt free to execute. The third proposal, a subsidiary one: to preserve that remnant minus one (verse 32b). Now Moses had conceived all of these plans in his own heart; apparently the ancient mediator had various "methods" at his fingers' tips. The method of a substitutionary suffering was his last resort, the one to be used only if the other plans were, God knows why, unacceptable.

Now it is plain that the man who approached God in this way was further removed from a paradoxical struggle than anyone conceivable. He was perfectly willing to suffer death but in dying he had to be the great aristocrat.

Now place overagainst this mediator of the Old Testament the better Mediator of the new. In Him there is not the least hint of a "system" of redemption which has been conceived in His own heart. In Him there is but one thing: the Word. I must . . . I must . . . it is meet for me — those are the terms of justice and redemption which He has gleaned from the Scriptures. Precisely because the way of redemption is but one way and precisely because the plan of salvation is but one plan He is being plagued very terribly and being placed in the terror of paradox. If only He could but for a moment have turned aside and detached Himself from the Scriptures and from what is written there about the person who is cursed without the gate, all of His sorrows would have receded from Him at once. Then He could have woven the laurel wreaths which would have been extended to the eventual, more than aristocratic man of love around His own head with a kind of blessed ecstasy. But the awful thing of the day is that the Word does not present laurel wreaths as prizes of honor; it gives away only emblems of shame to this Chief of those who love on the day of His greatest sacrifice. This grieves Jesus sorely. The word which is at once lofty and lowly simply must be expressed: Why? Why? He simply cannot reach, He cannot touch God. The system is so terrible because it is absolutely inevitable and is based on a relentless sovereignty. Moreover, who has believed His love? There is not a single one yearning for preservation who cares to look up to Him as the rest of Israel once looked up to Moses in his final approach to God. Here are two murderers who are mocking Him, the one on the right and the other on the left. He is suffering the mockery of hell. There is no form or comeliness in this non-apologetic Jesus. He sinks away into nothingness beside Moses. This is purely a question of grace.

Purely a question of grace. Just because it is that we love Him. For He proves to us that He is the final Mediator precisely by this paradoxical silence as He suffers hell's defiance.

That was the second point we made above: that He was the final, the perfecting Mediator. This Mediator had been thrust into the narrownesses, into the grottos of His paradoxical thoughts. This is but saying that He not only transcended Moses: He also solved the problem of Moses. Moses' "solution," painful as it may have been to himself, was a very easy one. His thoughts had not been limited but had remained free; in fact, they had remained too free. He himself had drawn up his plans: A preferred plan, and a subsidiary plan. Think how perfect Christ is as He stands overagainst this situation. His thoughts are completely limited. While He is bound spiritually by the Word, God and Satan turn the muskets of the spirit upon Him. Suppose for a moment that Moses' sacrifice had been accepted by

God. Then death would have approached him, borne on by a stream of fragrant incense, by the fragrance of a great, incomparable love. And can you suppose that fire and sulphur would have been hidden underneath the fragrance of this love? Had Moses ever thought of that problem? But Christ Jesus did not draw an opportunistic argument of defense from the empirical fact of His burning love; no such apology released Him from the pain of contradictory thoughts. His practical reason did not come to the assistance of His theoretical reason. He is not a Moses who can so avidly imbibe the fragrance of his bottle of nard, of his incomparable love, that its delicate scents, springing from his "beautiful soul," draw out the vapours of fire and of sulphur. But fire and sulphur were present in abundance in Christ Jesus, and the stench of these could not be suppressed by anything save the revealed Word. The terrible fact was that this dark vapour had become perceptible at all only because of the Word. As Moses enters upon his hypothetical death he drives the dank vapours ahead of him. But Christ struggles with God and with the Word and by His own authority draws hell into His spirit. He draws hell and all its dank vapours into Himself. He has kept all the commandments; nevertheless He must ask God: Why? Why? He had to labor for hours before He could bring Himself to the point of uttering even this one word. Moses thought he could pleasantly descend into hell, but Christ is shocked, and trembles, and has no apology to present. He is mute while the rabble heap on Him their raillery; He alone could say how the venomous vapours of fire and sulphur cut off all knowledge and self-assurance from Him.

Hence we conclude by looking upon Him as our Surety. He is our satisfying, our compensating, our paying Surety. The act of suffering the mockery of hell was the act of payment. Christ bore the mockery in our stead. The rasping language of that passerby, the conscious mockery of the leaders of the people, even the stuttering disdain of the man who hangs beside Him on the tree — all these are appropriate here, they belong here. This is the burden of God's justice which weighs down upon Christ. And this is true in a double sense: in suffering the mockery of hell He endures the natural results of sin (hell, after all is very natural!), and He also makes amends for the arrogance of sin. Concerning the first of these we must say that the sin whose penalty He bears for us has separated man from God not only but from his fellow man also. The bloom of social life can burgeon forth only in Paradise and can be enjoyed only in Paradise. And, on the other side, the disrupting influence of sin is perfected only in hell. Hence this same power of disruption had to devastate the Christ. In this, too, He had to suffer what we deserve because of our sins. The mockery which one condemned person hurls against another is not an artistically conceived "device" of the last judgment but a natural "apparition" of the first judgment, of the judgment, that is, which accompanies sin at its first advent.

Concerning our second consideration to the effect that Christ in suffering the mockery of hell, is compensating for and atoning for the arrogance of sin, we can say this. We may not permit our spirits to be guests at the banquet of those arrogant ones who with a painful punctiliousness are perfectly willing to state what that first movement of sin in the first Adam should be called. One such specialist will say that this first transgression represented pride; the other that it was unbelief; the third that it was doubt; and the fourth will name it something else. We prefer to be classified with those who do not further divide the general category of disobedience or lawlessness. But we can, at least, all agree that sin, that the first sin, included pride among other things. *Hybris* is the word used for it in these days; and hybris means — arrogance, pride. Yes, it was pride which induced man in Paradise to set up his ideas, and the ideas of Satan, overagainst the spoken word of God. It was pride in man which wanted to analyze the order of God's thoughts, and wanted to set man up as a critic of those divine ideas and their order.[1] It was by pride that man did the deed which issued naturally from this critical attitude and the standards which it set up. All this was included in the essence and

---

1. "Yea, hath God said?" He arrogates to himself the strength and right to construct a system of God's secret will in his own way without feeling bound by God's revealed will, and without standing awestruck in the presence of the idea behind that revealed will. Taking this course man soon arrives at a second autosuggestion. Then he claims that he has the right and the power to construct a system of God's concealed will which is in antithetical relationship to the expression of God's revealed will. And thus he finally arrives at the act of setting up such a construction, and of regarding it as something which has truth and reality. This is "being like God."

in the birth of the first sin. The name of this was *hybris*. It was arrogance on the part of the created and finite spirit.

Now the second Adam must compensate for this arrogance of the first; He must suffer for it and die the spiritual death. The pride of Adam is now being judged and punished in the paradoxical distress of Christ.

God breaks down this pride by means of the paradox. No, this is not saying that our pride is broken the moment we desire the paradox. To desire the paradox is to play with fire, to play with the bonds of the spirit, to play with what is hellish in character. And Christ did not desire the paradox. He dreaded it. He suffered because of it just as He suffers under all things which issue from hell.

Nor is our pride broken when we regard the paradox as our normal fate, as a sure symptom and regularly accompanying phenomenon of a pious life. For our fate, precisely by appropriating to itself the Christ of God as the Surety for our sin, must bow before the revealed word and the revealed promise. It must bow before that word which assures us that Christ by the captivity of His thoughts guaranteed liberty to ours and opened the doors of the prison in which our thinking spirits were held captive. We must bow before the Word which tells us that the captivity of Christ's thoughts assures us of the swallowing up of paradoxical stress and death by the vanquishing power of God's gracious Spirit, a power which in virtue of Christ's merits earned on the cross gives us fellowship with God and the solution of His decrees of grace above all that our spirit would divide and tear asunder. The faith of the Christian is willing to acknowledge that it cannot reenact the cross of Christ, nor earn it. This acknowledgment of faith which sees Him suffering what we may not want to suffer, leads us to the conclusion that His paradoxical grief was unique, that He has redeemed us from the distress of the paradoxical plagues, transplanting us to the fellowship of the transcendent God.

Thus Christ takes His place, the place of the Surety, driven into a strenuous narrowness. Thus we apprehend by faith what we cannot fathom with our minds: namely, that in the paradoxical distress of Good Friday He was completely humiliated by the binding of His thoughts, when these thoughts were driven to and fro. These thoughts contradicted each other not because He doubted the Scriptures but because of a successive, temporarily effected struggle with the Scriptures.

Thus the Lord caused His Servant to make atonement. If this Servant had played with paradoxes He would have perished because of His own guilt. Because He shunned them as He shunned the judgment, He could be broken by that judgment. In this He arrived at a nadir of the state of having no rights whatever, of a non-apologetical relationship to justice, and of silence. Nevertheless He thirsted for the Most High throughout. And this nadir was situated at the opposite side of the mountain top of Adam's tribe. O the depth of the misery both of the achieving of knowledge and of the earning of wisdom of the Saviour: how unfathomable God's judgments were to Him and how untraceable were God's ways! Even the obedient soul had not known the meaning of the Lord creatively — *schöpferisch*. The Grand Pensionary of the Love of God could not be God's counsellor in His own right. For of Him, through Him and to Him are all things. To Him be the judgment in all eternity. Amen. When Christ had arrived at this sub-paradoxical *amen* He had arrived at the nadir of His Suretyship. Then there was no more possibility of progress for His thoughts. Irrespective of the place at which His thought-conquest had begun, He again and again confronted this paradoxical confusion. This was His passion. It was His. It could be the passion of no other person. When God had become the "wholly Other" to Him, the transcendent One, and when Jesus no longer could experience the comfort of the immanence of God, He was in hell. The *hybris* of Adam was broken and conclusively condemned. The second Adam no longer found room for His thoughts. In this the proud conquest of Adam's spirit was avenged. All of Adam's *schöpferische* ideas are put to shame on Golgotha, are put aside, are mocked by God, by Raphael and Michael.

And Lucifer looks on, and gnashes his teeth.

And what man, pray, would not shudder in the presence of this reality? For God used those people standing there at the foot of the cross in order to put His Son in distress, and in order to disconcert His thinking.

Come down, come down, they shouted. It was a challenge to His power. This challenge had been hurled into Jesus' ears more than once. A wicked and adulterous generation frequently asks for a "sign." But Jesus must suffer under His own prophecy: No sign shall be given this generation, save the sign of Jonah the prophet. Now Jonah has been driven into his narrowness, and a greater than Jonah is here. O yes, more than once they ask that Jesus perform a miracle and show a sign. He never granted the request unless He was called to do so.

Never. But things had been different in the past than they are now. In the past when He had refused to perform a sign for which no official mandate existed, the "will not" was identical in Jesus' consciousness with the "may not." The limitation had its other side in the lordship, in the self-assertion of God's self-concious and goal-conscious Worker.

Today He hears a wicked and adulterous generation clamoring for a sign again, for the last, for the greatest, sign. He may not perform it. He looks at the coin of the prohibition, and lacks the courage to turn the coin around in order to learn whether the other side is inscribed with the free will of Jesus the Nazarene. He was not allowed to, inasmuch as for the first time He was without the gate. For the first time He lacked the courage to triumph in the pure and unalloyed Word. And Satan's wiles were not unknown to Him.

Only one thing He knows, and that is the justice of God. Yes, He had been a child and had had to learn the nature of life. Now He was entering hell; now He was a child living in the evil place. Again He had to learn anew, had to learn how to take the first steps.

But the hand of the Pedagogue hurt Him and led Him along dark avenues. The Head of the covenant had to be mute among the rebels of the covenant. He did not know what to say in response to all the reviling. He did not know because of the paradoxical plague.

Because of the transgression of My people the plague of the paradox came upon Him. Now He had reached the core of the matter. Now He faced the problem of whether thought was free or restricted in the world, in a world in which every thought is a *created* thought, although it wants to be *creative* (*schöpferisch*).

Golgotha: counterpart of Paradise: apologetic hiatus.

Yes, at no time had it seemed easier to defend Himself than it did now. The chances looked very favorable. Just visualize it: the speeches of mockery hurled against Him were the poorest ever heard in the world. They were a denial of the most superficial of human feelings. It was a contradiction of humanity and humaneness itself and a repudiation of the simplest logic. Barabbas, the Antichrist, and even I, we all can say, we could easily have opposed a good defense to these mockers, for they represent the world at its worst.

But Jesus held His peace. Even here there was nothing more to say. His name was the second Adam. That means He was the very beginning. Every beginning has its own laws. The hammer of the word had bruised, had annihilated Him. He who was hanged upon the tree was the curse. He dared not stand next to Job, for Job dared to put the crown of apology upon his head. Nor did He dare to punish Job by means of Elihu. There was but one thing to do: to be punished. And until He had suffered the penalty, He dared not speak. To speak while under the burden of *such* a punishment is to contradict. The paradox strikes one dumb before God. He who is not struck dumb has not known it.

Christ's Paradoxical Plague and His Forgotten Chapter

CHAPTER TWELVE

Christ's Paradoxical Plague and His Forgotten Chapter

> And saying, Thou that destroyest the temple, and buildest it in three days, save thyself. If thou be the Son of God, come down from the cross . . . .
>
> He saved others; himself he cannot save. If he be the King of Israel, let him now come down from the cross, and we will believe him.
>
> He trusted in God; let him deliver him now, if he will have him: for he said, I am the Son of God.
>
> MATTHEW 27;40, 42, 43.
>
> And the soldiers also mocked him, coming to him, and offering him vinegar, And saying, If thou be the king of the Jews, save thyself.
>
> And one of the malefactors which were hanged railed on him, saying, If thou be Christ, save thyself and us.
>
> LUKE 23:36, 37, 39.

WE return once more — and hope to do so again —[1] to what we discussed in our preceding chapter. We return to the subject of Christ as He suffers the mockery of hell. In that awful hour of mockery He felt the terrible plague of God, the Just One, bearing down upon Him. He was the incarnate Logos, He was filled with the Spirit, He was bruised by His people. As such He felt hell's mockery weighing down upon Him. Consequently we cannot pass lightly over this theme. We must devote our attention once and again to the plague of paradox which ac-

---

1. Chapter 13.

crued to Jesus, to the grief which the paradoxical motifs of His plagued thoughts placed upon Him from the outside.

Someone may feel inclined to ask: Why all this discussion? Has not enough been said about these things? Has not the mockery of all those people been sufficiently discussed? Permit us to answer that the question is stranger than any possible reply which we could give to it. We have pointed out in our previous chapter that we should not devote our attention to those mockers but to Christ, that it is because of Christ and not because of those who railed against Him that this moment of mockery upon Golgotha is so terrible as it is and that it deserves its own, unique place in our considerations.

But that is not the only reason. There is another reason which compels us to linger longer over this spiritual conflict of the expressed thoughts of men against the repressed thoughts of Jesus Christ. We must not forget that in this matter we are standing overagainst the greatest riddle that was ever given in the world. We allude to the riddle which God presents to us in the fourth utterance from the cross in which Christ laments: "My God, why hast Thou forsaken me?" It is to that fourth utterance from the cross that our ponderous thoughts would now proceed. We must go there. We must go through that fourth utterance. We must pass underneath it. But the moment we sense a little of the significance of this fourth statement from the cross it at once becomes a crystallized mystery to us. There is not a single riddle in the world which conceals so many unexplained things as this unique statement uttered by Jesus at this time, Why? Why? Is this the mystery that on the day in which He whose office it is to explain God Himself calls for an explanation? It is. He, the One, who was sent out to put all those who are asking their "why's" at rest, cannot find rest Himself — that is the mystery. By His "why" He leaves all those who would have an illuminating "therefore" in embarrassment. That is the great mystery, the embarrassing circumstance in which Christian thought here becomes confused.

The "why" coming from the mouth of the highest prophet really is the blind alley in which all Christian thinking seems to run against a wall; it is the great den of lions of Christian wisdom from which no one can escape by the ladders of his own thinking. That is why we consider it very important that Christ seems to us to be caught in paradoxes. He who is ensnared in the lassos of the paradoxically frightening God must perforce ask his many "why's," and he cannot escape from them unless he should leave God outside, God and the problem, God and the soul-rending paradoxes. But because Christ cannot relinquish His hold on God in all eternity He must progress from the many "why's" to the singular "why." He must utter the single "why" which raises the basic problem. Therefore Christ must continue to struggle, to battle, with all the paradoxical experiences and troubles which fiendishly accrue to His spirit today. These paradoxes are at enmity with Him; they are antithetic to Him in the holy war in which the incarnate Logos has become involved. Can you suppose now that it is "superfluous" to linger long over the Christ while He is ensnared in these paradoxical complications? No, we have not the qualifications to analyze His "why." The abyss of this acknowledgment of impotence which He is constrained to make, the abyss which stands at the very center of the world's primary conflict, and in which the paradoxically plagued Mediator confesses that He is defeated, is an abyss which no one will ever completely fathom. Hence, our only purpose is the hope that by the great grace of God, we may, if we believe, discover the lines which the Scriptures have laid down in delineating the manifest character of His revelation. We would discover these lines also on the *campus paradoxalis* upon which Christ has been smitten down, and on which He seems to be the plaything of the winds of the Spirit, beaten to the ground, as He is, by the efflux of hell, stifling under the venomous vapours which are belched from so many cesspools. What has Christ to say to us? Or if in the mystery of His paradoxical hour He has nothing to say to us, even if in this mysterious period He experiences a paradoxical confusion of thoughts which reciprocally consume each other — good, let it be so — what then has God to say to us? What has God to tell us by means of the Scriptures? The Prophet holds His peace. God refused to let Him speak in the world without the Scriptures. Hence ours is the task of carefully and discriminatingly following Him in His paradoxical confusion, by way of preparing ourselves thus to meet the plagued Christ later in that deepest nadir in which the fourth utterance from the cross must necessarily confront us.

In studying these things, three considerations demand our attention. This is the first one. Just what is it that those people who are madding around His cross have against Him? Yes, we know they are merely the loafers running about in the market-place of the spirit, but we know also that, in spite of this, they have proved to be instruments of the mockery of hell. Consequently, our first consideration must be: Just what is it that these people are saying to the Christ? And this is the second issue of importance. What are we to think of what these people say? What basis of criticism can a Biblical approach give us for appraising the content of their raillery? And the third and last important question is: How, both negatively and positively, does the soul and spirit of Christ respond to all these things? What effect has the mockery upon Him; or, to put it better, what does He, from His side, place overagainst their reviling? We shall consider each of these points in order.

Just what is it that these people are saying about the Christ? What charges are they making against Him? If we compare the several narratives of the Bible as we find them spread out before us in the gospels, and if we lay these several accounts next to each other, we see that they are raising six counts against Him. First of all there is that well known maschil which we discussed frequently in our second volume. The meaning of that is clear to us now. The maschil was the inciting word of Christ telling them that they could break down the temple and He would rebuild it in three days. Now they hurl the words back at Him: let Him begin this miraculous building, they say (Matthew 27:40; Mark 15:30).

In the second place these mockers at the foot of the cross raise the issue of the miracles which Christ had performed. They unmistakably acknowledge that He has saved others. Perhaps they mean that He has rescued them from the general distress of life. And it may also be that they are thinking of that master-stroke by means of which He as a worker of miracles robbed death and the grave of their loot. Lazarus! Hah! Let Him repeat that Lazarus-miracle! There are three crosses here; He has a triple chance to repeat it (Matthew 27:42; Mark 15:31; Luke 23:35)!

The third count they raise against Him concerns Christ's self-announcement as a King; it deals with the message of His royal qualifications. If He is the King of Israel, let Him come down from the cross (Matthew 27:42; Mark 15:32; Luke 23:37)!

The fourth subject which has a place in their raillery is Christ's personal faith in God and the mystical communion that has united Him with God. Yes, He has trusted God, has He? Then let God, if that trust means anything, give Him answer now and rescue Him, for he who is not a priest of Baal need not send up the prayer of Carmel in vain (Matthew 27:43). Observe this: they seem to be able to step into the atmosphere of Carmel in a moment; Carmel is not far removed from the sermon on the mount.

The fifth issue they raise is the theme of Christ's Sonship before God. He has said that He is the Son of God. That is at least what our translation states. But it may be better to take a different translation and to agree with the general observation, which asserts that these mockers really said: He said that He was a child of God.[1]

And the sixth and last charge which they have against Him is that Christ said He was the Messiah. At least He announced Himself as such. Now if He is really that let Him draw up His festive procession, and come down from the cross! We will gladly form a part of it (Luke 23:35 and 39)!

If we compare these various argumentations with each other, we must naturally begin by agreeing that they are all confused with each other. We detect several groups of mockers: the one group says this, the other that. The several groups are specifically named. The members of the Sanhedrin contribute, the soldiers make sure to add their part. Then there are those who are chance passers-by and happen to look upon the spectacle. These, too, add their bit. And even those who were crucified with Christ chime in with this well supported choir of hellish mockers and revilers. We believe that we would be going too far if we should, as some wish to, assign each specific piece of mockery to a specific group. On the contrary, we may accept as a fact that these six points mentioned by the Bible were confused with each other, and that the one group took up the cry of the other. This is the course the

---

1. See Grosheide, *Kommentaar op Mattheus*, pp. 352, 353; and see also what we shall say later about the centurion, and his utterance: Truly, he was a Son of God (Matthew 27:43).

mockery of hell takes. This is the false appearance of solidarity; it is the caricature of solidarity.

We know that these mockers represented various stages of cultural development. The one had attained a more complex level of general or theological development than the other. The one had a better familiarity with the concrete events of the day and of the outstanding moments of Christ's public life and ministry than the other. Consequently, it is remarkable that all of these groups can agree among themselves about these specific points. We want to point out three counts on which all of these mockers agree in their mocking.

In the first place, they all acknowledge that Christ has done miracles. They concede the fact that the man who is hanging on the cross has performed wonders. They do not deny that forces coming from "another world" — "another world" is a handy term for unbelief, that is, for an unbelief which refuses to call it by its real name — have been loosed in His life and that those wonderful potencies have come to expression in specific effects which took the form of miracles. The registration-book in which the wonders of Jesus of Nazareth were written has lain open to their investigation for some time — they speak pedantically of unusual events.

In the second place they all characterize their raillery and typify their own spirit by asserting that the conclusive miracle is still lacking, and that this one — alas — simply has not yet been registered. Yes, the Nazarene has exhibited various powers, and there are several entries of miracles in His journal. And, a person might investigate them and find that they were authentically reported. What of that? One wonder is still lacking. He has not yet saved Himself. That is the one thing which should still take place. Imagine, if you can, a crucified person, imagine this crucified person, coming down from his cross. If he could achieve that, it would indeed represent the acme of miraculous activity, and it would clear up all that which is still of a disputable character in his previous wonders.

The third point on which all these railers agree is that they can boldly demand that this last wonder be performed now. They suggest that if he does this needful thing, they will "believe" him.

But they suggest also that as long as this particular miracle is lacking they propose to reserve the right also to investigate those other miracles critically, and to think of them accordingly. They know all about it, they suggest. Beelzebub can also do tricks. There are those who in disturbing times perform miracles through Beelzebub, the chief of devils. And you need not think that good theologians are going to have the fleece pulled over their eyes so easily.

So much by way of a reply to the first question which we put.

The second question was this one: What must we think of these charges, these counts raised against Christ? What evaluation must a mind guided by the Scriptures place upon these revilings? In answering this we do well to bear in mind that we can give our attention both to what they say and to what they do not say.

What must we think of what these mockers dare to say? In answering this question let us first reckon with the opinion of those who think that an ethical seriousness still characterized these people who mocked the Saviour. And also with those who believe that an unfortunate and pitiable *misunderstanding* was responsible for their mockery. For there are some who hold that this was the case.

Some believe that the Jews at the foot of the cross were thinking of a passage taken from an apocryphal book, the so-called Wisdom of Solomon, or at least that a passage of that book is applicable to these Jews. The designated book is clothed in the form of an admonishment, artistically put into the mouth of Solomon, and directed to the pagan empires and pagan world-rulers. In this admonishment the learning of Wisdom is glorified. The book itself was not written by Solomon inasmuch as it has a later date. Opinions about the date of this composition differ greatly. Some think it arose in the time of the Ptolomies; some think of a more recent date; a few even adhere to the opinion that it was written after Christ. The conjectures vary between a period extending from 150 A.D. to 40 B.C.[1] You see that nothing has been definitely ascertained. Hence it would be quite unwarranted to suppose that

---

1. See R. H. Charles, D.Litt. D.D., *The Apocrypha and Pseudepigrapha of the Old Testament*, volume 1, Oxford, The Clarendon Press, 1913, p. 521. According to the argument of this book, Paul was familiar with the Wisdom of Solomon and alluded to it in his letters to the Romans and to the Ephesians (p. 519).

the Jews at the foot of the cross were thinking of the Wisdom of Solomon.

Nevertheless there is another possibility. It may also be that the content of the book inadvertently in one way or another runs parallel to or has a point of connection with the spectacle of mockery which we are witnessing on Golgotha, and, indeed, this apocryphal literature does touch on the mockery of hell which grieves Christ on Golgotha. The passage which is usually related to this panorama on Golgotha can be found in chapter 2, verses 12 to 20 of the book. There the issue of the relationship of divine wisdom to profane wisdom is raised. In the Book of Wisdom a polemic is conducted against certain Jewish, philosophical free-thinkers of the time in which it was composed.[1] First their argumentations and manner of conducting themselves is delineated;[2] then a portrait is given of those eminent but decadent Jews whose picture is also delineated in the Book of the Maccabees. These same Jews, we know, again and again are the theme of the writers of the psalms also. In general, then, we can say that the first part of this book outlined the battle which divine wisdom must carry on against the wisdom of the world.[3] It is in the midst of this peculiar entourage of this aprocryphal piece of writing that a very remarkable passage occurs. In chapter 2, verse 12, the wicked freethinker himself is made the speaker. In fact the company of these decadents is seated in council. They arrive at a kind of conclusion. They propose to keep a close watch upon "the righteous" because he is always standing in the way of these free-thinkers, and hindering them in their work. As a counter-stroke to the discipline which "the righteous," the law in his hand, always wants to exercise against the wicked (verse 12), this group proposes to subject him to a kind of judgment of God. The passage reads:

> He professeth to have the knowledge of God; and he calleth himself the child of the Lord.
>
> He was made to reprove our thoughts.
>
> He is grievous unto us even to behold: for his life is not like other men's, his ways are of another fashion.

---

1. E. Kautzsch, *Die apokryphen und pseudepigraphen des A.T.*, volume 1, Tübingen, Mohr, 1900.
2. *Op. cit.*, citation above chapter 1:16-20.
3. Ibid, p. 483; see also I Maccabees I: 53 and 54; and then again see the reference on page 483, both to Psalm 22:9 and to Matthew 27:43; and also p. 478.

We are esteemed of him as counterfeits: he abstaineth from our ways as from filthiness: he pronounceth the end of the just to be blessed, and maketh his boast that God is his father.

Let us see if his words be true: and let us prove what shall happen in the end of them.

For if the just man be the son of God, he will help him, and deliver him from the hand of his enemies.

Let us examine him with despitefulness and torture, that we may know his meekness and prove his patience.

Let us condemn him with a shameful death: for by his own saying he shall be respected.

You detect it at once: in this peculiar language which the author of the apocryphal book puts into the mouth of a wicked coterie, mention is indeed made of a certain judgment of God; according to the proposed test the righteous if indeed he is righteous will prove to be righteous by the outcome. But if he cannot by a miraculous escape from his distress prove that God is befriending him, his pretensions to being a child of God will be proved vain. Then the shameful degradation of such a person who is righteous in his own eyes will serve to these people as a gift of God. It will give them permission to go on in their careless way.

Some think that the problem raised in this passage in the Book of Wisdom was in the minds of the mockers at the foot of the cross. These interpreters graciously conclude that, especially among the scribes, a certain ethical and theological seriousness characterized the raillery they heaped upon Christ. Might they not in their own way have put the problem of the judgment of God here?

However, we said that another attempt was made, and that this one tried to ascribe the brutal and uncouth mockery to a certain misunderstanding which existed between Christ and His enemies. We are thinking in this connection of a book which appeared not long ago, and which speaks in detail of these matters. It is the work of a theologian who belongs to the so-called religious-scientific school. This theologian maintains[1] that Christ's familiar statement about the destruction and rebuilding of the temple was really

---

1. By reference to Acts 6: 13ff. (Stephen), and Amos 9:11; see also Acts 15:16.

a kind of protest against the temple made of stone. This is asserted on the supposition that the temple in Jerusalem was far too beautiful to suit Him. Accordingly, Christ's maschil was intended to be a kind of plea for a simple, unadorned tabernacle, which, so far from being a display of splendor, might serve as a spiritual dwelling place of God among His people.

Does anyone feel like asking how such a singular paraphrase of Christ's statement could possibly arise in the mind of this theologian? Well, according to him that other explanation, familiar to us, which the Bible itself gives, and according to which Christ meant His body by "this temple," is a Pauline, allegorical "distortion" of Jesus' statement. The writer referred to thinks that to the Jews it would have been a strange and unacceptable idea to believe that the body of Jesus could be acknowledged as a dwelling place of God, as a temple. On that basis, he argues that Jesus meant something quite different by His riddle than is the usually accepted interpretation. According to him, Christ wanted to protest against the temple as such in Jerusalem. The assumption is that the building of the temple of Solomon was a sinful transgression against God and the fathers. Christ in reference to those fathers would, according to this interpretation, have preferred to limit Himself to the statement: God does not dwell in a house made with hands and this, in turn, is taken to mean that God does not dwell in a house made of stone, but in a tent, a tabernacle. Christ, then,[1] was by means of the well known maschil condemning the proud temple with its splendid adornment and exalted dome. Instead of it He wanted to return to a tabernacle. The old

_____

1. According to this argumentation, a more or less conscious difference of opinion must have existed between the Jewish contemporaries of Jesus and the Saviour Himself. The Jews, deriving their argument from Exodus 36:8-38, appeal to the unusual beauty of the old tabernacle, and wanted even more splendor and adornment in the temple of God (now extant, or to be built by the Messiah), but Christ over against this desire for greater splendor wanted to adopt the line indicated in Amos 9:11-15, and to deduce from it that the ideal temple of the future should not be a proud and splendid one, but a simple and unadorned tent. The God of the fathers had not lived in so formidable a temple but in a tabernacle. What Jesus, then, had wanted to build in the desert during the three days which elapsed between the feast of the Passover and the exodus into freedom was a tent, for the worship of God by the faithful ones of the future.

tabernacle of Israel in the wilderness was as simple as the temple was extravagant. Now, as this interpreter sees it, Christ wanted to return to that tabernacle within three days. For Moses had also asked that Pharaoh grant them three days for the exodus of Israel into freedom and for the sacrificial feast in the wilderness (Exodus 8:27).

Might it not be that the obscurities of the temple maschil partly provoked the misunderstanding upon the part of the people and were a contributing cause of the conflict with the official leaders of the people? May we not suppose that behind the sarcastic word of the scribes this theological controversy lurked? That is the question they ask.

Inasmuch as this issue touches our subject, we want to linger a moment over this example of exegesis. We believe what follows will suffice to rule it out of consideration. If the interpretation cited above were the correct one, Christ in opposition to the Jews, who wanted to make their present temple even more beautiful and dazzling, was entering a summons to return to the simple dwelling place of God such as had been given the fathers in the form of the tabernacle during their journey through the desert. We deny the justness of this "explanation." For good reasons, we believe.

Christ was not taking exception to the temple as such. He did not come to destroy the temple, but to fulfil it. Moreover, Christ never stood in the way of the progress of the vehicle of the history of revelation. Hence He never advises a return from the temple to the tabernacle. That tabernacle had its place in the wilderness, but that does not mean that the temple was not a desirable house, nor that it might not be richer and more beautiful than the tabernacle in the wilderness could be. Just as Christ had no objections to supplanting the tabernacle when the time came for it, by the temple, so He has many objections to returning to a tabernacle after the temple has been built. The work of Christ never goes backward. Besides, it is unwarranted to say that a plain exegesis of Christ's maschil, an exegesis given by the Bible itself — saying that "the temple" is to be taken as His own body — is nothing but a "distortion" in the manner of Paul of a statement made by Jesus. Such an interpretation is in conflict with what we regard as the truth in reference to the Holy Scriptures.

We shall let that suffice, and shall not discuss other ideas which might be raised in refutation.[1]

Moving as some of the alien interpretations may be, they cannot alter our opinions. Even in full view of the objections raised, it seems to us that there is nothing in the mocking and reviling on the part of the enemies of Christ which can be characterized by an ethical seriousness or by a theoretical "misunderstanding." The mere fact that the mockery which they indulge serves to unite the most diverse human types, and that the genteel members of the community as well as the ordinary folk poured out the last remnant of their humanity upon the crucified Nazarene, goes to show that the commentary to be written about this occasion must not be drawn up on the grounds of humanity. We saw that there were various groups here. There were passers-by. These, in passing, could hear only a few words, but once they heard them they immediately joined in the chorus. There were the soldiers. A stray sound occasionally reached their ears also, a rumor about a kingship which the crucified one had arrogated to Himself. But they also take an eager part in the railing. How little of seriousness there was in their bearing (even though they as a group are placed on a par with all the other mockers in the gospel account), becomes obvious from the fact that they in a quasi-spontaneous manner offered Him vinegar[2] without by any means wishing to quench His thirst.[3] No, we cannot speak of ethical seriousness in reference to them, and not even of the most superficial sympathy. And we have seen before what we ought to think of the attitude of the Sanhedrin.

No, we cannot agree with the interpretation of those who would mix the "clear water" of genuine humanity with the filthy wine of demonic passion. The language employed by the mockery and the defiance today is too terrible for that. Frankly, is it not terri-

---

1. This consideration, for instance, that the "fulfillment" of the shadows of the temple by a worship "in spirit and in truth" rules out the forms of the tabernacle as well as it does the beautiful dimensions of the temple.

2. Some think that this item in this connection (Luke 23:36 and 37) tells us something which anticipates what is separately reported in Matthew 27:48, Mark 15:36, and John 19:29. Personally we believe, however, that this is not a just interpretation, and agree with the opinions of others, among them Nebe, who defend the attitudes presented in this study.

3. The Greek can also be translated to mean: They came to offer him vinegar; they came bearing vinegar with them.

ble to notice how they manipulate the word "faith" in their reviling? "Come down from the cross, and we will believe you!"

They cannot succeed in getting beyond that point. They want
a miracle and preferably one which corresponds to their improvised stipulations. Without having weighed the norms of the
concept of a miracle, they at once definitely stipulate the exact
shape in which the greatest of wonders (greatest and primary in
their estimation) ought now to take place. And, they claim, the
moment they see this stipulated miracle, they will believe. But the
true faith which is the essence of religion and which unites men
with God, and through Him by means of love bears fruit, is completely ignored by those theologians and their disciples.

As long as these mockers are in a position to get no further than
an opportunistic theory about the wonder and power of the miracle, they will always be able to escape from their own snares,
when they are unexpectedly caught in them. For before this time
they also explained Christ's miracles by assigning them to Beelzebub the chief of the devils. That they can do again if He should
actually perform the miracle, for the Nazarene has for days and
years spoken to them about the miracle and its source. The moment He had chosen to perform their miracle, the discussion would
immediately have begun anew. Even if Christ should come down
from the cross, they will not believe, and will prefer to assert
themselves by characterizing this last wonder by the Nazarene as
the deftest show which prince Beelzebub has yet presented.

Moreover we can see how little of theological earnestness was
in them by noting from the whole complex of argument which
they present that in their estimation the true king of Israel cannot be humiliated. If Jesus is the king of Israel, let Him come
down from the cross! So they concoct a kind of dogmatics which
leaves no room for faith in a king of Israel who is in a state of
humiliation. But their own literature has very frequently referred
to a Messianic King who achieves His glorification only through
the experience of humiliation. Their own literature contains references to it, but it is necessary to state that the problem there is
put much differently than it is in the letters of Paul, and in the
whole of the Scriptures themselves.

Go on now, and you will touch on even deeper abysses of sin.
We have already stated that their spitefulness reminds us of

Psalm 22:7. In that psalm also the poet complained about mockers who "shake the head" and say: He trusted on the Lord that he would deliver him: let him deliver him, seeing he delighted in him; let Jahweh deliver him, for Jahweh delights in him!

The question might be asked whether on this occasion there is a conscious quotation or allusion to Psalm 22:7 and 8. Certainly it is foolish to think that each of these gapers at the cross could literally have remembered Psalm 22 or have quoted from it. But what of the scribes? They knew how to quote Bible texts, and how to apply them in their own manner. Indeed we may accept the fact that among these there were some who knew that in Psalm 22 a righteous person is speaking to whom the wicked say that he must go through a judgment of God if he is to prove his conscience clear. And these scribes know also that according to the logic of that psalm this tormented righteous man cannot perform a single external sign by which to externally demonstrate his righteousness before God. If these scribes were thinking of this text, that is just so much more proof of their demonic mockery; then indeed they are playing with fire; then they most certainly demonstrate that they are tearing the psalm apart and are recalling only that part of it which will not incriminate them at once in the eyes of those standing by. But if they had known what it means to tremble at the Word they would have dreaded a flippant game of words as men dread death, especially a game of words in which the rôle of the wicked is delineated. They would have found it just a little too "risky" to put the words of the poet of Psalm 22 into the mouth of the Nazarene, for that poet, although he was plagued and forsaken by God nevertheless was a classic example of one who was righteous before God but whose apology would not be effective until it was presented in heaven. And yet David was used as an exordium of a salutary influence and life on an earth which simply will not understand.

In touching on this point we come to the second question which, as we said originally, requires our attention: What standards of evaluation does the Bible give us for appraising these mockers and their mockery, with a view to what they do not say. Why do they obscure the issue in Psalm 22? How does it happen that these fine heads can tear all problems into bits today? The reason is not unrelated to the general truth of the day: namely, they have no eye for Christ's priesthood. Their thoughts persistently ignore the great question of the ministration of reconciliation, of the idea of the offer, of the ministration of satisfying, compensating love. We can say that God is being wounded anew in His soul because no one of all those who are shouting so loudly ever touches on the subject of His "forgotten chapter."

Just what was that — that "forgotten chapter" of Christ? What do we mean by that phrase? We have used it before. We referred to it in so many words in the second volume of this work, but we alluded to it also in the first volume. In our second volume, you remember, we discussed Christ exlex and His forgotten chapter. We noticed that this "forgotten chapter" was the priesthood[1] of Christ; it was the law of satisfaction, of reconciliation with God by means of a satisfying sacrifice. Throughout the trial not a single word was devoted to that subject. The kingship, yes, and the prophetic office of Christ were referred to, but the priesthood was not once raised in the discussion. But in our first volume also we already confronted the tragedy of the "forgotten chapter." It was necessarily a part of the chapter which bore the title, "Christ Welcomed — and Travestied." There too we notice that the people who are madding around Jesus like to glory in His might and His wonders, are perfectly willing to linger over the concept of His kingship, but refuse to devote a moment's attention to His priesthood, to His will for reconciliation by satisfaction.

The same theme returns now. Read those speeches of mockery again. There are references in them to Christ's prophetic office, for those who mock acknowledge that the wonders are signs, and the prophet becomes manifest in the sign. They also allude to the kingly office of Christ, for they acknowledge that His wonders are "powers"; and it is the king, the bearer of might and force who is manifested in these "powers." But there is no one who thinks of Christ as a priest; no one even alludes to the idea of the priesthood; no one thinks of the miracles as a gift, as a gift in the absolute sense, as gifts of a sovereign love, whose giving is always absolute, and whose receiving therefore is impossible. No one thinks of the fact that in the wonders of Christ a love is coming to the fore, a love which gives, a love in which influences of

---

1. *Christ on Trial*, p. 428 f.

healing are given expression, influences of healing which will presently consume the physician himself. For if they had thought of that, their defiance would no longer have been significant. Then all their fabricated learning or banal ignorance would have become immediately apparent; then all could have seen at once that they were miles away from the real problem of the day.

Surely, this was a tragic omission. For now we can point to three moments in which Christ was publicly placed overagainst the people, and in which the issue of His priesthood proved to be His forgotten chapter. These *three* moments have been assigned to each of the three volumes respectively. The first of these was that of the entry into Jerusalem. Then the crowd spoke of Christ's deeds and powers,[1] but not of His priestly sacrifice. On that occasion we saw *Christ glorious* — and His forgotten chapter. The second moment took place when in our second volume we saw the rulers and the people together speaking of Christ as the eventual King and Prophet, but being deathly silent upon the subject of His priesthood.[2] There we saw *Christ exlex* — and His forgotten chapter. And so we come to our third volume and find Christ ensnared in the paradoxical riddles, find that He is being mocked even unto death, that He is being cast into the mockery of hell, and that He is mute among all these people who speak of everything save His priestly love. This is *Christ paradoxalis* — and His forgotten chapter.

Well, if the whole mass of Christ's executors completely deny His priesthood then it is apparent that the defiance, the proud mockery which they heap upon Him does not even touch the essence of His own problem. We knew this beforehand: now it becomes obvious also. Mockery could never be as shallow as it is here, never as stupid and ridiculous as it is now. One step farther, and we would indeed touch on the hellish; and one definition of what hell is can be said to be this: the acme of the ridiculous. We are not trying to write exciting literature, but have wanted to contribute an answer to the second of the three questions we originally asked.

In the last analysis, of course, we are not here to judge these people. A better question — our third question — demands an

---

1. *Christ in His Suffering,* p. 121 f.
2. *Christ on Trial,* p. 428 f.

answer: How did Christ respond to all these things, and what was His reaction to them? The answer to this huge question is this short reply: *Jesus held His peace.* No, this time we are not citing a "bible text." We do not find those words actually written. The fact that we do not find it seems remarkable to us at first. In the account which the gospels gave us of the course of the trial we hear it said again and again: But Jesus held His peace. And as often as we paused to consider these words, we noticed that they contained a profound significance. And it is not surprising that we should at first expect to find this characteristic comment included in the narrative of Golgotha also.

But it may be that the Bible this time purposely omits mention of Christ's holding His peace because — here upon Golgotha, "without the gate" — His silence may be taken as self-evident.

Yes, indeed, the silence of Christ during the mockery which He suffers in this dark hour is self-evident. That becomes apparent if we simply pause to appreciate the conclusive significance of this particular moment, and the difference between His legal status before and after His passing "through the gate." For what is more "natural" than the silence of the exlex, of the man who has not the right to present an apology? The first thing to excite our marvel was Christ's silence in the presence of His judges. We wondered at that. Why? There He still had the right to speak; in fact, He was expressly asked, summoned, to speak. But here, upon Golgotha, Christ sinks to a plane beneath that other one; the question about whether He may or may not speak is no longer a disputable issue. He is sinking down into "bottomless" slime, He has become for us a lost person who, precisely because He endured the mockery of hell, no longer has the privilege of free speech, inasmuch as He no longer can think freely and thus set up His self-defense. *Pro domo* — that is the most useful term with which to describe a person who would speak for himself. But how can Christ pronounce a *pro domo* here? He is here in the stead of all His people, and inasmuch as His people in their lost condition cannot but be silent as they listen to the charge of God's vehement wrath, Christ also stands mute. This is the hour and the power of the children of hell; these are bringing Him the deserved wages of sin, the anti-social power of death.[1]

---

1. *Christ on Trial,* pp. 142-194.

Christ is silent; He leaves the mockery of hell unanswered. In so doing He is revealing His passive obedience, His endurance of God's ministration of punishment. Unhesitantly He spurns self-defense. His thoughts which have been frustrated in their course do not even conceive of an apology, or think of entering one where none belongs: the place of absolute excommunication. He reads all the proverbs of the Scriptures, also all those which shut off every avenue of escape from one who is hanged upon a tree on the other side of the walls. He does not contend with the world, and does not begin at the beginning. He has just performed His "extreme service of the Word." Now He comes to the Judge who has been basically maligned by His own, by His mystical body.

Christ's silence therefore means something different now than when we saw Him stand mute before. His silence before His judges proved to us, in our second volume, to be a legal act. It was an insistence upon the maschil,[1] that is, a prolongation of the judgment of separation, of sifting, set loose by the Word, and a calm re-authentication of all the obligations which Israel and all its colleges of law, and in another sense Pilate also, had not yet satisfied. His silence was an act of authority[2] as long as He stood before the judges. In His silence He condemned them more firmly than they Him; within Him He was conceding the same thought which, some day, having arrived at the end of the revelation of the Scriptures, He would say, He would inspire in Revelation 22:11: He that is unjust, let him be unjust still; and he that is filthy be filthy still, and he that is righteous be righteous still; and he that is holy let him be holy still. Such was the law of separation; such was the eschatological law of sifting.

But the situation is different now. Christ's silence upon Golgotha was a vital and powerful and significant appropriation of the curse. He who as an accursed person no longer had the right to apologize, refuses to take that right now by stealth. His silence now is an expression of conscious weakness. It is judgment.

Weakness — this is a word which we easily misunderstand. Therefore we wish to add at once that in using it we do not refer to a weakness of "character" (if we may set this theological piece

---

1. *Christ on Trial*, p. 104 f.
2. *Ibid*, pp. 104 f., 112 f., 357 f., 364 f., 399 f., and 403 f.

of folly down on paper); it was not a subsiding of courage; it was not a disheartened relinquishment of a struggle which seemed to be "useless anyhow." For this kind of "weakness," this kind of defeatism, would immediately have thrust Christ outside of the possibility of fulfilling His messianic task. No, in calling His silence weakness we mean by that to refer to the absolute helplessness of one who in very justice bears the judgment of God. It is God who fetters His lips and who forbids and practically hinders Him from speaking out against God on the basis of the right of His nature, His human nature, as if these had any rights at all outside of their connection with law and justice. His human nature is not a phenomenon *"an sich."* For today Christ must speak and maintain His silence purely in terms of His office, an office which was instituted by justice and circumscribed by justice, an office which has delineated and delimited Him in all His movements, including the movements of His spirit. Everything He is still to say after this time, all those utterances from the cross, all those explosions in the spiritual world, will have to be uttered by force of an inner convulsion and uttered before the tribunal of the Chief Lawgiver. Every privilege of free speech which He is to exercise after this, beginning at once in the second utterance from the cross, must be expressly earned.[1] It must be a Samson's burden for which He must struggle with God. And hence Christ may not antithetically make Himself as He is in His naive "nature" a sort of focal point for a group of accidentally congregated spectators who in that specific little spot of the world, under a given constellation, raise the question of the Nazarene and His peculiar "case." Golgotha is not "a specific little spot" of the world, for Christ now is in hell; and the moment of Golgotha is not "a given moment" in the history of the world but it is high noon of the one day of the Lord, the Day of Jehovah; and the group at Golgotha is not an accidental conglomeration of people who raise the case of a historically conspicuous Jesus in their discussion. What we have here is simply and solely the great dialogue between God and creature, between God and man, between God and the covenant-breaking communion, between Him whose privilege it is to demand and those whose duty it is to comply.

---

1. We shall discuss this and the power to earn this privilege in the next chapter.

If that is the situation, "a certain Jesus" has nothing to say, for "a certain Jesus" does not exist; He who is here is the second Adam, and He is arriving at the critical point of the workday of the world. Consequently, the "historical Jesus" has nothing more to say; that is, no "specific" word, no "specific" expression, no "specific" datum, no "specific" count, no "specific" action which might become the subject of discussion among such a chance aggregation of people. But one thing is in order here; and there is but One who draws up the program of speakers, and who assigns the roles of speaking and of being silent. That One is God; He is in charge of everything; and He opens no discussion which would be an unrelated "part" of the whole.

Therefore Jesus is silent as these mock Him. It was self-evident. For these people talk about a certain text, about a certain allegation, and about a certain remarkable predication which has struck their dull attention. These they have gleaned from the discourses of the Nazarene. If Christ were to respond to such mockery after He had ministered the last service of the Word, now that He was in the curse, He would be speaking out of order. Then He, now that the great, fundamental problem of all thinking and living and speaking is being discussed, would have been acting like someone who takes a specific subpoint from the periphery of a problem and accentuates it as a way of distracting attention from the main issue. Then Christ would immediately have departed from the imperious style of the hour. Hence Jesus holds His peace. This becomes so clear to us, that after His last service of the word, He did not once address a direct, antithetical condemning speech to men. In this He appropriates to Himself the right of God who is transacting everything, that is, the *one* thing, in this hour of His condemnation. He is so essentially silent, that mention is not even made of the fact.[1] Never was anyone so essentially mute; not even He Himself at any other time. We know, then, that Christ did not give a single detail of His messiahship to the argumentative people for discussion. Neither antithetically nor by way of predicated thesis did He raise any one of

---

1. Before someone raises a question about it, we wish to remark that in a later chapter we hope to speak of the place and the mutual relationships of the other utterances from the cross, the statement to the murderers, to Jesus' mother and disciple (in which the "particulars" of daily and personal life are also given their place).

the six "points" they named. Formerly, when He was their teacher, He always traced everything back to the main issue, and now that He wants to be our Surety He maintains His silence in reference to that same fundamental major issue. Now these people are forgetting that "chapter" of His office which is called the priesthood. They are forgetting the idea of the sacrifice, of God's will to minister, of the Messianic self-surrender prompted by burning love. And having forgotten that, nothing they may say besides concerning Him can have any worth. Therefore Christ assumes the burden of His destiny, He assumes the denial confronting Him, and bows low under the misery of the punishment of hell. And a rule of hell is that the people who understand the secret, the mystery, of no one have the most to say about everyone.

By assuming the burden of this silence Christ became the Man of sorrows in the strongest possible sense of the word. We said before that as a proposer of His maschil He had to become entangled in the skeins of His own yarn.[1] Now this is being fulfilled in its most terrible sense. For Christ has fatigued the people with His riddles, has, in the form of a servant been wandering around with the Chief Wisdom, and by presenting the problem of the three-day restoration of the temple has incited the animosity of all theologians by profession. Today, on Golgotha, is the day of the reckoning. Now all those riddles are turned against Him. He must experience the fact that even that small suggestion of respect which all proposers of riddles generally may count on does not exist for Him, inasmuch as He has made a "great mistake" in the estimation of the people. He did not increase the number of the riddles, He did not solve one problem by presenting another, nor cover up one mistake by another, after the fashion of the interesting proposers of problems belonging to the school of false prophecy. But He always forced these poor ponderers and pedantic professional people back to the one problem which was not yet solved. He raised the maschil about the temple again and again as a problem throughout these years. Who had ever seen so arbitrary a master of riddles? Away with Him!

Now the masses avenge themselves after their own fashion. The crowd knows nothing, and therefore acts as though it knows

---

1. *Christ on Trial*, pp. 92-94.

everything. The man on the street without any investigation whatever poses as though he knows all about it: there are six counts against Him! But He assumes His fate, He accepts the profoundly human grief of this suffering, the suffering of being travestied and mocked in the most peculiarly personal intent of His life. He stands silent overagainst those people, because He is so essentially mute overagainst God. Whoever has entered into the great dialogue with God does not have to cover his ears against what those who are standing next to him are muttering; for he has an ear only for God.

This is the passive obedience!

But this silence is also characterized by an active obedience. How shall we describe the task of this active fidelity? Perhaps we can visualize it best by thinking of what the Bible calls "committing himself to Him that judgeth righteously."[1] Yes, we are all familiar with that text: "Who, when he was reviled, reviled not again; when he suffered, he threatened not; but committed himself to him that judgeth righteously." But do we give enough attention to the power, to the activity of this act of "committing Himself?" Well, if we read this word in reference to the Lord Jesus Christ in the light of what in our "sensitive moments" we regard as edifying for ourselves, then this essentially powerful word "committing," even though it is used here in reference to Christ, takes on a prosaic and frail significance. So frail does its connotation become that it communicates nothing to us but a kind of dull resignation, a kind of "letting it go at that." Then it means nothing more than to do nothing, to be passive, to be inactive. But if we look upon the word from the viewpoint of Christ (the right method!), "committing" means a definite act, a deed, a deed which is persisted in, and is repeated again and again.[2] Committing may be taken to mean "giving oneself over." Well, the act of "giving" is indeed an act; hence that of "giving over" connotes a conscious surrender. It suggests going to the judge, begging audience from him, and then purposely presenting our case to him. Whoever "commits" his case in that way cannot remain passive,

---

1. See I Peter 2:23 (imperfectum); active deed.

2. Dr. S. Greijdaanus, *Kommentaar op de brieven van Petrus, etc.* (Amsterdam, Bottenburg); see comments especially on I Peter 2:23 (persevere in perfectum).

for a passive person remains at home and does not try to obtain an audience with the judge. The active person, on the other hand, does something. He calls on the judge, and declares himself incompetent, he achieves the active deed of "committing."

Hence we can say that Christ is busy. Precisely because He is "without the gate," and because He acknowledges the punishment of God which allows Him no privilege of free speech, He goes actively upon the way of the incompetent, the way to the only Judge. Step by step He goes, actively, in His thoughts. He is actively obedient and in being this reckons with the time and manner of it. His thoughts have been driven into their narrowness; this was His paradoxical plague. His thoughts were not allowed to go on; He finds Himself in the one, in the absolutely real dialogue; God has entered into the crevice and he who has become a Balaam cannot get through the passageway. But He has seen God and the sword in time, and He does not strike at the dumb beast, or at anything or anyone in the world. He is silent and does the deed. He puts the case into the hands of the judge. He has pondered all these things, and speaks to God so basically that He does not say a single word audibly; because of that it is that He can be so essentially mute overagainst these people.

In this obedience He separates Himself from all the children of hell who in their mockery wish to annihilate Him, that is, who wish avidly and eagerly to entice Him into their circle. But it is just the fact that He gives His case into the hands of the Judge which does not hold true of these children of hell. If only there were one soul in the realm of eternal darkness who would put the case of the revilings and mockery into the hands of the Judge, then at that point the bottom of hell would be split wide, and a human being would begin to be rescued from the claws of Satan. That would be the case even if he were to do nothing more than to say something opposed to the mockery of the others, something desperate about the disruptive influence of hell, that great and wrecked community. That is, of course, if a beginning and a "becoming" were still possible there. But no one there will ever do what Christ is doing here.

That, then, is one thing. Christ isolates Himself from the children of hell. In the second place, He also vanquishes them by that means, He overwhelms them, He purchases for Himself the jurisdiction over their coterie. By actively giving Himself, together with the world, over to the righteous Judge, the Servant of the Lord, the second Adam allowed God to remain the Judge over the whole world. And this kingship of God He acknowledged precisely in the spiritual world: there the principles of the fundamental law are being maintained or denied. In that spiritual world, where it was most difficult, He transferred to God and the Father the right to rule. This He does before He plunges into eternal death, just as He will do it again before He conducts everything into eternal life.

Now this active obedience again, as ever, merges with the passive obedience in a single act. We said before[1] that Christ isolated Himself in the catastrophic curse. The bitter fruits of this self-isolation He assumes now in the moment of this silence both in its active and its passive side. He eats that which is His; He eats His own food. At bottom there is no such thing as real isolation, save only among the lost. To be the object of the mockery of hell — that is to be isolated. Reverence Him now: He began the isolation of His curse in the form of prayer: Father, forgive them. Now He has completed it by actively committing all that was His to the Judge of heaven and earth. Thus He persevered in prayer. In His silence, also, He persisted in the prayer of the first utterance from the cross. He prayed perfectly, for prayer at bottom is committing oneself to God. It is actively proceeding towards the prayer which will constitute His last utterance from the cross: Father, into thy hands I commend my spirit. Prayer is to acknowledge in faith (an active deed therefore), it is to acknowledge God as He is in exercising the right of infinite or[2] of the elemental election, of the prime decision. Prayer is an active self-expression to the Father and a simultaneous, conscious attachment of the self to the Judge. To pray is to put oneself in the right position overagainst God, and therefore involves accepting the consequences. For Christ it means that He be given the privilege to put all things in the right position overagainst Himself. Thus Christ was isolated in the curse, as He prayed the "messianic" prayers of the servant. He was alone. And He who stands alone is silent.

---

1. Chapter VII.
2. In this connection these two are the same.

May the church now praise its Surety, who held His peace in hell and there recognized God as the Judge. Now we dare to speak of the "Suretyship"; now we know that in our stead He suffered the mockery of hell. When His spirit was driven into the one, unique, and utter[1] narrowness, when He suffered the conflict of thoughts, and the inhibition of the stream of His thoughts, He consciously bound Himself to the ideas of God. At this time He did not dare to pronounce His maxims aloud unless God Himself had written them upon His conscience as the articles of the Constitution of the Kingdom. In this we see the Christ as one who dared to transcend His own confusion only by the grace of God. He had been cast into the paradoxical confusion. He wants to transcend this, He is eager at heart to conquer it. But only in obedience. The "Satz des Widerspruchs" could not, as a quietistic argument which would distract His thinking from God, comfort Him for one moment. He was not permitted to find peace in a self-determined sabbath. God was His sabbath and for the remainder — there was only the plague of His suffering.

In a separate chapter we shall in fear and trembling try to say how He conquered this plague of suffering. We shall not discuss that now. Today we wish to ponder but one thing. We want to see that Christ in the plague which came upon Him because of the paradoxical strife entertained the forgotten chapter of the love of His Suretyship in His own soul and spirit, and preserved it there for Himself and His people. Today it suffices for us to know that He did not in order to cling to it have to look upon the idea of Suretyship according to which God determined His priesthood, and His priestly sacrifice, and the opening of His heart to all that was lost, antithetically. He did not have to look upon that idea of Suretyship antithetically in order to preserve it overagainst the people who reviled Him. Instead He grasped that idea anew, struggled with it again, clung fast to it, and reorientated Himself to it in His own personal struggle. This He did first before God and then before the people who were bound to His spirit. "Set me as a seal upon thy arm," says a soul who is looking for a bride's comfort. "Put your name upon my back as the mark of a burn-

---

1. Eschatological.

ing brand," said the Slave[1] who was here exercising religion before God. His saying was first, His saying counted.

How glorious is He who by means of His own human[2] spiritual faculties always kept clearly before His mind that which every one forgets; He kept it before His mind constantly, unintermittently, continuously, permanently.[3] Is He not the most Beautiful of the children of men? Wholly different — as far as sin is concerned?

For we human beings if we are honest must acknowledge that the man who rails against us, and persecutes us, that the man who mocks and defies and pursues us with his ugly caricature, very frequently is as necessary to us as bread, inasmuch as he in spite of himself often does us a great service.

Does us a great service? Yes, for there is such a phenomenon as "ressentiment"[4] in psychology. We shall not enter upon the question of whether those who in our days talk about this most[5] are leaving things in their proper positions. But in general it is true that many people raise a given subject again and again in the presence of others or in their own minds simply because the oppositions they encounter in their enemies, or the mockery which clever caricaturists employ lingers in and incites their mind to constant defense. There are people who can cling to a subject only so long or can elaborate their pet thesis, or can furbish their playthings or their instruments of battle only so long as their spiritual property meets with opposition. They are active in these things only when some other person actually or, as they imagine, takes up a position directly opposed to them, or contradicts them, or puts their thesis in a false light. Here is a man, for instance, who ardently defends the "Christian activity" when a real or supposed enemy thwarts his path. There is another who can pursue an ideal so long only as another stands in his way. The moment the opposition weakens the zeal wanes. Over there we find still a third who propagates the positive demands of the kingdom of heaven, the Christian school, Christian politics, a Christian "radio" and other

1. Christ "in the form of a servant" (Philippians 2) ; in spirit also.
2. This will be discussed further in the following chapter.
3. Imperfectum; see note 1, p. 262.
4. This can be defined in one way as a constantly recurring, negative, emotional, often unconscious response to another person or to something else.
5. Nietzsche, E. Dühring, A. G. Hübener, and especially Max Scheler.

Christian movements, solely because Christianity still has to conquer these things by means of an active struggle. It is not a pleasant truth, but we must say it nevertheless: the existence of "the world," and much talking about "the world" is very necessary to a weak church because it incites activity, keeps people alert, and serves again and again to raise schemes for consideration which our apathy, in case there were no active struggle, would rarely touch on. The entire history of the church, and also the history of Christianity in our own day, is proof of this. And he who is honest and is willing to trace the concept of sin down to its deep source, will have to admit that many Christian voices in the world would immediately be silenced if the world itself did not make so much ado.[1] It is a fact that there are many in the camp of Christ who would immediately cease following Him if there were not an Antichrist and a Pseudo-Christ.

This is not the place to discuss this further;[2] here it is our duty to put in the foreground the fact that we will not have our reward if we must be incited to "act" in the kingdom of heaven on the basis of such a negative stimulus. In such a case we are not driving our own steeds, but are letting Satan bridle and conduct us.

But enough of that. Overagainst all this apathy, negativism, and decadence by which we, especially in our "busiest" moments, must seem very poor and meager and ridiculous in the eyes of the angels, we have need of keeping the High Priest of our confession before us. Look closely upon Him. Presently, right after this, He will give the love of His Suretyship to the "murderer" and thereby prove that He is burning with love even in hell; and He will prove also that He has ignited the fires of His love Himself, that He has blown it into a flame with His own breath, that He has fed it with wood gathered by His own hand. Observing that, we

---

1. The opposite is also true.
2. Naturally the instances cited are not sufficient to typify the phenomenon being discussed. It takes other forms also: criticisms of the vices of others, for instance, because one regrets that he cannot participate in them himself; a glorification of specific ideals, in an attempt to escape from the imperative of other ideals, etc. That which people are discussing recently on this theme tends more and more to become a part of the doctrine of suppression: the conflict becomes an inner one, the antithetic attitude to the outside world does not become as conspicuous then as in the examples cited above; but we chose those examples advisedly for this connection. See Max Scheler, *Vom Umsturz der Werte*, volume 1, 1919.

must acknowledge that there was not a hint of "ressentiment" in Him.[1] In this, too, this High Priest is without sin. God be praised: His love was not sentiment, but a struggle of the Mediator, a will to fulfill His office, an instance of obedience, of being a servant, of faith; it was a revelation of Christ's being completely contained in God. "For such an high priest became us, who is holy, harmless, undefiled, separate from sinners" — and He became us also as He was in putting His problems.

For again He has overcome all. "Ressentiment" can lead to a situation in which we constantly evade[2] specific subjects because some other person uncongenially opposed to us, or in a manner unpleasant to us, or with an effect disagreeable to us is discussing them. Human beings are alike throughout the centuries; is it particularly foolish to suppose that the silence of the priests on the part of Christ's priesthood[3] also was born of "ressentiment"?

Nevertheless Christ was victorious over them in this respect also.

We can be sure of this: Christ while suffering the plague of paradox, although bandied to and fro between "doxa" and "doxa," between meaning and meaning, between thesis and thesis, did not take refuge from one bias in another, from one "doxa" in another, from one thesis in another, from one word in another, but remained what He had ever been: the Word of God, the man of God, the unbroken man of God, the pure soul, the unbroken soul, the guileless spirit, in whom there was no diversification of whole and part. It is from this fact that the secret of His transcending the distress of the paradoxical struggle must arise; but of that later.[4]

Hast Thou been in hell, Lord Jesus? And hast Thou stood in the fire of thorns prepared by the mockery of hell? And didst Thou there, my Saviour, preserve and blow into a flame that other fire of Thy priestly love, the love no one would name, the love no one would recall, because no one saw or sought a place for it in the con-

---

1. This theory must be maintained overagainst those of Nietzsche (in a broader sense), and especially of A. Gustav Hübener (*Christentum und das Ressentiment*; see Scheler, p. 74).
2. The "forgotten chapters" of the ecclesiastical press, for instance.
3. We refuse to countenance the suggestion maintained by many that there is a contrast between Paul's Jesus and the synoptic Jesus.
4. In our following chapter.

stitution of things above or below? Then we would take courage, and believe that in heaven a song of love will be composed and sung which will be done in figures of speech very different from those of Solomon's song as recorded in the Bible. The Song of Solomon reaches the point beyond which our thoughts could not go when it writes as follows: Many waters would not be able to quench love, the very flame of Jehovah. But the praise of the angels will sound loftier and the litany of the redeemed people will be more sublime as they together marvel at this great miracle in which the many flames of hell did not mingle with the flames of love. It is a great thing to know that many waters cannot extinguish the fires of love but it is a greater thing to know that the many fires of the passion of hell did not consume the flames of the Lord by the glowing coals of their destructiveness and did not even make them invisible. Lord, Thou art the second Adam; for since the first Adam fell, there has been no one who could withstand the opponent in love. Those who mocked Thee were not an inducement to Thee to recite a psalm, a hymn of love. By way of thesis and not by way of antithesis Thou hast related Thy forgotten chapter to God, without being provoked to do so by any single voice coming to Thee from below. As I open the treasury of books composed by human searchers for beauty, I find a well known poem[1] which tells me that in the battle of angels and demons the angels can avail to make the spirits of hell recede. When angels softly and delicately strew rose leaves (symbols of love) upon the backs of these upstorming devils, they by that means gain the victory; for how could the spirits of evil bear the symbol of love?

But now I have heard Jesus being silent, and now I have seen Him struggle in the campaign of His love, deriving His materials from His own treasury to which all the winds of earth had contributed nothing, even when He was in the house of hell. And now I know that the rose leaves of love are helpless to achieve anything in the garden of the world. But that figure is not strong enough. Many waters — ardent fires, and a groaning called a whirlwind, because it issued from Jesus' mouth, that is a more suitable figure. Paradoxical winds are blowing. It causes the rose leaves to twirl about in the air and to settle on the devils,

---

1. Goethe's *Faust*.

blowing past these punctilious people. The leaves go with the will of the wind. But in the winds of paradox the Rock of Love stood firm. The winds blow from beneath, and all of them have been released together; they are paradoxical. But the wind of the Spirit, the firmly-driven wind of the relentless, priestly influence proceeded from Himself. This whirlwind did not arise from nature, and consequently could not be dependent upon the natural laws which hold for the earth. God's wind coming from God's storehouse — what more can we say? The powerful whirlwind of the spirit of Christ as it is in the priestly campaign of His Suretyship conquered the vicious circle of all the blowing winds. He did not spring from nature, nor from man; He is of God.

Come down from the cross, they said, and we will believe you. But they did not understand that He Himself had planted the cross; that His own hand driven by the Spirit had planted it. It is not a Saviour who comes from the cross that compels us to believe, but a Saviour who ascends to the cross — He is a wonder in all eternity.

Again: come down from the cross, and restore the temple! That is what they said.

But they did not understand that this was indeed the building of the temple. Surely He who can still see God and the people redeemed by the priest, He who can still see these in the community of hell, and who can cry out "My God" and "My people," so that the sound of the crying transcends the screams of hell's mockery, He has traced the plan of God's house upon the floor of hell, and He has had the whole structure with all of its dwelling places of love before His eyes, even when He descends between satyrs and demons, between bandits and revilers, between the doomed fellowship of you and me as we are by nature. Great art Thou, Lord, and greatly to be praised, for our eyes, seeking for the temple of love, seek ever restlessly, until they are fixed on Thee.

Christ's Super-Paradoxical "Amen"

CHAPTER THIRTEEN

Christ's Super-Paradoxical "Amen"

● *And Jesus said . . .Verily (Amen).*
LUKE 23:43.

B UT Jesus held His peace. This was strange and yet very natural.[1] Such can be the summary of what we have been discussing in our latest chapters. "But" Jesus held His peace: it was a wonder in our ears. "Therefore" Jesus held His peace: it was reasonable religion. To be silent in the dialogue with God, to stand mute before the Judge, to hold His peace in hell, that was reasonable religion.

Jesus very simply held His peace. He had nothing more to say; the hour of abandonment had come, and no one had heard the clock striking the hour. In eternity the pulsebeat weighs as heavily as the stroke of a clock. Jesus held His peace because of His heart and His God; in His case we can put it that way. He could not speak, because the prayer which had been on the lips of all the poets of the psalms would have done injustice to the knowledge of being abandoned, being forsaken by God. The psalmist had prayed, Deal justly with me, O God, and avenge my enemies, and those who revile me. But Jesus could not pray that prayer. Therefore He was mute.

But His silence was not His last act. Very soon we will hear Him speaking again. The statement He will make at that time will be one of great power. It will be an assurance of firm confidence. He who could not succeed in forcing a single thought to the door of heaven, presently by means of a confident gesture throws open the gates of heaven, and says to a murderer — now you have

---

1. Strange if observed from below; natural if observed from above (from the viewpoint of God's justice). This, therefore, is not a paradox!

guessed it—: you are sure to enter; come, thou blessed of my Father, and inherit the kingdom. He who Himself had to be silent while surrounded by the mockery of hell now governs a thousand angels who are singing their litanies, and He does not ask whether these might wish to have His guest go elsewhere. He speaks firmly; He speaks so boldly and so loudly that the heavens quake because of it. He says: Amen!

This is a strange thing. We know that this "amen" comes after the mockery with which He was afflicted and which buried His living spirit. That this, however, is the chronological order becomes apparent from the indication that the "murderers," regarded as a group — we shall consider the particulars later — took part in the mockery of the many others. Jesus said nothing to the one fellow crucified person, to the one who perseveres in mocking. Overagainst him Jesus remained profoundly and essentially silent. But when a little later the other murderer speaks, and addresses a reprimand to the blasphemer next him, and then says nothing until, somewhat shy and embarrassed, he directs a prayer to Christ, we know that much time must have elapsed between that moment in which the mockery took place, the mockery also of this fellow condemned, and the moment in which Jesus by His address to the second criminal, again speaks, and, with a voice full of assurance, introduces this second person into the paradise of heaven.

The very fact that Christ pronounced His "amen" after He had suffered the mockery of the people, tends to enhance for us the sense of His poised power. "Verily" He says. And in the Greek the word used here and at other places where our translation uses the word "verily" is the familiar designation "amen." If ever the little word "amen" was used as more than a stop sign or a dignified ending, it was here. Here it was living and powerful, a word borne up immediately by faith, by sure knowledge, and by firm confidence. This "amen" was spoken at mid-day of the Day of Jehovah, the great day of the Lord. It challenges our attention for three reasons.

It challenges our attention because it is another instance of speaking. Jesus opens His mouth again; He listens again; He has something to say after His profound silence.

The word challenges our attention because it is firmly, positively, confidently spoken. It represents firm assurance. "Amen" is a word taken from the vocabulary of faith. It really is a Hebrew word; the root from which it is derived means: to hold a thing true, to trust (overagainst a person), to feel assured. The word has this function throughout the Bible. Jesus used it often, as often as He said "verily, verily," for "verily" means "amen." But we also find the word (after all it is a Hebrew word) in its root form in the Old Testament; and always in such cases in which faith is being described. The word used in the Old Testament for "believing" comes from the same root from which "amen" was derived. We read, "Abraham believed God." In the original, we really read that as follows: Abraham stood in an amen-relation to God. It meant that a full confidence in God had naturally elicited the "amen" from Abraham; the word was part of the man; it typified his relation to God. Now this faith of Abraham, this amen-relationship in which Abraham stood to the living God, is, as Paul says in the letter to the Romans, the cause of His justification with God. We can say that Abraham entered into an amen-relationship with God in a moment of time. This took place in history; it was conclusive, radical, definitive, and it took place because of the irresistible work of God in that moment of time. Since then Abraham remained in that relationship, and it was reckoned unto him for righteousness.

We all understand, of course, that the word "amen" is not always used in this sharply delineated and firmly circumscribed sense when it is used in the Bible. On the contrary, there are also places where the word "verily" or "amen" is used to indicate only a very ordinary assurance. But now the word comes from Jesus' lips. That means that the simple "amen", just as all His words, can be explained solely on the basis of His specific relationship to God. It is true that the word is used by the Saviour to give assurance to a human being; nevertheless the word according to its origin and birthright must arise from His perfect assurance about the universal acts of God. Jesus speaks to a malefactor crucified beside Him; His "amen" opens Paradise to him. We shall discuss the particulars of this later; now we have enough to do to think of Christ, using His "amen" as a self-aware Prophet, and Priest, and King. As a Prophet He sees Himself opening up the avenues of blessedness to the desolate present circumstances of this lost son. As a Prophet He establishes the relationship between heaven and earth, between the man next Him and the counsel and will of God. Hence, Christ is prophesying; He says "amen," and is perfectly certain about the axioms of God's heavenly ordinances. As a Priest He puts this lost sheep to rest by means of His "amen." Hence He must be completely assured about His relationship to God and about the inner influences of His mercy. Finally, we can say that by means of the power of a King He throws open the gate of the heavenly Paradise to this fellow sufferer of the curse; that act also testifies eloquently to an awareness on His part of His own powers of isagogics.

This astonishes us. Out of the eater came forth food, out of the strong came forth sweetness. And an "amen" came from Him who suffers the paradoxical plague. It is a short word but it wrenches clouds asunder: "amen" — the Assurance. Never had an "amen" echoed so clearly as did this one. No "amen" ever was such a miracle as this one. Even the preliminary "amen" of the angels, of the blessed, of the "beasts," of the "elders," in the heavenly-paradise[1] are not as powerful, as active, as self-sufficient as the "amen" of the Crucified. He who spoke it had long been silent, because He knew no more . . . it is a wonder in our ears.

For these two reasons alone, this "amen" deserves our fullest attention. But there is a third reason for devoting careful study to it. We are almost embarrassed by our own first gladness. The "amen" seems to subside very quickly, even though it was so positively expressed. A moment ago it seemed very firm and overwhelmingly confident to us but a very different word is to follow upon it: the word, "Why." Where now has the power and assurance gone? "Amen" — surely that is as far removed as possible from "why." And besides being very far removed from "why," "amen" transcends it. At opposite poles from "why," failing to comprehend, stands the "therefore," the expression of those who understand. And those who add the "amen" to the "therefore" have added insight to understanding, and faith by its own laws gives them assurance. Hence the "therefore" means much, but the

---

1. Revelation 5:14; 7:12; 19:4; 22:20.

"amen" means more to those who live in the revealed Word of God. "Amen" does not oppose, but strengthens the "therefore" of faith as it is maintained overagainst the "why" of the uncertain. "Amen" signifies more than laying down the relationship of the will to the content of assurance, and the god of good pleasure who has internally given us confidence; for when I say "amen" both the thing I am certain about and my certainty are founded on the presence of God. Hence the "amen" serves as a loud speaker for the expression "therefore" as well as for the assurance "that." And this in faith.

Now if this is true, how shall we go about explaining Christ's "amen"? His fourth utterance from the cross asks "why." "Why, my God, hast Thou forsaken me." These are the words of the man Christ Jesus. Again He confronts a wall and cannot pass through it. By means of His "why" — He has struggled for three hours to reach the point at which He could utter it — He hurls Himself and us to the other side of His sublime "amen." All of His confidences and assurances have disappeared in a moment. Disappeared? As He saw it, they have been forfeited. For to Him everything here seems just.

But Lord, how can this be? He who says "amen" one moment and "why" the next, and in both cases about the same relationships, must be regarded by heaven as an abomination, for, as it seems to us, He has disturbed the amen-relationship. This, if we may be allowed to use the language of men, is a living offense and foolishness. Yes, indeed, also in reference to the words He speaks, and to His interludes and pauses, we seem to be driven again to I Corinthian 2: Christ, the offense, the great foolishness. For it is indeed true that the fourth utterance from the cross with its "why," at bottom makes the very same things disputable which the "amen" of His second utterance from the cross had established as being certain. The fourth utterance from the cross also treats of the relation between God and the creature, of the relation between heaven and earth, of the relation between the ordinances of God and their corollaries, on the one hand, and the soul that loves God, on the other hand. For Christ together with the murderer has been elected of God, and awakened to the love of the Spirit. The issue at stake in the fourth utterance from the cross also concerns whether the doors of heaven shall be open or shut. Fundamentally considered, the second and the fourth utterances from the cross deal with the same elemental problems. That fact precisely constitutes the difficulty. The very Saviour who by means of His powerful "amen" had hacked every knot in the rope of the murderer next Him to pieces is in a position three hours later to unravel His own knots, and to pronounce His gloomy "why." God, He says then, I am not certain any more.

Be as cautious as you will now, you will not for the sake of Paul's wish — for he wrote I Corinthians 2 — and for God's sake — for He inspired I Corinthians 2 — succeed in restraining the question: But, if this is so, was the "amen" of Jesus worth anything? Is that which we have called the strongest language possible to faith perhaps nothing more than a hollow phrase? Can it be that the "amen" which Jesus pronounced at 12 o'clock of the Day of Jehovah is a brutal anticipation of those declarations of heaven, for which the Father of all truth, and of all integrity, has thoroughly punished Him? Can it be that it was simply to take from Him His confident assurances that God punished the Son of man who was so very certain in uttering His "amen," by means of uncertainty — even though He allowed the murderer, who, after all could not help it, to enter in.

Yes, yes, Paul, this is foolishness and offense. A new guest is being introduced to the heavenly banquet, but He Himself must presently ask why He is being locked out. This is foolishness and offense. We have here one who is assured, and one who assures, and the latter, after a few hours have gone by, has no certainty anymore. Now it becomes very difficult to hear Him say "amen," without clenching the fist or bursting into laughter.

It was very difficult for the man who had been so easily comforted by means of that "amen." It was very difficult for the bandit to whom the word was addressed; someone[1] has suggested that the man must have had a very difficult time when Jesus died before him. And this person discriminatingly adds that the murderer had to believe in a dead Saviour. We have no objection to a person who says that a dead Saviour must have been a problem to that man, but we would like to suggest that in reality the problem begins earlier than the death of the Saviour. We would like to

---

1. J. van Andel, *Bloemlezing uit "De Avondster,"* p. 172.

put it this way: Presently the murderer must believe in an amen-sayer who is asking "why." It is quite possible to enter in at the eleventh hour as that murderer did, but there is no possibility of escaping from I Corinthians 2 at the eleventh hour.

These then are the three reasons for which the "amen" of Jesus is of the greatest importance to us. Their simple natural-ness is so convincing that it seems inappropriate to overlook this "amen." However, it has frequently been overlooked.

This neglect was owing to two causes. On the one hand our Christian thinking continues to have this weakness, that it looks too much upon the suffering of Christ as a bodily distress, or, to put it more delicately, as soul distress. Christian thinking too in-frequently struggles with the problem of the spiritual distress of Jesus Christ. By that we mean the distress in which His human spirit and His mind become involved. A fact which is frequently ignored by many is that the redemption, the Suretyship, the earn-ing of the right of free thought by means of a limitation of thought was also a part of the program of the Surety on Good Friday.

Nevertheless it was on that program. But if we prefer to look upon the suffering as taking place primarily in the body, or in the sorrow of His soul — and of His soul as understood up to this time — it is very natural that we will not soon, or rather we will never, busy ourselves intensely with the spiritual struggle which had to take place in Christ. This spiritual struggle has two sides: on the one hand, He must passively listen to the sarcastic words of the mockers; on the other hand, He must pronounce that confident and self-conscious "amen." A second reason, or cause, for over-looking Christ's "amen" is that our emotional Christian world prefers being stirred by a narrative about an interesting "murder-er," one who is brought to repentance, and that *almost* too late, rather than consciously and purposely and proleptically always proceeding from Christ Himself. An "eleventh hour" object of eternal election is more interesting for people — they would say "more edifying" — than the spiritual struggle of the Messiah who had to leave the legal basis for election lying just as it was. No wonder, they say, when you present the contrast: The one is good matter for a moving story, and the other is "nothing but" a dogmatic construction of which we read nothing "in so many words" in the Bible.

Nevertheless we shall have to be on guard against this double mistake. It is a comforting thing to speak about that comforted and redeemed bandit but it is our duty to proceed from the Christ. And it is also necessary for him who is looking for "suspense." Which is the greater: the suspense in the person who listens to the narrative of that proselyte who almost comes too late (the one who listens forgets that for God the "almost" was by no means a "surprise"), or the suspense of the Christ who must now struggle in order to earn a legal basis upon which He can introduce this man who had been elected from eternity into heaven? Yes, this is tension, this is extreme suspense. The "amen" of Christ's spiritual triumphs — for it was the beginning of His spiritual victories — is a turning point; the embattled God later drives Him back from this position which He has gained.[1] That is why this event deserves its place in this book before we can consider what is to follow. The question is not whether we can succeed in avoiding this "amen," without thinking of the distress of the poet of Psalm 42. "All God's waves and all God's billows" have gone over Christ. The poet of Psalm 42 time and again admonishes his soul to pronounce an "amen," but he must ever repeat the admonishment. Now this short-time amen-sayer admonishes the spirit in the one verse to redeem itself from the paradoxical experience and complication of soul which he is experiencing, and by faith in God to work his way upwards; but before long his "amens" will again be interrupted. Just so Christ passes from His "human," all too "human" hurry and paradoxical confusion to His reprimanding and encouraging "nevertheless," and thus to an "amen" of regained certainty; thereupon follows the relapse with its: Why, O God? "My rock, why dost Thou forget me?"

Let us approach reverently and try to understand some of these things. The question at issue will be one which even touches on the inspiration of the Scriptures. The poet of Psalm 42 is not singing his own psalm so much as he is struggling to earn and release it. The Author experiences his own psalms and emerges from beneath them.

---

1. Darkness, and "why"; the fourth utterance from the cross; we shall discuss that later.

We have stated already that this assertative "amen" of Christ is a cry of triumph. By means of it He emerges triumphantly from His paradoxical plague. By means of this "amen" He regains the top of the very mountain which had caused Him to be driven into the grottos and crevices of oppression, and into the valley of contradiction before.

Let us for the sake of clarity summarize the main things that were said before. In the first place, we observed, Christ had to be absolutely sure, as He kept His eye fixed on the Scriptures and on experience, that He was innocent in the sight of God. He was not allowed to be in doubt for a single moment about His own purity and virtue.[1] In the second place, we noticed that Christ had to be absolutely sure, as He kept His eye fixed on the Scripture and experience, that He was repulsive in the sight of God, that He had been made a curse, that He had been made sin. In the third place, we are confronted by the difficult question: How was such a paradoxical concussion of thoughts possible in Christ's human nature? And thereupon we also had to ask how, inasmuch as this conflict was given, He could vanquish it and emerge triumphantly from it. Hence the question now is: How does He come up from the valley of the "why" to the mountain top of the "amen"?

Some interpreters evade these problems by appealing at once to Christ's knowledge. For them it is enough to assert that Christ simply saw everything "systematically" and plainly before Him. These aver that at every moment of His passion the whole book of explanation was with Him in head and heart, and that He consequently never stood embarrassed before a closed door. He had the key which immediately fitted all locks. Christ, they say, always saw the whole plan of God, the whole work of God. He saw it stretched out before Him, and consequently He could have no

---

1. We asked on page 215, "Why?" To recapitulate: if Christ had no longer been aware of His own purity and sinlessness then (to say nothing about many other unacceptable deductions) His suffering would no longer have been the active deed of the Mediator; then the "why" of the fourth statement from the cross loses its keenness, precisely because it is explicable at all only on the basis of His awareness of being without sin; then Christ would have had to regard Golgotha as a daily recurring symptom of injustice in the world, or as a judgment upon His own sin, or — if He had thought that He could redeem without a *conscious* conviction of perfect obedience — He in the act of His final satisfaction for the covenant would have broken the terms of that contract (for one of those terms is the imperative of perfect and self-conscious fidelity to the commandments).

problems, but immediately brought everything He knew to bear upon everything He experienced.

It will very likely be apparent to all those who read our first volume with approbation that this interpretation is not ours. There we tried to indicate at great length that Christ's thinking as man always represented a unity,[1] that it always remained pure, and also that it always remained completely human and therefore relevant to the laws of time. Because of that we were permitted to speak of Christ's sorrows as having their own peculiar origin,[2] their own peculiar severity,[3] and their own peculiar end.[4] What we remarked then must, in a different connection, again be brought into connection, again be brought into discussion here. Why, indeed, should we still have to speak about these things as though they were disputable to a person believing the Scriptures? The mere fact that Christ Himself asks "Why" is conclusive. Either we must reduce this "why" which He uttered in His dying grief to the level of a rhetorical question (which would be making it blasphemy) or we must take out of it its devastating quality, or we must let it stand in its full strength, and then acknowledge at the same time that a grievous oscillation between the walls of the work-room of God's righteousness and truth was possible here in this history in which God's counsel is being fulfilled; we must acknowledge that it was possible for Him to be pushed back and forth between heaven and earth, an oscillation caused by His real and difficult search to establish a connection between God's revealed and hidden will, between a creative and a created knowledge, between a righteousness which establishes standards and a righteousness which maintains standards, between decree and experience, between a nomothetical and a nomotactical work of God in history, between a logical and a genetic judgment, between the books written in heaven and the journals written on earth, between an *a priori* and an *a posteriori* way of thinking. He was hurled back and forth in His real search to establish a connection by means of His life-taking struggle between one end of His

---

1. Synthesis (without the added idea of the relationship of heterological elements: Kant).
2. *Christ in His Suffering*, p. 289.
3. *Ibid,* p. 349.
4. *Ibid,* p. 379.

thoughts and the other, in His effort to find a higher harmony, approved of God and effected in His soul.

Surely, if Christ on His cross had stood outside of the possibilities of paradoxical confusion and dissipation, if He had lived beyond the chances, beyond the possibilities, of the pain of paradox, and — imagine the possibility — if a true "why" could not have come to birth in Jesus' soul, then — we are taken aback at the very thought of the word — then Golgotha would have been a mere display, and a mere appearance. The very people who are so eager to discuss Christ's blood, and who write many books about the worth of only a single drop of that blood, and who dedicate sermons and poems to it should have busied themselves long ago with the tremendous worth of the struggle and the passion of Christ's human spirit. Take the spiritual confusion out of Christ's suffering, especially His suffering on the cross, take the oppression which He suffered in His human experience and the confronting of problems which He encountered in His human nature out of Golgotha, and Golgotha will become nothing but an unsuccessful attempt; then Golgotha represents an effort to enter into human suffering, without ever achieving a real participation in it. Then Golgotha at very best, if it still represents a service to all, certainly cannot represent the service of the second Adam.[1] Then Christ is not in our stead suffering that which we by our sin deserve, but then He — imagine that this were possible — is bringing us something as a "prize" which He has "earned," a prize, understand, which had never been a debt demanding to be paid. For a part of the suffering of the wrath is the binding of His ideas, the confusion of His spirit.

Consequently we cannot avoid the question we put above in this way.

But now others approach us, and say that they too do not want to look upon the matter thus. Nevertheless, they add that they propose to overlook all these curious questions simply by taking refuge in that statement of our faith which says that in His hu-

---

1. Second Adam: for the first (think of the probationary command) was also duty bound to establish the relationship by means of a conscious and active deed of religion between God's hidden and revealed will, etc. (See p. 282). We shall not discuss this further at this time, however, because the issue of the Suretyship as it functions in the paradoxical suffering of Christ was touched upon in the preceding chapter and therefore need not be taken up here except in an indirect way.

man nature Christ's suffering was supported by the divine. Those who prefer to adopt this attitude like to believe that the thinking of Christ is too difficult for us to follow (a fact which we readily admit) because (and in this their attitude differs from ours) we cannot possibly know anything about it. They say that Christ was not only a human being, but also God; in Him therefore there was not only human experience, and human thought and feeling, but also divine knowledge, divine sovereignty of decision, and divine foreknowledge. And in Him there was, besides, a constant knitting together in each specific moment of all the threads which merge in each specific decree of God. Therefore — they go on — it is not appropriate for us to go into these things farther. "We ought not to be wise above our own conceits." Even though we know that the soul and spirit of Christ were vexed by the passion and by the problems which depressed Him, let us — thus their admonishment — let us comfort ourselves in general with the truth that the divine nature supported the human, and that, for the rest, all questions must necessarily remain unsolved in this admittedly unsolvable mystery.

Now it is the least of our wishes to gainsay the element of truth contained in these remarks to the extent that they have been spoken with reason and justice. We, too, acknowledge the fact of the mystery, and frankly state that we cannot fathom it. We do not know and we never will know how to span the gap between the divine and the human in the Christ. As He hangs on the cross, we confess that He is our Lord and our God. To confess Him as such in this terrible hour necessarily commits us to a full acknowledgment of the unfathomable, of the mystery in this hidden relationship. If ever a person should undertake to give a "conclusive" explanation of the relationship between the divine and the human in Christ's mind, we could say that this effort would be as foolish as the effort of those who think that they can "prove" God's existence, and that they can exhaustively set down a characterization of the works of God.

But this does not take away the fact that precisely by calling the mystery a mystery we are but becoming more deeply entangled in our problem. The core of that problem we remember is this: the paradoxical in the human which remained pure. Now we cannot escape from this. It does us no good to say that Christ's human nature "must have" been sustained by the divine also in its spiritual struggles; for that is a remark which includes the suggestion that a further "application"[1] of it must not be undertaken. The very fact that reference is made to supporting, is an acknowledgment that Christ's being vexed in His human nature is the real problem.

Now is it allowed to man to investigate this human passion in the light of Scriptures. Allowed to man? No, the Christian must investigate it. We are called to see the second Adam who struggled for us as He was in His thinking; we are called to investigate that in the light of the Scriptures and it is our duty to keep that which has been given us to know about it clearly before our eyes.

Just what kind of "comfort" is it anyhow, and what kind of ethical seriousness is there in that facile gesture to dismiss all the difficulties of the problem of Christ's spiritual ascents and descents, of His "amens" and "whys," by a mechanically applied theological knowledge according to which the moment a difficulty arises for us we dispatch it by a reference to the support given Christ's human nature by the divine? We must not think of this support in so mechanical and abrupt a way. We may not use the mystery of the relationship between Christ's divinity and humanity as an argument which, after the fashion of a *deus ex machina,* can be drawn into the discussion at any time to help us out of our difficulties. For that mystery, that relationship, between the divine and the human created a certain condition, a condition which was ever present and remained for years, a condition which was Christ's in His youth, in His temptations, in His miracles, in His sleeping, in His calm deliberations, in His eating and drinking, even in His vacations. We must not think of the relationship between the human and the divine as something which periodically intervenes and then recedes again; it is not a spasmodic interference on the part of heavenly influences which explodes out of the clouds each time difficulties arise for us. Hence anyone who would forbid us cautiously and reverently to investigate the problem of Christ's human, spiritual confusion by an appeal to the relationship between the divine and the human in Him, must also act on his assumption when he discusses Christ's birth, and child-

---

1. The application is that the problem be left untouched.

hood, and youth, and such other things as were named above.

No, we prefer to acknowledge that in each instance Christ was true man, and that it is both warranted and good to discuss His purely human temptation and victory, provided that in the discussion we limit ourselves to the data of the Scriptures. Whatever the connection and relationship between the divine and the human nature were, Christ nevertheless suffered all His passion completely and exclusively in His human nature. This, therefore, also holds true of His spiritual struggles, of His paradoxical difficulties, and of the triumphs which He achieved in His "amen." Every attempt mechanically and abruptly to call the relationship between the divine and the human into the discussion by way of explaining this or that, is, to anyone who has fathomed the fundamental principle of Calvin, nothing but a hardly concealed heresy. For it takes offense at the truth that the suffering of Christ was completely endured *in* His human nature.

Accordingly, we shall limit our discussion solely to the *human* nature of Christ. We want to raise two considerations. The first is the fact that Christ is true man; the second is the thought that Christ is sinless man. And we want to attach two conclusions to our problem: first, if Christ is true man, then it is possible for Him to be steeped in paradoxical conflict. Second, if Christ is sinless man, then it is impossible for Him to remain in a condition of paradoxical conflict.

Our first consideration, accordingly, is that as true man, Christ can be steeped in paradoxical conflict. In view of what we said about this in our first volume we can leave the discussion here after having made a few remarks.

Christ as a man born in time, and, living, suffering, and dying in time, was subject to the law of growth, of change, of mutation. True, His being was characterized by unity but the unity of His being, of His essence, did not exclude the breadth of His experience. It is true that He always stands as an essential unity, perfect, undivided, unblemished, overagainst the pluriform, vacillating things and influences of human life. But His mind is subject to the law of growth, and also to that of time and succession. His mind is genuinely human and consequently cannot isolate itself as a separate entity from what for Him as for us are gradually developing and evolving areas of knowledge. All the things which are external do not impinge upon Him simultaneously but successively. For Him, too, life does not arrange things in a harmonious order. For Him, too, the Scriptures are not a concordance, with an adequate text-and-subject index. He, too, must learn, must penetrate, must organize. Hence when His human nature confronts the things which He must meet, and when He fastens His heart upon God's means of revelation, He also establishes a relationship between what He experiences and what He knows about God; these He puts into living relationship with the things of temporal experience, with the vacillations of earthly life, with historically progressive human experience. Thus He puts Himself before a gradually unfolding Scripture. Christ's attention does not wish to be dissipated or scattered; neither is it an immovable, immutable greatness; it is simply bound to the scattered condition of things, and to the scattered condition of the Scriptural data. In the last analysis Christ as man did not have to devote Himself to the hidden things, known only to God, but to the revealed things. Each moment, overagainst everything which He sees and experiences, He must consciously and by means of an ever new deed, fix His attention upon the Scriptures, upon the spoken and written Word given us "at sundry times and in diverse manners."[1] This He must do with powers that are ever growing and with a mind ever becoming firmer, a knowledge of God which takes on strength with His increasing knowledge of man and life.

From this we may infer that Christ, even as we, met with influences and realities in this our human life, with antithetical forces and things, whose deeper unity God only knows, but whose inner reconciliation is given no human mind to know. There is much in life which seems contradictory to us. Now His consciousness was also impressed by the things coming from without as having this apparent antithesis, this apparent duality. When these mutually contradictory things confronted Him, He had to span the gap between the one pole and its opposite, between one side and its opposite, between truth and temporary truth. He had to span the gap, He had to bridge the gulf, as does everyone. The material for that bridge God gave, as He ever does, but He first had to gather it together. He Himself had to estimate the length, the arch of

---

1. Think of the significance of this expression (Hebrews 1:1) as Christ must have read and assimilated it.

the bridge. In order to do this He had to concentrate on what He knew about God, about what He read and believed in the Scriptures.

This was all the more exacting because Christ is not in an abstract sense a "theologian" but is first of all the one who is the motive force of religion, the one who is the great religious soul. The fact that the man Christ Jesus is active theologically, the fact that He lives and reads in the Scriptures is but a result, an expression, a "good work" of His religion. This religion we must understand as being pure and unbroken, as a service of God manifesting itself in all things. For this reason it is impossible for Christ to set up an experiment with an "abstract" theological system of thought, and to combine the manifestations and scattered data of experience and revelation without entering into awful spiritual conflict. In Him the knowledge of God does not come "from" experience but is itself experience, life, and service. Precisely because He is the motive essence of religion itself He is a theologian. Ours is not a Christ who by means of abstract human thinking constructs park benches where, unmoved by the apparent contradictions, He can sit, resting quietly, and making Himself believe that He is "enjoying" God. Nor is ours a Christ who by means of the apparatus of His mind constructs His arcs — arcs by means of which He binds together the outlying mountain-tops of God's revelation — in the manner of an architect who by means of a mathematical computation and the aid of a few scattered data works out his blue print for a building. For, besides constructing the blue print, besides drawing up the plan on paper by means of square and ruler, He must experience His constructions. He must bring what He has projected in His mind to bear upon living reality. These He must carry into the farthest recesses and the inmost chambers of the universe of the works of God.

An immediate consequence of this fact is that paradoxical experience is possible to Christ. For He came into the world as true man, and as true man He came into the Scriptures, and both the world and the Scriptures reveal their unity only to those who obediently investigate these in time. Gethsemane is the example of that, by no means the only example, by no means the first, but possibly the one which speaks most loudly to us.

Now there was paradox in this human course of His obedience, in this dual experience. Here was the consciousness of His just rights on the basis of the revealed Word; for the revealed Word testified well of His works. And on the other hand, there was the consciousness of His being abandoned, of His being forsaken, of His being condemned, of His real repulsiveness to God — and this again on the basis of the revealed Word, which specifically assures Him that the curse attached to him who hung upon the tree.

In this way, then, we may know that it was possible for Christ to be steeped in paradoxical entanglements.

We consider next the fact that, as sinless man, it is impossible for Him to remain in this paradoxical confusion. He cannot stay caught in it, He cannot remain resting in it. He cannot abandon the problem; He cannot admonish His soul to overlook the problem, and without a super-paradoxical answer to rest in a "why."

At this point we must make two predications. First, the paradox cannot evolve in Christ from within. Second, Christ cannot objectively ascribe the paradox to God, or explain it on the basis of God's essence and works.

We said that it was impossible for the paradoxical confusion to arise out of Christ's own life. This has its immediate consequences, for — speaking generally — that which cannot evolve out of man (unless it is a new creation,[1] a thing which we shall presently deny about the paradox) cannot be a remaining condition of the human life, it cannot be an abiding, ever accompanying manifestation of his life.

The fact that the paradoxical confusion cannot arise from Christ Himself needs little contention; at least not to the person who shares this interpretation of the essence and the origin of the paradoxical. If we can define the paradoxical as a division of the ways of thought, by means of which the unity of thinking is broken, and as a result of which two attitudes or theses persist in contradicting each other in our minds, and concerning which we dare not say *yes* to the one and a conclusive *no* to the other, then we can safely say that such paradox cannot possibly have its origin in Christ's human constitution.

---

1. Such as regeneration, and the effects of it.

Christ is one. Sin may have seized upon our human mind and have steeped us in paradoxical confusion, but Christ who was conceived by the Holy Spirit and in whom sin at no point introduced perdition or disruption — Christ, even though He was heir to the weaknesses of the human constitution, never found the cause of these residing in Himself. His thoughts were never driven apart by an act of His own spirit. Never did He on His own part shift His point of view, His point of orientation, from the center to the periphery. He never sought for bias, and never carried faulty weights in His hands. Hence the paradoxical cannot arise in Him; it can only impinge upon Him. He was never antithetically opposed to Himself, and consequently He never "saw" an antithesis unless God had placed it there. True He saw a clear and sharp antithesis between God and Satan, between the divine and the satanic, between good and evil; but He never recognized an antithesis as the result of a flaw in His own thinking, never in this way saw a contradiction in the Scriptures, or in God, be it in nature or grace. We must never convert the weakness of Christ's human nature, a "weakness," in which life as He experienced it, and in which His apprehensions and His spiritual development were bound, into a spiritual "sickness"; for weakness and sickness are not identical. No, Christ's thinking was not faulty, and He was not Himself responsible for the parting of the ways of His thought. His thinking "creates" no antinomies. "Weakness" and "sickness" are not identical; and "weakness" and "strength" are not identical. The "weakness" of Christ's human nature is not a positive influence or principle; it cannot set Him to thinking "creatively." We cannot ascribe His knowledge about the Most High to it any more than we could imagine a phantasy about a God broken up into antinomies, or about a revelation thus broken up as having arisen in Him because of it. His "weakness" prevents Him from climbing up to God's altars but does not itself build an altar to an unknown god who conceals himself in antinomies. The weakness of Christ as a human being can operate as a hindering influence, and as such it can be an obstruction in the way of the ascent of Christ's thoughts. It can also detain Him in His struggle to arrive at that sublime condition of rest which He desires not at the beginning but at the end of the labor of His thoughts, at the end of His inquiries which both proceed from and work towards His God. This weakness, this human and temporal limitation, can stand in the way of triumphantly feeling that the mountain top of accomplished thinking has been attained; it can prolong the struggle of His ideas. But it cannot introduce a flaw into His thinking. It cannot teach a false logic; it cannot serve to impart a false dialectic which ascribes unreasonable things to God and traces antinomies back to Him.

We do well to note the difference between the beginning of Christ's thinking and the results of Christ's thinking. We admitted above that as true man He was susceptible to the struggle and conflict of thoughts. As the second Adam in objective reality, and as having a mind which functions purely and genuinely, He must now achieve knowledge, He must earn the content of thought; and this He must do along the ways of revelation. For Him, too, nay, precisely for Him who must go the whole way of the probationary commands of Adam, precisely for Him the rule was inviolable that the revelation of God contained no paragraphs in which specific loci, in which specific chapters of dogmatics, or paragraphs of philosophy, or completely prepared material of knowledge were fixed and arranged in a logical order. The opposite is more true. The first and second Adam are duty bound to gain for themselves a synthetic judgment and unified knowledge about what God reveals in the Word, in nature, and in history. And in this we detect a difference between the beginning and the end of the learning process of both. At the beginning both have as a given a pure, and genuine capacity for apprehension, an unspoiled mind, a normal attitude toward everything. Thereupon both are asked whether they are, as religious people, willing to take the way of obedience to the rich reward of knowledge (regarded now as the content of thought, as the object of knowledge). It was in this way of obedience that Adam fell but the second Adam remained inaccessible to sin. The sin of passive acquiescence in the paradox[1] consequently could not be His. Such acquiescence would be possible to Him only if on His own part He had yielded the center of His area of knowledge and had no longer believed in the unity of God and the work of God. He ascribes no antinomies to His God, even though the appearance of these can distress Him and assault Him.

---

1. A form of despairing of God, or despairing of conscious fellowship with God.

We note, then, that the appearance of paradox — for this appearance does exist — can accrue to Him, but that He cannot acquiesce in this semblance of paradox for a moment. Just as a healthy body reacts to infectious materials, so a reaction must immediately arise in Christ against every phenomenon of life by means of which God or Satan prove or tempt Him with the semblance of antinomy. A passive attitude toward the appearance of paradox in God's words or works is as He sees it a sin, a repudiation of God, and an instance of unbelief.

This opinion is based on our firm conviction that acquiescence in the paradox, taken in its strictest sense, is an instance of arrogance. We stated previously[1] that God can use the experience of paradox in order to break down one's pride; in fact, we derive from this thought our right to conclude our previous chapter with the thought: Christ our *surety* in the paradox.

We must remember, however, that this coin has its opposite side. When God while disciplining me by means of the trial of paradox, strikes me to the ground in order to break my pride, I must not myself want to manipulate the instrument with which He struck me down. That would be to confirm my arrogance: God's instruments do not fit my hand. Nor must I take the instrument which God hurls against me in His loving warfare and conjure it into a different thing by means of an unctuous faith; I may not, preaching the while, convert it into an instrument of peace, but I must pray that His proving me may not become a satanic temptation: lead me not into (paradoxical) temptation, but deliver me from evil! It is folly to take the instrument which God uses for disciplining and to convert it into one for building up, or for cultivating a field. It is folly to convert a disciplinary device with which God can humble my arrogance into a means of education by which He can in His school teach me the genuine elemental relationships existing between things. It is folly to oppose the salutary effect of shame caused by ignorance (in paradoxical conflict) after the conflict (for then the shame follows) by regarding ignorance as normal. The abnormal — my sin — is indeed broken by the disciplinary means of God's proving, but this last remedy of dis-

---

1. Page 234.

cipline must not be praised and glorified as the normal bread of life.[1]

It is this last consideration which is the error of those who proclaim that as long as the world and time exist, the paradoxical is normal inasmuch as God is "wholly different" from man. Overagainst this thesis we maintain that God goes give us a sense of His revelation in our human life, causes it to bear fruit in our human life, inasmuch as in this life we are aware of communion with Him as conscious human beings and enjoy such communion. Now we want to add that those who take this attitude can never ascribe the paradox to the revelation which God gives, or to the manner in which that revelation is given. Clashing with these paradoxes arises from our limitation, our weakness, our perdition, but not from God. It may be true that He humiliates us by this means, and "mocks" us as dwarfs who in our proud journey have gone astray in the forest of paradox in which we, like so many children, have been overtaken by darkness. But His is not the guilt for our straying; for His revelation was one. If we were to accept the paradox as a fate, a fate which God as the Creator and Revealer has laid upon us from the time of Paradise to the end of time, we would not have believed in the unity of God's thoughts and works or in the unity of His being, or in the unity of His revelation. Then we would have been taking an attitude of doubt, an unbelieving point of view, towards the transparency and manifest character and unity which, according to these themselves, characterize the Holy Scriptures. Then we would be taking a critical attitude towards the belief that the Scriptures are adequate, not to "solve" all kinds of scientific problems, but adequate to lead us as religious people to the goal which religion puts before us.

If we carry these thoughts to Golgotha, we will be able to understand what the response of Christ must have been to these things. God had never taken an arrogant attitude towards God, and hence

---

1. For then we forget that the disciplinary remedy of proving (a) coincides with a satanic temptation in the form of an act of war; (b) that, from God's point of view, this remedy is applied at all because I have recognized the revealed Word too little, and must be driven back to it now. The first of these was no part of the Christ (not sufficiently recognizing the Word before the paradoxical conflict); but it is true of us. Because of that He must make atonement for us as our Surety now; therefore He must by means of the conflict of paradox work His way back and up to the Word. For this purpose the Word first had to be broken into pieces: text "against" text.

He at no time could for a single second countenance the thesis
that God had spoken to us unplainly, or that God had plainly contradicted Himself, or that He had talked to us in a way we could
not understand. The Saviour never found rest in the experience
of paradox; for such an experience cannot represent a Sabbath-
experience; and the spirit of Christ longed for the great Sabbath-
rest with the Father of all spirits Himself. The appearance of paradox cannot arise from the positive will of God. As long as this
plagues Him "His heart is burning within Him." The content of
God's speaking is a single, undivided thing. Consequently He
must take His paradoxes to the Scriptures, even if it was the
Scripture itself which had placed the paradoxical problem before
Him.

We even dare to accept the thesis that Christ in the conflict by
means of which He would consume Satan's temptation[1] and deliver His thoughts from the burden of paradox, was pointed solely to the revealed Word, solely to that revealed Word. His Messianic consciousness was not a superb, divine knowledge, which He
had taken along out of heaven, and which, for the rest, at no point
touched on His human thinking. It was not a naive intuition,
which could stand as a second factor in the motivations of His
life beside the Scriptures as a first factor. Every attempt to "explain" these matters in that way must necessarily lead us back to
the manner of thinking alluded to above,[2] which ascribes Christ's
human obedience in part to His divine obedience; but the divine
excludes obedience; God does not obey. No, when Christ entered
the world, grew up into a lad, a youth, a man, when He suffered
and died, He had to be satisfied with what was His in the Scriptures. The doctrine of the adequacy (*de sufficientia*) of the Scriptures takes on new glamour and new depth if we look upon it as
being the spiritual property also of the true man Jesus Christ. The
second Adam could learn from the Scriptures that obedience, that
the fulfillment of the commandments, was pure religion; and He
could also learn that religion is always communion with the
Father. Moreover, He could learn from the Scriptures that the

---

1. A struggle, too — this time of Satan: See Cremer-Kogel, Bibl.-theol. Wtchch.
d. Neut. Gräz. 10, p. 914, for the difference in the original between *dokimazein*
and *peirazein*. This must not be regarded as a purely intellectual struggle by
reason of paradoxical temptation, but as a battle for life.
2. Page 285.

unique human life which could confess every moment that it had kept the commandments could only be the life of the one Messiah for whom the centuries had waited, and to whom the Great Mission had been given by the Father. Thus Christ, confessing with a blessed joy His own sinless existence every day, and confessing with blessed joy His own perfect faithfulness to the commandments, could move upwards knowing with certainty that He had to be the great elect, the Messiah, the second Adam, He who had been called from eternity to the great labor of redemption, to the law of the covenant of grace.

In very truth, then, the Scriptures were adequate to Him. His Messianic self-awareness was conditioned by their adequacy, and *vice versa*. The adequacy of the Scriptures, was, we can say, His great axiom, His first and great conviction and belief. Because of this it was impossible for Him to look upon a paradoxical experience as being normal, and impossible for Him to find peace in such an experience for even a moment. And when the passion of that paradox came upon Him, along the one route on which it could accrue to Him, the way of descent into hell, the way of being the exlex without the gate, He — this was His obedience, and thus He became our Surety — exerted all His living effort[1] to take exception to that paradoxical experience. But the effort He exerts is an exertion of obedience. Thus do the Scriptures drive Him to the Scriptures; thus words impel Him to the Word. "Comparing Scripture with Scripture" — that is what took place here. The wrestling of Psalm 42 in which the soul admonishes the soul and the spirit the spirit was absolutely fulfilled in Him there.

Now we shall not ask further to what extent His divinity supported His humanity on this occasion. We believe that it did, but we can never say a word about the manner in which this took place. It does not grieve us that we are unable to say anything about it, for we cling to the heartening knowledge that in His humanity, that in His being Adam, He had enough not only to be susceptible to the confusion accruing to Him as a paradox from the outside, but also by the exerted strength of His perfect religion to assert Himself against it, and to fight against it so puissantly

---

1. See note 1 on p. 294.

and effectively that He finally gave voice to that super-paradoxical: amen!

Amen — "It shall certainly be so!"

Now there are some who abandon this Scriptural chain of thought in favor of entangling themselves in such poetry of the Middle Ages as, by means of a false science of esthetic, an unspiritual eroticism, compared Christ to a nightingale singing a song in the May-tree, or warbling because He cannot do otherwise in the joyous May of His natural, native, impersonal, unspiritually apprehended love — a song of love[1] for that poor "murderer" hanging next Him. For he who abandons the other interpretation in favor of such a phantasy has bartered the riches of God's truth and the riches of a truly architecturally constructed dogmatics[2] for a poor and helpless science of esthetic.

Perhaps someone will call this a singular unbosoming. It is. But it can be explained on the basis of our firm conviction that this is the only way we can believe in an amen-relationship[3] which has, by means of a proving[4] of the second Adam, been put in the fire of refinement; this is the only way we can believe in such an amen-relationship between God and the Christ as the head of the covenant of grace, as the Great Maintainer of the covenant of works.

Now we want to see the dogma converted into a poem; now, by losing the paradoxes,[5] we would gain them. For the "amen" which the Christ addressed to the murderer is fully informed by glorious contrasts; but, since we understand the background, we know that these contrasts have their deeper unity in Himself, and in God, and in the Word.

We can say that the "amen" of the Saviour is: first, although full of tension, nevertheless very "ordinary"; second, although empirically it may be regarded as a moment of experience, Scripturally it may be regarded as sound doctrine; third, although it is super-paradoxical, it is humbly believing; fourth, although uttered

---

1. *Christ in His Suffering*, p. 269 f.; also see this volume, chapter 14.
2. A dogmatics which has left ample room in it for this "mystery."
3. Probationary command!
4. To be "proved" again presently from God's side by the darkness which lasted for three hours; to be discussed later.
5. Not now, naturally, in the strict sense in which paradox was set aside above.

by the emptied Christ, it is an expression of the perfected, plero-matic Messiah; fifth, although uttered by one who was com-pletely broken, it is a cry of triumph. We pause to consider each of these predications.

We said that although Christ's "amen" is full of tension, it is very "ordinary." By this we mean, that as He saw it, it was per-fectly "natural." It has become apparent long ago that it is full of tension; it represented a cry of triumph after a paradoxical conflict; and it is to be followed very shortly by a "why" of utter distress. The "amen" may therefore be said to be situated between two wars. On the other hand, it is also very "ordinary"; for in all this, we have seen the Christ as a true man, who in order to utter this "amen", needed nothing more than that which God had given to every man: namely, the Word, and for the rest the revelation of God in the history of life. Everything in this wilderness conse-quently was as common and usual as was every moment in Para-dise for Adam. Perhaps we can say that Christ did not stand up before our astonished eyes on the stage of Golgotha in order to fulfill His calling there in a mystery drama motivated by divine knowledge and kept poised by a super-natural strength, but He proved in all these things to be true man. We have not seen His Messianic self-awareness as a detached mental construction which always lay fully explained before His mind's eye, and which He had taken with Him ready-made from God's hidden council, or by way of recollecting the council of peace which from eternity and all times had been set up between the Father and the Son. No, Christ had no means at His disposal which the first Adam did not have. We have seen the Christ as a true man who in His Messianic self-awareness in the last analysis had sufficient for Himself on this day, and as a servant had to have enough for Himself in the two data: the Scriptures, and His perfect, self-confessed, histori-cally manifested obedience. We can say, therefore, that Christ as Servant, as Mediator, entered into the most difficult of battles in no other armor than suited Him every day. He fought as man; what God was to do besides, in order to support Him, that was God's prerogative and work; but He, from His own side, did not reckon in terms of that. In this most unusual, and unnatural hour, He remained "usual" and ordinary. Then He uttered His "amen" and the utterance was not foisted upon human experience by divine knowledge; nor was the "amen" an "aristocratic" gesture of certainty on the part of one who without super-human strength could not have rescued His spiritual property, but it was the expression of one who was true man, and who made use of no armor which had not been given Him at His birth as a servant and a man.

Therefore we can say that this "amen" of the Christ in the last analysis is a maintenance of what, three years ago — at the beginning of the ministration of His office — He had told the devil. Then, three years ago, when Satan tempted Him in the wilderness —no people were present at the time—Satan told Him: Leap down from the pinnacles of the temple, and they will believe you. Satan said: Perform an ostentatious sign, a miracle, and they will believe you without the cross. But Christ said: "My "amen-relationship" with God prevents me from doing that; get thou behind me, Satan, hallelujah, amen! Today the situation, but with a sharper delineation of the problem now, recurs. Again there is the voice; no, there are many voices, there is a chorus of voices, of human voices, saying to Him: Come down from the cross, and we will believe you; perform a miracle, expressive of unusual might, and we will believe you. This time the problem is a more difficult one. These are not devils, but these are men; and that aggravates the situation, as we have seen before.[1] In the second place, the cross can no more be evaded, for the cross is here now. Only death can be avoided. However, the problem may be more complicated and the tension severer, but it is the same old problem, the same problem now which existed then. The question is this one: Will Christ by an ostentatious miracle, cut loose from utter obedience, request and earn faith in Himself. This helps us to understand His answer for the first time. It is the answer which He has given during three years of discoursing, and it is the answer which He is giving now by silence. The answer is: It is written: Thou shalt not tempt the Lord thy God. To Him this means: Thou shalt not perform any extraordinary miracles, any miracles not written in the revealed Word; Thou must accommodate Thyself to the lowly, to the ordinary, to the things written in the daily program of the kingdom of heaven, to the extremely "common"

---

1. Pages 226-28.

attitude of one who simply does his duty, and cares to know no more than that.

Christ did not "tempt" God, but chose the "ordinary" way. He kept choosing it also as He hung mute while suffering the mockery of hell. As He did so, He saw the way lying clear ahead of Him. It was the way of very ordinary things. By that route He arrived at His "hallelujah" and His "amen." The heavens quaked because of this "amen," but the heart of Jesus did not once beat faster because of it. On the contrary, His heart regained its normal equilibrium again precisely when He could utter the "amen," and his soul was the more ready to offer itself now to death. He who gives God room is able to breathe the more freely. This "amen" is fully informed by the conscious activity (the utter tension) and — let us use the predication very cautiously — the heavenly naivete (the very ordinary).

We said that, in the second place, the "amen" of Christ, although it can be designated empirically as a moment of experience, can also be designated Scripturally as the sound conclusion of sound reasoning. It is indeed a moment of experience; for while Christ was in the state of being forsaken, and of being rejected without the gate, He was in a state of extreme distress. Difficulties of experience crowded His hours and consumed His soul. Nevertheless, in order to save Himself, He must let the Scriptures speak, He must let all of the Scriptures address Him. The difficulties which the Scriptures themselves disclosed to Him, He solved by means of the Scriptures. In these His victory must have its point of departure. Just as Christ, a few days later, after His resurrection, will comfort those travelling to Emmaus, and will lead them to victory by admonishing them not to listen to a single statement of the Scriptures in reference to a specific event, but to let all the Scriptures witness about all the events, so He Himself now turned Himself to the whole of the Scriptures, and referred the whole of the Scriptures to the One Word. Between the one datum of the Scriptures which asserted that God cannot despise the absolutely faithful soul and the other Scriptural datum which asserted that He who was without the gate was to be legally despised no bridge seemed possible, and this, we said, seemed to us to be the paradox. Now Christ who for the sake of God and His own distress, had to bridge that gulf, proceeds to construct the bridge not by means of an abstract philosophy about possibility and non-possibility. Instead He allowed the Scriptures themselves to gather their data into a synthetic whole, and thus He climbed from one mountain top of Scriptural wisdom to the other by passing through the connecting valley of what was also Scriptural wisdom. "He was not foolish, and slow of heart to believe all that the prophets, all that the Scriptures had spoken aforetime." "Ought not Christ (the Messiah) to have suffered these things, and so (along this route) to enter into His glory?"[1] Yes, indeed, this all the Scriptures said. There had to be one, and that one the Messiah,[2] for whom forsakenness and abandonment would dig a gulf to acceptance, for whom the curse would be the route to the perfected blessing. Now all the days, and this last day also, and this last hour even, had been concluded with the perfect assurance: "I have kept all the commandments." Therefore He knew: There can be no other Messiah than I; hence for me utter distress can be the only way; utter abandonment the only method of acceptance. Thus He entered into the Scriptures and thus His "amen" was the result of His Scripturally authenticated wisdom.

In the third place, although Christ's "amen" is super-paradoxical, it is also humbly believing. He assumed the burden of the Scriptures and the Word. This had to be, this sank deeply into His soul today. It had to be, He sang to Himself in His soul. It was meet for God, He told Himself, and now He asks no further questions but believes along the way, along this route, His Messianic triumph must come. And He believes that He is being obedient when He, doing the work of the Messiah, opens wide the gate of heaven to a lost son of man who is praying in His ears. Hence He opens the door as King and nevertheless knows that He is servant. Just as even in this moment Christ still governs the world from heaven as the servant of the Lord, a servant in exaltation also, so, as a servant, He has the law-book open before His eyes, and the commandments of God in His heart. Thus it was that He uttered His "amen." That "amen" represented the self-control of the servant assuring himself that the work He had done was compatible with the counsel laid down in the Scriptures.

---

1. Compare Christ's statement to those who travelled to Emmaus.
2. A posteriori thinking about what God decided a priori. From the second conclusion (by God) to the first (by God), from the fruit to the root; practical piety, theology as religion.

In this again we see Christ transcending Moses, for Moses dashed the tables of stone to pieces. By this we mean that Moses not only robbed the sermons of confession of their text, but he also robbed his sermons of promise and comfort of their text *a priori*. Moses hurled the first proof of the Scriptures (the engraved tables of stone) away from him, and then he made the first great, "messianic"[1] attempt, the first messianically intended effort at substitutionary suffering. Hence Moses' offer of substitutionary suffering was in no sense to be authenticated as essentially religious. The experience of Moses was not legitimate, for it was not based upon the Scriptures; and that which was Scriptural in Moses (in reference to the substitutionary, messianic sacrifice) was not "experienced." But by means of genuinely human experience Christ gave a place to God's sound Word, and *vice versa*. He transcends the paradoxes, He emerges from them, because He, while steeped in them, searched all the Scriptures and pressed the tables of stone against Him. He did not neglect to read one jot or tittle.

Our fourth point, closely related to the third, was that Christ who utters His "amen" may be entirely emptied, and completely exhausted, but His Messianic self-awareness is pleromatic nevertheless. And He demonstrates that precisely by uttering the "amen." We must refer to Moses again. When he climbed the mountain to present his notion of satisfaction to God for further elaboration (mark the folly in those words), he could give the people nothing better than a "maybe." Before he climbed the mountain, he said: "Peradventure (perhaps) I shall make an atonement for your sin" (Exodus 32:30). Twice he used the "peradventure"; to men first, who had to hear him say it; and then to God, from Whom he must hear it said in order to be mediator. Yes, indeed, he even approaches God with nothing more than possibilities, not with certainties.[2] This man, this Moses, and his "peradventure" is contrasted now with the man who says "amen." "Amen" means sure and certain; but a "peradventure" leaves everything uncertain and unsure. Such is Moses. Not so Christ Jesus. He is completely exhausted, entirely emptied. In this con-

---

1. Moses is called "mediator" in the Bible; see this volume, p. 228-33.
2. The three plans: see p. 230.

nection that means that He is without any external semblance of persuasion, and without any externally attractive right of apology, and without any divinely immediate, uncontested certainty. And this Christ says not "peradventure" to the murderer, but "amen."

This is His Messianic fulfillment. Moses is like an architect who does not know how to find rhyme or reason in his own print. Moses had three plans, and had presented them all to God. But a master of architecture, a man who sees and dominates the purpose, the environment, the time and situation and elements of the house to be built, and whose spirit, moreover, is disposed to present a completely adequate blue-print for its erection, can only submit one such print; he would regard a second as an unbecoming experiment on his part. The better the architect, the stricter the form of the plan. Such an architect of God is Christ, and such a builder is He. He is the Master! He can only submit one plan; in this plan the unity of all the Scriptures and not only one specific idea of the Scriptures will be fully expressed. Hence He is the only one who can conquer the "peradventure" of Moses — and of others — by His curt "amen." It shall certainly be so; it cannot be otherwise; only in this way does this detail fit into the scheme of the Lord. Simply an "amen."

In the fifth place, although Christ is entirely broken, His "Amen" is a cry of triumph. He is entirely broken and beaten down. Even in spirit He is that. Hence He recognizes His "God as being God"; His "amen" consequently is in conformity with God because it is uttered in conformity with "all the Scriptures." At the same time, however, His "amen" arises from Himself (by a complete mastery, a complete appropriation and assimilation, of "all the Scriptures"). It is a triumph in which the slave who because of heaven has been rejected, can now introduce another person into heaven. He who has nothing more to say on the basis of His own worth or merit, to the extent these are a human phenomenon, has nevertheless so absolutely included and worked His way into the legal status of things that He, in the hour in which He knows Himself to be the accused, does the work of the judge. Having begun as servant, He concludes as Judge. He manifests to the lost person hanging beside Him all the majesty of the Judge, of one who is in charge of heaven's throne. He pronounces His simple "amen" and then proceeds to bleed until He is quite empty.

Yes, this vision is also an "esthetic" one, and is full of tenseness, but this is an esthetic which has conformed itself to prophecy, and which could not depart from it. God shines through Golgotha, that perfection of ugliness, most dazzingly. My Lord and my God!

For all these reasons we know that Christ is now in a state of triumph. Paul teaches us in the second chapter of the Philippians that Christ was lifted up as a reward for His humiliation. But that exaltation began on Golgotha. This "amen" is a glimpse of His Messianic glory. No wonder. Now that He has Himself by means of His struggle gained everything from the hand of the Judge, the Revealer of all the Scriptures, He can celebrate the triumphs of His "amen." The day of His death in other moments, too, permits Him to reach out ahead to the exaltation in the very moment of humiliation.[1]

Thus in Jesus Christ the paradoxical humiliation earned its perfect logical exaltation. He hurled the "amens" of the angels[2] who go before, here on Golgotha, and so Himself became "the Amen."[3] By maintaining the Scriptures as a means of rescuing Him in His own thinking, He earned the right to inspire Scripture. The Logos, the incarnate Word, is standing here at the division between the Old and the New Testament. This Word incarnate long before this time, under the old covenant, had given the Scriptures of the Old Testament, but now He earns the right to do that as Christ, by being paradoxically tried because of the Scriptures, and by singing His super-paradoxical "amen" after the conflict of obediently following the Scripture.

Thus He according to His merits becomes the rightful inspirer (by His Spirit) of the New Testament, and also of the Old Testament. He earned the right to send out the Spirit, who inspired Scripture, as a gift given by Him; this right He earned because

1. Think, for instance, of Christ's surrender of His spirit to God, of the signs which accompany His dying, of the new grave in which no man had yet lain, of the third utterance of the cross (requisition) and of the fifth, in connection with John 19:28.
2. "Amen" also before the Lamb (Revelation 5:14); this must be taken in connection with the Lamb of Revelation 7:12; see Revelation 7:9, 10 also.
3. Revelation 3:14.

He was forsaken by the Spirit when He was in His human spirit and nevertheless, although abandoned, believed in the manifest character of the Scriptures. Moreover, as man and servant, He became really one with all His own, also in the absolute assimilation of God's Word. He earned the right to admonish the "foolish and slow of heart" on their way to Emmaus to search "all the Scriptures." He bore the Scriptures and loved them even when He Himself presented the problems. This is faith in God and in the Word: to know that God as the God of the Word proposes a riddle, and nevertheless to cling to Him. In the "amen" of Golgotha we have the breaking through of the Christ together with the Scriptures, with His own Scriptures, with His own God. It is the climax of perfect faith, breaking through the vicious circle of empirical appearance.

However, this hymn of praise still seems dangerous, immature, subject to pollution, for we have not answered one of the questions which we originally proposed. We have refused to say that the "amen" of Christ seems to be worth so little. It was easy for us to praise Christ as having transcended Moses, because Christ says "amen" and Moses "peradventure." But all those words do not take away the fact that Christ — and this is the question we have not answered — after a few hours again gives expression to His "why." Then He utters a "why" in which His "amen" sinks to a plane lower than that of Moses' brave "peradventure." Again we ask, Did the "why" of the fourth utterance from the cross completely supplant the "amen" of the second, did it completely push the second aside and empty it of its triumphal content? Can all those doxologies which we have just been singing about the Christ be sustained as we consider the bitter "why," as we consider the "Why hast Thou forsaken?"

Indeed it is true from a human point of view that Christ's "why" is an annihilation of His monumental "amen." But He who relates His thoughts by means of faith's assumption to the Scriptures, also to the question of the relationship and coherence between Christ's experience and Christ's faith in the Scriptures will find the solution to that problem also. The fact that Christ triumphs now in His "amen," and sinks to a very humiliating plane again in His "why" cannot be due to Him, as He is in the moment of His confident "amen." The cause of this descent must necessarily lie in the external circumstances. Something new must have intervened; not He, but "the situation" must have changed.

If you seize on this thread in the maze you will be guided to a vantage point from which a very wide perspective is opened to you, and you will marvel anew at the sublime style, the divine harmony, which fully informs the history of the passion of Christ. Then you will see that Christ was twice placed in the sieve; once without a direct act coming from the outside, and once because of an intentional, and if you will "mechanical," intervention of a new force coming from without, which struck Him down in order to test Him again on the question of His utter obedience.

In order to make our meaning clear we shall have to go back for a moment. When Christ was oppressed and grieved in Gethsemane, He, all alone, had to fight out the conflict and master it within the walls of His own soul's dwelling place. Only after He had been attacked within (without the intervention of people or powers coming from without) and only when He had conquered there,[1] did the externally accruing trials come upon Him. The secret of Christ's sorrows in Gethsemane arose not from the fact that fetters were binding Him from the outside, but from the fact that He was putting the problem to Himself, and was struggling with it, and was solving it in faith. And only when His own spirit had escaped the bonds did the murderer descend upon Him from without in order to take Him captive.

Another line ran parallel to this one. In Gethsemane Christ first had to force His blood out of Himself by a process which began within and worked to the outside. Only after that was the blood driven from Him by human hands. Only then did the influence coming from without, working to the inside, accrue to Him (the scourging, after the sweating of blood). Each time, consequently, that He carries a conflict which arises within the walls of His own spirit to its goal, to its end in faith, there follows the distress which comes from the outside, and which steeps Him in distress anew. Christ must treat all His fundamental problems twice, and must conquer them twice; the first time He must do this without, and the second time He must do this with mechanical force.

---

1. *Christ in His Suffering,* pp. 369-372.

Such is the law of the conflict of paradox. First this conflict accrued to Him without "anything strange" (something that did not belong to the schedule, to the program of the day). The mockery, the dice, the scoffing laughter, alas, these all accompanied the cross. These could have come to Isaiah, to Peter, or to anyone. True, there was a problem in all these things for Christ, but it was a problem which He Himself had to sense, which He Himself had to ponder, and which He Himself had to solve. This He did by making the events of the day paradigms and revelations of infinite necessity and its law. He followed the conflict to its conclusion in His own soul's dwelling place and thus arrived at the utterance of His "amen." But then it is necessary that a strange, mechanically intervening force thrust Him back into that same struggle, and then it is necessary that this force come from the outside. This new intervening movement coming from without is the darkness of three hours which we shall discuss later. Up to this time the darkness was not present. That which came upon the Christ from the outside was, once the sentence and the cross were given, a very "ordinary" thing. They could be "expected"; these people, their spikes, their words, their gestures could be expected. If Christ Himself had not borne them into hell, Golgotha, as far as the external things were concerned, would have witnessed nothing unusual. Then all the events would have flowed logically from what had gone on before.

But now it is God's turn. Now a mechanical force comes down from above. This is something which does not lie in the natural course of things or in the "logic" of the events. The sun covered itself; a miracle took place. Nature also set up its camp against the Son, robbed Him of the gift of Diogenes, the gift of all paupers. He was allowed a light no longer. For three long hours the order of nature opposed itself to Christ. Darkness came at noon.

In this God cast Him back into the conflict a second time. The paradoxical stress returned. Again the struggle to cling to the knowledge of His righteousness before God against the appearance of things recurs. He utters a bitter "why" after three long hours. Ah, how distressed He is! First He had reconciled the "ordinary" course of actual history as He had endured it up to

this time overagainst the revelation of the Scriptures and the revelation of events. Now this new element comes, this darkness!
It referred to the beginning of the Scriptures, for light was called
into being by God's first created word; it referred to the beginning
of history, for God begins the course of history by calling light
into being; it referred to the beginning of common grace, that
course of life which came after the advent of sin, for the first
miracle after the fall was that the sun continued to shine! And
now He is being proved by this very first thing. The sin of Adam
could not put a stop to the shining light, and could not extinguish
the lamps, but God darkens the sun for Him. Thus God calls into
question His right to life and light, His demonstrability, His
right to the privilege of the poorest of men; thus God proves the
Son by means of a paradoxical appearance a second time. Paradox again, yes, not in Jesus' own soul this time, but in the most
general revelation of God, in nature, and in His own most special
and most recent experience. This is a catastrophe caused not by
nails and spikes but by the deeds of Genesis I. And in this second
struggle which covered the same difficulties as the first Christ had
to triumph again, and in such a way that He eventually can say:
It is finished. By that He will mean that the program, the schedule, the sequence of events has been maintained, that nothing
strange has accrued to Him. Father, into Thy hands I commend
my spirit.

   In this way we arrive at the legal intention and dispensation,
at a delineation of the historical place of the darkness which lasted
three hours. It seems to be an irregular hiatus in the pulsing activity of Golgotha; nevertheless it now demonstrates the awful
harmony, the divine style of the day of the great sacrifice. Thus
we arrive at an answer to the annoying question which we have
been putting, to Christ's "why." Now we can answer, and can
state the reason for which the "why" of Christ does not make His
"amen" worthless, and does not supplant it by vitiating it. Our
answer is: It does not! The "why" did not destroy His "amen,"
but confirmed it, and is an evidence of the fact that God recognized Him. For God was awaiting that "amen" before He could
oppress the soul of Christ by means of His externally interjected
darkness. First the Son had to endure the struggle alone; and

when He had really defeated Satan within the walls of His own soul's dwelling place, and by means of a self-achieved and puissant "amen" He had stunned the devil, then God could introduce His darkness. This He could do, not to tempt the Son, but to prove Him.[1] Christ puts His "why" overagainst His silence in that first "organic" process, and overagainst that second, mechanically imposed process. Overagainst Christ's "amen" as the conclusion of the first immanent process of the plague stand His sixth and seventh utterances from the cross as the triumph over the second process of paradoxical spiritual struggle.

Now the fourth statement from the cross is more intelligible to us. There is a harmony now between the two abysses of Christ's humiliation and abandonment; it is a harmony determined by the strictest necessity and by the austerest divine style.

We can say, then, that the "amen" of the Lord Jesus Christ was purchased at a precious price. It unchained, it set loose, the last power of annihilation which sought Him from without and which was kindled against Him, bent on consuming Him. The divine command, "Sword, arise against this shepherd," had been forced to wait for this dynamic "amen," as evidence of the fact that the first struggle, the immanent conflict, had been completed. Only then did God (figuratively speaking) stop the sun in its course, and drive the clouds together over Jesus' triumphantly lifted head. Yes, indeed, the "murderer" was compelled a little later to believe in a Saviour who asked His "why's." That is what we said a moment ago. But there was no other way of salvation open to Him save this way of foolishness.

For us, too, there is no other way than this one. We have advisedly been attempting in the last three paragraphs to enter into those abysses of the spirit out of which the fourth utterance from the cross had to be borne. This had to be the case. The descent into hell is not a separate activity which we can limit to the three

---

1. From this it also becomes apparent that the period circumscribed by the first trio of utterances from the cross (socially considered) delineates the descending (struggling) and the ascending (the amen) line, and that thereupon the second period, circumscribed by the four last statements from the cross (considered only in reference to Christ Himself) gives expression to the same descending (fourth and fifth) and ascending line (sixth and seventh) (the fifth constitutes the transition).

hours of darkness during which God closed the doors, but is the drama itself. Perdition may come upon the head of the Son of man by means of never so many leaps and catastrophes, by means of never so sharp a contrast of convulsions overagainst calm devastation and thus develop both inside and outside of Him, but the descent into hell never becomes one of the activities in the drama; it becomes the drama itself.

And in this drama Christ is compelled to fight out the controversies twice: first in the microcosm, the little world of His created humanity; then in the macrocosm, the great world in which the play will begin with the action of the Son and with nothing less cosmical than that.

Consequently, Thou hast not yet done, Thou who utterest the "amen" in the house of Satan. Thou wilt have to suffer unspeakably for this confident "amen." This is the hour in which death demands its consequences. These had never been granted it, nor the one who drove death on: namely, Satan. Thus the sorrow moves from within to the outside, and from without to the inside. Consequently the Son is quite alone, for He is suffering consequences; and the consequences have ever been withheld until now. We, too, O Saviour, cannot follow Thee. We shall leave Thee alone. But speak a simple "amen" in our ears. That will be enough for us; and that will be enough for Thee. Whisper Thy "amen," before the hour has elapsed, for today Thy "amen" is no longer being contested. The sun of the Passover continues to shine; there it is always mid-day. Set us as a seal upon Thy arm; for, amen: it certainly shall be! No matter how high distress may arise, Thou wilt destroy the head of the enemy, and annihilate every dragon. In all this Thou art more than conqueror through Him whom Thou hast loved. Amen, yea, amen!

Yes, indeed, we too want to shout "amen" very vigorously. He has taught us this Himself; He has given us this Himself. However, our giving does not correspond to His. Nevertheless this does not rob us of our comfort. Give Him His honor in the dynamic of "amen-saying" — and give us for Christ's sake the grace of the amen-relationship, O God of all grace and comfort. For the Son of God, Jesus Christ, who was preached among us, was not yea and nay, because He was "amen" and "why" — yes, both

of those and in righteousness. "Why" and "nay" are not identical;
they are to be essentially distinguished. Thus He was to us yea
in Him. For all the promises of God in Him are yea, and in Him
amen.[1] This the amen, the true and faithful witness, now made
manifest as the beginning of the creation of God:[2] Amen, thou
with me in Paradise.

1. See II Corinthians I:19, 20.
2. See Revelation 3:14.

Christ Confronting the Dead Judas With the Dead Scoundrel

CHAPTER FOURTEEN

Christ Confronting the Dead Judas With the Dead Scoundrel

> *And he said unto Jesus, Lord, remember me*
> *when thou comest into thy kingdom.*
> *And Jesus said unto him, Verily I say unto*
> *thee, Today shalt thou be with me in Paradise.*
>
> LUKE 23:42-43.

IN OUR first volume, and again in our third,[1] we alluded for a moment to a legend of the Middle Ages according to which the Saviour was likened to a "nightingale" which sings a song of pure "love" in the May-tree of the cross. And we did not neglect to deny every attribute of genuine beauty to such a "vision" because the true significance of the crucified Christ and the power of His love is denied in it. Will it still be necessary for us, after the immediately preceding chapters, to develop our objections to such a legend further? We do not think so. We pay attention now to the second utterance from the cross;[2] it was directed to the scoundrel who was hanging beside Christ. That singer of the Middle Ages also gave attention to this theme:

> The nightingale is singing
> Out of the thorny tree;
> His heart is full of loving,
> He sings for you and me.
> The rapist cried, Peace I pray,
> And he was given the prize.
> The nightingale sings on: Today
> With me in Paradise.

But we shall not contend against this any longer. We merely repeat that the love of Christ was not a natural emotion seeking

---

1. See *Christ in His Suffering*, p. 269; also this volume, p. 296.
2. We shall not discuss further the "verily" of verse 43, inasmuch as chapter 13 dealt with that.

an outlet in *self-satisfaction;* it is official, personal religion. His is not an uncritical love, but one which very critically distinguishes and separates the various relationships.

The love of Christ is a distinguishing, a discriminating love. For Christ, hanging between the two malefactors, accepts the one and not the other. Two condemned shall be dying on the hill of a single cross: "The one shall be taken, and the other left." You see that there is distinction, selection here. Christ who is today being confronted by the dead Judas[1] in the other world, presents Himself at the beginning of the session of the gods[2] of the universe in the company of a dead scoundrel. He asks the privilege of speaking first and He takes that privilege. He says: Give me Judas; I confront the dead Judas with this dead bandit. And He let all the gods hold their peace. A hand wrote an awful word on the wall: the sovereign good pleasure. The devils grimly suppressed their wrath; they had no apology to present.

Well, then, for the sake of Christ, we shall consider first the scoundrel and his embarrassed questioning.

I hear someone say: Be very careful in your treatment of that brother-scoundrel. He mingled fragrant incense with the stinking vapours of hell; into these he introduced the sweet incense of prayer. However we must say that the offering he gave was exceedingly meager. Thoughtful Christians may not make the prayer of this man more beautiful than it is. Those who say this are quite right, and it is to be hoped that they really wish what they say. We may not forget that this time the nard was contained in an ugly vial; the bottle had not been rinsed before it had been filled. Unclean thoughts. Confused ideas. Inadequate elaboration of saving grace. The contents are none too good.

But there is the form! God likes beautiful forms. But in this respect, also, everything is equally meager. The voice is a crude voice, the face is distorted, the spirit giddy, and the hands are not even folded. One almost feels like joining in with the Pharisees who, a few days before His death,[3] asked Jesus whether He was actually going to be charmed by the prattle of children. "Hearest Thou what these say?" they ask in disgust. And, adopting their

---

1. *Christ on Trial*, pp. 239-259.
2. See Psalm 82.
3. Christ in His Suffering, p. 133 ff.

manner, we at first sight would ask: "Hearest thou what that fellow says? It is but the grumbling of a scoundrel. Say now, canst Thou take the man seriously?"

And that is but the form of the prayer. But alas, the content, the essence of the prayer! Is it really prayer? Yes, someone hastens to say, I am sure that it is; for his approach is very beautiful. He calls Jesus: Lord. In saying this, one, however, forgets that there are manuscripts which have the word "Jesus" instead of the designation "Lord." In these we read: "Jesus, remember me, when Thou comest into thy kingdom." But the mere use of this name and nothing more does not warrant the inference that this speaker thought through the salutation of the prayer by a sound logic and in fidelity to the revealed truth.[1]

Yes, someone now adds, but the man certainly shows unusual courage by confessing Jesus and by asking a favor of Him. Surely, by putting his body and soul into Jesus' hand he was acknowledging to the judges and the people that he found Christ beautiful and good. He blesses the One whom they curse; he calls aloud to Him as to the lord of a definite kingdom, to the very One whom the Jewish authorities have thrown outside of the gate. Can it be that such a protest against these judges is not a virtue? Is it not an act of faith on his part to choose against his people, and to oppose the man who is hanging crucified with him by asking him why he does not stop reviling Jesus?

Thus there are some who wish to infer from all these things that the prayer of this man was truly a prayer. In response to this we must reply that these particulars as such by no means constitute evidence for the ethical quality of the murderer or for his piety and religious sense. This man had lived for years by way of protest against judges, against a majority, against the half plus one. Very likely the man was one of the many rebels against the Roman authority; in any case, he was one who had never taken very nicely the attitude of the majority and of the intent of the government. As a matter of fact, he had always been among the objectors. Hence the fact that he is opposing the people at the foot of the cross by no means constitutes evidence of a sincere repentance. Jesus had better be careful, we would almost anxiously advise

---

1. Even this reading (punctuation) is not definitely ascertained.

Him: there are so many people who agree with Thee simply and solely because they like to disagree with others. Who, consequently, can infer from his opposition that this murderer appreciated the mystical union?

We know that the man asks Jesus to remember him when He has come into His kingdom. With respect to that, we would say that if we write the text on a little piece of paper and then examine it carefully without thinking of Christ Jesus who replies to it, what it says tells us nothing about the soul of this murderer. It might very well have been selfishness which induced him to say a good word for Jesus, or to ask for a safe place.[1] We know them all too well — the people who during their lives have no regard for the rights of others and then when their own hour is at hand are extremely anxious for themselves. Try to imagine Jesus' answer as not extant, and you will be able to exploit the question of the embarrassed rascal by writing a gripping chapter of a book, entitled: *De mortibus persecutorum*. Being interpreted, that means "Those who let blood" — and how anxious they sometimes feel when approaching their death. But, yes, take the favorable position that the man had good intentions and that he really wanted to honor Christ and not only safeguard himself. Even then the thing that motivates him may merely be an "impression" and an impression received at the last moment. What a moment to receive an impression! Jesus, mother Mary — we still know the exclamations — and do we not all have reasons for mistrusting that man? We read that both of those who were crucified with Christ when they first were hanged reviled Jesus[2] just as did the others. These murderers also asked the question pertaining to *might*: they also inquired whether Jesus would be able to give freedom. And now — is that one murderer changing sides? He keeps back his reviling; he takes thought; he ponders the question concerning the might of Jesus; and finally comes out with a servile question in which that same issue of Jesus' might is again lurking around the corner. There is to be a kingdom, and the ruler of that kingdom will be able to hand out good positions. Strange, is it not, that it is again the consideration of might which comes to the

---

1. We shall consider the question itself presently.
2. In our opinion Matthew 27:44 when compared with Mark 15:32 does not admit of a different interpretation.

foreground? What about considerations of justice? Christ, remember Thy forgotten chapter.[1] Yes, we know, the man is praying a prayer. To pray, according to the Greek, means to ask, but
according to the Greek text all that we know is that the man said
something. The account could not possibly give a more neutral
impression. Can it be said in any sense that the man's request has
the earmarks of virtue? Be careful, people! In any other case
you would shrug your shoulders and at best leave the matter in
God's hands. We know that the time in which the murderer might
have proved the integrity of his prayer was not allowed him. Very
soon he must believe in a dead Saviour, we said.[2] But even now
all generations must believe in the life of the dead murderer.

The matter becomes even more dubious when we pause to consider the words which the man spoke. He is talking about a kingdom, about a kingdom of Jesus. What can he possibly mean by
that? The disciples for three long years were willing to open their
ears to the words of Christ and, nevertheless, after that time they
still had such foolish and impossible ideas about the kingdom of
Christ. That being the case this man certainly will have very
strange notions about the nature of that kingdom. He sees something very vaguely at a distance. But a clear recognition of the
reality God has in mind and is even now busy creating, the man
did not have. This becomes specially evident from the fact that of
all the questions about Jesus the one point he raises first is the
very same which has been in the foreground throughout. During the process of the trial of Jesus, to the extent he heard of it
on the way to the place of crucifixion and afterward, he has repeatedly heard the issue of Jesus' might spoken of; we have referred to that before. Can He, or can He not? That was the question. He is called a king; then let Him come down from the cross.
The charge against Him was suspended over Jesus' head. That,
too, contained a reference to the alleged kingship. There was not a
man who believed in it. At first he himself did not, and now that
he finally does believe it, he, like a typical man (it is 19 centuries
ago), thinks — well, perhaps a case of arrogant rebellion against
the majority. Very likely the man was one who claimed time and

---

1. The priesthood; the satisfaction: see *Christ on Trial*, p. 428 f; also this
volume, p. 256.
2. J. van Andel, "De Avondster," p. 172; see also this volume, p. 278.

again that right belongs to those who are rejected by the majority. All rebels and revolutionaries begin their speeches that way. But what, concretely considered, is the kingdom of which he is talking in the dire stress of his death? We do not know. We do know that one important word is not mentioned here. The word "priest" is not named. The priest-king[1] of Zechariah 6 — that is far, far beyond his sight.

In addition, the man speaks of "remembering." Jesus, remember me when Thou comest into Thy kingdom. What is the significance of that word? We can say this to begin: he makes the "remembering" indefinite, does not limit it to a specific time. Even if he had been thinking of a messianic kingdom he would not have dared to look for its coming until Jesus after many miracles would have arisen over his cross-knolls and king's graves and Caesar's thrones. When that will be? He prefers to leave the time indefinite. Moreover the use of the word "remembering" warrants the suspicion that his notion of the Lord Jesus Christ was still very vague and confused. For it does seem that the request to "remember" him may mean a prayer for a "good" position in that new kingdom.[2] In that case we could make this the point of connection to which to fasten the contention that he saw the Messiah, and not merely one of the harbingers or saints — in Jesus. But if it was intended so, we should certainly think that he was beginning to dicker for an honorary position a little too abruptly and early; then his longings would immediately have soared in a flight which is hardly appropriate to his embarrassment. Moreover the prudence we ascribe to this man can be appreciated better as a request for intercession. The word "remember," then, must be regarded rather as a petition for a "good word" than for a "good position." Something of the concept of intercession shines through his petition. Jesus must serve as his intercessor with God, for he has nothing to lose any more save that one thing which men call everything. But what are the implications of that? We know that many Galilean mothers brought their children to Jesus in order that the rabbi of Nazareth might place his hands on them and bless them. These women proceeded on the assumption that Jesus was able to put in

---

1. *Christ on Trial*, pp. 429-432.
2. Think of the familiar question put by Salome in the interests of her two children.

a good word with God.[1] Now this request that He intervene between God and them, amounted, of course, to a virtual ignoring of Christ's own authority as the Messiah to forgive sins and to take over the kingdom. Just so, now, this malefactor in his confused thinking may have looked upon Jesus as an upright man[2] who because of His pure life and unusual holiness enjoys the special favor of God. Such a Jesus, then, could serve as his intercessor. But that he recognized the Messiah in Jesus, the Messiah who in virtue of His own justice and merits governed the keys of the kingdom is a fact which is by no means evident from the words which he speaks.

What we want to say, therefore, is that the prayer is by no means perfect. Even though it is possible to discover the essence of true prayer in the words, we must also say that Christ was able to detect the bad odors of sin in the fragrant incense of the petition. Remnants of the old man, the foolishness of a diseased theology (if indeed a "theology"), and the earmarks of human misunderstanding characterized it. Now if anyone, whether somewhat angry or not, should ask us why we choose to emphasize all this so pronouncedly, this would be our reply: It is not our intention to take anything pleasant out of the picture. But we must ask what the source of the pleasantness is, and how we can discover it. Phantasies are not pleasant on Golgotha. If the account is to become very dear to us, we must not let the embarrassed bandit say what we want to hear. That which the man asks might — if I simply exegete his own words — have been asked just as well by an unconverted man. His prayer, taken simply as it stands, does not contain a single bit of proof to show that this poor fellow who cannot even express himself in the vernacular of the visible church is a living member of that church, and a true believer in the Christ.

Only when we have told ourselves plainly that we cannot prove the virtue of this prayer by pointing to its own forms will we get something pleasant in return for that which was first subtracted from the picture.

Now it is our turn to explain. Fortunately, we cannot derive a bit of evidence from the malefactor himself for saying that his

1. Dr. F. W. *Grosheide, Kommentaar op Mattheus*, p. 228.
2. "This man hath done nothing amiss."

prayer was real and genuine; for the evidence lies in Christ. Not the unconfident word of a crucified malefactor, but the confident statement, the absolutely binding promise, of the Messiah is conclusive evidence for us that this corrupt son of Abraham was the object of the favor of grace. Christ accepts him. This means that Christ recognized him as His heir, and that is proof positive that the truths of eternal election have germinated here. Such fruit cannot be determined on empirical, psychological grounds and cannot be inferred from a prayer. This must be accepted on a basis of faith, and be believed on the basis of Christ's word of promise. Not a religious psychology, but the words, the promise, the statement of the Messianic awareness of the Saviour, provide the constructive answer to our problems. The amen of the answered prayer provides the exegesis to the amen-relationship of this praying malefactor who has not the amen-formula,[1] that gives the explanation of this bashful and embarrassed man who seeks refuge with a Jesus who has been put to shame. Be quiet, embarrassed brother; we believe the integrity of your prayer not because of you, but because of the Lord. We believe that Christ, under the paradoxical confusion of the developments of God's decrees ever and again, as He speaks of the decrees of the God of election, finds the sure bottom of His sovereign good pleasure. And we believe that on the basis of that He assigned you a place in Paradise. He gives His admission tickets to Paradise, only with the stamp of the foreordination of God on them. We learn nothing about this admitted applicant by following the bypaths and avenues of a psychological route; we learn everything along a theological road. This more than suffices us.

And now that we have discovered and acknowledged this new brother as a member of the mystical union of the second Adam, now, on this basis, we know that at bottom his protest against the people who reviled his king was not an assertion of his old nature, but a revelation of his new one. Now we know that although his prayer may have been mixed with the elements of a diseased theology that prayer also was in essence a true prayer. We know that he was broken by the Spirit of Jesus Christ and that his diseased brain would even "today" be given healing, the moment his puls-

---

1. See for an explanation of this "amen" and for the concept of the "amen-relationship," p. 273, 275.

ing heart had been silenced. Now we know that his exception to the people surrounding the cross included in itself a self-accusation; we know that although he did not "understand" Christ he did "know" Him, he accepted Him in faith as He truly is. We know that in the roots of his being he did not allow himself to be guided by the false light of his confused thinking, but that he vanquished such thought. He *surrendered* himself. To whom? To Christ. By what means? By the hearing of the preached word. Small bits of the revelation of Christ Jesus had fallen into his "heart." Was it not a beautiful thing that he joined himself with the very last things which he himself heard and saw in Jesus? Christ Himself, as intercessor, has revealed Himself as such in reference to His enemies, and His revilers, in His utterances from the cross which had immediately preceded this one. True, the malefactor understood very little of the eschatological and history-making significance of Christ's intercessory prayer. But so much he understood: a host of mockers and revilers on the one hand, and the vital and living energy of the intercession on the other. O God, he himself had been one of those who had reviled.[1] But God had placed the intercessor next to him, had given him spiritual support, spiritual sustenance — how shall we say it — God had looked upon him. And now he reflects upon the most recent revelation. At once he takes the initiative and lets himself be heard. At one leap he stands head and shoulders above the theologians of the nation. Thou, who art the intercessor for Thy murderers, I too am a murderer, I too. Be mine, also be mine. Give me the crumbs, Lord. They are still falling from the table of the children, are they not? Remember me, Jesus,[2] when Thou comest into Thy kingdom some day. Can it be that this man is thinking about Jesus in much the same way as Joseph thought about the butler when he asked the butler to remember him when he should presently be serving Pharaoh again? Ah, ask no such questions. There is such a thing as coming to God through Christ with our

1. Both Matthew and Mark report that the two crucified malefactors *reviled* Him: only of the one who hardened himself do we definitely read that he blasphemed (Luke).

2. The translation "Jesus" named possible in the discussion above is not being set down here with absolute certainty; see Nebe, *Leidensgeschichte*, volume 2, 1881, p. 266.

CHRIST CRUCIFIED

human heart. The man believed God and it was reckoned unto him for righteousness.

Was he converted, you ask? Surely, he is converting himself. When he first came here, he himself sanctioned that cry of the blood:[1] save thyself and us. A rude question, an unbelieving question, that. Now he speaks a different language. The great miracle must accrue to him now, not on this side of death but on the other side. The Christ must not help him down from the cross, but must bear him, cross and all, into His kingdom. See, he is already coming out of his byways and alleys and he will leave the matter of getting suitable clothing for the banquet to the King himself. He is going along at once, just as he is. Surely, this is progress, this is gain, this is development, and it comes all in a moment. This is to take refuge in the mediator of God and of murderers, this is to accept Christ just as He has revealed Himself. Can it be that he is exalting himself above his spiritual kin? Has he suddenly become too "important" to count himself a murderer? How can we say that? He is asking for nothing more than he knows Jesus is willing to give to — murderers! For he has understood the first utterance from the cross. That first statement from the cross was a prayer for the murderers, and now he is simply asking to share in the blessing which Christ had for murderers. Who can say, now, that he is nurturing pride? He is not denying his kin, for he takes his stand as one of those blood-thirsty ones, of those murderers. He does not choose a lofty vantage point, from which he, as a spiritual new-comer, arrogantly condemns others; and he is not active now, as we first deemed possible, in his old negativistic rôle. No, he just takes his place at the table of the condemned; he is satisfied to have Jesus give him something of that which He gave to those who crucified Him.

Yes, the answer recognizes the question. *Prayers* have been conceived and born. Prayers, for, according to the Greek text, the poor fellow prayed repeatedly. Jesus, Jesus, art Thou not listening yet; may I be in Thy kingdom? Dost Thou say nothing,

---

1. "Of the blood": Nebe points out (p. 258-9) "that (see our present volume, p. 151) the execution of these two may have been advanced somewhat, because they were eager to put Jesus to death quickly. In that circumstance it was for His sake that they now had to die, unexpectedly. This is a possibility with which we must reckon, inasmuch as it makes the reviling of both easier to understand and less demonic in character."

Jesus? I wanted to ask, wilt Thou be my intercessor there? Jesus, Jesus, Thou canst be mute so long, and, alas, I have deserved nothing; but wilt Thou remember me in Thy kingdom? Jesus of Nazareth, king of the Jews, I know very well, I can plainly see that Thou hast too much to be anxious about, but alas, pray for me too! Wilt Thou speak for me in that kingdom to which Thou didst allude?

The man persisted in prayer. That goes to show that Jesus allowed him to persist. He knew when to be silent, and He did not disturb the birth of prayers. But when the man who prayed had eventually opened his soul entirely, and when his hoarse voice had finally exhausted the last word in his distorted mouth and he could go no farther, the Mediator of God and of murderers raised His sublime voice and said: Amen, I tell thee, today thou shalt be with me in Paradise. And from this we know that not only Jesus' kingship but also the idea of Christ's Mediatorship as a priest seized on this broken heart. The man understood the core of the matter; he said: Remember me, remember me.

His faith removed mountains. It believed and embraced an intercessor who presently was reduced to asking His "why's." And that was even more wonderful than the acknowledgment of the dead intercessor, for, in order to return to His kingly power,[1] Jesus — and he knew this very well — first had to be submerged. No, it was not the physical but the spiritual death which frightened the man, if, indeed, he was still in a condition to experience fright. But there were mountains for him to move: he was to be in Paradise; the fourth utterance from the cross did not put him to death.

Enough of this man now. What is there to see in the Saviour on this occasion? We begin with the general truth. In this we see Christ's strong faith. Christ opens Paradise to the man in His communion. Paradise is the name used here for life in blessedness with God, such as awaits those who fear Him, after their death. Well, the Saviour is absolutely certain that He will enter Paradise; He also takes upon Himself the right of introducing others there. He has faith in God and in Himself.

To this we must add that Christ's response to the malefactor is a pedagogical reply. It serves to purge the imperfection in the

---

1. "En"; not "eis" (Greek).

questioner. The man asks something about the kingdom; in answer he gets a promise about the Paradise. The kingdom is an "institution," the Paradise an "organism"; the kingdom (in the fallen world) is a luxury which has been achieved by struggle; the Paradise is a restoration of natural grace. The human in Christ is glorified in the kingdom; the divine with all its glamor and blessing is again returned to the human in the Paradise. The kingdom of "Jesus" comes at the very end of Christ's struggle as Mediator, but the Paradise of "God" was at the very beginning of God's creative campaign prompted by His will to peace. The kingdom (of Jesus), the "murderer" says, is an anticipation of the end of time; Paradise (the Paradise of God, for such the Saviour intends it) is a recalling of the elemental beginning of time. The kingdom is a representation of Christ at the end; Paradise is the manifestation of God at the beginning. Because the word "Paradise" refers to the beginning, to the beginning of creation (the period which preceded that of the re-creation, the conquest of the kingdom by "Jesus"), it refers also to the new world which is to harvest the fruits of Christ's service as Mediator. Presently Paradise will refer to the communion of the blessed and of God; in that communion the renewed mankind will be allowed to enjoy the luxury and the riches of presence with God in a restored order of life. Paradise — as long as history has not yet come to an end — is a name to indicate the condition of rest which is reserved behind the clouds of the ever "becoming," the ever developing kingdom of heaven which must still experience its struggles here on earth under the clouds. Hence, when the murderer asked for the intercession of Christ in His kingdom he was attaching himself to the person of Jesus. He says: Remember me; that is: Reserve a little place for me, behind you. But in His answer, Christ uses the word: With me; thou shalt be with me in Paradise. Not Christ, but the eternal God, is the First and Last here. Jesus must "decrease," but God must "increase." Thus He who gives puts Himself on a plane with the one who receives, the Lord sits next to the servant, the One who takes the lead places himself on a par with the one who follows. "With me in Paradise." In this promise Christ does not subordinate the one who prays to Himself, but co-ordinates the petitioner with Him. Brother, he says in effect, together we shall go — to God. The king in Christ takes a position behind the servant of the Lord. The Mediator does not put Himself on display, proudly parading in His kingly robes; He gives all the honor to God.

Therefore this word is also a true utterance from the cross; it faithfully preserved the style of the cross. The Mediator is present in it, but in a position of concealment. He does not exhibit Himself or parade until God expressly gives Him the privilege to do so. But just now God is busy with Jesus in the matter of justice, and God will not break up the clouds which cover His glory before the time has come. "With me," not "behind me." Yes, that is true, but that is putting it very neutrally. By adopting this manner of speech, the Most Beautiful of all the children of men goes into humiliation and concealment. He says nothing about "remembering," or about His most peculiar kingdom. He speaks very calmly, and clings so firmly to the veil which God has on this day thrown about His beauty, that He, the General, chooses a word as simple as the language of His privates. And is it not true that every simple, pious person who lives by grace can say the same word to everyone who, he believes, is also God's, should they both die on the same day? No, Christ is not expressly referring to His priestly intercession here; nor is He quoting Daniel 7:13, as He did, directly or indirectly, in the presence of the Sanhedrin.[1] He does not manifest Himself as the Son of Man who is to enter into His power at the right hand of His Father. On the cross He makes use of a *vox media*. He leaves to God the glorification of His Son and tells the murderer precisely as much as is necessary to unite the man with Christ, yes, but especially with God, and to put the murderer in obligation to Him for all eternity.

From this, Christ's word proves to be extremely obedient. He has gained new spoils. Someone is coming up behind His chariot of victory but that chariot has not become to Him the stately coach of Satan. He did not, because of His rejoicing over these spoils forget His cross or the struggle of justice which He is suffering. He simply gave the spoils to His Father; He was a mighty hunter, but always before Jahweh (the Lord). The second utterance from the cross did not profane the style; this one, just as was every

---

1. *Christ on Trial*, 140 f.; see Dr. J. Ridderbos in *De Bazuin*, 78th volume, number 31 (August 1, 1930).

other, was an instance of revelation in concealment. The will awakens; the sovereignty assures itself of itself; but that which is heard besides is so lowly, that my age-ravaged grandmother can say it on her death-bed to every old person who together with her enters upon death in God's name. The word is so peculiarly an act of concealment, that "Hopeful," the character who supports "Christian" in Bunyan's *Pilgrim's Progress* as they together wade through the dark waters of the Jordan of death, can literally repeat it if he wishes to.

Learn of Him, for He is "meek and lowly." No one will ever enter Paradise unless He has pleaded for the guest. He is still using the language of the *guests,* and not that of the Lord of the banquet or of the Paraclete of the guests. He says nothing about sitting to the right or to the left of Him, as He did when He was still "within the gate." He does not manifest the bearing of one seated upon a throne, but that of one who takes His place "with" the least at the table of God. "With me, with me," you and I, we together. O God, He still remembers: the language suits His place, it is spoken outside of the gate. When God has taken all adornment away from Him, He will not put Himself on display crowned with a Mediator's crown. The figurative customary language which very facilely refers to the "pearls" in the crown of the Mediator — He made no use of that as He stood at the gate of hell. He selected no adornment for His crown, for He simply did what His office required. He has no time to turn the coin around and to see that the other side of the burden is the delight. The private in the vanguard of His camp should listen closely to Him now; this servant on the great day of days will say precisely the same thing to the least of God's poor, when the Antichrist kindles the fires against both, or when God will draw both upwards into heaven.

Plainly, He who does not parade His words, is a perfect man. O Christ, Thou who dost not insist upon Thy rank in the state of the curse, and who dost not make a display of the pearls in Thy crown! O Servant who risked a maschil on this child but newly born in the house of Thy Father! For it was the language of the riddle, of the maschil. It said enough, but it concealed and kept covered more than enough. That is what we would say; we are fond of saying verse at a death-bed.

Yes, *today thou shalt be with me in Paradise.* Now because of the concealed sublimity we love the words. We had to struggle a long time before we[1] could sense the awful struggle of ideas lying behind it. Now follows the "amen," great and full of energy; but the self-announcement of the Archegos[2] of our salvation is so small and restricted as it can possibly be. He went through His paradoxical mountain passes; finally He climbed His height and spoke His first word. That word could not have been simpler. In fact, it can very well teach us to make our words few.

Therefore Jesus' second utterance from the cross is His own and our salvation. Our salvation — that means the salvation of murderers.

Yes, it was His justification. If Jesus had by an untimely display of majesty inappropriate to the authentic style of Golgotha impaired His self-concealment He could have saved neither Himself nor the murderer. But now, inasmuch as He obediently remained concealed behind the veil of humiliation, He achieved His glory.

Moreover, He achieved His apology, not in words this time, but in facts. There are times when *words* do not suffice to defend a person. Blessed is he who at such times is justified by *facts*. It is in that way that Christ Jesus is justified by the fact today. Not by words. We have already given much space to the consideration that on Golgotha, when burdened by the mockery of hell, the right of apology had been taken away from Him: He had to suffer *without the gate*. That was the first line of thinking. Just now we discovered the continuation of that line: As Mediator He pronounced a word which is indeed a wonder as far as the consciousness of the speaker is concerned, which is quite unique in the world,[3] but which as far as its external form goes, was so ordinary that everyone who believes can say it to any other believer. It is matter for rejoicing to us to discover this glorious harmony between what we learned in the foregoing chapters and that which confronts us now. Our thinking of that can point out the way we should take next.

---

1. See the immediately preceding chapters; especially the one concerning the "amen."
2. "Chief Leader."
3. The "super-paradoxical amen," chapter 13.

In the calm deliberativeness which characterizes the second word from the cross we honor the pure response of Christ's spirit to His legal status at the moment. Just as it always does, so each word which Christ speaks now stands in immediate relation with what accrues to Him from God. The Mediator, although called upon as the Mediator, nevertheless is quite silent about the honor and name which as the Mediator is justly His. He does not announce what He is doing, or what He is going to do, or what He can do, but only what is to accrue to Him together with the murderer. The answer which He gives, in short, is not that which eternally *distinguishes* Him from the man who petitions Him, but that which He will eternally have *in common* with the man. True, His statement gives expression to the triumphant certainty that Paradise is awaiting Him, but this very assurance serves but the more to amaze us because of His controlled silence about His status as the Mediator.

We cannot recover from our amazement until we see the Christ as a Mediator who is governed completely by the legal relationship of things, by the legal status of everything which accrues to Him here. Christ's glory as a Mediator is so cautious, so pure, in singing its own praise because it would not play with a crown in the moment in which God is taking His splendor away from Him. No, His glory would not even play with a crown constructed entirely of *words.*

Strange, mystical confusion this; strange manifestation. They exchange garments: the Saviour, and the man who has been rescued as a brand from the burning. The murderer hopes that Christ will plead for him, will witness for him before God, but Christ bears this murderer as His vindicating witness into heaven, and feels free to present the man there as such. Does not this strike you as strange? The soul of the servant Jesus, did not depise the benefit of a good witness. His complete subjection, felt to the very marrow and bone and reins, to the compelling logic of the authentic fact that He Himself really is the accused, the *one* accused in the whole universe, becomes apparent from the fact that He did not despise having a witness, when this witness justified Him by fact. In this He could rejoice as a child rejoices. If it does not gladden Him, He is but playing a rôle. That man, hanging there in his pitiable misery, and nevertheless soon to be a guest of Paradise — he is in very fact a witness for our accused Advocate and Paraclete, for our great Witness, Christ Jesus. Was His not the right to present an apology? Well, if He must hold His tongue in check, let the facts speak. Here is a man who was burned by the flames of the same fire which drove Judas Iscariot into a spiritual death. But look at the result. Judas hardens himself, and by means of his obstinate death — probably at this same moment — accuses Christ as an impotent redeemer before God; this "murderer" stands up on the other side as a witness for Christ. And he comes to declare that Jesus of Nazareth can not be the cause of misfortune, of perdition, of misery in any man.

May no one be surprised to see that we allude to Judas again at this time. We are not resurrecting him from his grave, for he is just stumbling into it. God sees the crosses standing right next to where this happened to Judas. We have already observed[1] that on the day of Christ's death the trial of Christ Jesus caused a disturbance in the world of departed souls. On the same day as that of Jesus the soul of Judas passed over from the visible world into the invisible, and concerning the complications of life on earth this last infallible sentence was uttered. And that immediately.

Now there is a *third* soul here. This soul will be with Jesus in Paradise today. This soul was also greatly perturbed because of Christ. It is the soul of this praying bandit, of this broken-hearted rebel. On the one hand, then, even as it is to Christ's own consciousness, the Saviour is confronted by the dead Judas. But, on the other hand, He can confront Judas with this converted murderer, *coram Deo,* before the great white throne, around which are the souls, both living and not living (Revelation 20:4, 5, 11).

There were points of similarity and points of difference between Judas and this "murderer." The point of similarity is that both of them took offense at Christ. Judas took offense eventually, and the other man at first sight,[2] of a Messiah on the cross. Moreover, and it is this consideration which invites the comparison, both made the kingdom of Jesus the problem of their life. The kingdom is the great concern of the last hours of both, and greatly perturbs both. In addition, we can say that both ponder the "kingdom" at the cost of "Paradise." The kingdom, the im-

---

1. *Christ on Trial,* pp. 239-259, especially pp. 244-249.
2. Both murderers reviled.

mediate, visible, externally effective power, the reliable institution, the imposed force[1] — it is that which interested Judas, for which he yearned, it is that which he would rather have had today than tomorrow. But this man who prays from the cross keeps referring to the kingdom also by his last words.[2] Last words are weighty ones; you can see how anxious he is about that kingdom. But neither Judas nor the crucified malefactor gave an equal amount of attention to the Paradise, and to the concept of Paradise. Judas preferred not to indulge any fancies about the "next world" as men foolishly say; he disliked the fact that Jesus was always referring to that "other world" and seemed always to want to solve his problems by referring to it. As for the "murderer"— he too, apparently, had breathed very little of the atmosphere of Paradise. The "other world" could not charm him either. Hence Jesus' benediction contained a silent protest for him. He was straining hard to reach a kingdom, and he finds that he is standing on the border-line of Paradise. This had never occurred to him; Jesus' carefully selected word makes him think about it. Is it not true, then, that there are several points of similarity between Judas and this malefactor as far as their questioning goes?

A further point of similarity inheres in the fact that Christ opposed them because He had to. Just as Christ opposed the murderer — see what we have just said above — so He took issue with Judas. Making His appearance in this world, and maintaining His prerogatives of God as God, He did not hesitate to oppose Judas and He said that this world cannot be rightly seen nor rightly placed unless there is a preliminary acquiescence in God's holy order, an order which must still struggle in this world to penetrate the chaos but which has already created the blessed condition of a beautiful Paradise behind the clouds. He did not hesitate to point out to Judas that one can achieve the kingdom only if one begins at Paradise. Consequently there was no antithesis for Jesus Christ

---

1. It will not do here or elsewhere to oppose the concept "kingdom," as the New Testament speaks of it, to the concept "empire" as if to say that "kingdom" refers to a voluntary organization of people naturally drawn together by ties of culture, birth, race, or similar interests, and "empire" to a form of external force which artificially and artistically creates and forces national unities. The Greek language employs the word "king" even for the most autocratic despots, tyrants, or world dictators.

2. The word "kingdom" takes on richer meaning when we remember that the man persisted in his petition (see p. 323).

between the concepts "this world" and "Paradise." God would govern both, would join the two together, and would be served in both. But Judas had fixed an antithesis between two "worlds." He knew of but two types of people: zealots of the kingdom or idiots of Paradise. This is no idle fancy; the word "idiots"[1] means those who have no office, idlers, good-for-nothings. So Judas regarded things. He who fought for the kingdom, had nothing to do with a Paradise "today." For the kingdom demanded actual and visible effort here on earth. But those confused people who mumbled things about a Paradise did nothing either constructive or productive and therefore amounted to idiots. Thus spake Judas Iscariot. That citizens of the kingdom could possibly think that they were colonists of Paradise[2] and could derive the inducements for constructive labor in the kingdom from that fact was a thing he could not understand. So Judas thought and lived and so the murderer also thought and lived. If the murderer was in very fact a rebel, a revolutionary, this is even truer of him. Thus they together took offense at Jesus and opposed Him. That which Jesus had against Judas, that which He wished to charge against him as the total of things opposed during the three years of contact with him, is epitomized in His answer to the praying recruit who would enlist in His service. Both, Judas and the malefactor, raised the problem of the kingdom; this problem was not stricken from the agendum but Jesus says that the problem of Paradise comes first. Such was His protest. It had most important consequences, for both Judas and the malefactor looked only to the hand and to the mouth of Jesus of Nazareth for action. This Jesus had to accomplish the great deed. He had to make history. But Jesus recedes in the presence of God. My son, give God the honor. This is His answer: God himself has been proclaimed as the End and Goal of all things, and also as the Beginning, and as the Maker of history. Jesus enters into the evolving kingdom, but He leaves the completed Paradise (I Corinthians 15:24, 28). This Judas did not understand; he had no patience for such things. Jesus took His place with the simplest in the visible world; He used the language of "Hopeful" in His

---

1. According to the Greek (also the Greek of the New Testament).
2. "Our conversation—our *politeuma*—is in heaven; from whence also we look for the Saviour" (His "coming" from there "into" His kingdom: see p. 323 note 1. Philippians 3:20).

critical, fundamental moments, He went about (as with this murderer) with defenceless ones in Paradise, and He referred everything to the Father. These were precisely the things that fatally offended Judas. And these were the things which were given the "murderer" as the hard and unalterable truths. Was there *similarity* between the two? We see the problem of Judas returning in the murderer. Judas' obstinate opposition to Jesus continues. The man goes to hang himself; but his plaint is still vague here, anew, at the cross. That man simply will not die; his demon seems to have entered into a crucified bandit; plainly the bandit has a piece of it in his throat. The kingdom, O God, the kingdom. A former lesson in catechism and now this recent Jesus! But does this Jesus fit in these lessons in catechisms?. He talks of Paradises. It almost seems as though Satan, who has been driving Judas and has just now most actually realized his work in him, would now inoculate the error of Judas into the murderer, in order that he tempt the Saviour with the problem of Judas. And if not, perhaps the man, grim and stoical, like him of Kerioth, will turn aside from this unreal guest of Paradise.

That raises a question. Will Satan really place Judas *next to that murderer?* Will it really be true that on one day in Hades two witnesses will rise up in judgment *against* the Nazarene? No, that will not be the case. A great gulf of difference is fixed between Judas and the murderer. The points of similarity between the two were many and striking; but the difference is incomparably great. Judas took refuge in himself when he faced these problems and he suffocated in the stench of his own contaminated atmosphere, but the other went to Jesus. What he understood of the Messianic concept, he used. His problems were the same problems, but his attitude was different. He, too, — especially if it is true[1] that he joined in the reviling first — had to struggle in conflict with the idea of a kingdom which saw its Sovereign pass over the hill of the cross. But the problem did not destroy him. That which destroys man is not this or that problem; it is his unbelief.

And now the fundamental difference between these two finds expression in their fruits. Judas wanted to see that which he desired at once, "today." In the morning he said: Jesus, today I

---

1. See pp. 274, 317, 322.

would be with Thee in Thy kingdom. But he gets nothing today. And tomorrow — alas, let us say nothing of the morrow. But this late-comer, who, unlike Judas, had the patience to wait for a distant future,[1] gets his reward today. Today shalt thou be with me in Paradise.

This then is the apology of Jesus Christ. The *facts* spoke a conclusive language about Him even in the hour when His thought and His words and deeds were bound. Living history vindicates Him in every complication. Two witnesses rose up in judgment against Him. One of them, Judas, we might have called a "sympathetic" witness. But for the other no man has any respect. Judas at least struggled for three long years in the company of Jesus; and he gave others much of what he himself possessed.[2] But that murderer asked for something for himself alone; he had neither time nor room for anyone else, at least not in the kingdom of — Jesus. But in the world in which the law of Paradise has been restored, and in which the sequence of God very naively unfolds itself in the transparent facts, the "sympathetic" Judas will prove to be a false witness, and the frightened murderer will be declared acceptable as a true witness.

He will say many good things about Jesus there, for Jesus Christ saw the same sin in him that He saw in Judas, and He had meant the same to both originally, and He ministered the same Word to both. Moreover, He lodged the same protest against each. Now the one who charges Him with idleness is sent away from Him empty because of his own perverseness. He is turned away; he is sent away without office, an idiot against his will, from the eternal bliss of Paradise. But the other who allowed Christ to speak until He had spoken out completely, and who surrendered his soul to Him, was redeemed eternally by that same Saviour. He became an office bearer; he was given a crown in the kingdom which became Paradise after Christ's return.

Thus Christ entered into the gate of Paradise. His case could not be adjusted in terms laid down by men. But they understand Him readily in Paradise. Mark how joyously He raises His voice, a glimpse of gladness in His eyes. Amen, together we will go to

1. Page 331.
2. *Christ in His Suffering*, p. 168.

Paradise. Not a word too little and not a word too much. An angel supported Him in Gethsemane and then left Him alone again. A human being comes to Him at Golgotha, a witness, and this one accompanies Him later, and will say good words among the angels about Jesus Christ. The Advocate of all souls is grateful for this gift. God who comforts the lowly, gave Him close attention in order to determine whether He was lowly, so lowly that He would allow Himself to be comforted by the advent of this poor creature. Now He rejoices, for simplicity of heart is still His. Come, speak, brother-stutterer, speak right out, and firmly, and say something good about Jesus. Do not be embarrassed by the angels; just leave that to Him. As for you, the angels are very eager to read your heart. Present your testimony about the Son of man very simply here in Paradise. There they will at once conclude that this Jesus has done nothing amiss, that He simply proclaimed the Word and that He, for the rest, did not disturb the fundamental law for the life of the world, the constituency of the sovereign good pleasure.

Now, as far as we are concerned, we can not be present when the books are opened in the world behind the clouds, when Judas is to be confronted with the murderer by the strictly constitutional Prince whom he reviled as a rebel.

What, then, shall we do for edification? We shall read His Word, and confess to ourselves that everything will remain uncertain here, under the clouds, unless we believe His Word. Yes, indeed, if we abandon our hold on His Word, everything will remain unsure and infirm. Then everything will be a prayer which cannot be proved to be a prayer. Then we will have a repentance which is not fundamentally distinguishable on the basis of human argumentation from hardening of heart. There will be a confessing person who might very well be the most flagrant of egoists. There will be an election which represents too closely the other object of reprobation. So much for the outside, for the external. Who can prove, by any other means than by Christ's own word, that one murderer is any different from any other one? Take Jesus out of the midst of them, and the two outside crucified persons immediately become kin and remain kin, and both equally obstinately will deny Jesus the right of self-explanation. Take the word of Jesus out of the picture, or refuse to believe it unreservedly and the three crucified persons together will constitute a lugubrious society of death, a sterile college of babblers.

But if you begin on the basis of Jesus' Word, and if you let His light fall upon all, you will see at once that Christ is one who judges between the living and the dead, between the elect and the reprobate, between faith and unbelief, between repentance and hardening of heart. Again it is His Word, and His Word alone, which proves that the dying of these three is not a conjuncture of nature achieved *within* the circumference of the vicious circle, of interplay of death and life, of righteousness and unrighteousness, of zealotism and idiotism, but a product of that mysterious decree of God, eternal election and eternal reprobation.

Surely the comforting word of Jesus is more than the music of natural love. This is what Calvin calls the *mysterium tremendum*; this is a concealment which should cause us to quake before it.

No man hath seen God at any time, but the Only Begotten Son of God who stoops to the heart of a murderer, He it is who has explained God to us, and has *recognized* God in it. Lord, depart from me, for I am a sinful man. Stay near us, Lord, for the night is falling, has fallen; it is getting very dark here. Remember me, Jesus, now that Thou hast come into Thy kingdom.[1]

He will hear, and He will say to His little ones: *With* you. And they, answering, will say: *Behind* you. Yes, a preposition is an annoying thing in the sensible and intelligible world. My Catechism knows all about it, but does not solve it.[2] Nor is that necessary: He does my thinking for me, before He has come into His kingdom.[3]

---

1. A short poem of Anna Bijns, included in the original, is being omitted in the translation.
2. Lord's Day 13.
3. In an incidental way we discussed the self-revelation of Christ in saving the malefactor on page 158. The comments made there are related to what was treated in the immediately preceding pages, but we shall not discuss the matter further at this point.

Christ Substituting Himself

CHAPTER FIFTEEN

Christ Substituting Himself

> ● *Now there stood by the cross of Jesus his mother, and his mother's sister, Mary the wife of Cleophas, and Mary Magdalene.*
>
> *When Jesus therefore saw his mother, and the disciple standing by, whom he loved, he saith unto his mother, Woman, behold thy son!*
>
> *Then saith he to the disciple, Behold thy mother! And from that hour that disciple took her unto his own home.*
>
> JOHN 19:25-27.

MARY AT THE CROSS. That is the way many, especially esthetic natures, begin their discourse or their sermon when they set out to explain the passage we have placed at the head of this chapter. Well, in doing so they can appeal to old authorities. The classic

Stabat mater dolorosa
Iuxta crucem lacrimosa

has since of old in the church placed the figure of the oppressed mother at the cross, whose soul was pierced by the sword, in the center of the meditation. And in later days there has been no lack of poets and homiletes who felt the spirit of this "Stabat Mater" burn in their souls and who have written or spoken in the same spirit.

Indeed the picture in which the Bible sets off Christ in the company of His mother and His relatives is a moving one. At this point the drama is more stirring than at any other.

However, in our case, that is not our purpose. It is not the *mater lacrimosa,* but the *filius lacrimosus,* not Mary's maternal

339

heart, but the passion of her Son, of God's Son, her Lord, which is being proclaimed to us here, and which must save us. The moment we put Mary and her grief at the center of our thinking, we have done injustice to the Son, and — fortunately! — to Mary also. It is not the fact that the *mater dolorosa* stood there, but the fact that Christ *dolorosus* hung there that is of significance in this preaching. A cause of our salvation is not Mary's silence and Mary's departure, but Christ's speaking, and sending, and remaining where He was.

Again, therefore, by means of the statement Christ addressed to His mother and to the disciple whom He loved we want to find our Mediator and Surety, just as we have wanted to find Him throughout this book. We cannot agree with the claim of those who write of the suffering of Christ in a spirit of love, and who, as they approach the third utterance from the cross remark: "Yes, the first statement which Jesus pronounced on the cross, He spoke as the Mediator, the second as the Son of God, and the third as the Son of man who is anxious about the relatives He is leaving behind.[1] In fact, we can say that in general we have objections to this attempt to point out the "qualities" which distinguish between Christ's utterances from the cross. For we believe that Christ made all His statements as the Mediator, as the Son of God, and as the Son of man. And we also have our objections to the contention that Christ in this third utterance was laying a special stress upon Himself as a man among men, that in this statement He was placing His humanity "in the foreground." In the first place, and speaking generally, it is an exegetical and dogmatic error to present Christ as though He turned Himself towards His mother on the cross, pointing His face as it were to the domain of "natural life," and thus turning His back upon His "official life." The domain of natural life, even its outermost recesses, is for Christ the domain of His office; besides, the argument itself as indicated in the few words which we cited as being typical, is unwarranted. It is said there that Christ is anxious about the "relatives He is leaving behind." But that cannot possibly be right. Surely He had more "relatives" than His mother, and, if we work on this assumption, we face the question why Je-

---

1. P. G. Groenen, *op. cit.,* p. 498.

sus, in this respect, does this work now, and not before.[1] Or, again, why now, and not — though it may sound strange — later.[2] Obviously, Christ knew that it would not be right to speak definitely of "relatives being left behind." The Friday evening was at hand, the Sunday morning almost dawning, and on that Sunday morning Christ would be living again. And, even if after the resurrection His attitude to people and the world would be entirely different, there certainly would be time enough then to care for His mother, and to do this tranquilly and calmly. Indeed, if we think that we have exhausted the significance of the words which Christ addressed to Mary when we have explained them in the way indicated above, many questions remain unanswered.[3]

No, it is plain that in the historical events which have their manifestation now, in these as they are in their naked reality, our Saviour is coming to meet us, to meet us all. We are His "relatives" if we do the will of His Father. He is seeking His church, now also, His church and especially His God.

Nor must we distort the historical record which John gives by playing an allegorical game with it. Some do that. There are those, for instance, who present Mary as a type of the Israel which has remained faithful, as "the mother of Christendom." Thus they look upon Mary in the struggle in which she is involved today. Hence they see in John the type of the new Christendom itself. The conclusion then follows naturally: "Mary" and "John" must find each other. The Israel which has remained and the new Israel must support each other, and must enter into the relationship of mother and son.[4] "He is our peace, who hath made these two one . . ." Go one step farther, and you can use the narrative to point out an alliance between Roman Catholicism and Protestantism and this, too, has been done.[5]

---

1. John was in the room of the Passover; the burial was directly mentioned (in the anointing).

2. After the resurrection; the departure on Good Friday is (if we regard these things as they really are) preliminary; the departure at the ascension is definitive, is final.

3. We must state in fairness that the author mentioned in his further exposition of Christ's statements suggests much broader perspectives than it is possible for us to indicate in the words quoted.

4. Niebergall, *Praktische Auslegung des Neuen Testaments*, p. 254; Holtzman, referred to by Groenen, *op. cit.*, p. 501.

5. We by no means wish to say that these two stand in the same relationship to each other as do Israel and Christendom.

However, we shall say nothing more of the interpretation. We come not to see Mary, but to see Christ. At bottom Mary can do nothing but accept, but receive — just as we all. Today she cannot even be with Him in Paradise; the Son does not grant her this privilege.

Now it strikes us at once that Christ by addressing Mary is making a selection. His mother was not the only one who stood at the foot of the cross looking on. Besides Mary, we are told, these others were present: the sister of His mother; Mary, the wife of Cleophas; and Mary Magdalene.[1] Four women: first, Jesus' mother; second, Salome, the sister of Mary, and aunt of Jesus; third, Mary, wife of Cleophas, and inasmuch as Cleophas was the brother of Joseph, also the aunt of Jesus, just as Joseph was the "father" of Jesus in relationship to the law; fourth, Mary Magdalene. This was a small group but it "represented" all family ties. Here were the physical mother (Mary), and the aunt (Salome). Here were the aunt according to the law (the Mary of Cleophas) and the intimate relative according to the Spirit (Mary Magdalene) who learned to "do" the "will of the Father." In addition other members of the family were present. From further information given in the gospels it appears that the family circle was very well represented. John himself was there; Salome and the other aunt have already been named; besides, there were many women, who had followed Jesus from Galilee and had served Him; and — the expression used in Luke 23:49 is as general as possible — all His acquaintances stood at some distance. Now it strikes us

---

1. There is a difference of opinion among interpreters about who are meant here. According to many the sister of Jesus' mother is the same person as Mary of Cleophas, but if that is correct two sisters both had the same name (Mary). This fact, besides many others, results in a great many suppositions about the identity of Mary (the wife, or the sister, of Cleophas) and the relationships of the families in general. We agree with Groenen, *op. cit.*, 491-494, and with Dr. S. Greijdanus, (an article "Salome" in the *Chr. Encycl.*) and with Dr. C. Bouma (*Korte Verklaring des H. S.*, "Evangelie van Johannes," p. 232) who says: "It is not likely that John is mentioning three women. Were that true both sisters would have borne the same name. And it is quite in accordance with John's effort at anonymity for himself and his family that he does not name the sister of Jesus' mother. By comparing Matthew 27:56 and Mark 15:40 it appears that the mother of John stood at the foot of the cross, and that her name was Salome; and, inasmuch as John names three women besides Jesus' mother, apparently the same, it seems likely that John's mother was the sister of Jesus' mother. Jesus and John were cousins. According to Hegesippus, Cleophas was a brother of Joseph, the husband of Jesus' mother. This would make Mary, the wife of Cleophas, an aunt of Jesus. Therefore those who surround Mary Magdalene at the cross really represent one family. Thus we can say that there were four women at the cross."

that the Saviour addressed none of all those persons save his mother and the more intimate disciple John. And Jesus addressed Himself to John only to the extent that He was brought into connection with His mother. Christ spoke to no others in the circle of the family and acquaintances. Nor do we find that anything was said to the group in general. We must say, therefore, that Christ's address to His mother has peculiar significance. It represented a sovereign choice.

This is all the more striking if we remember that the last word which Christ spoke in the state of humiliation to men was this address to His mother. The remaining statements from the cross are all about Himself.

In this He is very obedient. The last word by means of which Christ enters upon the domain of the second table of the law (the domain of the neighbor) is addressed to her who, according to the first statement of that second table, deserves the first attention according to the rank which she enjoyed in natural life. His thirty-three years of life, of life given to the fulfillment of the law, are being typified in this today and are being found acceptable to God and men. Observe how he gradually individualizes more and more. His first three statements affected men. He begins with those farthest away from Him (the enemies), follows by a reference to His friends (the murderer), and concludes by an address to the mother who had been placed first in the second table of the law (Joseph the father seems to have died already). A holy order, this. It does justice to the neighbor. Thus He passed over — just think of the fourth utterance from the cross — to the first table of the law. He came to God and had no other gods before Him even though God robbed Him of everything. This upward struggle of Christ toward the second, then toward the first table of the law, and this prophetic-servile emphasis on the first words of the two tables, is new evidence to us of His obedience, and of His faithful service to God and His mother. "He that loveth not his brother, his mother, whom he hath seen, how can he love God whom he hath not seen?"

This alone suffices to point out the division we referred to above to the extent that we human beings are able to "explain" anything here. In one sense, Christ addressed Mary "pro omnibus": He spoke to her for all. He spoke to her, not because this mother had to become "the mother of the church." The church has no mother; the church is itself called the Bride; and it has besides a head, a father, a king. The church has no mother; she must herself become a "mother" (Galatians 4). Nor did Christ intend, by addressing His mother, to raise the "natural" relationship in which He stood towards her to the plane of the most important relationship in which He can ever stand towards men. We shall point out after a while that just here Christ is subordinating[1] the natural to the spiritual, that He is putting the natural in the service of the spiritual, and that He makes the ties of blood subservient to the bonds of the Spirit. Christ does not permit Mary to come to the foreground here as the first among women because she had been His mother and because that fully accounted for her service and for His. For, to repeat, we hope to see that His statement to Mary is but a subordinate part of this relentless process of Word and Spirit, in which His mother as mother is thrust into the background, and finds her glory and her consummation not in the exceptional circumstance which raises her above the plane of all women (the motherhood of Jesus), but in that which she shares with all women, that which she has in common with all believing women (her being a member of the church).

No, the reason for which Christ while dying directs His last statement given to men to His mother is that the law commands Him to do so. The law placed father and mother in the foreground in the second table of the commandments, and the law as the revelation of the Word would be so unreservedly trusted by us as to have us believe that whoever does justice to its first charges (for father and mother are that) thereby proves to be doing justice to his neighbor in all of the relationships of that concept. Whoever does justice to father or mother has fulfilled the whole second table of the law and has in principle kept the first table also. The paradigms of the law suffice because they are not paradigms but such as demand the whole service of the whole man. In the primary relationship existing between parent and child the beginnings of life unfold themselves, and the first imperatives of the law in reference to our neighbor there manifest themselves, and in them God comes to us in the forms of authority, and excites

---

1. Not in the sense of "inferior."

conscious life into being. The I-you relationship connects us with
our neighbor, and more closely with those two who according to
the will of both nature and Spirit are primary to us, namely, the
father and the mother. Thus Christ, by means of His immediate
sense of the harmony of the law, directs His last statement to His
mother. To Him, she stood on the boundary line between two
worlds, the two worlds He had to traverse today. In a certain
sense He is speaking to her *pro omnibus*. If He fulfilled the law
in reference to this closest neighbor He has fulfilled it in reference
to all.

Nevertheless, even though this statement by which Christ seeks
out His mother has a general bearing it also has a more specific
tendency. Christ places Himself in a specific, individual relationship overagainst mother and disciple. For both He had a command, for both He had a mandate. He Himself, as standing overagainst these two, has received a mandate in respect to them from
the Father of all. He puts Himself on a plane above them and on
a plane beneath them also inasmuch as He bears their burdens before God, inasmuch as He takes upon Himself the cross for both
of them, and inasmuch as He leaves them. Why does He leave
them, why does He keep Himself at a distance from them? Because He, not today only, but in the days to come also, presently,
that is, after the resurrection, must in an absolute sense be busy
in the things of His Father and in those of all His people.

We do not know to what extent Christ saw His brothers as
He hung on the cross. We believe that we must accept the fact
that He had brothers, both according to the law and according to
the birth given them by Mary.[1] Were these brothers present? It
is possible that these were numbered with "all His acquaintances"
who "stood afar off." Now if it is true that these were actually
present at Golgotha, the choice, the selection, the division which
He makes between family and family, and relative and relative is
the more striking. He does not choose one of the brothers according to the flesh to care for Mary. He looks over all His brothers
as they pass by Him one by one, and He chooses John, the "in-

---

1. We believe that we must on various grounds reject the interpretation of
those who say that "the brothers of the Lord" were not children of Mary and Joseph.
However, there would be no point in entering into a discussion of that issue at
this time.

timate" disciple, the candidate for apostleship, the young man who within a few weeks will not only be the spiritual brother of Mary by reason of the resurrection of the Prince of the Passover, but, by reason of the spirit of Pentecost, will also be her apostle. *Apostle* is a weighty concept. It means that John will be entrusted and fitted out with official authority over Mary as a member of the church; it means — think of Ananias and Sapphira — that he will have official authority over her life and death.

Now we can come to grips with the real issue of this matter. Yes, Christ, as He addresses this last statement to His mother, does so as the Son of man. For this name does, in the last analysis, include the general meaning that He is a man among men. As the Son of man He is identical with all men, but He is also the Mediator of God and of men; He is the Surety for His own; He is the history of all times; He is the Prince of the church and the world. As such He performs the work of His office: He compels the natural to serve the spiritual. He remelts the ore of natural life in order that it may again become an instrument which the spirit can employ as the great Worker of religion. He forces the blood into the arteries of the Spirit; He puts the mother on the ways of the apostleship; He makes natural birth the servant of spiritual birth; He makes the specific (Mary's individual honor) subservient to the general (the formation of the Church). And thus He arrives at His essential business: namely, to provide a substitute Himself, as a blood relative and as an historic wanderer upon the earth. He puts John in His own place and thus fulfills the law of the Kingdom of heaven, fulfills it in and for Himself, and fulfills it in and for those He loves.

Those were weighty words; they were full of significance. But now let us observe their content by pointing out their meaning from the Biblical account read in terms of the unity of all Scripture, and in terms of the *analogia fidei*.

The story looks domestic and consequently is well known. When Christ, hanging upon the cross, saw His mother standing there among all the other relatives and acquaintances, and saw John standing next to her, He made some dying stipulations about His home. Well, that is also the *municipium* of all who are about to die. The Christ becomes one of these. And still we must correct our phraseology; for while giving His family those commands

He is again in the state of His concealment. Giving His family
commandments? But it was not His family; it was not His home.
He could give His home no commands, for He had none. Foxes
have holes, and the birds of the air have nests, and the Son of man
lived under the law: the house, the home, remained that of His
mother. Well, then, He gave the home of Mary certain commands.
And, inasmuch as He is far more qualified than either you or I,
He at once goes farther. He also gives commands to the house of
Zebedee and Salome, the parents of John and James. He boldly
interferes with the program of that home. He demands that the
son of Salome support His mother. Woman, see thy son; son see
thy mother. The statement does not include two commands, but
is a double view of one and the same command. Mary may not
with her own hands draw the sword away that is piercing her
soul; this is to remain the privilege of her Son. It was for
His sake that the sword had originally been thrust through her.
He gives the care of His mother into the hands of John. This is
the simplest possible meaning of the words. The mother must now
give up her own son; for His sake she has been called blessed
among women; He has made her life a thing to wonder at. Let
the wonder also characterize the separation now: at His behest
she is to have another son in His place. As if the wonder could be
repeated! Yes, there are mercies which are very brutal. This
other son is to be John. Undoubtedly John is the best whom Jesus
can choose for this tender charge. Not that we can decide that
positively ourselves; but we know that Jesus' choice is infallible
and is not an experimentation. He selects the disciple whom He
loved especially; He chooses the son who was related to Mary by
ties of blood as his aunt and to Jesus as his cousin.[1] Him the
Saviour places next to Mary, and sends them on their way home
together; may the sorely wounded soul permit itself to be soothed
by the most loved disciple and by the most trustworthy nephew.
Thus these two went away hand in hand. And it was evening.
And it was night. Thy people are my people, thy God my God.

---

1. See what was said above in the note on page 342 and also the article of
Dr. S. Greijdanus on "Salome" in the *Christelijke Encyclopaedie*, Kampen, Kok,
volume 5, p. 22: "The sister of His mother, then, is Salome (compare Matthew
27:56 and Mark 15:40) and she, accordingly, proves to be the sister of Mary,
the mother of the Lord." Moreover, she was the mother of James and John
(Matthew 4:21). In this connection, see also the note on p. 358.

Sometimes that must be said in this way: What thy God conceals, my God will conceal; what they people mock, mine will mock. This is a love greater than the love of Ruth and Naomi. Can this be the reason for which they conceived of no new name for Mary, and never called her Mara?[1]

But let us say nothing further about their love lest we forget the lost Son. It is for His sake and because of His love that the Holy Spirit is in action now. This Spirit admonishes us to look closely, for we may not accompany Mary and John before we have seen Christ ministering His office again, before we have seen Christ serving in the capacity of His Messianic office. Yes, He is in His office. Again He exercises the old law which held for all of His work of revelation up to this time. Again He is concealing Himself to "the flesh"; again He is being overlooked and misunderstood in His true essence; but to faith He lays Himself bare. To the believing person He manifests Himself as Prophet, Priest and King. In all these things He lays Himself bare, "even"[2] in the things of the home, the garden, and the kitchen as the Messiah and the Surety.

We mentioned a moment ago that Christ undergoes a *concealment* as far as the eye of man is concerned. You wonder what we meant by that? It is indicated in the title of this chapter. Christ is providing a substitute for Himself by putting John in His place.

Christ is concealing Himself. He is even concealing Himself from the members of the family. And is this the farewell of the One who after a few days will be the Prince of the Passover? Is this the tone which He adopts who, three days later, will greet the women and speak to Magdalene and John, and give them a message of life and eternal youth which they are to communicate to His mother also? Once His brothers "did not believe on Him." And no one knows with certainty whether they have come to the faith since then. Perhaps they have, but we do not know. It may be that they have, but if so this last statement of Christ, unless God prevents it, can again sweep them on in the course of unbelief. He speaks as if He is not to be found again in all eternity. He acts precisely as does everyone who must postpone the "meet-

---

1. Ruth 1:20.
2. "Even"—between quotation marks. For the Mediatorship reaches out to all things in its passionate nisus towards redemption.

ing again" until the day of judgment. He is hanging among His family and He is silent about the sweet mystery of His resurrection on Sunday morning. You say, He could not speak out freely because of the unbelief of the crowd. If only, then, He had said nothing to His mother. His silence, then, would not have been half so painful as this suppression of the idea of resurrection which now characterizes His statement. In the presence of the whole family He selects a substitute for Himself, a substitute in the home of His mother. Surely this seems to suggest: I am going now, and for the rest you can do nothing except to buy balm, and to let me lie until the last day; for the rest, look to the bosom of Father Abraham. *Woman, see thy son* — with these words the Messiah *conceals* Himself by virtue of His Messianic power. As we see it, He is not being "friendly," the Messianic secret is preserved unimpaired. It is kept a secret even from the family. He seems so cold and distant — dare I use those words? — He leaves the family with the Scriptures as their only support. The Scriptures speak of the resurrection of the dead and of the Messianic day of life. For the rest these relatives had better deal directly with God, and, exercising their faith in the Bible, struggle with the concept of resurrection. This is *the great concealment!*

It is a concealment; also for John. It was the *tenth hour* when John had come from his former teacher, the Baptist, to Jesus, that Lamb of God, who takes away the sin of the world. Well, he had thought to himself that now the kingdom of peace would dawn and that now, after the powerful statements of the Baptist, sweet honey would flow from the lips of the "Lamb" of God. This must have disappointed Him; the new "teacher" accepted this nephew-disciple with an even stronger term: son of thunder, Boanerges. That is what he and James had been called by the new master. And he had accommodated himself to it, had struggled with the eloquent epithet; this much of it he had understood, that he had to bring much violence and tumult to bear upon the world, that he had to be a son of thunder. For three long years he had pondered the Messianic issue of how human beings make thunder, and how God lets the lightning strike in. But today! Where have the Master and his eloquent epithets gone. Alas, He Himself is quailing in the sombre night; and to the son of thunder, He serenely says, Son, see thy mother. Is this the world mission: to comfort a widow[1] inside the four walls of a home and for the rest to await the salvation of the Lord, *ad kalendas Domini?* Of course, it may be a part of "religion" pure and undefiled to "visit the widows in their affliction" (James 27), but after all, if one has been called a son of thunder, one expects to receive weightier mandates. Jesus, why dost Thou conceal Thyself?

Yes, He conceals Himself. He vanishes from the vision of His people behind the vessels in the home of a widow. Once this word had fallen from His lips so that the bystanders heard it, He could not escape the consequences. Now the mockers knew that He did not expect to come down from the cross. He is making His arrangements; He is talking to His mother. It is the preparation of His testament. There is not a single voice to suggest the sign of Jonah the prophet. Is He to be cast into the sea presently and then to be spewed back on dry land again? No, He is adjusting His business, and, to all appearances knows nothing about the great fish and the wonder. So forthrightly does He acknowledge that He Himself is expecting death, and so publicly does He avert His eyes from any sign of redemption, that the mockery, still to be heaped upon Him, will really be a rather flat and uninteresting kind of scoffing, for they will say: "He is calling Elijah; let us see whether he will come."

Thus He conceals Himself. To what end? "In order that seeing they may not see, and hearing, they may not hear." Mother, see thy son. What else is this but a reassertion and further maintenance of His maschil,[2] here, among these unbelieving? Now this self-concealment of the "Christ" has its culmination in "Jesus'" substitution of another man for Himself. This is a strange matter: His place is to be taken by another. Can He be supplanted by another? He? Surely the Christ can have no adequate substitute. It is impossible to suppose that anyone in His stead could be His substitute, could fulfill the task of Jesus either partially or completely. Nevertheless, it is a part of the law of incarnation that He as Jesus, as an historical person who moves about on earth at this particular time, and lives here and there in Palestine, is to be supplanted by another in part. In His human

---

1. According to general belief, Joseph, who is never mentioned again throughout the whole narrative, had already died.
2. *Christ on Trial*, p. 103 f., 363 f., and 388 f.

activity, in His social relationships, He subjected Himself to the law which God laid down for all.

Yes, indeed, to a certain extent, Christ can choose a successor to Himself. We are not going beyond the bounds of reverence or faith when we say that, superficially considered, Jesus' substitute in caring for His old mother could take much of Jesus' work from His shoulders, could possibly give her even more than He Himself could. For Jesus in these last days surely could not have "meant much" to His mother. The office which God had assigned to Him laid its claims on His entire time. It carried Him far from home; it made Him the servant of all. The more the years elapsed, the more basically Mary had to relinquish her first born. Thus it is quite possible that on a "calm Saturday," in which John gently comforted Mary, he gave her more of companionship and consideration than Jesus had given His mother for some time. Therefore, considered in general, much of the ordinary human contact between mother and son could be transferred to John; this would be quite possible, if only the substitute understood the soul of Mary, and if only he belonged to the "remnant of election" which in those day was concealed in Israel and shattered at the cross.

Nevertheless all these considerations do not remove the fact that Jesus as He was in essence and as He was in His true calling could not possibly have an adequate substitute. There is no "Seth" to take the place of this Abel for Mary.[1] Together with Him the great mystery entered into Mary's life. Angels sent a ray of light down to her house straight from heaven. The power of the Holy Spirit overshadowed her. The wonder accompanied the Child. She was unique among women, but only because He was unique.

Now if it is true that Christ is allowing His place to be filled by His nephew John, what can we say of this except that it is a further instance of His self-concealment? "The" Son of man gives His afflicted mother an ordinary solace, as though He were "a" son of man. His name was an ordinary name, His house, His life, His business were as ordinary as those of others. So was His departure. In it a son was caring for his poor old mother.

If you would fathom the riddle contained in this, place the first mother on the first page of the New Testament next to the first

---

1. See Genesis 4:25.

mother on the first page of the Old Testament, place Mary next to Eve. Only by introducing both members in that way can we justify ourselves in comparing the one with the other. Both mothers stand at the beginning of a new epoch of time. But there is this great point of difference: The one mother bears sons which have adequate substitutes, but the other mother was given her firstborn son as one for whom there could never be an adequate substitute.

Eve had her Cain, and she had her Abel, and Seth came to her in Abel's stead when Cain had put his brother to death. Seth is the substitute, the successor; the name which Eve gave him indicates that beyond a doubt. "I name him Seth because God hath appointed me another seed instead of Abel." Give Eve the privilege of saying this. She bears sons solely by reason of "the will of man." The one can substitute for the other to the extent that is possible among men. For, Eve's is the wealth of the poor. She has the many; her children are numerous; men can count them and give the number. And that which can be numbered, that which can be assigned a "number," can be given a substitute. The limited and finite can fill the empty place left by the limited and finite. At least "to a certain extent." And maternal feeling doubtless will not quarrel about the reasonableness of the phrase "to a certain extent."

Now return to Mary. Hers is not "a" son but "the" son. She has given birth to the great Son, to the "man" child who was "to rule all nations with a rod of iron" (Revelation 12). The relationship of Eve to Mary cannot be seen rightly unless it is seen in the light of Revelation 12. In that transporting chapter all the mothers who bore the "seed of woman" into the world are subsumed under the one visionary image of the "woman" who has her head in the clouds, the moon under her feet, filling all heaven and earth, she who gives many birth, but really gives birth definitively but once. She gives birth to many, for there is a reference to the "remnant of her seed." Yes, there are many. However, there is but one definitive birth. For in the fulness of time she bears the one son, the man child, who by His power will dominate the clouds. That one is the Christ.

In this way everything is given its proper position, and in this way the relationship contained in the birth registers of the seed of the woman are properly delineated. Thus Eve takes the right position, and Mary also. And thus the mystery of the third utterance from the cross is disclosed.

For who is the woman of Revelation 12? She is not Eve, and she is not Mary. She is not a queen of heaven who happens to have been given a human name. For, all mothers giving birth by the Spirit for the church and in the church are included in this one woman. She is the church, and Eve and Mary are members of this one great body which is the church. Eve is one among these many; and Mary is one. To the extent, now, that Eve and Mary have been incorporated into the mystical body of the one church the maternal travail and the maternal joy of the one is set on the same historic plane as those of the other, and both become of co-ordinate importance together with their children. On the other hand, however, this chapter teaches us also that a great difference exists between these two mothers and their children. It is an eschatological difference, a very important difference. The son of Mary is the great One among all sons. He is the man child among those many anonymous persons who have been classified under the common title: "the remnant of her seed." These others are incompetent to perform the "masculine" deed of turning the world upside down and ruling it.

To the extent, then, that this one masculine Son cannot be adequately replaced by any of "the remnant of her seed," that which Mary accomplished by her travail as God's religious woman can be compared with nothing. It is a unique thing. In this way we can find the connection between Revelation 12 and Luke 23. Here on Golgotha is "the man" son who was to rule the heathen with a rod of iron. Now He has become the weakest son of all. He sinks to a plane below "the remnant of her seed." Never was any of them so weak, so emptied. He is "a worm," and not a "man child." He is the object of mockery and disdain. This is His objective concealment. Now, by means of His utterances, He is appropriately fitting Himself into that objective pattern. By means of His third utterance from the cross He is fitting Himself in with the legion of anonymous ones. These are the little ones who can possibly find their name mentioned in the books of history, but who are too insignificant to be specially mentioned in the apocalyptic vision of Revelation 12. The one man child takes one of those many anonymous sons, and substitutes this one for Himself. Thus He hides Himself, He who is unique among many, He who can be assigned no "number," but is the head of all, and therefore irreplaceable in all eternity. He is the center, but He speaks as though He were the periphery. He is "the first of many brethren," but He acts as though He were an ordinary brother, one who can be replaced.

Nevertheless, even in this concealment, He is revealing Himself to those who believe. It is precisely for those who believe that He asserts Himself as the unique man Child, whom none can replace, as Surety and Mediator. "Woman, see thy son." He must help you to overlook him, and to understand the Great Son in His Messianic essence. Son, see thy mother, — but see her in faith; it will consume the honor of being my substitute, and give me alone the honor. Yes, Christ ministers His office, and, accordingly, does the work that can be transferred to no one. Faith detects its Prophet, Priest, and King, and in these constantly detects its Surety and Mediator.

Christ speaks as prophet. This is the work of a prophet: to place historical and natural life in the light of the eternal, the creative, the sovereign good pleasure of God. Thus Christ prophesies now. What is the salutation He uses? He does not say "mother" but "woman." Is this a lack of respect? No, it is an assignment of position. Precisely by assigning another son to her and thus basically separating Himself from her eternally as far as the ties of blood are concerned, Christ is delineating the future and illuminating the present by means of eternity. Mary is no longer His mother; accordingly, she is put into her place. She is a member of the body of the church; her travail has gone by, but that of the church not yet. As for her, as a church member among many members she is given a general, and not a specific and individual name. From this time on she will no longer be regarded in a concrete, actual, historical connection as "the" mother of Jesus, but as "a" member of the church. Hence she is called "woman." The Angel of the church, the King of the church, assigns a chair to her in the great congregation. The chair given her is not a chair of honor, such as Rome has provided for her, and such as Rome each day takes the trouble to dust off anew. For Mary must completely sacrifice herself. She, too, must spurn every display of glory which would place her in the center of things, which would darken the sun of Jesus. Her chair presently will be standing in an inconspicuous corner. That becomes apparent from the first chapter of Acts; in that chapter an irony sufficient to perturb us greatly is speaking. Presently a little group will gather "in an upper room." There they are to await the feast of Pentecost (the return of Christ). There the company present are named in a significant order. The men first and the women afterwards. First the apostles, the office-bearers who have been called to their duty; after that those who were related to Jesus by ties of blood — Mary and the brothers of the Lord. First the spiritual family; then the "natural" family as members of the spiritual communion. Mary is seated in the background. The apostles now are seated in the place of honor; theirs are the best positions; their names are written first in the register, not the name of Mary. Mary no longer has a special position of honor, but the apostles, John included, are given a special mark of honor, a special privilege which distinguishes them from others. At the time Mary had been called to an exceptional service in the domain of nature, in the domain of flesh and blood. Now the apostles are to be called to a special service, and this time in the domain of the spirit. They are given an office which can be transferred to no one in the world. This office will be just as untransferable and incapable of substitution as Mary's motherhood had been. Theirs will be the calling of the direct ministration of the office, of prophesying the Word, of ruling the church; this spiritual charge has been given them in a specially sealed letter of privilege. Mary, too, will presently have to bow reverently before this apostleship.

Now it is true that not all of this is proclaimed in the salutation "woman," for Christ is concealing Himself; but that salutation does make room for these consequences. As often as Christ called His mother "woman" He wanted to assign Himself and her their respective positions in relation to the office. What we have here, therefore, is an instance of prophesying.

Thus the third utterance from the cross puts Mary in her place. In Luke 2 and in Luke 23, next to the manger and to the cross, she is standing on ground which has already been covered; there she stands head and shoulders above the others. But Revelation 12 sees this exalted figure dwindled into smaller size. Only a member of the church remains. These are the two methods of revelation contained in the Scriptures: the historic and the apocalyptic. The third utterance from the cross, together with its salutation, constitutes the link between them, and illuminates the connection between them. Step aside — this is an instance of prophesying. Woman, relinquish your hold on me and take another son. Endure the fact that he is to accompany you. Do not touch me, do not cling to me, that is what He will say to Mary Magdalene on Sunday morning. But in the complicated form of this self-concealing word He is already saying it to His mother, to her who formerly was His mother. Let go of me, Mary, do not touch me, for the ways of the kingdom of heaven, and the campaign songs of the Lord God which impinge upon history eschatologically, make for schism. Woman, let go of me; I am yours no longer; hereafter I belong to everyone; thus it is meet for us to fulfill all righteousness. I am still descending to Satan, ascending to my Father.

Thus He comes to His second office and becomes Priest. He gladly gives away the gifts of God. He gives Mary hers; what more can she ask? No man can live by that which distinguishes him from others; he lives only in fellowship with the common gift. Thus Christ blesses His mother. He gently leads her from the natural union with "Jesus" to the mystical union with "Christ." He removes the form of "Jesus," in order that the figure of "Christ" may take form in her. He does not lead her into temptation but delivers her from evil. She was being tempted — more than Thomas — to isolate herself from others because of her special experiences, to exalt herself above the apostles, to appeal to her beautiful past. Now He puts an apostle next to her. Very gently the Son leads the mother to the feast of Pentecost; there He will be returned to her, but to the others at the same time. He accepts the member of the church, and therefore He relinquishes the mother. He cuts the ties that bind Him in order that they may continue to bind. He thrusts her *back,* but essentially He strengthens her. He rescues Mary.

He has gifts for John too. John has been called "Jesuphile" in contrast to Peter who was given the name "Christophile." The names were intended to show that Peter tended to elaborate the idea of Christ as God's office-bearer, whereas John loved intimacy with Jesus in His historical manifestation as friend and rabbi. However, we shall not accept this distinction. Jesus, who chooses His intimates with great care, condemned it. It was John who had to sustain her in that conflict of soul which resulted from her relinquishing "Jesus" and accepting "Christ." Thus it was John's duty to help Mary become "Christophile."[1] Thus the Priest also puts John in his place. He ordains him for his work in life. As a mild Patron, He does this step by step, stage by stage. Just now John, as a son, is still subordinate to Mary. The priest keeps John in a condition of subservience because it is good for him. It is not the day of Easter yet, and therefore John, too, may not enjoy a premature Easter gladness. But, in the meanwhile, Christ prepares for new situations, and arranges these according to His good pleasure. John is subordinate to Mary now, for one person must anoint the feet of Jesus with nard, and the other must shed tears on Mary's veil, and both must do it in preparation for His burial. Now the maxim still reads: Woman, see thy son; son, see thy mother. But after a few days, when Easter has come, these two will be the equal of each other in the exalted Lord. For in the "Kurios" there is neither man, nor woman, nor "mother," nor "son." Then the maxim will read: Sister, see thy brother; brother, see thy sister. And on the day of Pentecost — think again of the first chapter of the Acts — the relationship existing today will be reversed. Then John will be a prince of the church to Mary and she will be without office in a growing fellowship of church members. Then the maxim will read: Church member, see thy apostle; apostle, see thy church member. The Priest is in God's house here; He assigns each to his own place, for in the house of the Father, here below also "there are many mansions." And meanwhile, by virtue of the satisfaction He by His priesthood has achieved, He awakens their religious talents in them, and willingly takes the gifts of the Spirit from their trembling hands. O marvellous deed of the Priest. He Himself enters His catastrophes, but He saves His own from them. He sees to it that — in spite of their many troubles — the *homogeen continuum* of service is assured them. He sanctifies them.

Have you seen your Priest properly? For He is the Priest of us *all*. He relinquishes His mother, for He does not wish to belong

---

1. We shall return to this point presently.

to her by fleshly ties any longer but by spiritual bonds. O gentle
voice of a priest. I hear Him saying softly but positively: *Let
the dead bury their dead,* but do you two arise, and follow the
Christ by seeking Jesus no longer. Perform your actual service
in that way, for this before God is religion. Who is my mother,
my cousin, my brother? He that doeth the will of my Father, he is
my brother, and my mother, and my sister, and my cousin.

By this statement Christ also asserts Himself by virtue of His
kingship. He is King on this occasion. You remember how often
we related His kingship to the exercise of His right of requisition.
On this occasion He proves to be a royal Requisitioner fully conscious of His authority. As a matter of fact, this third utterance
from the cross is the crown of all His acts of requisition. Salome,
the mother of John, and John himself are here. Now Salome, according to the belief elaborated above,[1] was the aunt of Jesus, the
sister of Mary. Always Christ demanded and laid claim on that
which seemed best for Him, for His own official ministration. He
interfered with the business, with the big business, of his uncle
Zebedee, when he told James and John (two brothers), sons of
Zebedee and Salome, and Jesus' cousins: Follow me. They abandoned their father's business and followed this remarkable cousin.
This was the first act of requisition. By it He was saying to Salome: Aunt, woman, overlook thy sons; and He was saying to
John: Son, overlook thy mother. He that loveth father or mother
more than me is not worthy of me. That was the beginning. And
then? Christ also interfered with the finances of the family. Not
only did he take two representatives out of the firm — for they
were active in their father's business[2] — but He also made demands on their capital. Salome gave him some of her goods; and
it certainly was no easy thing to let thirteen people live for several
years without working. And now — as if that were not enough —
this moment. First He took Salome's two sons from her, then He
demanded money, and thus He interfered with the future of both.
Now He is hanging on the tree, everything seems lost, but He
does not hesitate to exercise His right of requisition, and take
Salome's son from her beforehand for the period to follow His

---

1. See again the article "Salome" by Dr. S. Greijdanus in *Chr. Enc.,* volume 5,
p. 22, in which, however, we must not overlook the phrase "it seems likely."
2. This thought is based on the indication that hired servants were kept for
the business (Mark 1:20).

death. John must leave his house and his ship behind for all time, must take Mary with him, and must take care of the aunt instead of the mother. Still it was true that John's mother had also been wounded in her soul, for she had also loved Jesus greatly.

Such is the will of the king. But who is there who would dare to contradict? He does not make His demands for Himself; His royal act is also the act of the priest. True, He acts in conformity with His dominant style. He began the week of the passion with a double demand. The first was for the city of Jerusalem by way of stating for the last time how matters stood (the foal of an ass).[1] The second came by way of telling the church how[2] matters would stand in all eternity (the room of the Holy Supper). Now He makes the last demand of the week. He makes a love-feast — an "Agape" the first Christians called it — of the Holy Supper. Just as the first Christians in their gatherings added the love-feasts to the Holy Supper; that is, they added the natural care of the needy whom Jesus had left behind (mark that modification here), to the proclamation of His death. And just as they in this united the requisition of the room of the Passover and of the soul of cousin John for Aunt Mary, so Christ willed that it should be. He is proclaiming ecclesiastical law, He, the King of the church. This represents a holy order, a lavish love; and at the same time it represents a regulation of the new church which is to arise out of this blood. Indeed this act of requisition is already a self-display of the coming prince of the Passover.

Hence we can also say unhesitatingly that this act of requisition is not less marvellous than Christ's super-paradoxical "amen."[3] His last "amen" is being followed by a super-paradoxical requisition.

At this point the tendency of our thoughts returns to the point from which they departed. It is beyond doubt that the person who makes claims and the person upon whom the claim is made are two different people. And it is also true without any doubt that the person who demands and accepts the gifts of souls for himself is more than he who is claimed. The (absolutely) claimed one is the one who can (relatively) be replaced; but the absolute Requisi-

---

1. *Christ in His Suffering*, p. 106 f; see also p. 150 f.
2. *Ibid*, p. 150 f.
3. See page 245.

tioner is always the One whose justice and beauty dazzle us. No one in the world can substitute for Him. To take something, if we follow it to its logical conclusion, is to take something absolutely; it is a simple deed, the deed of one, and not the deed of two or more; it is the deed of my Lord and my God. Therefore we say, that Christ, although He concealed Himself from the Jews and from "the flesh," revealed Himself beautifully and gloriously to those who believed. He triumphed also in this act of requisition. His right to lay claim — we elaborated upon that to a considerable extent — was completely challenged and at bottom was denied.[1] When His coat was raffled, this denial, this acute, sharp, bitter and demonic denial issued in the extremest possible consequences. Nevertheless Christ, although He was completely naked, fully exercised His right to requisition in the presence of the rafflers and dickerers. Surely, this is triumph. He comes up out of the abysses of paradoxical conflict in triumph as a thinker when He utters His super-paradoxical "amen," and in His super-paradoxical act of requisition He comes up out of the eternal abysses as the Owner. In the great, fundamental issues of the state of privilege and of the possession of privilege, Christ gloriously asserted Himself overagainst all appearances.

In all this He is our Surety. Blessed is he who is not offended by such a Surety. As Surety He proclaims the place of the history of revelation, the place of His death. That first. And as the Surety He also enters into this death. That next.

As the Surety He puts His own death on its proper plane by means of the third statement from the cross. He gives Mary and John work to do. He has no patience for letting Mary or any other person be troubled by His "death," from the late Friday evening to the early Sunday morning (a day and two parts of a day). He does not want them to suffer because of the death in itself. Nothing exists "in itself." He does not want to see a single day lived in lamentation about the death of Mary's lost Son. His mother may not be a Rachel, for Rachel refuses to be comforted because her children are not. Woe to Mary, if she, a second Rachel, should make the death of her Son the uninhibited cause of comfortless sorrow. A Benoni is not acknowledged in God's house. We are the

1. See chapter 11.

children of *His* sorrow; let us not reverse the order. Thus He presents a Benjamin to His mother; He cannot die in God's house. He places that disciple on her right and on her left side who was chosen of all men by the spirit of God to write the profoundest things which were ever said in the world about the interrelationship of God's thoughts in the historical life of the man Jesus. He has His mother supported not by a "synoptic" soul, but by the spirit of John. John was the disciple who up to this time understood most about Him, and who was permitted to write about the Word made flesh under the impelling drive of the Spirit. John had apparently been predestined by the creative father of spirits in his thinking and being for that task from his birth on upwards; he had been prepared for it by virtue of predestination, and this man, Jesus places next to Mary. This is the quiet Saturday. That was a day in which John 1:14, the great prologue of the great gospel of John, was already approached by two seeking souls. On that day the Holy Spirit overshadowed those two who could say the most about the Logos made flesh. The flesh was Mary's; it was torn apart by God. The spirit was John's; it was torn apart by God. The one, Mary, knew how fleshly the Logos was; He had assumed her flesh and blood. The other, John, knew how truly the Logos had entered into the flesh: the Logos had assumed his spirit, the spirit of John, son of Zebedee. Therefore Jesus gave His mother the best He could give: He assigned the death suffered in His Suretyship to the right place. In other words, He strictly forbade these two intimate persons, intimate according to the flesh and intimate according to the spirit, to accentuate the moment of His death in a way cut loose from faith, or while their backs were turned to God, the God who implants faith in human souls. This third utterance from the cross resembles "natural" love (*philein*); but from A to Z it is spiritual love (*agapaan*). Christ's most devoted care for His mother Mary is a strict command, carried out on Good Friday, not to look upon His death "erotically," not to approach it "psychologically," or "sensually," or "naturally," and not to become steeped in it by way of impossible grief. Francis of Assisi is helpless overagainst this utterance, and all erotic souls of every epoch are being summoned here to convert themelves to the spiritual love. Christ proclaimed His death as the death of His Suretyship (again on the assumption of faith). He said: This death is the way; it must take place thus; and therefore John, *doctor dogmaticus* that he is, and already waxing strong in the spirit, must support the *mater dolorosa* until he shall sometime write an account of the gospel. For it is not the nature of flesh and blood, but the spirit born of God, which can see the death of Jesus in the proper light, and can struggle through the transition from the last Sabbath to the first Sunday on a quiet Saturday.

So much for the first point. And this for the second. Christ also assumed His death in speaking that third utterance from the cross. To suffer shame in the presence of those nearest us, to see those nearest us as the ones who are really the most distant, is also an instance of the passion of the Surety, for it belongs to the essence of the penalty. In hell each person turns aside from every other, because there no one can love. Christ is not such; He can love, and He does. And hence He, by an effort, sets the others apart from Himself, and Himself apart from the others. But this active obedience is again related to the passive obedience. He is being segregated from the others, from those whom He loves. This is His suffering; this is His suffering of the penalty for our sin, a penalty which takes the form of disruption. What is sin at bottom but the primary and elemental principle of schism. It introduces segregation between father and mother, parent and child; it puts the single individual to shame in the presence of the most intimate communion which life knows. This penalty, and this punishment, He now assumes, looking it full in the face. Thus He suffers a spiritual death. However, He suffers as the Surety, that is, He gains the victory over the spiritual death. That capacity to unite by means of which He draws John and Mary together, consumes the disruptive influence of sin. This it does at the right time. For this power of disruption which is of the essence of sin had just accrued to Him on that stage of mockery which we discussed before. The mockery of hell with which He was afflicted was a clear manifestation and assertion of the disruptive power of sin. Hence we can say that the third utterance from the cross refers to the past as well as to the future. Rejected and abandoned Himself, our Surety makes a great effort to bind the disrupted together again. He unites disparate entities; He unites the profound spirit of John with the sensitive soul of the mother; He unites the man with the woman and makes sons out of cousins. The robbery which He commits against Salome becomes a blessed delight to her. This is because of His Spirit. He triumphantly metamorphoses the reflection upon the day of the definitive death, into a preparation for the most beautiful of days, the dawning of Easter.

In all this, however, the Surety assumes His isolation. For He cannot dispose of these profound feelings of love to anyone. His love is so spiritual (*agapaan*), that they can find no adequate forms in which to express themselves (*philein*). Such a love is a consuming love. At least it consumes human nature. Hence He must be consumed because of this love. No wonder, therefore, that it carries out its fatigued command immediately before His *descent into hell*. His love can no longer express itself without a struggle; He is approaching the edge of hell. He is alone. Another moment, and it will be dark upon Golgotha, and the darkness will last for three hours; thereupon the last struggle will impinge upon Him from the outside; when that happens Love will have forsaken Him entirely. Nevertheless He assumes His lot and His isolation. It is remarkable, is it not, that before the darkness, and before the great exclamation of the fourth statement from the cross, He sends His mother away. Did He know what was still coming? Did He feel it? We dare not say any more than we know, but we believe that He wanted to be in a right relationship with all men, with all forces of the earth, before He sank away in the bottomless abysses of the griefs of hell. And He knew that these would come.

Thus He enters upon His isolation.

At the Valley of the Shadow, we say, all friends forsake us. Yes, that is the way we put it. But He could not say it that way. When He enters upon the valley of death, He bids His earthly friends adieu, He puts Himself into a state of isolation. Again I understand Him better now as He says, not "mother," but "woman." Hereafter He will have no mother anymore. Even on Easter day and on the day of Ascension He will give His mother conspicuously little, much "less" than many others. The austere logic of His own sublime diction subsides not at all. Yes, woman, just go now; I am taking leave of mother for all centuries, and for all eternity.

.Thereupon Christ entered upon the final trial. But by sending His mother away beforehand He in the final act as a Priest creatively fulfilled this stipulation of the law: Greet no one upon the way. In the hour in which one must serve God directly, no one must be spoken to enroute. Greeting God, one automatically greets all those who are His. And this must suffice for them, whether they understand it or not. Greet no one upon the way. For souls and movements of souls may not pause on the open routes of the Spirit. Just as a priest in Israel may not grieve because of the death of those dear to him, inasmuch as a priest may not allow himself to be interrupted in the ministration of his office,[1] so Christ forbids, by way of making the command and its austerity even profounder, that any lamentation be made for Him without faith. The High Priest sends His mother away before the utmost of the penalty is demanded of Him, and before the extreme of punishment tortures Him. He did not pause on the way; His eye was steady in spite of the proximity of His mother; He kept His gaze steadily upon His helplessly embarrassed people.

Accordingly, we can say that this substitution on the part of the Nazarene was an instance of church-service. The family received the *official* ministration of religion. It grieved Him greatly, it caused Him extreme pain to minister this service. We alluded to Eve a few paragraphs ago, but the conflicts of Eve are explained here. When Adam had seen the light of evangelical grace dawning over a cursed world,[2] he changed the name of his wife. First she was called Woman, but after God had pronounced the blessing of the Redeemer which should be born of her seed he changed her name to Eve, for she was to be the mother of all living. This in Adam was faith. The name *woman* is a name for the present. The man is for the woman, and the woman for the man. They play together in the *present*. But the name *mother* here is an eschatological name; it represents a struggle for the future, and a reaching out for benefits to come. God Himself had said that redemption was to come from their children, from their future. Hence Adam now names his wife not after herself, but after his posterity. She is no longer here in order to play an Arcadian game with him in the present (man and woman), but they

---

1. *Christ on Trial*, pp. 161, 162.
2. In the familiar mother-promise: Genesis 3:15.

together are here to suffer and to travail for the future which must produce the seed.

However, his faith was still groping, was still uncertain. *When* was the Great Child to appear? Alas, Eve is the mother "of *all* living." Hence it may still take a long time. . . .

Now that great birth has finally taken place. And the mother, she who could really be the mother of this prince of life, of this great seed of the woman, might stand here . . . but stand next to a cross. The woman has entirely disappeared, and the game, the game of life, has ceased. The *mother* arose; she was entirely broken, and the Great Son sends her to the house of hard consolations. He sends Himself into death. If Adam could have seen this hour from afar the name of the mother of all living would have died on his lips. But the second Adam who conceals all His strength in the words of His self-substitution, still asserts Himself as the Prince of life. The game had died out; but thus it was restored again. For, now that the issue is squarely confronted, it appears, not that the Child is to be explained in terms of the mother, but the mother in terms of the child. And hence the Child leaves the mother in obscurity. Only faith can remove the darkness.

Thus Christ is our peace also, in nature, in flesh, and in blood. Adam and Eve are explained today. The Son explains the parents. Yes, this Son explains His fathers and His mothers, all of them together. Father David, also, finds his explanation and fulfillment in David's son. David, during his life, had also been aware of an afflicted mother who directed a question to his house. We are thinking of Rizpah (II Samuel 21), who took her place next to Rachel, and who stood on the boundary line between the house of Saul and the house of David, weeping.

When Saul fell, he left a gloomy legacy behind: an unconfessed evil, the core of a curse. He had defiled the oath of God. And when in the time of David, this curse was destroying the people — for no one[1] had given any attention to it — they took seven — the sacred number — of Saul's children, including two of Rizpah's, and hanged them on a tree of shame. These were declared to be exlex: each was an exlex in his accursed death. But the curse proved not to be destroyed by this sentence: the plague

---

1. Not even David!

(a famine) persisted. David's sacrifice no longer had the potency to satisfy.[1] Was David himself praying too little? Was the old tension present no longer? Be that as it may, there was one who felt the tension, and that one was Rizpah. She struggled long in prayer with the Lord. She kept watch by the seven gallows, in order that the curse might be removed, and those who had been hanged might be buried honorably. Her persistent watching and her dramatic wrestlings in prayer with God, begging Him to hear and to allow the miserable remnants of Saul some little vestige of honor in the form of a decent burial — this persistence of Rizpah we said was a good thing still. It was a salutary counterweight[2] overagainst the apathy and indifference of the many who were satisfied with the *opus operatum*[3] of an accomplished curse-judgment. But for the rest, how pitiable, how miserable! David had not avoided Saul's sin; neither had he made satisfaction for it. And an *afflicted* mother must support and complete the inadequacy of King David.

Back to Golgotha now. Mary is here. Her child, her royal child, is hanging on an accursed tree. In Him David himself is being accursed. But there is a difference, and the difference inheres in this: Mary, in contrast to Rizpah, has nothing to do; she has been dismissed. The struggle of Rizpah's soul was the necessary complement to an *opus operatum*. True, the house of David is making sacrifices, but is itself playing with sin. And although the house of David can follow Saul into his death, it cannot break the curse. Hence Rizpah did something. Her tension and her perseverance overagainst Jehovah completes the sentence, and assists in compelling the blessing to come. But Mary — the second afflicted mother standing by an accursed tree — can go home. Today Jehovah can be inclined to favor the country without her. The sacrifice of this day is not an *opus operatum;* Christ surrenders Himself "through the eternal Spirit." He Himself puts the

---

1. There was sin in his own house precisely at this time. His sons (we read in the Hebrew) were called priests. This may have been a mere gesture in the direction of priestly honor by means of the royal house (the evil which had caused Saul to stumble returned to the house of David). Disobedience in the fulfillment of the office; concealment of the messianic image.

2. "And after that (Rizpah's struggle was a contributing factor) God was entreated for the land."

3. A religious act satisfactory when externally effected even though insincerely done.

tension of prayer into this sacrifice of the curse. There is nothing for Mary to do; the mother can go home. The Son has now finished everything, everything. Not only does He have the knife employed in the sacrifice, but He also has that tension of soul required to drive the curse out of the atmosphere. These two had been separated in David but are united in the Son of David. Rizpah: the ecstasy of complementary sacrifice; the public intercession. Mary: a calm dismissal; a hymn of praise lifted up about the adequacy of Christ, who gives His mother nothing to do by way of atonement, but, as the Son, consumes in Himself all of the evil committed by David and by Saul when Saul or his condemned generation, and the remnants of David, believe in Him.

Thus Christ takes leave of men. He kept His two staves in His hand, the staves of Beauty and Bonds. Having come to nature in the power of the Spirit He remains its peace.

Now we have pondered half[1] of the utterances Christ pronounced from the cross. The harmony of these was beautiful, was it not? In the first utterance He asked God for time and indicated His will for the time which would then ensue.[2] By means of the second statement He opened eternity to a person who was lost to time and made known His will to him.[3] Now, in this third utterance from the cross, He has subjected time to eternity, subordinated the days of men to the law of the day of the Lord; in this statement He caused two people in a quiet home on a quiet Saturday to ponder the dark mystery which later would be defined and described by John. John would write of that later. John, driven by the Spirit, could then teach Mary that in the beginning was the Word and the Word was with God, and the Word was God. The same was in the beginning with God. And the Word was made flesh, and both of us beheld His humiliation, an humiliation as of the last begotten of Eve, but full of grace and truth. The great substitution comes by way of the great absolution. For the Eternal, the Infinite, moved to redemption in time among finite values. In this way Christ's self-substitution represents the fulfillment of the washing of the feet. The Master became as one who serves. The Master cannot be replaced, but servants (slaves) could be

---

1. See pp. 130-31.
2. See pp. 134-35.
3. See pp. 275, 302.

bought in those days. These could be replaced; adequate substitutes could be found for them. Thus Christ washed the feet and the eyes — it was all the same. The Lion became the lamb; food went out of the eater. This is a riddle you will not guess. And when you say "I give up," the great Samson will clothe you in His own change of garments. He wove them with His own hands, and He did not kill a single Philistine to get them for you.

Christ Exlex in the Darkness: Christ Outside of the Gates of God

CHAPTER SIXTEEN

Christ Exlex in the Darkness: Christ Outside of the Gates of God

> ● *Now from the sixth hour there was darkness over all the land until the ninth hour.*
> MATTHEW 27:45.

I N ONE of his books Nietzsche has his hero Zarathustra say: "There many suns are cavorting in space; their rays have a message for all that is dark, but to me they are silent. Ah, such is the enmity of light against everything which itself gives light!" These are well turned phrases, but phrases in which the arrogance of the speaker is evident. Regarding himself the while as a bearer of light, he glories in the fact that the world's bearers of light have nothing more to say to him, and by way of self-glorification (perhaps it would be honest to say by way of an unconscious attempt at self-vindication) he creates the fable of the jealous suns.

How very different is Christ Jesus. He who Himself is the Light, calls for light. He avidly accepts the luxury of light which the mount of transfiguration offers Him, and even after that He cries aloud for a ray of light, for a kiss from heaven.

> Redeem me and give me a trace,
> Of the light of Thy comforting face.

Hence for Him it was suffering and not the cause of a false glorification when light was taken from Him for the space of three hours on Golgotha. Now all the generations may rejoice because of that darkness and say: "In Thy light we see the light." Hence we must follow Him into the darkness.

The context of the story is well known to us. When Christ, while hanging on the cross, has suffered the first affliction, the acute act of the crucifixion, He enters upon the second phase of His suffering. From the catastrophe of the crucifixion He enters into the passion of being crucified. Gradually but certainly His blood ebbs. Gradually His wounds become swollen; these pained Him grievously; His blood congeals because it cannot course freely; fever consumes His body. The work has been done; the social act, save for the extreme sacrifice, has been finished. The intercession for the soldiers, the opening of Paradise to the murderer, and the assignment of the mother to John — these have taken place.

When this work had been completed, God said: The preparation is finished; now follows the essence of the sacrifice itself; now He must enter upon the darkness of night. After the six preparatory seals the pre-emptory seventh seal of the book of death and the curse is broken. A hand intervened in the clouds; it hung a veil before the sun and receded again.

Then it was dark. It was dark and that was all. Silence everywhere. A drop of blood fell to the ground. The centurion plainly heard it falling. It was quiet and that was all. That and the passion. And silence everywhere. Silence above, and silence below. The mockers dared go no farther. The tumult subsided. The chest of the murderer was heaving audibly; they in the back rows of the spectators — no, of the bystanders — could hear it.

What shall we say of it, you ask? Not too much learning, perhaps, and nothing, surely, that can serve to "explain." Attempts at an "explanation" of this darkness have been undertaken, but they mock themselves. There are people, after all, whose pet ambition it is to "explain" by natural means what God does by miraculous means, — as if God and nature were antitheses, as if nature were not as miraculous as a miracle. But let that be. People of this temper have said: Very likely it was an eclipse, a very ordinary eclipse. No, all alarmed believers hasten to reply, glad that for once they can boldly take issue, that is impossible. Easter, they say, coincided with the full moon, and when there is a full moon an eclipse is impossible, the moon is then directly opposite to the sun, a circumstance which cannot make an eclipse. True, others admit, but are quick to add: Then the darkness must have been caused by an aggregate of particularly dense clouds, or by a sudden rising of mists from the earth. These point to the fact that each year in Jerusalem, especially in the month of April, dark days frequently occur, usually called "black siroccos," during which the atmosphere is hot and full of dust. In fact, Origen committed himself completely to this supposition."[1] However, although we do not regard this possibility as being excluded "in itself," we believe that the word "darkness" has been too strongly accentuated to warrant such a natural explanation.

In any case this at least is of the greatest importance to us: that we must see an intentional and direct influence of God in this intervention of darkness.[2] Or, if we want to put it that way, we can say: This was a wonder. God spoke objectively.

Naturally, God is first of all speaking *about* and speaking *to* His Son, the Surety of our soul. For this is "the hour and the power" of darkness. He said so Himself, and consequently He must experience it as such. Hence God comes to express this truth which in its essence touches on the invisible world, in visible forms also. In Bethlehem night was once converted into day; on Golgotha day is metamorphosed into night. In Bethlehem there are many angels whose light dispels the darkness. On Golgotha there are many devils who — as it seems — gain a triumph in the conquest of darkness over light.

How could we possibly see the proper relationship of these things except in terms of Christ's descent into hell? The darkness in which Christ now hung suspended accrued to Him, impinged upon Him, in that second of time in which His sorrow became so aggravated that it finally had to give expression to the statement: My God, My God, why hast Thou forsaken me? He was suffering the pains of hell. What God wanted to say to the Son was this: Have you desired to suffer the passion of hell? Then you must do so fully aware that you are doing so.

Therefore we can say that the Father, as Judge, now continues what the Son, as Accused, has begun. When Jesus first came to

---

1. P. G. Groenen, *op. cit.*, p. 512.
2. We may call attention in passing to the fact that various testimonies which men have tried to glean from sources other than the Bible by way of confirming this historical datum of the Bible, can contribute nothing to explaining this darkness. Men have appealed to the letters of Polycarpus and Apollophanes. References have also been made to Phlegon, to Thallus, and to others. We shall pass over all these things without consideration, inasmuch as they do not affect the gospel account, and inasmuch as these testimonies are quite superfluous to the believer.

the hill of death, He refused the drink of wine mingled with myrrh. He did not want to be dulled by the sedative. He chose to look the Father full in the face, even while the Father thrust Him aside.[1] Now God keeps Him to the course He Himself chose at that time. He who would be alone with God and would feel the eye of God burning down upon His own, must be in the dark. Where else can one see God, save in the dark, at least in that which the people of today call the dark? Was not the night always reserved for the prophets and the poets who were taken away from God and forsaken of Him? Now Christ comes as Prophet and Surety. He enters upon the extreme penalty. Consequently, the night is meet for Him.

It could not and it might not be otherwise. True, it is possible for God to give someone the privilege or the imperative of looking into heaven or hell on a brilliant day, but when this happens, it happens only in an instant of ecstatic transport. Such a transport immediately dims the eyes. When God takes Paul, and gives him a vision of the third heaven, Paul is experiencing a trance-experience. When John is given the imperative on Patmos of looking into the second heaven, he does so on a brilliant day, but while he is "in the spirit." When Abraham is called upon to see God on the day when God wants to disclose the history of the future to him, Abraham also is in the spirit.[2]

Consequently, God could have showed the terrors, the realities, of the other world to Christ Jesus upon a brilliant day, if only Christ had been "in the spirit," if only He had been in a state of ecstatic trance. For then, too, Christ would have been attentive solely to the things of heaven or of hell.

But that is not the manner in which things must take place for Him. Trance experience, and the condition of being "in the spirit," makes a person passive; it excludes his own activity. Christ may not be passive merely; and He may not be that merely in relation to the things below. No, He must remain active to the very end; He must be busy personally, must keep Himself in suspense, must continue seeking for His God, and must descend to Satan by His own act. He must not, like John, Paul, and Abraham, be made attentive solely in a passive way, but must by an act

1.   Page 96.
2.   Genesis 15: The light in the smoke.

of His own cause His eyes to penetrate every obscurity, seeking out God and the devil. His ears have been "opened."[1] He can listen very attentively, He can be very alert, and must faithfully accept the calling of being that now. By an exertion of His own effort and not by a mechanical compulsion He must receive the sounds coming to Him from the other world. An ecstatic Christ cannot redeem us. If the Saviour had been "in the spirit," His activity would have been lost in compulsion. Then the unity of His work would have been broken. Then He would have been a servant who because of His limitation could see only that which had been placed before His eyes. That is the condition of those whom God puts "in a trance." They do nothing themselves; they draw nothing to them, neither God nor devil. If Christ had been like them He would not have descended into hell by virtue of His own energy, but would merely have been forced past it. Or, to put it more strongly, then hell in its various aspects would merely have passed by Him. Such would not have been an act of redemption. Such is not to see God or to see the devil. That causes nothing more than a mechanical convulsion, one which can take the body and soul captive, but which cannot by means of body and soul permit Him to take captive the devil and his straight-jacket, and God and His sublime book of law.

Hence the reason for which God now puts His Son in darkness is to keep Christ faithful to His own work in the office of His Mediatorship, and to try Him as such. The second Adam may in no sense enter into a coma. The covenant of works has just been placed upon the table. The dialogue is beginning. God and He are to stand overagainst each other. Now the curtains must be drawn; God can be spoken to only in the dark. Light serves to unite people living on a single horizontal plane, but it cannot unite men with the other world. Light is a medium of intercourse, it is "social." But God is not our *socius*; He is the *Other*. He can be found in the dark — the others must step aside then. And what, pray, can Christ do in the cleft of the rock in which He is to meet God and the devil, what can He do there with a medium of intercourse employed among men? Thus far He has done His work among men. He has dealt with and dispatched the last point on the

---

1. Psalm 40:6: Mine ears hast Thou opened.

"social" program of the day.[1] Light does not make sense to Him any longer. There is nothing to do now, except to achieve the great sacrifice. As far as He is concerned, He has been shut out of the range of communion. The Mediator who comes to achieve His most unique function no longer needs an intermediary. The light is a means of communication; what can one do with it after the great excommunication?

The last question forms the transition to a *second* consideration. The darkness gives expression to the burning of the *curse* which is accruing to Christ. He has been robbed of the light; affliction suffered in the dark is more. Affliction in a night which has been "made," which has been intentionally made for Him at mid-day — that is everything. Things cannot go any farther on earth. The darkness creates possibilities for the severest suffering possible, and accordingly is an expression of the extreme curse.

We know that light was the first gift of God's preparatory[2] creation. This very first gift — which was still the privilege of everyone after the fall — is now withheld from Him. "God causes His sun to shine upon evil and good." But He does not cause it to shine upon Him who as the Surety and Mediator is "less than evil." Even this world has no garment which would fit Him, for the best it can do is to oppose common grace to the common judgment, and hence it cannot isolate the Surety in the absolute judgment. Accordingly, God brings a portentous sign to bear upon Him: He takes the light away from Him in order to indicate by this act of stripping the Surety that the Surety is sinking beneath the level of the first of God's gifts and media. The person whom God has robbed is cut off from access to the primitive gifts. To-day He is that man. He is made the equivalent of a Thief. The curse is coming, and it is coming with catastrophes.[3] Three days of darkness in Egypt, and the first-born die, the first fruits of Egypt's might. Three hours of darkness, and the first-begotten dies, the first-born of the power of God.

But the advent of this strange darkness affected not only the nature but also the degree, the intensity, of Christ's suffering. We

---

1. See pp. 366-67 (the first three utterances from the cross); see p. 130.
2. There are two kinds of "creative" activity: the making, the constructing of the world (Genesis 1:1), and the preparing or furnishing of the created earth-world (the work of the six days of creation).
3. See p. 114 f.

must know that the intensity of His passion is a separate problem. For — as we pointed out previously — the Mediator confronts the humanly impossible task of suffering an infinite burden of penalty in a finite period of time. Time, and an hour of time, must necessarily have an end. Else that moment will never come, that point of time, in which the historical process of God's work of grace can be transformed from suffering into triumph, from cross to crown. And then the "payment" of the Surety cannot mean a cancellation of the debt. Nevertheless, the burden of the suffering must necessarily remain infinite; for the burdens which God's unrestricted, and "unrestrained" wrath brings to bear upon those who are outside of Him is infinite. The Mediator is being required to suffer, not for something else, but for the same guilt which sin has deserved, a suffering beyond human computation.

Now the suffering of Christ receives its infinite value first of all from His Person. His human nature is related to the Person of the uncreated Son of God. However, this suffering must be characterized by an intensity which exacts the utter extremities of His capacity for awful tension. Just as the successive periods of time (three hours) must be subordinate on this occasion to the intensive suffering, everything depends upon the fact that this intensity wholly consume the Man of sorrows.

And is it not true that in this world the hour of darkness is peculiarly the time of intense experience? The daytime and the daylight speak to us in successive, in quantitative language; these count out their hours and their minutes, and permit us unintermittently to measure time and space. But darkness and the night, and especially the strange darkness, the artificially created night, suppress the succession of moments from the active consciousness (to the extent that they can) and permit the influences being brought to bear on us to have their full effect of intensity (to the extent that they can). Counting is the work of the day; weighing is the work of the night. The night puts the concept of depth in the place of the concept of length.

Now, precisely because in Christ's burden of suffering length must give way to depth, and intensity is more than a passing of time, night and darkness take on significance. The burdens of His spirit are infinitely heavy upon Him. Therefore God thrusts Him into the dark. He must experience what is meant by the term "outer darkness." This was one of His own teachings: outer, extreme, darkness, a darkness unknown on earth. He had always genuinely and purely exposed the content of this doctrine. Today He must experience it, and the experience of darkness demands a medium of darkness.

Indeed exegesis must go hand in hand with experience for Him. Once John the Baptist testified of Him: He may teach us about heaven; for when He tells us of the house of light, He is talking about something which He has seen and heard; for He was in the house (John 3). In other words, the exegesis which as a man He gives of heaven, is one and the same thing to Him as the experience which is His as the Word, as the Logos. Today this word is being changed into its opposite. Does He, as the Logos, wish to learn of hell? Would He present the exegesis of this sombre concept through His Word? Good, but then His "teaching" of the hell, house of darkness as it is, must become a teaching of that which He has seen and heard. He must have been in the house of hell. The exposition of hell, which He gives as the Logos of the Scriptures by means of the apostles and prophets, must be made His experience which He must undergo now as a man. He must experience the darkness.

Say nothing, pray; He is experiencing it already. He is experiencing what chaos is. He is caught in the caesura of that inclusive "day of the Lord" which circumscribes and comprises the history of the world. God brings darkness on at twelve o'clock. By this means God proclaims that the normal condition of a lost world would be just such abandonment, such desolate suspension in unfathomable darkness.

Thus Christ experiences the absence of any comfort. Once one of the prophets had said: *At the time of evening it shall be light.* A comforting word, indeed, but now He confronts the exact opposite: at the time of light, at twelve o'clock noon, it shall be night. In the "day of the Lord," it is noon, it is twelve o'clock, the time for a chaotic interference with the cosmic scheme. Just as the spikes and the hammers of the soldiers were by Him placed between the beautiful beginning and the chaotic ending of the world, and just as He, when He prayed for the soldiers, consciously took up His position between the first day of the world-harmony and the last day of its chaotic disruption, so He is here. The Son hangs suspended in darkness at midday. At midday, you understand, not of one specific "date," but of the history of the one day of the world. Thus His attention goes back to the beginning and to the departure of the history of the world. It goes back to the beginning first of all. In the beginning of the great "day" God opened the doors of the world by creating light. And these doors He left open, even after the fall of devils and men. But that which was in the beginning and remained afterwards, is denied to the Son. He feels and He knows that history is being made here, that God is doing something new (*chedasjah*), and that He is permitting the Son to be swallowed up of it. For this darkness is also pointing ahead to the evening of the world. Listen to the voice of Joel (2:10) : The sun and the moon shall be dark, and the stars shall withdraw their shining; it is the day of the Lord; therefore the Lord shall roar out of Zion, and utter His voice from Jerusalem, and the heavens and the earth shall shake (3:15-16). Again listen to the voice of Isaiah (13:9). Behold, the day of the Lord cometh, cruel both with wrath and fierce anger, for the stars of heaven and the constellations thereof shall not give their light: the sun shall be darkened in his going forth, and the moon shall not cause her light to shine. And again (50:3) : I clothe the heavens with blackness, and I make sackcloth their covering. And in all this the Lord hath kept from me the tongue of the learned, and I must lament: why, why? I know that I am not in the place of God; I am the brother of the blind and of the cruel. Day of the Lord, day of days: It shall come to pass in that day, saith the Lord God, that I will cause the sun to go down at noon, and I will darken the earth in the clear day (Amos 8:9). Christ in the catastrophic curse! He stumbles — there is a fall; the abyss of outer darkness confronts Him. He has stepped over the border-line; He has no valid passport.

The "day of the Lord" has been in Christ's soul. He did not *count* the years in their succession, nor, looking back upon them, reckon them, but these years weighed down upon Him, and He experienced the tension of history in all of its gravity. Just as a dying person, according to the opinions of some, sees the panorama of his life's history flitting past in a second, and just as a seer intensely experiences what the daily people merely pass through extensively, thus Christ experienced the whole of the history of the world and of the history of redemption, and each moment was equally present in His attention. With this addition: for Christ it was not a dream, and it was not an apocalypse. He awoke in the dark, and He worked, and He felt Himself being thrust outside of all God's gates. The gate of Jerusalem had suddenly grown as wide as the whole world.

For — to elaborate the last point — the darkness affects not only the nature or intensity, but also the legal significance of Christ's suffering. That moment in which Christ was driven outside the gate, a moment we have discussed so often, now takes on a universal significance. The sentence becomes reinforced and at the same time is declared effective for the whole universe at this time. Without the gate of Jerusalem — that now became the equivalent of: outside of all gates, not only of the gate of Jahweh, the gate of the covenant and of redemption, but also of the gate of God, the gate of creation, the gate of light.

Yes, indeed, this darkness has something to say about Christ's relationship to the law, His struggle with the law, and the fulfillment of the law. God barred the way along which the Son was passing. Every alley and every bypath was closed to Him. Personally and absolutely, God closed all His gates to Him. God now calls in a loud voice over Jerusalem, over Judea, over Palestine, over this world, and presently over all the stars and all the world: Is there a gate anywhere; then let it cast Him out. Now the scapegoat which was sent away really suffers. This is the great day of atonement; the day in which the scapegoat must be sent into the wilderness. And can we say that there is any real wilderness in this world that we know? Wilderness, faithfully translated, means hell. Accordingly, Christ must be cast outside of the gates for He deserves to descend into hell.

We must return for a moment to the beginning of this volume. There we spoke of the legal significance of Christ's being cast without the gate as an exlex. There we emphasized the fact that in Israel, among the people of revelation, the casting out of a condemned person, and the rejection of such a person from the domain of legal activity, of legal words and deeds, to the extent that men could see that domain, contained a confession within itself. It was an acknowledgment that human words and modes of punishment were insufficient to give adequate expression and application to the essence of the punishment and of the sin committed. Neither the words nor the legal execution of guilt completely reached the fulness of God's justice and wrath. Even the revealed law, even the materials of punishment that had been drawn up after the example displayed on the mountain of the lawgiver, were not adequate to execute the full measure of the law. For human beings there is an inexhaustible remnant of divine wrath; this appeared to us to be the great assumption underlying and also the clear confession contained in the institution of the exlex who is hanged before Jehovah without the gate.[1]

This wrath which could not be expressed in human language *now* accrues to Christ. The darkness has something to say to Him. It gives Him its extreme message. It is the form in which the Lord gives expression to the wrath of hell. It is also the ministration of that wrath; it belongs to such materials of punishment as human beings have no access to. Darkness is that, certainly is that, even though it is not that alone. The inexhaustible remnant of wrath now descends upon the Christ. Human beings can make a cross; but this is mere child's play when compared with the materials of punishment which God now applies. He lays His hand on the suns. His taking away the light is an extension of the worst that human ingenuity can devise for an accursed person. The language which God speaks by means of this darkness is so absolutely devastating, disarming, stripping, erosive, and consuming that the legal sentences of Pilate and the Sanhedrin, and the mockery of Golgotha, are as nothing as compared with the language of God which places the exlex in the dark. Yes, we know that Christ had by the act of His own thinking, and by His personal "fear of the Lord" transposed all these human methods into a hellish and eternal intensity. But now God makes His approach from the other side. The Son had transposed the penalties of man, but now He is confronted by the impositions of the Judge, by the inexhaustible remnant of wrath, by the unutterable puissance of wrath, by the super-earthly, by the extra-mundane, by the infernal in the language and deeds of the irate Judge. This, and this coming from Him, now accrues to Christ. The darkness coincides with the descent of the Son into hell. It is a form which God's unmitigated wrath chooses of all things created to make

---

1. Page 20.

Himself known and to satisfy Himself. God molests the Christ by means of the possibilities for molesting which His human nature and the whole of created things offer Him as the Judge. For the rest, who shall say what the *body* of Christ suffered? Who shall say what was going on in His soul, in His spirit? Who can say to what points His thoughts were stretched? In this way Christ was thrown outside of every gate, outside of every sphere of life, outside of every world. We hear Him say that this is to be *forsaken*. And from that we infer that this act of the darkening of the sun has a negative as well as a positive influence of devastation. It presents the Christ as one who is brought to justice in an extra-mundane, that is, in an infernal way. Extra-mundane: that means that no single "world" may receive Him. A "world" is a thing which belongs together and which remains together. It is an organism. But He, the Great Sinner, can find no place in any organism. Adam is passing through all the worlds, and heavy darkness surrounds them all. Consequently Adam sinks down; the exlex becomes an exile; He has no *ground* under his feet any more. He passes out of time, yes— even though His heart is still beating in time. He has been thrown outside of space, even though the cross is still standing, its beam still planted in the ground. And now that He knows that He has been cast out of all organisms, now He descends into hell. That is the simplest because it is the only result. It is the opposite side — we might say it is the translation of "not being acceptable to organic constituencies." That is by no means saying just how it is, but is at best suggesting how it is not. There is no light, and there is no sun; there is the absence of God's first and greatest gift: namely, the light. But to the struggling spirit of Him who immediately gives all things a covenant name, a religious name, this negative element immediately indicates a positive act. It is not as a king but as a recruit, not as the head, but as a man, not as rabbi, or prophet, but as apprentice and proselyte to the angels that He is being degraded before the universe; and so essentially degraded that the first gift given to all, the gift of light, is taken away from Him. This is extra-mundane suffering.

And this is converted into the positive, into the infernal, into the hellish. No, beyond this point we cannot go, because we cannot write of hell unless we have been there.[1] We shall not strain to find words, God forbid. We cannot get beyond the word He used in His own teaching: outer darkness. Now the Saviour has been completely disarmed.

We human beings think it is something to see the eye being "broken" in a dying person. Well, presently Jesus' eyes also break. But before that takes places, His eyes are made useless. Is He blinded? No, it is much worse than that. Seeing, He sees not, and hearing, He understands not. He had frequently spoken of that Himself. There is concord between the eye and the light, and life sustains the harmony. But here this concord is broken, not because life fled, but simply because God said: He has been made sin. Thus God spoke to all angels: Cut off every thread connecting Him with other things; leave no avenue open to Him. The conduits, the aqueducts[2] of nature lead everywhere but to Him. No longer need *He* pray to God that the avenues of grace be opened to Him.

No, no, He need not pray for that any longer. For it is precisely when He lets Himself be made sin, and curse, and pollution, when He lets Himself be truly made that,[3] all "conduits" have been cut off from Him. The world always depends upon these conduits. But now there is no access for Him to any good, not even to common grace. Now He has been excluded from everything, even from the benefit of dying from exhaustion. Not long ago a book appeared in which someone who had been tortured — in Russia — in a dark prison, told how it had been possible for him not to cry aloud under the impact of the most terrible tortures, and not to lose consciousness. He decided — at the suggestion of another — to keep a point of light steadily before his eye, a lamp, a shining thing, something of copper or of brass, or the like; so long as he could keep that point of light within the focus of his eye, he could remain himself, not lose himself, nor be crazed by the pain. No one who reads the book can say how much of truth there is in it. But even this last resort was not available

---

1. The next chapter will discuss this theme further.
2. Ezekiel 31: The waters under the earth, that nurture the trees; see page 57. The darkness as an answer to "Christ's extreme service of the Word."
3. II Corinthians 5:21.

to Jesus Christ. His was not the privilege of light, nor the privilege of sight; O God, how can He preserve Thee and Himself?

Nevertheless a very clear light has been kindled in this darkness for us. For Christ performs His service as Surety; and God admits Him to the weightiest of all service. Those are two separate considerations; we must study each in turn.

The Christ is *performing His service as the Surety.* We know that the extra-mundane suffering, which released itself infernally upon Him, is the suffering *which we have deserved.* Today Adam is taking his own place.

Why do we preach, and why do we think, ten times, no, a hundred times, about the transfiguration on the mount to once about the darkening on Golgotha? Is it not self-evident that we should put these two contrasting moments into relationship with each other? You remember that the great theological problem which was raised on the mount of transfiguration[1] was this: Where is the possibility, where the reality, where the legal basis for an unhampered progress of the "kebood Jahwe," that is, of the glory of the Lord? The greatest representatives of the Old Testament, Moses and Elijah, had experienced the glory of the Lord in themselves, but could not give it to others, could not pave a way for it in Israel. They could not provide the route by means of which the "kebood Jahwe" might pass on to the people of revelation, to the people of the covenant. Therefore they came to Christ on the top of a high mountain, and asked whether He could do that. They asked Him whether He could let God's people partake of the illuminating "glory of the Lord."[2] The light of heaven which could find no passageway under Moses and Elijah, could find no route along which to pass to Israel, that right Christ had to provide for all the world, and that effectively and justly.

Thereupon Christ swore with a precious oath upon the mountain that He would do this, and that He would lay the legal basis for this. Now this oath is being exacted from Him. He must confront it now. Therefore He sinks to a plane lower than that of Moses and of Elijah, and is deprived of the light. This is an antitype of what happened to Him on the mountain of transfigura-

---

1. *Christ in His Suffering,* chapter 2, and especially chapter 6.
2. *Ibid,* chapter 6, p. 91 f.

tion. Then the night was made day,[1] but here the day is made night. He hears a voice saying to Him: "See to it that Thou doest it all in terms of the promise Thou gavest on the mountain; see that Thou doest this even though God is changing the pattern shown Thee on the mount. See to it that Thou purchasest the privilege of light by entering into outer darkness Thyself. Make sure that Thou canst cause the "kebood Jahwe" to go out from Thee, by first of all radically choosing it Thyself." Then the mist fell; it could not be penetrated. He is not asked what the people asked Moses. No one asks Him to cover the glory of His face, for the eyes of none ever suffered pain because of Him. True, a veil is thrown over His countenance, not because He is too beautiful but because He is too terrible. He is too much for the eye not because of super-abundant light, but because of ghastly death. His dulness became unhuman, became sub-human. But when the bearer of the light had been denied by the light, He gave us both light and life. The *glory of the Lord* receded, the light returned to its source, the foundations were removed, He was bound to the pale horse, and the first preparatory act of creative providence was withheld from Him. Thus our Surety earned the right to a beam of light. To a beam of light, and to the line of a psalm: God's friendly countenance beams, in joy and light.

Joy! And light! For, in the second place, we must make the point that the Surety was admitted to the *severest of possible examinations*. Up to this time He had been acknowledged as Surety. The sound of rejoicing echoed through the air. Certainly, admission of any person to the heaviest possible service, is official proof that up to this time He has passed his course with good success. Thus we can say that the darkness takes the form of a kind of honorary diploma for the thirty-three years of Christ's ministration and activity on earth. For it was not Christ who caused the darkness; it was God. From Jesus' point of view, and in the way Jesus sensed it, this darkness came upon Him mechanically.[2] By means of this wonder the Judge acknowledged that the curtain can be raised for the last act. He Himself summons Christ to carry out the severest and the last examination. This is God's approval of the thirty-three years. Christ gets His credentials. The

---

1. *Christ in His Suffering*, p. 26.
2. See pp. 305-9.

Son of man has carried out His work satisfactorily. This means that three of the seven utterances from the cross have also been accepted as good utterances. And inasmuch as these three statements spoke to us of His relationship to men, God is by this act testifying that Christ has dealt justly with all men. Now the final question must be asked, the final examination given. He must prove His merits to God, and the Judge will say, thereupon: It is enough. Now that God is personally ushering Him into the torture chamber of the universe, God is saying to Him: Up to this point the service was perfect. Rejoice all ye heavens, and be glad, for, although a curtain was placed before the sun, the light of the Passover is already breaking through. The time remaining is but a short time, for we are now to witness His last act. With one hand God strikes the heart of this man, but with the other He puts the hands of the world's clock to one minute before twelve, the turning point of "the day of the Lord."

In this matter the simplest Christian is wiser than the Greek philosopher Diogenes. Of him they tell the tale that when a usurper of the world asked him what he wished, he answered: "Only that Your Majesty be pleased not to stand in my light." Diogenes thought light was his best gift. Well, this choice of one of God's gifts was inadequately motivated and not entirely sincere. But that does not concern us now. Let us transcend his wisdom and learn after Golgotha to look upon a ray of light as a gift of grace. The sun shines each day for Christ's sake. Christ's first utterance from the cross was a petition not to stop the sun's course. Christ proved to be the great Joshua, who caused the sun and the moon to stand still for the sake of the battles of the Lord.[1] In fact, Christ took the position above that of Joshua. But now He is a lesser than Joshua. As far as the sun is concerned, Christ has been robbed of the privileges which every armour bearer and officer's valet may call his own. Now that He has borne this, the sun of His grace sings a song. Psalm 19 is an intensification of His hymn of joy, sung after the "twelfth hour" of the great Good Friday; and Romans 1 is its threat.

We know, of course, that this sun cannot say a word without Him who explains it. The sun can make its language intelligible

1. Page 147.

to us only if we have read the Word. God does not want to have His Christians instructed by speechless suns, but by the living proclamation of His Word. No, the sun is not disclosing its own pauper. The children of the Samaritans and of the Batavians kept on playing on Good Friday. We know that the darkness did not cover the whole earth,[1] but only the (Jewish) "country," only this particular "region"; it is hard to translate the original otherwise. In other words, no intentional mission was entrusted to the sun. That mission was reserved for the Spirit of Pentecost, by that Spirit Himself.

Nevertheless, God does have something to say to those people who are gathered here. He leaves the pagans at rest for the time being, but speaks only so much more eloquently to the people of revelation which has gathered in the holy city for the feast. It was enough that God spoke to Israel; for the veil over yonder had not yet been rent and Israel still enjoyed its privileges as the people of God's covenant and revelation. God addresses the children of Abraham and gives them what was promised: "the sign of Jonah the prophet." This He gives them in the last act. This He gives them as He sinks out of sight in the depths, in the darkness.

But even this sign will not be intelligible without the Word. The rule still applies: "In order that seeing they may not see." And in this case, the statement may be reversed: "In order that seeing no more, they may nevertheless not doubt that they are seeing rightly." The great question remained: If the darkness was a sign of wrath, who is being admonished by it? If God by placing

---

1. See Grosheide, *Kommentaar op Mattheus*, p. 353, 354. There are some who are eager to cling to the interpretation that "earth" is the proper translation, in order to think of it as a striking symbol of the fact "that the whole world" is suffering convulsion because of the "murder" of Christ. They regard the universal scope of this darkness as one of the travails of the last judgment. However, we cannot accept this thought. Up to this time, only the people of revelation had been addressed; for confirmation, consult the text. Moreover, the concealment is as apparent in the suffering on the cross as is the revelation, and the domain of the one constantly defines that of the other. Moreover, the interpretation is in conflict with the history of revelation, for it would see catastrophic events affect the whole world before the spirit of Pentecost has completely become effective, and it would accept a sign, when a sign is unaccompanied by the word. We could with equal justice contend that the light on the eve of Bethlehem has to illuminate the whole world. Or that the metamorphosis on the mount of transfiguration had to be a public spectacle. No, the issue here, is not a garment of mourning which God wishes to throw over the whole world, but the imposition of judgment on the Christ. The share that men have in this must be considered but must also remain secondary.

His hand on the sun and the Son, wants to threaten, who is it He wishes to threaten? The Christ or His judges. Is this eclipse of the sun a confirmation of the sentence passed upon Joshua of Nazareth or does it call down judgment upon that sentence? That is a question no one will answer except by means of the Word. The Scriptures alone can answer it, "all the Scriptures." Presently the Nazarene Himself will complain that He has been forsaken of God. Then all the judges can breathe freely again: Look, they can say, He certainly is taking it hard; He knows very well that the Father of lights is opposed to Him. It is not impossible that in the evening someone defended capital punishment on the score that execution sometimes succeeds in moving a person to repentance at the last moment.

But, if we read the Scriptures, we see in the darkness that God is adressing Christ's murderers. Say now, you beautiful priests, is Easter the great feast of Egypt's fall? Once it was dark in Egypt, and Goshen was lavished with light. But today it is very dark around you; as for Goshen, well, where was Goshen?

Ask no more questions. They did not repent. They said to each other: Be quiet; let us see whether Elijah will come. They suppressed all their questions, and acted brave and confident.

But what of those who believe? Has the Lord something to say to them? Yes, indeed. Everything which the Suretyship preaches to them about the content of faith. But not that only. He wishes to tell them also of the method of faith, something about the way by which one can attain to faith. When Christ suffered the pain of hell no one saw Him. Not in Gethsemane, for He stood at a stone's throw away. Not on Golgotha either. No man saw what terrors distorted His face, or how the affliction of hell entered into His body. God attracted His children of Pentecost to Him by the thousands, but He attracted not one of them by means of a "glance" at the wound. He allowed no one to look into hell.

Accordingly, we return to the mountain of light, to the mount of transfiguration. There also we saw light playing around the head of Jesus. On that occasion, the last word which God spoke to men, and to the candidate Pentecost-preacher, to Peter, was this word: *Hear Him, hear Him.* Hearing was the *sine qua non.* The thing that mattered was not seeing the light, or not seeing the light because of the darkness, but the *hearing of the preached word*. Therefore feel free to step out of the darkness, feel free to open all the shutters, and to light your lamps at night. Light is a good thing if enjoyed with thanksgiving. Open your Bible, and explain this intermezzo on the day of the Lord in the light of all the Scriptures, and of the dogmatics of the heavily laden Paul. Then come and recite your psalm. Now, however, you can sing on earth: God's friendly countenance gives light and joy to all. You can be sure that the voice of Christ in heaven is saying to the Father at this hour: One day in Thy house is more than a thousand without Thee. For He had been in hell. One cannot keep the count there. For the accursed exlex there the thousand days are as a fragment of one day, and three hours are as a thousand days. Hence He lived separated from God a thousand days. Nevertheless the house of the covenant is opened and the watchers at the gate are approaching. Meanwhile a certain Paul is learning at the feet of Gamaliel. He is learning to decline the noun *light* in all of its inflections, in order that he may presently write an epistle which will extend far beyond the country of Judea. The content of that letter will be distributed farther than the rays of the sun; it will contain a mystery about the inheritance of the saints in the light. When they read John, the narrator, those who listen to him will say:

> My heart sinks within me
> At this sight.
> Who would think *this* of thee
> O eternal *light!*[1]

But when Paul, the exegete, will have done speaking, these same auditors will add: The people who sat in darkness, and who therefore did not notice the darkness, have seen a great light: the light in the dark. Such was the order; thus everything was in order.[2]

---

1. Justus de Harduyn.
2. We shall not discuss the part taken by the darkness in the suffering on the cross as an organic whole at this point. Concerning that, see pp. 305-9.

Christ Thrust Away But Not Separated From God

CHAPTER SEVENTEEN

Christ Thrust Away But Not Separated From God

> ● *And about the ninth hour Jesus cried with a loud voice, saying, Eli, Eli, lama sabachtani? that is to say, My God, my God, why hast thou forsaken me?*[1]
>
> MATTHEW 27:46.

THOSE of us who have attended a rendition of Bach's *Passion of St. Matthew* very likely can recall the moment in which "the evangelist" announces the fourth utterance from the cross. In many programs this announcement does not harmonize with the immediately preceding moment, in which the other soloist interprets Christ's words by singing that fourth utterance. The first announces that Jesus cried with a loud voice.[2] But when the second soloist interprets that which Christ said he generally presents it in a restrained voice, and the organ usually accompanies the solo in hushed tone.

This seems to us to be an unfaithful interpretation, if not of the composer certainly of the Biblical evangelist, the first composer. The fourth utterance from the cross was not spoken softly and in a restrained voice, but was cried aloud. Those who cause the organ and the human voice to subside at this point misunderstand the matter entirely. There was violence in Jesus' crying; He exerted Himself to raise His voice. Never did the world quake as it did when the Saviour cried: Eli, Eli, lama sabachtani? His utterance rent the clouds and again pushed back the sun, which at first did not break through because it might not and there-

---

1. In this chapter we shall discuss the significance of the "why" only indirectly. We have discussed that already in chapters 12-13, especially the last. The reason for this method of treatment is indicated on p. 309; see also pp. 25, 242-3, 282 f., 305-8.

2. Und um die neunte Stunde schrie Jesus laut.

fore could not. It was a super-individual expression of a super-individual emotion. The whole church was groaning in this cry with groanings that cannot be uttered. And the Spirit groaned with groanings that cannot be uttered. Heaven and hell were included in the same act and were placed in the proper relationship overagainst each other in a single cry. However, on their part this was not made possible for the *anima sensitiva* of our Lord Jesus. Hence His crying with a loud voice was an extreme demand on that voice. In this portentous hour the highest demands on exertion possible to human nature were given outward expression.

Accordingly, we must say that the power which Christ puts into His cry is a bitter admonition to us. He wishes to suggest beforehand: No one will be able to understand this today. It is as if He wishes to suggest that at best we are but groping for the significance, inasmuch as a revelation, even though it is itself now preserving its manifest character, impresses upon everyone the undefilable character of its mystery.

Accordingly, we shall be able to "comprehend" nothing of what we say now. We shall not be able to "explain" the content of the fourth utterance from the cross, at least, not the essence of it. Of course, that is also true about everything else which we have written here concerning the suffering of Jesus Christ. But the impossibility of an expression which explains the essence is more firmly impressed on our hearts at this point than at any other. A well known saying has it that those who would understand the poet must go to the poet's country. And now the Poet par excellence is appearing on Golgotha. Be quiet, for Jesus is speaking. The creative spirit. The sensitive soul. And the Author of the psalms. Now He will sing, will *recite* His severest hymn — and no longer endure His own verses. You all remember that the fourth utterance, to put it that way, is a "quotation." It is literally the overture of Psalm 22. The Son of David is repeating the song of His father David.

Recently a book appeared written by an Israelite about Jesus of Nazareth. The man wrote that very likely the account of the fourth utterance from the cross was not historically reliable. Why not, do you suppose? Well, he said, because a person who is suffering the extreme passion of dying does not "quote."

We are already contradicting the general bearing of this objection, of course. Anyone who understands anything of the piety
and mysticism nurtured by the Scriptures will know better. Pious
people in anxious moments of life almost naturally quote the
Scriptures. There are many of those who pray, and who, when
they reach the point of strongest feeling in the prayer, immediate-
Scriptures is more effective at the ministration of the Holy Supper than a "beautiful" discourse. Death beds succeed in eliciting
more and more texts from the soul in proportion to the extent that
the wall texts in the dying room become paler and paler to the
breaking eye. Whoever lives in the Scriptures will, precisely in
moments of great stress as in moments of great joy, speak in quotations. So much in general. But we must say something also of
the Saviour in particular. He speaks in quotations because in a
strict sense He never uses quotations. The Scriptures are the product of inspiration; the author of the Scriptures is the Logos
through His Spirit. Thus the Logos is the poet, the creator of the
thoughts and of the poems in the Bible.[1] Accordingly, when as
man, that Logos feels back, goes back, in experience to that which
as the Logos he announced beforehand through the Spirit, we can
say that the specifically human in this experience can undoubtedly
be characterized by saying: Notice, He is quoting. But on the
other hand, Christ, who as a Person remains the Son of God also
in His human nature, is not quoting. As a human being He does
indeed refer to a statement of the Bible, but as God, as the Supreme Wisdom He once Himself announced the very statement
He quotes. Accordingly, He is not "quoting" another person whom
He recalls, but He is repeating His own words which He had
ly start using the phraseology of the Bible. A citation from the
spoken beforehand concerning Himself, and which, as man, He
now fulfills and realizes in Himself. Now they prove indeed to
sion between the divine Person of the poet, on the one hand, and
have been written and spoken with Him in mind. Now the ten-
the human nature of the man Christ Jesus who is struggling with
His own poem, on the other, is given expression in the loud, harsh
cry: My God, why dost thou forsake me? Thus He perturbs

---

1. *Christ in His Suffering*, pp. 273 and 275 ("The Author Sings His Own
Psalms").

Himself again.[1] He stirs His own waters with His own staff. He moves His own spirit. The Word became flesh, the flesh has recourse to the Word, experiences its own inspiration, and is in the same moment the one to receive and the one to conceive thoughts and poems. Thus He accepts Himself at this moment, but accepts Himself as He is being thrust aside. Thus His God *has* not forsaken Him, but He is busy primarily in maintaining Himself and confirming Himself in His own words. This is a great thing: to maintain Himself as He is in His own words. To God that is everything; if He does not do that He is not God. Hence God the Lord, God the Logos, exercises, maintains His own words. However, inasmuch as His own words of abandonment are speaking their message, His self-maintenance and self-insistence upon His own words is also self-rejection. God thrusts the man aside, because the Logos cannot thrust Himself aside, but is searching for Himself in His own Scriptures.

This is mystery. We cannot appreciate it because — to refer to what was said a moment ago — we have not been in the country of the poet. His country was heaven, and it is hell. We have not understood the poet, will never understand Him, because He is God, because He is in heaven, and because He therefore in His speaking transcends our comprehension. Nor will we be able to think as we should about the poem itself, for the poet is now in hell. Whoever would understand Him as He is in His hellish torture must have been in hell; and may God forbid that. Yes, God Almighty forbid that we should ever enter into the country of this poet. May He protect us from a comprehension of the fourth utterance from the cross. God forbid that we should concoct a theology of experience for we shall have to pay the expensive price of damnation for it.

In fact, even if someone after this life, and in the real suffering of the lost condition, should want to reflect upon the torture of Christ, which He experienced as God forsook Him, he would find that an eternal impossibility still. For whoever is in hell outside of Christ is there as a sinner; his pollution has not been annihilated. But Christ suffered the pain of hell as the holy man, and besides as the Person of the Eternal Son. No one ever was in hell

---

1. John 11:33; also pp. 432-33.

in that way, and no one will ever be there in that way. The fourth utterance from the cross is unapproachable to every creature on earth, in hell or in heaven.

All that we can do, therefore, is limited to this: to try obediently to appreciate the revelation, even though it does not permit our comprehension, and, in doing this, to follow the lines which the Scriptures have laid down for us.

They tell a story about a man who had thought for a long time about the fourth utterance from the cross, and who finally arose with the cry: God forsaken by God; who can say anything about that?

Now we can say at once that although we cannot comprehend the mystery, we can say what it was not. It is plain that it was not what the man said. God did not forsake God; that is an eternal impossibility. Even in the moment in which the Son as Christ was rejected from God in His humanity,[1] God yearned for God, and accepted God. Even in the moment of forsaking the Surety as Man, God's desire for Himself expressed itself eloquently and maintained its yearning. We said that a moment ago, but now we add this: precisely because God desires Himself, He willed the redemption: His own world might not be allowed to escape Him.[2] And inasmuch as the way to this usurpation of the world had to lead over Golgotha,[3] and over the point of being utterly forsaken, therefore God in this very moment is busy maintaining and asserting Himself.

No, it is not God, but man, who is here being forsaken by God. The man Christ, as the sacrifice for sin, *He* is being abandoned. And it is of this that Christ is speaking in His human language.

Now the language of men is inadequate for exhausting the eternally real and the really eternal things. We have said this so often that we need not elaborate it here. However, we do well to be impressed by this fact in connection with the fourth statement from the cross. A clear sense of that will at the same time aid our progress by inspiring humility; he who humbles himself as a thinking person, shall be exalted.

---

1. Presently we shall discuss whether that objective can be understood, p. 401.
2. Infra-lapsarian terminology which does not wish to contradict the supralapsarian idea.
3. It "was meet for God" (Hebrews); "it was necessary" (Matthew, Luke).

In human language Christ complains that God has forsaken Him. The language of the fourth utterance from the cross can therefore at best give but an inadequate and incomplete expression to what He experienced. We know that the abandonment of no single person, not even of the poet of Psalm 22, was complete. No person in the world was ever completely forsaken by God as a giver of gifts and as a preserver. For we can say this of "the world" in general: it is still included in the plan of common grace. God's worst enemy can still pluck fruit from its trees, and wear the clothes which God Himself has woven. The generals and the recruits of Satan's camp are all going about in armour which heaven provides. Abandonment, called such not because of its ethical or legal bearing but because of the consequences, abandonment, therefore, defined as complete disarming, is not possible in this world. Now you ask whether such abandonment is completely realized in those lost persons who have already left the world and the answer must be: no, it is not perfectly realized in them. For no one has as yet been steeped in the complete affliction of the torture of hell. Hell will be exposed to the raw winds of God's wrath completely only when the day of days shall have passed by. Hence, the complete content of the concept "abandonment," of the concept "forsakenness," is not yet known in hell.

We think, finally, of the *children of God*. They, too, sometimes speak of being forsaken. But in their case also this abandonment is never entirely real. They have been accepted of God. They have been regenerated by His Spirit; they live in Him eternally. Abandonment in principle is impossible to them in the absolute sense. It is true that they sometimes speak — and in speaking follow the Bible in part — of "spiritual forsakings," when a fever afflicts their heart, or when the comfort and the fellowship of God wanes or is swallowed up — but surely this is something different from an objective, divine act of forsaking, inasmuch as it is purely negative. They lack a certain amount, a certain degree, a certain fulness of the Spirit. But God does not thrust them aside, He does not deny them, He does not close His doors to them. Even though their spiritual lack does not exist independent of His providence, inasmuch as He takes that means to be their pedagogue both negatively and positively, a pedagogue who lets them feel presently that they have need of Him (see p. 234), nevertheless He does not positively allow perdition to accrue to them. And when He has led them back it becomes apparent that "their being forsaken by God" was but the other side of God's being forsaken by them. They themselves had retreated on the way which His grace had paved between Him and them. He, on His own part, can say: My child, my child, why have you forsaken me? As for Himself, He still extends His hand to them. And that which had actively accrued to them from Him during the "period of abandonment" was a subordinate part of a process of acceptance.

Not so the situation for Christ. For Him everything is different. Compare Him first of all with the lost people on earth, and you will see the difference. *They* eat from the table of common grace; He lacks that privilege now; even the rays of this sun do not caress Him. He wears no armour which God Himself has prepared for Him; for His spirit and body and soul are radically broken. Next compare Him with those who are even now steeped in the torture of hell and you will see the difference again. Their torture is that they are incomplete there; their body is not there; wrath cannot express itself in their body. But Christ is hanging on the tree in His body and the plague accrues to Him as He is in His whole human life. And, finally, compare Him with the believers, with a believer such as the poet of Psalm 22, and again you will detect the difference. They on their own part have forsaken God, and do not know how grievous it is to do without Him. But He has not forsaken His God on His own part, is not yet forsaking Him. Heaven has no charge to lodge against Him: My son, my son, why dost thou forsake me? Moreover, overagainst the Christ, God is not the mild pedagogue, who by letting Him feel what it means to forsake Him is really leading Him back to the state of favors and privileges. For Christ has been forsaken here because of His relationship to law. God is ministering the full wrath of justice to Him. Hence the distinction is very sharp: when the believers think they have been forsaken of God, they can return to Him, and must return to Him, and have no need of laying down a new legal basis for the return. Woe to them if they should refuse to undertake the return to the gate of heaven. But Christ in His abandonment is not warranted in accepting God's hand on the old legal basis. He must now set up the legal basis for the return. He must wait. He must suffer. His abandonment is not a phase of a latent process of acceptance, but is the essence of the process of rejection itself. And this last process cannot be divided into "phases," for suffering is infinite, and that which is infinite is not cut up into phases nor measured in periods of time. Besides, He Himself as He is in His Person is infinite; the awful significance of that is terribly impressive. And, inasmuch as Christ nevertheless was forsaken in time, this was not a phase of God's approach to Him, but of His messianic achievement of God's fellowship by means of His power as the Mediator. He was allowed to seek God's hand, and had to seek it, but He had to wait until it was extended to Him again. It is the same hand which is never withdrawn from the grasp of the believers.

Therefore we can say that the situation is fundamentally different for Christ than it is for the others, than it is even for the poet of Psalm 22, even though this poet gives expression to a unique poem. For this poet, apparently David himself, the abandonment is a relative one. For Christ it is absolute. For David it is a feeling that he lacks the blessings of grace; for Christ it is reality. David is the type, Christ the anti-type; in other words, David must refer to the Christ, but the Christ is the real. In the case of David, God is far removed from his "roaring"; in the case of Christ, God is completely removed from it. True, David misses the external support, but in the same moment the Spirit inspires him, and in the same moment he exercises faith and prophesies. But Christ, besides missing the external support, misses the internal sustenance also; and although He prophesies, His prophecy is one which was attained at the cost of struggle by arduous conflict (remember His "why") and without any help. Compared with Christ, David is the child. A child's hand can be filled easily and can be emptied very quickly. But Christ is the giant; in Him "deep calleth unto deep." David senses that he is in danger of death; Christ is in the midst of eternal death. David does not live under the curse, but under the blessing; the fact that He can compose a psalm proves that he is in a state of grace. But Christ is under the curse; He has neither grace nor glory; He would have been a repulsive spectacle, if God had not hidden Him in darkness.

All this, accordingly, was very strange. The like of it will return neither in time nor in eternity. For this Christ, God in the absolute sense was the "wholly Other." That, and the wholly and diametrically Opposed One. The human language was strained to the breaking point of its capacity for expression in the utterance of the fourth statement from the cross! It gave expression to something which it had never heard. In spite of that, however, this most mighty of statements was expressed in the Aramaic vernacular, in the language used daily by Jesus and the people. The official priests could quote Psalm 22:1 much more beautifully and better modulated than He. But our High Priest puts it very ordinarily in the language of the people; He had never learned the official Hebrew employed in the temple.

Therefore we can say that the law of the incarnation is again being fulfilled in this fourth utterance. Hell lies wrapped in bonds. And heaven also. The demonic is given expression in Aramaic. God speaks in dialect. Eternal reality is put in the language of the men at the market and the girls in the kitchen. Things are moving in the direction of Pentecost,[1] but for the time being we cannot comprehend it.

Nevertheless we want to come closer, and attempt, if we cannot understand, at least to become acquainted with these matters.

One question which arises very early is this one: Does the fourth utterance from the cross give expression to something which is really true, or to something which Christ "felt" was true. We sometimes say that the gross sins of God's children remove grace, and yet not grace, but the sense of grace sometimes. Similarly, we can ask now: Was Christ really forsaken of God, or did He simply feel that He had been forsaken? Is His word a prophetic statement; does it disclose an objective reality or is it a subjective expression of feeling? To this question Reformed interpretation, in the language of Bavinck, answers: "Some have regarded this utterance from the cross as a cry of despair giving expression to the fact that His faith had been lost and that God had forsaken Him . . . and others take it as an expression purely of His human feelings, of the psychological pressure suffered in that moment of greatest pain. Others again compare it, even though in broad out-

---

1. The ordinary language of daily life is declared adequate for the holy things; the official (limiting) Hebrew of the temple is no longer prescribed.

line only, with the cry of a mother whose heart must break because of the shame of her child, but who, nevertheless, motivated by her great love, assumes the shame herself and bows before the judgment of God. But all these interpretations do not do justice to the Word, and conflict with the continuous description of Jesus' death as delineated in the Scriptures. The lament of Christ is not a subjective, but is an objective, abandonment. It is not only that He feels Himself to be forsaken, but that He actually is forsaken of God; His sense of it was not the product of imagination, did not rest on a false assumption, but corresponded to reality."[1]

Yes, what Christ gives expression to here is, in the first place, a *fact;* in the second place this fact He senses genuinely and to this fact He gives genuine, if, as throughout the Scriptures, anthropomorphic expression.

The abandonment on the cross therefore was an *objective abandonment.* That in the first place. *God* is doing something. Now the forsaking by God as an act can be described negatively and positively.

Negatively considered, this forsaking may be regarded as a complete withdrawal from Christ of all those gifts by means of which God through His common and special grace has comforted and sustained His creature. The sun was gone. His honor had been put to shame. He was too repulsive to look upon. He had neither form nor comeliness; in fact He returned to that acosmical condition of a person broken in the presence of God. Moreover, spiritual fellowship has been withdrawn. There are no angels to support Him. The Holy Spirit does not comfort the Office-Bearer; the Holy Spirit neither confirms His being ordained to the office, nor His qualifications for it. The Holy Spirit comforts Him neither by whispering to His heart, nor by opening His eyes as in that portentous hour in which Christ saw Satan falling from heaven as a lightning. Christ had never received the oil of anointing, but where was the spiritual comfort, the *vocatio interna*[2] as a restful and delightful feeling? There were paradoxes, too, but that was another matter. And the Spirit which gave no comfort, gave no strength either. Influences and sustaining forces do not issue from Him—but stop here . . who shall ever be able to state

---

1. Dr. H. Bavinck, *Geref. Dogmatiek, volume* c, pp. 431-432.
2. Internal calling.

plainly what the withdrawal of the gifts of the Spirit means for a sinless heart? The matter is a riddle to us, and would be that even if we were standing overagainst other men. For no one can accurately describe the manner in which the spiritual world, the angels, the Holy Spirit Himself, influences human souls. We know that such an influence exists, but do not know how it "functions." We can write about it, but we cannot define it. And because we do not know how it takes place, we can not say in what manner and by what specific means it can withdraw itself and check its influence. How much more, then, are we embarrassed now that God stands in a specific, never recurring relationship to the sinless, human nature of Christ. And we must remember that His is a human nature which multiplies its riddles inasmuch as it is impersonal.

We stand abashed and scarcely dare to open our mouths. All we know is that the religious passion in Christ cried aloud for fellowship with God and upon a crystally clear internal testimony to the fact that He desired God. But that which God caused to accrue to Him from the outside was not an adequate response to this internal passion. "Thou dost not answer"; we can hardly get much farther than this negative phrasing (Psalm 22:3). But exactly this negative element turns everything topsy-turvy within the pious soul of Christ.

The issue, consequently, was not one of uniting, but one of indwelling. It was not one of uniting. In Christ the two natures are united, but God is not challenging that. Being forsaken means in a person where uniting has obtained, disruption, antithesis, eternal relinquishment, the breaking of the bond. However, next to the uniting of the divine and human nature there is such a thing, we know, as God's indwelling in man, in the man He has chosen, and in the man Christ Jesus. "The unity of the Divine and human nature in Christ is essentially distinguishable from the indwelling of God in His creatures and in the believers."[1] Christ as man also shared in this indwelling. And although the union, referred to above, allowed of no change, of no schism, the indwelling is indeed susceptible to various degrees of strength, and can at times be withdrawn entirely without surrendering "the house" in which

---

1. Bavinck, *op cit.*, p. 331.

God "dwells" eternally. The concept "dwelling" leaves room for variation, for more and less. For the union, designated above, this law holds: everything or nothing, eternally or never. But for the indwelling of God in Christ there is a law of more or less, of ascension and descension. Therefore we can say that each withdrawal of God's grace, each retraction of heavenly energies and divine acts of fellowship, can oppress the man Christ Jesus. These take Him out of His element, make disputable His whole right to life and His power to life from a human point of view and raise the question whether, inasmuch as God is divided against Him, He is not also divided against Himself, and whether He does not therefore fall back into the chaos of a life not nurtured and strengthened by God. External affliction this.

But the forsaking of God is also *positive*. God is directly sending the torments of hell against the Christ. A cry of pain surges up in His soul: lead me not into temptation, but deliver me from evil. And when God fails to hear this prayer, and persists in the failure to answer it (thus negatively withholding Himself, Psalm 22:3), Christ knows with immediate certainty that the representation of an inactive, and negatively withholding God by no means exhausts the truth. God is also actively busy in this inactive supervision. Just as an active influence of God leads us to the battle ground of temptation, and just as in the admittance of sin God the Almighty Himself appears as active inasmuch as all sin can exist only by means of the active permission of God, so the action of the Father against Him is simply unmistakably known to the Christ. It exists. It is God who looses the devils against Him, the devils and the four winds of the earth. The spirit of Christ, as it battles against the forces of hell for three hours, sees the devils rising up against Him, and as He sees it, God is taking the role of the supervisor in the arena, and it is God who releases the lions, the bulls and goats and cattle of Bashan, and it is God who releases the dogs (Psalm 22) against the great martyr with an agonizing calmness. It is God who lifts the doors of the cages. There is a voice, a lamentation, a mourning; there is the sound of groaning; deliver me from the lion, deliver me from the roaring lion and from the dogs. Plainly, He who really prays that, has acknowledged that God is doing something, that God is not afar off. Just as the martyrs in the arena saw the man who opened the doors of

the cages, and maintained the supervision from that point on, so
the Saviour saw God in His arena. God did not do much; but He
did everything that needed doing; He released the dragon. The
same Saviour who once saw Satan falling like lightning from
heaven, now saw Satan coming up out of hell. All the winds of
God's storehouse blew in one direction. All were blowing
against Him. *Afflavit deus, dissipatus est*: God has released His
winds; the son, the shepherd is being destroyed. Listen to the
summons of the Lord of heaven: sword, awake thou against my
shepherd. No, the doctrine of an inactive God can afford no
solution.

In very fact the forsaking, the great abandonment, was *objective*. In the second place, this objective abandonment is *genuinely
felt, subjectively,* by the Christ. And, what is more, this subjective feeling is genuinely and purely, if anthropomorphically, expressed. We notice that Christ's statement "corresponds" perfectly to the content and the form of that which has just proved
to us to be an objective reality.

The diction of His reply is a response to the negative element
in the "abandonment" of God. Even though He knows that the
devils are descending upon Him, and that the gate of hell is being
flung wide by this supervisor of the world, He does not complain
about the attack of the devil or about the abandonment of God.
We read of the attack by dogs and bulls in Psalm 22 also, but
Christ does not recite the whole psalm; He simply states the theme
of the poem, simply quotes the first verse of the psalm. That which
is dominant in this first verse is not the declaration of what the
devil does, but the proclamation of what God does not do. There
lies the possibility, and not in what the "dogs" do. In the last analysis the devils and the "dogs" are but the "second cause"; God
is the first cause. And he who would say something about the essence of a fly or of the cross, of a match or of a stroke of lightning,
about a child's wagon or about God's chariots winging their way
through the cosmos, must begin *a parte dei*. He must proceed
from God, must begin naming things by naming God first, and
must put God in the center of his thought complexes and of the
turmoil of his words. And doing that, he notices that God is withholding the commandment which could serve to stop the dogs.
Had it not been so, the "dogs" would not have had a chance on the

steps of the forum. The question is not who the devils are, who the dogs, who the bulls, who the people. The question is who is not here. It is not the coming of God in wrath, but the recession of God's love which determines the diction of the fourth utterance from the cross.

But the positive element in God's objective act is also reflected in the concrete statement. Christ says that God has forsaken Him. A person who has been related to us at any time cannot leave us without performing an action, without turning aside, without taking a different position overagainst us from the one in which he stood before. In other words, Christ is applying to Himself that which the Bible, anthropomorphically speaking, expresses when it says that God "repented." Now the idea contained in this repentance of God suggests just this change of position. It is true that back of this change in external relationship there lies the unimperilled unity of God's counsel and decision. But these belong to the hidden things. And inasmuch as Jesus by His "why" definitely indicates that He is not asking about the hidden thing, but that He is arduously struggling with the revealed things, with the expressed works of God, we must also find the explanation in a similar manner. Now there is another thing that we know. He hears God saying to the angels — not even to Jesus: I regret that I made Jesus king. Or again: I regret that I made man. We must even go a step lower before arriving where we should be: I regret that I have made man a slave, saith the Lord, the Almighty (see Psalm 110:4: Hebrews 7:20, 21).

Is it true that this matter of repentance has a bearing upon the real point with which we are concerned here? How could it be otherwise? Forsakenness implies fellowship. It implies fellowship between God and man. We know that the fellowship between God and man is a religious communion; it creates a unity, not of essence or influence, but of fidelity to covenant. The covenant has been placed between God and man. From that covenant, religion arises. By means of the covenant the relationship existing between Creator and man becomes a personal relationship of love. By that covenant also the fellowship becomes a consciously known communion; the fellowship recognizes itself, confesses itself, and enjoys all the times and seasons which the Father of love has in His own power appointed. In that covenant, in which God

Himself fixed and declared and announced all the terms and forms and postulates — for He never ceases to be Sovereign — God accepts man, His creature, as a friend. Man, who exists in a relationship of duty, now stands in a relationship of privilege. Man, His pure product, He now makes a producer. By this means God makes His own servant a friend. It is in that covenant that He now has religion in all of its entering in and going out, in all of its movement, become a communion, a medium of fellowship, and a manifestation of the union of God and man.

Christ as religious man was also placed in that covenant. He serves His God: that already represents the covenant relationship. He serves God as the Head of the covenant of grace, and as the supervisor of the covenant of works. By that the covenant relationship is in an absolutely definitive sense made central. Throughout His life Christ felt this relationship, and this union, this fellowship with God. It blessed Him, it gave the blessing, it colored and determined the blessing, it was the blessing. "Father, I thank Thee that Thou hast heard." "But I knew that Thou didst always hear" (John 11). But now, in this hour, those words with which He opened the week of the passion[1] stick in the Saviour's throat. The unity between God and Him no longer attracts, is active no longer. No wonder, we zealous students in His own school dare to say, no wonder, for now He was being treated as a covenant breaker, and therefore the union had to be cut off. Yes, yes, that is easy to say, but, even though the statement does name a legal basis for the broken relationship, it does not explain everything; in fact, it explains nothing about the legal basis for that action, nothing about the way which this dispensation of justice takes when it proceeds to remove all Christ's rights. The manner of it simply defies description. The only thing which we are able to confess to ourselves is that the meriting of the covenant relationship by the covenant interdict, that the achievement of the peace of the covenant by the suffering of the wrath of the covenant, was an infinite grief to the Christ, a return to the origins of the world, to the beginnings of religion, to the bases of all joy, and to an acknowledgment there of His own essential excommunication.

---

1. *Christ in His Suffering*, p. 56. This gives a further perspective to the narrative: John 11: 41, 42 stands overagainst this fourth utterance from the cross; see p. 418.

Even the Scriptures cannot help Him here, for the Scriptures were given in and by means of the covenant of grace, and although they speak of the covenant of works, they speak of it only in its relationship to the covenant of grace. These find their point of orientation in the covenant of grace which has entered the world since the fall of Adam and which explains itself in the course of the history of the church and the world. But in this astonishing hour Christ lacks not only the covenant-relationship as it was preached to the Israelites in terms of the covenant of grace, but He also misses the form in which it presented itself to Adam in the relationship of the covenant of works. He always "worked" in conformity with the demands of the covenant, but the reward which the "working" carried with it is consumed by the *supplicie*. Hence God is now referring to the epilogue of the sixth "day of creation." God says: I repent that I made Adam a sharer in my covenant. That is God's unexplained word. The covenant was monopleurical in character. It was announced by God; hence the Son can do nothing but endure that this same God from His own side can, in His sovereignty, proclaim that broken man retains nothing save a confused "why."

At this point, however, we hear someone saying that the expression about God's "repentance" is a mere anthropomorphism, not particularly serious inasmuch as it was not quite true. The person who raises that argument by way of claiming that the spiritual struggle of Christ was less severe than it is here presented — by use of the word "hellish" — means by His "anthropomorphism," a manner of speech in which God, and the divine, are represented to men in human figures. There are well known instances of such usage. God is a spirit, and still He is represented in human figures as a God who has hands, feet, as one whose eyes comprehend the whole earth, as one who senses sacrifices, and as one who sometimes repents. No one accepts these modes of expression as an adequate statement of what God really is. In fact, when we hear them, we feel at once that they are somewhat unreal.

Arguing in that manner, such a person draws his inferences in connection with this point also. He will say that in the last analysis it is but an anthropomorphic expression which presents God to man as one "who forsakes." Christ is really accommodating Himself to the Biblical diction, and consequently is expressing Himself by means of anthropomorphisms. The significant conclusion follows quickly: the "forsaking" was meant only in a figurative sense, and consequently was not as serious as it is sometimes made.

We completely reverse the rôles. Precisely because the Scriptures speak of God in an anthropomorphic manner and precisely because Christ makes use of their figurative language, the suffering was much severer for Him than we can ever imagine.

Just what, generally speaking, is the significance of the anthropomorphic in the Scriptures? In answer, we must indicate that it includes two elements: a humiliating, and a comforting element. Yes, the anthropomorphic element in the Scriptures is humiliating. It tells us in so many words that we cannot know God, that we could not know Him if He spoke in His own language, and in His own language gave expression to His unique completeness. He must condescend to us, He must address us in our own language, must make Himself known to us in images taken from our sense experience in order to enable us to understand Him at all. In other words, we are treated in the same way that a pedagogue treats small children. But the anthropomorphic manner of speaking also contains a comforting element. It proves to us that God in His love does wish to make contact with us, and that in doing this He is very merciful, inasmuch as He takes account of our capacity for comprehension, even though His sermons must necessarily be freighted with significance.

What, now, was Christ's relationship to these anthropomorphisms — Christ, that is, as man, as a creature limited by time. This much is certain, for Him the comfort inhering in it for us was not present. And the humiliation, the terror, included in this phenomenon, held for Him in an absolute import.

Yes, He had to forego the element of comfort contained in the anthropomorphic figures of God. If someone is doing his very best to make it plain to us that he no longer wishes to do his best for us, can we call that comfort? By no means. If he were to leave his brutal message shrouded in a cloud of obscurity, very vague, and quite beyond our reach, it could not possibly hurt us. But because the speaker is actually exerting himself to make it very clear to us that he has rejected and denied us, he wounds us grievously by the very intelligibility of his cruel word. Now this was the case for the man Christ Jesus. The Scriptures out of which He as a man of God had to learn His own ways, also speaks of God's wrath under the unmistakably anthropomorphic figure of *being forsaken*. Accordingly, God does His very best to teach the Son of man that He has no good word to say to Him. The very transparency of revelation is an agonizing message to Christ for precisely this reason at this time.

And that is why nothing remained for the Christ but sheer suffering, precisely because He was addressing the Scriptures in anthropomorphic language, and precisely because He had to express Himself in such figurative speech. For the reality about God is always much weightier and more powerful than the anthropomorphic figure of speech can express. And this is true also of the forsaking. The phenomenon of forsakenness among men is never something absolute, is never given without reservation, and is never infinite in scope. But for Christ it was all these things. Being forsaken among men is never a fundamental rejection, is never the act of a perfect sovereignty of justice, is never an absolute withdrawal. But for Christ it is all these things. Hence being forsaken never represents being put to death among men, and if to be forsaken does mean to be put to death, the cause of the death is never the abandonment solely, and it is never the cause of an eternal death. For Christ it was all these things. And hence His suffering was infinitely greater than the anthropomorphic way of speaking could indicate.

Listen closely, Second Adam: God repents of having made Adam. No humiliation remains, only the servile attitude. God is a terrible God, His sword cuts deeply. Christ listened to the psalm of David and conformed Himself to David's God. He did not cry out His lamentations in the language of His experience — had He done so all prophets would simultaneously have been consumed — but in the language of the anthropomorphic Scripture. Adam was here, and God was here, and all the doors were closed. Let that which is dying, die. Thus God had spoken and He had turned His back. This is to be forsaken! But precisely because Christ assumes the law of anthropomorphic revelation, He is the greatest sufferer among the prophets. Now the word characterizes Him also: Thou hast overwhelmed me. The statement fits Him as an auditor and as a speaker. It fits Him as a bearer of the message, and as the suffering victim of the message. There is no weightier theology than the theocentric theology; there is no more significant theology than one which proceeds from God. For this is the kind which now proceeds from the Christ. We have observed already that He made no mention of the second causes — of devils and of man — or of the powers which God's active permission allowed to descend upon Him, but that He spoke only of God Himself. In this His words about the "dogs and bulls" are placed under an awful tension, for He proceeds from His God. Now it may be, as we hope to point out later, that this is a manifestation of obedience inasmuch as it will save our souls, but for Christ it nevertheless is the root and cause of His passion. He who cannot get rid of God, cannot take a sedative, cannot dull the ends of the goads, cannot break the point off any lance, necessarily aggravates all His contrasts to the point of infinity. In this fourth utterance from the cross Jesus Christ is the absolute victim of the sermon on the mount. His theocratic thinking and speaking has placed these griefs upon Him. Only by means of such thinking and speaking can the "forsakenness" take on a positive content and a negative; only in that way can it prove a real perdition, paradoxically grieve His spirit, cut off every approach to God, and disrupt every scheme of organization within Him.

Now we must note that the expression of God's objective acts of commission and omission, the saying aloud of the fourth utterance from the cross, was a separate and necessary element in the suffering of Christ. He not only felt and pondered the fact that God had forsaken Him, but He also *stated* it. Why, you ask, is the expression and the pronouncement of this abandonment of such significance?

We can appreciate that fact better if we think, for instance, of prayer. The physical shape which we give to our petitions, the outward expression, the actual phrasing of our desire, is a separate element. We can say that in the last analysis prayer is an attitude of the spirit of man; we can give the name "prayer" to our desires, and God can reckon them as such, even when they still have only the form of unspoken thought and desire. But it is a part of the technique and of the essence of prayer to make it verbal, and to present the completed expression of it to God. A complete prayer is a speaking prayer. Not the objective need, or the awareness of it, not even the subjective sense of need arising from the desire, or the ideational approach to God determines the essence of prayer. A mature prayer is put into language, is expressed in words.

This is true for more than one reason. The oral presentation, the express form of prayer, is necessary first of all to keep the prayer pure and genuine. The cautious formulation of the petition, the oral phrasing of the desire, makes concrete a need which is first vaguely felt, and puts it into human language. In other words the spirit of man presents itself after preparation; it exerts itself to express adequately its needs. The naive upsurging of need disciplines, controls, and conforms itself to God's speaking, and forms words. The naked soul looks for a cloak. It cannot appear before God in a frolicsome gait, because it knows the nature of its sin. The soul hides itself behind a cloak, feeling justly ashamed of unwarranted boldness, and making the approach in humility. It shapes its words, and adapts its phraseology to the revealed word. By speaking its own words in conformity with the word of God faith conquers false shame, and converts every feeling of such shame into a genuine manifestation of humility. That is why the oral presentation is necessary to prayer.

That should suffice to make clear why the oral expression of His forsakenness constituted a separate and indispensable element in Christ's suffering. He preserved the essence of prayer. Now the psalms sung in churches may raise the song: Hallelujah, amen! The High Priest did not for one moment defile the essence of prayer. His distress did not make Him curse and, surely, the vitiation of prayer is called cursing in heaven. He has *spoken,* hallelujah, amen! His soul was like a parched land. This He had in common with all purely natural life, the natural, created life which has no tongue, inasmuch as it was not foreordained and created for a covenant relationship and therefore had no capacity for speaking in a covenant language. But He also gave oral expression to His thirst. He spoke in human language — He has no other — and gave physical shape to His experience. Thus He gathers His ideas together, now, when they are downright terrible. He is very ashamed of Himself, put on display as He is before God's angels, but His shame does not become a false shame False shame never wants to give expression to itself; it stands

mute, or it talks about every other thing, in order to divert attention from its own unworthiness. Consequently, it is disobedient;
it can neither pray nor confess, it asserts sin, and rejects virtue,
for virtue serves with simplicity of heart. But Christ in this nadir
of His suffering must still speak, for only in that way can He preserve His prayer intact and pure, and still be qualified for prayer.
He fully appreciates all that God is doing to Him; He acknowledges that this is called rejection; that He no longer represents a
mission, but a dismissal. Thus His shame remains holy. It is
weak, yes, but it is not sinful. He has not on His own part broken
the covenant by spurning language. He kept on speaking, even
when God was mute. He continued to speak. Never did any man
speak so shamelessly. The unrighteous Judge of the parable — ah
no, he cannot be found in this reality; however the righteous
Judge will have to arise from His tranquility. Here is a creature
who persists in speaking, even though the First Speaker long and
essentially held His peace.

Even that, however, does not exhaust the matter. A second
reason exists for which Christ had to speak. And that precisely
when God refused to answer. The first reason, you recall, is that
the prayer had to remain prayer. The second reason is that the
prayer must remain *subservient*. It must remain so absolutely subservient that it confesses God to be the first cause of created life,
independent even of the covenant. It must remain so subservient
that it continues to seek Him, even when the man, the original en-
joyer of the highest possible scheme of creation (the domain of
the covenant), is steeped by the silence of God in the lowest possible scheme of creation in the humility of the purely natural life
which must acknowledge the duty of serving and seeking God.
And that even though not as much as a single privilege ever
accompanies the imperative of duty.

Have you noticed that Christ comes to God in spite of the fact
that He is not called to do so? That is the nadir of the suffering.
When I as a human being am called to do a thing, when I have
been summoned, I know that a covenant relationship exists between me and the one who calls me. And a covenant always is
accompanied by those privileges which man in distinction from
the other creatures has received. But the covenant is monopleurical; in other words, the predominant element in the covenant is

that God is sovereign, that man must refer the enjoyment of the covenant to the duties of the creature. "Even though He slay me, I shall have to come to him . . ." Even though God takes the grace of enjoyment and all the forms of fellowship from him, even though He mocks these by virtue of a light inaccessible to our broken thoughts, does not this duty-bound servant remain a creature? Is he not one who has been thrust into existence by a sovereign good pleasure and a monopleurical will? Even though every enjoyment and every delight recedes, is it not the duty of all things made to honor the Maker?

Here now is your Saviour. God no longer answers Him, but He continues to speak. He clings to Himself as a creature, He excavates the ground of His own covenant until He comes upon the created foundations of His humanity, and dares to become one with every creature, and to say: Maker, why dost Thou reject me, Thy creation? In this He confesses His God in terms of "the whole creature."

This was His nadir. Now that Christ can no longer enjoy religion as a covenant relationship but continues meanwhile to acknowledge it as the duty of the creature, and now that He because of this duty undertakes to speak to God even though God does not speak to Him (Psalm 22:3), now the problem of His suffering has become the problem of every created being. And now the utterance of the fourth statement from the cross is one which proceeds from the deepest profundities of an unreserved (if need be, joyless) obedience and of absolute (without regard to special privileges) dependence and pain. He seats Himself at the table of all created beings and takes the lowest place for Himself.

Now we recall the discussion of anthropomorphism previously indulged. Every covenant relationship demands oral expression. Covenants serve to open the mouth. In a covenant relationship there is a fellowship between personal beings who declare their love to each other. Thus they stagger joy to higher levels. By means of the word they surrender to each other, by means of the word the association and fellowship are lifted to higher levels, and by means of the word spontaneity becomes conscious, a song of love becomes a psalm of love, life becomes a confession, and life is logically celebrated in the spirit. Hence the covenant fellowship of religion is a fellowship of speech. God calls and answers: man answers and calls.

But we noted above that the language of the covenant is an anthropomorphic language. Such is peculiarly the language of the covenant between God and man. In this very anthropomorphism we discover an element[1] which humiliates man, which forces him to condescension, which keeps him humble, and another element which comforts, exalts, and buoys man up.[2] The thought that the covenant between God and man in its deepest manifestation is monopleuric in character, inasmuch as God in it proves to be the Sovereign, the "wholly-Other," the one who in Himself is unapproachable to us, the one who cannot be understood unless He condescends to us in anthropomorphic language — that thought, we find now, is in conformity with the humiliating element of anthropomorphism. But there is also something to correspond to the second element and this something is the reality of the covenant as covenant. By means of the "anthropomorphically regulated" communication, God exercises fellowship; by that means He exercises and permits us to exercise it. Therefore Christ had to speak, His speaking preserves Him and the whole of creation. By speaking at the place of natural creation He arises together with her to the plane of the covenant. The speaking is a part of that. Just because the idea of a forsaking God is anthropomorphic, and just because it cannot be exhausted in the depths of its terrors, Christ has to speak. He must speak, even though God remains mute. He must speak, not on His own authority — the creature has no authority — but on the authority of the Word. We can say, therefore, that the anthropomorphism is the thin thread which He obediently grasped in order to climb from the plane of the natural creation to that of sonship.

By speaking to a silent God, Christ confesses that He does indeed lack religion as a covenant gift but that He still clings to it because of His duty as a creature. Having arrived at this nadir, the creature asks for the rights of a human being, and the human being for the rights of a covenant child. The duty-bound crea-

---

1. The first predication is appropriate after sin (the covenant of grace); the two second predications are appropriate before sin (paradise, the covenant of works).
2. As in note 1.

ture does not ask for release from duty, but he asks for a manifestation of a communication in which duty is pleasure. The unashamed prayer of the creature is the profoundest language which humility ever spoke. God be praised, He keeps the shame holy, relates it to religion, and manifests faith even in the extreme temptation and rejection. He is redeemed by His *theocentric* insight and His *honest* speaking.

By His oral communication with the God who has forsaken Him, He becomes *the Corrector and Atoner of the first Adam.* The first Adam hides himself among the trees, and does not make his appearance until a voice of God definitely summons him and asks: Where art thou? This is the false shame. This is a loss of language. But Christ is the unsummoned One; no one pays any attention to Him; all voices are mute. Nevertheless He opened the gates of heaven by calling up out of hell, by calling to God. The uninvited guest stood at the gate of heaven and knocked. Pray, He admonishes Himself, and you will receive; seek and you shall find; knock, and it shall be opened to you. The creature in the garb of a widower knocks at a door behind which the celebrated judge is celebrating a feast and is now sleeping. He says to himself: Would God not deal justly with a person predestined to be a creature, and open the door again? You see that this being forsaken, that this not having found, that this empty heart and empty hand, and that this locked door have not yet been explained. All these are still punctuated by the question mark of the "why" "why"? But above the fact that the abandonment is inexplicable stands the fact of the certainty of His wanting to and having to approach the gate of heaven, even when there is no voice to summon Him or to invite. Must His approach to God be an entrance into the "wrath of the covenant"? Then it must be that, but He will come, and He will also say that He is coming.

We feel at once that the turning point of the thought has been reached here. Up to this time everything issued in the idea: Christ is being rejected. Now we must amplify that epitome and add: Yes, He may be rejected, but He has not yet been separated from God. The tie which united Him with God continued to draw Him, and He Himself as a mere creature preserved that bond.

Therefore Christ's speaking in the state of His soul's distress is the reinforcement of our thought. At this point His own redemption and ours begins. The uninvited Guest redeems us. He takes us in behind Him. He who by His speaking condescended to the creature which was silent, ascribed no unreasonable things to God. The paradox, the apparently unreasonable did not drive Him away from God. He did not derive the notion of being from the notion of reason, and the notion of duty from that of thought. He lived on the principle of God's glory and honor. Surely, God cannot condemn His creature, for the name of God is written upon it. This the Saviour knew not on the basis of extensive argument, but on the basis of faith. The fourth utterance from the cross is a practical denial of deism.

Moreover, when Christ by His crying aloud to God lays Himself bare as a needy child, who cannot live in His abandonment, He proves to take no delight in that which is not of God. "Whom have I in heaven but Thee" — in those words I recognize the psalm of Golgotha. Did He despise the hell? By no means, but He hated it terribly, and feared it mortally. Why? Because the penalty grieved Him? No, not for that reason. He hated and He feared because God is great and good, and because our heart is restless within us until it finds rest in Him.

Again: why does He lament? Because of the pain, because of God, of Satan? No, in the last analysis He does not lament, He does not complain. He merely *asks*. Not even the fact that He is the victim of hell grieves Him. But the fact that He has been surrendered to hell by God, that wounds Him terribly. He Himself had the high courage to deduce chaos from God, and to look for the principle of its explanation in Him. In other words, He denies the chaotic in the chaos. He denies that the hell is another world of equal worth, standing sovereign overagainst the world of God. He takes His "why" to God whose justice and power and will assert themselves also "in the element of hell."

This is obedience, and it is a primordial obedience. He does not speak of a possibility, but of a fact. He says nothing of what can be, but much of what is.

> A person often suffers most
> from an imagined care;
> the grief he thus anticipates
> burdens him with heavier weights
> than God gives him to bear.

We human beings very often say, do we not: God will forsake me now; alack, He is forsaking me already. We often shout aloud our anticipations of abandonment, and convert these into the realities of being forsaken the moment we feel the first suggestion of the suffering coming on. It is not so for Christ. He did not say: My God, wilt Thou forsake me now? but Thou hast forsaken me. There is a fact, and the fact creates a circumstance. No, this person does not bear a greater weight than "God gives him to bear." That would be impossible anyhow, for He had been given every burden, and when one has everything, one cannot speak of "greater" ones. But what we mean to say is that He suffered nothing but that which God gave Him to suffer. His suffering never became mingled with unbelief. He reverenced the fact even in hell.

As a matter of fact, we are told as much by the words of the text: Christ cried aloud in the ninth hour. First we have been told that darkness came and lasted from the sixth to the ninth hour, that is, from midday until three o'clock in the afternoon. For three hours, therefore, the son struggled in torture and held His peace. He did not utter this statement until the end of those three hours had come.

Hence He is not guilty of the sin of the poet who created Psalm 39. The poet of that psalm was one who had wanted to hold his tongue in check lest men should see that he was no longer able to cope with that which God sent down upon him. That was the man who could not hold his peace in the calmness of faith because he derived his strength from God, but one who by means of a false manifestation of strength overagainst the people virtually tried to conceal his restlessness.

Christ is not such. For when He finally does speak, the message is an honest acknowledgment of His being defeated, and of His condition of defeat. He camouflages nothing: He cries with a loud voice. He cries so loud that the cry of victory which He had allowed Himself at the grave of Lazarus is now absorbed. For the sake of the people — you ask whether He takes account of the people! — for the sake of the people He had said: I know that God heareth me always (John 11:41-42). That had been the first impetus given the government by way of rousing them to thrusting Him out.[1] And now He again says to the people: God does not answer; I have been forsaken. I aroused Lazarus, but I cannot save myself. When "his heart is hot within him" it is burning with a holy fire.[2] Moreover, in this He also transcends the singer of Psalm 39, in that He first speaks when God has done speaking. The darkness receded in the ninth hour, and Jesus opened His mouth the ninth hour. He allowed God to have His full say; He did not hurry and act impatiently overagainst heaven and God.

Christ is obedient especially because as the theocentric theologian He exercised religion in His theology, even when the majesty of God was subduing Him. He did not address "God" but "His God." "My God, my God, why dost Thou forsake me?" It was a "quotation," but nevertheless absolute experience.

We can say now that He was in hell as the perfect stranger. He did not belong here, He could not acclimate Himself to that place. There was not a single reality of hell which He did not gainsay. His strangeness overagainst hell was not something negative, but something positive. He was a stranger in hell, because He remained a son and member of the family of heaven, because He remained theocentric in His thoughts, words, and deeds.

Therefore He shuddered in hell. He shuddered and trembled. True, the devils also tremble (James 2:19). Nevertheless, the difference is infinitely great. The devils tremble because they are divided against God and against each other. Christ trembles, because God is divided against Him, yes, and because He cannot sustain Himself independent of God any longer. But He Himself is not divided against God, and therefore not divided against Himself. He fears and trembles, but "fear and trembling" are not the same in Him as they are in Satan; they are not evidence of a destructive life, but means to a constructive end, a positive comprehension. "Fear and trembling", that is a phrase which assumes its classic significance, the significance it always has when used in the New Testament, when it means exacting suspense, awful tension, but a suspense, a tension, which accomplishes something.

Brethren, we are saved by this means. Christ descend into hell solely because that is necessary. To descend into hell means to

---

1. *Christ in His Suffering.* p. 56; this volume, p. 407.
2. See the confession of Psalm 39:4.

perform a personal deed, and to put oneself into hell by an act which results from personal choice is an abomination, and an instance of terrible haughtiness — unless it is necessary. Forget for a moment that Christ *had to* because of the theocracy, and the predication He descended into hell means: He played with God and with fire; He repudiated His God. But now that we know that it had to take place, and that while in hell He asked in God's name why He was not acceptable in heaven, now we can say that He was a stranger in hell, hallelujah!

Brethren, we are redeemed by this. He passed through, He emerged from the darkness. He lived in it for three long hours, and then passed on. Observed from a human point of view, this represented a period of time. He Himself knew nothing of such a period of time; to Him it represented eternity. Before Abraham was, I am, He said. He said it to people who measure time by periods, who use such words as "sooner" or "later." But He hung suspended in darkness for three hours, and was able to speak again only after these had elapsed; therefore He cannot distinguish between a "sooner" or "later." He said: Abraham lives, and I am dead. He did not say — not now: I die. He did not say: I shall die. Nor did He say: I died. He no longer was familiar with the imperfect, past, or present tense. All that He knew was the *perfectum absolutum*. I am dead. God has completely forsaken me. Yes, we designated it right. He passed through hell; He emerged from it. There was no scream, and no one heard an explosion when the darkness fell, when the darkness fell on Him. A scream was no part of His sublime character; it had become a second nature to Him to let God have His full say. Nor did He start with sudden fright, for He sank beneath the possibility of fright. The possibility of being frightened was suddenly lost to Him; this was worse, this was very different. . . . A person who becomes suddenly scared, who is frightened of a sudden, will scream, will be "changed in an instant of time." But Christ gave expression to a full predication, He gave voice to a question, after what for you and me was a period three hours long. Satan simply could not frighten Him, not even when God the Lord confronted Him with a sea of darkness at bright mid-day. We are redeemed, for no one stumbled into hell. He strode through it; but His eyes were sad. His eyes were turned towards Himself; not that He was absent-minded, not that, but, yes, I hardly know how to express it, I simply wanted to say, that this one question was written large on His eyes; but for the rest He strode on, He passed on, He emerged on the other side. He was not subject to fright, and nevertheless He was true man, and not acclimated to evil. In His case we would not even dare to talk of becoming used to hell. . . . He could not be frightened, for the situation was much worse than that. It was not an obsession; it was much worse. It was not a stroke, it was not a broken eye, it was not a convulsion, it was not even a combination of the seven travails, of the seven woes. The reality of this was below the reality of those. It was an endless woe, and it is just possible that human thought can best appreciate it from a consideration of these negative suggestions. It was not this, it was not that, and for the rest: God alone knows the mystery of the One.

Brethren, we have been redeemed by this. This was the second death, this was what the others had to suffer after the first death. This it was about which Revelation says: "The rest of the dead live not."[1] Ah, the comfort of that, for that, too, is "but" a negative predication.

Brethren, we have been redeemed. For now it is high time to remind ourselves that He at one time also taught us about the nature of hell. He told us about it by referring to two symbols: that of the worm, and that of the fire. The worm, he said, would not die there, nor the fire be extinguished. In saying this He was speaking in agreement with Isaiah. He, too, at one time depicted an irresistible death, the second death, the death of hell, by referring to these two symbols. First, he said, there is the worm. This symbol indicates that law of death which is the law of disruption. In this disruption death proceeds from the inside to the outside, for the worm — we may as well be honest about it — when you think of the worm you think of a dead body, which reaches the stage of decay, which disintegrates, and does so without any effort on anyone's part. It "just happens," because the blood is contaminated and the body simply relinquishes itself in all of its parts. But there is a second symbol, the fire. The fire refers to a

---

1. Revelation 20:5. Dr. S. Greijdanus; "did not become alive"; "sinking away in eternal death"; "lost in all comprehensive sense." De Openbaring des Heeren aan Johannes (Korte Verklaring der Heilige Schrift), p. 302.

devastation which does not proceed from the inside to the outside, but which consumes and devours the condemned person from the outside. Fire is something which is ignited externally, which burns the outside first and then scorches the inside. Accordingly, we have a picture of hell given us in these two signs, a proclamation of death in two ways. In the first place there is the worm. No man will ever be consumed by the fire of God's judgment unless an influence of death, a disruptive influence has been active within him beforehand. Death begins within: sin is perdition, it is the principle of disruption, and the worm does not come until the end, and then it gives an honest picture of the condition. Only after that does fire have a place as an objective, an externally consuming and scorching influence. In the figure of the worm we get a picture of the human being as already dead, and therefore a voice comes to us from the fire saying: Let the dead be consumed by death: flames of the Lord!

Therefore, brethren, we are saved in Him. Now a vision of the truth begins to dawn upon us. Christ was in hell, not according to the law of the "worm," not according to the law of essential perdition, but solely according to the law of the fire, of the external perdition. His fourth utterance from the cross, theocentrically speaking and theocentrically expressed, proves to us that He did not for a single second repudiate God. Hence He was not disrupted by a perverse influence operating from within. The worm was not in Him; there was no sin in Him; all that was present was the fire. And when the fire of God's wrath devastatingly accrued to Him, that "fire," that objective death, found no "worm" in him; it found no subjective death in Him. Only the fire was there. There was no correspondence between His external attitude under the judgment (the fire) and His internal attitude under the same judgment (the worm). Death consumed Him from the outside, but was not present inside Him. In the case of all human beings, and in the case of the devils, the fire comes only where the worm has been active already, and the objective death follows upon the subjective death. In the case of these there is death within and death without. Not so for Christ. And hence death was swallowed up in these three hours of absolute abandonment. He could go no farther. "Something new" had accrued to Him. At first it devastated Him from without, but it found no contact inside. Then death died; it had become exhausted. Where the correspondence between the external and the internal relationships is wanting, no hope for death or life is possible.

Death found no contact within. As for life? God simply could not break the contact. Just listen. Out of the depths of the affliction He cries aloud with His mouth and with His heart. He cried aloud to God: *Eli, Eli.* Eli, Eli — the whole of church history is concerned in this, and the two natures, and heaven and hell. And no one can learn that grave and sombre hymn, either in heaven or in earth or in the abyss which has been passed. Beware, do not recite it; and if you can, think of heaven, of hell, and of the earth. Think of heaven — a hand was extended from hell, laid itself on the steps of the Throne, and the Throne was not polluted. Think of hell — there was a fire which could find no inner contact and could go no farther and was extinguished.

Think of the earth. Do not say too much, but ponder this. Someone once wrote, and many are eager to read: a hundred and forty-five sermons about the bruised reed. But how many sermons do these same people desire about the green wood that was put into the fire? Of course, it is not a question of number, for those who have understood at least. Each man is weak in the things in which he is "clever." A hundred forty-five sermons — but He is too great for even that. My God, my God, why hast Thou accepted me? I live on the earth, and in very fact I have not denied it, neither it nor its numbers. I confess that I myself have busied myself a hundred and forty-five times with my own ego as compared with——how many times that I suffered, and labored for His sake. I dare not determine the proportions, but I am much ashamed. I hear a voice saying there is forgiveness. But twenty centuries of the history of the church and of dogma certainly should suffice to make us aware of our duty.

Christ Adapting Himself To His Death

CHAPTER EIGHTEEN

Christ Adapting Himself to His Death

● *And after this, Jesus knowing that all things were now accomplished, that the scripture might be fulfilled, saith, I thirst. Now there was set a vessel full of vinegar, and they filled a sponge with vinegar, and they put it upon hyssop, and put it to his mouth.*

JOHN 19:28-29.

The rest said, Let be, let us see whether Elias will come to save him.

MATTHEW 27:49.

"H E gathered his feet into the bed" — that is a way of expressing the death of a patriarch in the Old Testament. A man who was old and full of days sat upon the bed. He has run the course, he draws up his feet into the bed, greets the world, and meets his God.

Now it is rather difficult to compare a cross with a bed. But the great "patriarch" and Captain of our confession who lived and worked in the strength of Father Jacob-Israel[1] will also die in the strength of Father Jacob. He arranges His feet upon the cross, and dispatches His business well. He cannot, like Moses, mount a hill, in order to give Himself up there to God. He has already climbed all of His mountains. Nevertheless He does a deed which transcends the deed of Moses in its strength. He takes, He demands water of the people, water designed to clarify His thoughts in these last moments, in order that with a clear mind and with a clear voice He may commend His spirit to the Father and stride out of this world to the Father's bosom. Observe closely. Jesus is drawing up His feet upon the bed. That this is but figurative language is something that you may feel free to forget this time.

1. *Christ in His Suffering*, p. 400 f.

You wonder how He was able to surrender Himself so peacefully. The narrative tells us this, The Saviour on the cross was suffering from a parching thirst. That was quite natural, we all say. Yes, indeed; the last time Christ had taken a drink most likely was in the room of the Passover; and the gruesome crucifixion, the preliminary abuse, the scorching sun, the tortures of the cross, the spiritual struggle — all these tell us enough.

But there is another thing which strikes our attention. Not the fact that Jesus is thirsty, but the fact that He says so causes us to wonder a little. Those who stood by heard Him complain. And the question must have arisen: Does He regret that He refused a little while ago? For He refused to take the drink concocted of wine and myrrh. And did He have in mind now to recall His haughty and positive refusal? Look how avidly He drinks now. The reason cannot be the exceptional quality of what has been given Him, for it is not perceptibly better than the other. Myrrh was bitter, but this "vinegar," this sour, acrid, bad wine of the soldiers is not much better; just some water and some vinegar . . . and yet how eagerly He drinks it. Just a moment ago He could still lift the cup to His mouth with a free hand and then — He did not want to. And can you see now with how great difficulty He bends His head forward in order to keep the sponge from slipping from the reed? Does He regret His former action?

By no means. We shall see that Christ by calling for a drink, so far from indicating regret, was maintaining Himself as previously manifested. But in order to see the harmony of His thoughts as He drinks and refuses to drink we must first of all determine the place which this utterance from the cross occupies in the whole context of things.

It seems that the "I thirst" was uttered after the fourth statement from the cross. We know that mockery, while Jesus was being given the drink for which He asked, sneeringly said: Let us see whether Elias will come. The name Elias is a wicked punning on the text of the fourth utterance from the cross: Eli, Eli, lama sabachtani? This makes it plain that Jesus lamented His thirst after the period of the three-hour darkness, the period which was concluded by the fourth utterance.

The Saviour asked for a drink. Thus He returned to the world. You wonder whether this thirst had not caused Him to suffer before. Naturally, but the hellish suffering gone through just now had sunk to a plane so far below that of human suffering, that during the course of those three hours not a single word came from His lips. Then too He thirsted; then not for water, but for the living water, which, when men drink it, they live eternally. That thirst had been sub-human; it conducted Him into the next world. There a cup of water is nothing, is far beyond sight. And Christ's asking sustenance for His body now is in a certain sense evidence to show that Christ has come up out of the deepest abysses. He is among us again in this peopled world. He feels His flesh again. He can pay attention to the material of the sacrifice again: praise be to God.

However His turning around in order to see the materials of the sacrifice was a work of Christ's spirit. He becomes aware of His body by means of the spirit. Both of these are necessary for the sacrifice that is to come now. Be quiet, people; the last thing is about to happen.

The Gospel itself points out these things. Christ's thirst-motivated cry, John says, can only be felt and appreciated if we make a spiritual problem of it. No, we do not mean that this thirsting should be "spiritualized." By no means. The Saviour is suffering from physical thirst, and He is given the ordinary wine of soldiers; and He gladly accepts this. Why, then, should anyone wish to "spiritualize" this cry for a natural drink? It is not necessary; it is foolishness. For everyone, and also for Christ, in fact, for Him first of all — the spiritual is present in the natural, and God demands to be served also in the natural functions of life. The natural is immediately related to the spiritual. That becomes very apparent from what John says in connection with this story. The fact that Christ's request for water is not a purely natural expression such as the bleating of a dying animal might be, but is a spiritual problem, is apparent from John's indication that Christ in His short utterance knew, first: that everything which He had been asked to do was finished; and, second: that He had in mind to fulfill the Scriptures. Now both of these things are two strong achievements of His spirit. He knows something, and He wills something. His knowing extends itself over the whole of His past life, and His willing extends itself over the whole of His coming death; and He has the desire withal in His dying to remain faithful to the course of His life. We said that His knowing comprises His whole life, including the difficult work of this day. He has finished that which was given Him to do according to the Scriptures. As for His willing: He intends to relate the death which is almost upon Him now to His life, by means of remaining faithful to the Scriptures also in His dying. As He dies, He assimilates a Scriptural problem, He follows the direction pointed out in the Scriptures. It is a small indication, hidden, often forgotten, lodged between so many other words. But in that tiny indication Christ's whole life is opened up for us. For, precisely in the manner in which He died He had ever lived.

Christ knew, therefore, that everything was finished. That is a most significant piece of information. In other words, the content of the sixth utterance from the cross (It is finished) proves to be present in Jesus' spirit and soul when He utters the fifth. In speaking the fifth one, He is already eager to utter the sixth. Thus He lays all His stones one by one in the walls which He is building by His death. He arranges and rearranges His words: He builds a temple of the Word. The fifth utterance from the cross builds the sixth, the sixth lies concealed in the fifth, and the fifth is explained by the sixth. And not only that, but the fifth statement referred to the fourth and to what preceded that. We have stated already that the fourth utterance from the cross was the turning point of Christ's dying. In making that statement He arrives at the bottomless abysses, and arrives there as Conqueror. That which must follow now is lighter than that which has gone by. First He suffered the pain of hell, and died the eternal, and the spiritual death. But that has gone by now. All that is left for Him to do now is to surrender the body, to give up the instrument, the tortured instrument in which and by means of which He had faithfully served God. In this instrument and by means of it He also as a spiritual man accomplished His hardest work: namely, the descent into the affliction of hell. The body too suffered in that descent; it did even if we cannot say anything about the manner in which it suffered. And now that the work assigned to Him has been completely finished in the body, it is the most natural thing in the world that He Himself should give up this body to the God who gave it.

But how can He do this? Not according to the law of the former Paradise, in which the body would have developed to a higher form of existence without an intervening death, but by the law of the fallen world in which the curse takes its course. Surely the curse takes its course also in breaking down the body, in segregating and cutting off the soul from the body. The dissolution of the instrument — the body — is also a part of the punishment.

Christ knows that this last part of the penalty has now almost come. He feels that He is to die now.[1] Now the thought contained in the special note that Christ knew that all was finished is evidence to us that He did indeed understand the significance of His own complexes as a Mediator.

In speaking about the darkness of Golgotha, we pointed out that this darkness represented an objective expression of God. It was a humiliating, and at the same time a comforting, intervention; it was an acknowledgment that up to this time Christ had faithfully finished everything.[2]

Frankly this last observation, even though it gives us a necessary and logical link by which we can relate the darkness to the whole of the passion, nevertheless would have been too bold a contention on our part if it had not rested on this remark of the evangelist John. But John assures us that Jesus as man knew that He had finished everything. His conscience says a good word to Him about Himself.

And when Christ in that darkness felt Himself called upon to begin the last arduous struggle, He entered into the battlefield and He sought out death and the devil in their own home. The result of that? Well, if the advent of the darkness for Christ spells that moment in which God according to justice sends Him into the worst of devastation, then the moment in which light breaks through again, and the darkness recedes, must be an objective testimony to Him that God regards the struggle as having been satisfactorily finished. If the coming of the darkness indi-

---

1. We will discuss this presently, p. 439.
2. See p. 385.

cates an admission to the severest examination and trial, then the recession of the darkness indicates the presentation of the diploma of justice which tells Him that He has passed the examination. Jesus descended into hell when it was dark; God Himself draws Him up out of it when He again sends light down upon Golgotha. Again, you see, Easter is here in principle. Above the clouds they are already feeling for the ropes by which to sound the bells to the coming feast. Just as the resurrection of Christ from the dead on the first Sunday morning to follow will be a public, legal acknowledgment of Christ's being declared acceptable — He and His work and His justification, acceptable to God — so this new advent of the light is evidence to Him that God acknowledges Him as the Worker and Second Adam justified in reference to His last arduous struggle, the passion of the pain of hell.

Accordingly, Christ *knew* that the suffering of the pain of hell was the severest suffering; He knew that this was the eternal death, the second death. He knew that He had emerged from this second death and He knew that He had not yet been subjected to what the Scriptures call the first death, the dissolution of the body, the silencing of the heart, the withdrawal of that life which one has by virtue of birth. Very definitely a worse time could not be forthcoming any more. The turning point had been reached; the about-face, the upward flight, this time to eternal life, simply could not be prevented any more. There was but one thing to do besides — to die. That which takes place first in the life of men, takes place last in the life of Christ. He had to suffer their "second death" consciously before their first death, if His life here on earth was not to end in vanity. But now that He has suffered the "second death," now He can die in the body; His death in the body is already being regarded as a conquest of eternal life.[1] Listen to the utterances from the cross still to follow. They will be confessions of life, and of power, and of the deed. This is the first approach to a Passover hymn in the form of a fugue.

Therefore everything which is still to happen is to be His *praeparatio ad mortem*: His preparation for death. The cry: "I thirst," must be related to this, and derive its explanation from it; so much

---

1. By which of course we do not mean to deny that the dying belonged to the *sacrifice*. Read, for a consideration of the relationship between this and that, chapters 20 and 21.

the reader of John knows beforehand. The Saviour again carries His spirit in His own hands. He is again *compos mentis,* that is, He is master of Himself again. He has loosened His soul from the clutches of hell. God be praised : the Christ can exert Himself again.

And as He does so the work of religion which He believes is most peculiarly *His* now is that He devote His full and fine attention to the body and that He care for it. For within a few moments now everything will converge upon that, and everything will end in that. The Christ had done with the spiritual death. Now the body was left. O God, the last act of the Priest must take place now. Therefore provide Him with means which can help Him to make this act perfect and complete before God. O Greatest Majesty, clothe Thy Priest in righteousness. He is performing the last deed. Fill His hands; give Him the material with which to sacrifice; put vinegar in His mouth, and praise, and whatever else is necessary for this last thing.

Do not be too hasty, too hasty. John makes a second comment. He knows so certainly that Jesus by His fifth utterance from the cross was fulfilling the Scriptures and He knows just as certainly that He definitely intended and willed to do this. Literally He says : Jesus knowing that all things were now accomplished, that the Scripture might be fulfilled, saith, I thirst. At least, that is the way our Authorized version puts it.

There are three interpretations. Some think that Christ by means of the words "I thirst" and by means of those alone wished to refer to the Old Testament. According to these interpreters He announced His thirst in order to cause a word of the Old Testament to be fulfilled. For the Old Testament reports that a pious person had also cried because of thirst.

This is an interpretation, however, which has its difficulties. It is not easy to suppose that this very short sentence, a single word in Greek as a matter of fact, was a quoted phrase. Moreover, who will point out the words in the Old Testament which Jesus actually quoted? You can find them everywhere and nowhere.

A second interpretation is that Christ did not wish merely to give expression to His thirst and to nothing more, but that He wanted to elicit from the people all that they did in answer to His cry, in order to fulfill the Scriptures in that way. In other words, the vinegar's being handed to Him (in answer to Christ's lament) comes into consideration here. These interpreters point to specific words in the Old Testament; for instance Psalm 22:15:

> My strength is dried up like a potsherd; and my
> tongue cleaveth to my jaws;
> And thou hast brought me into the dust of death.

Or to those of Psalm 69:21:

> They gave me also gall for my meat;
> And in my thirst they gave me vinegar to drink.

This second interpretation has something appealing about it. It does indeed establish a relationship between Jesus' statement and the historical report in all of its implications. To that we must add, besides, that Psalm 69 comes to the fore more than once in the Gospel of John (2:17, 15:25) and that Psalm 22 also required our attention in the account of the passion.

Nevertheless, we have objections to this interpretation also. This kind of "quoting" has too little of quoting in it; it is just a little too mechanical.[1] If this had been the intention we should have expected that John, after reporting that the vinegar had been extended to the Saviour would have written: Thus was fulfilled that which was written in the Scriptures of the Old Covenant. Nevertheless, it is very plain that Christ intended that which He does and says as a means by which He on His own part intentionally and expressly can fulfill the Scriptures. The events here certainly do not indicate a fulfillment of the Scriptures which is unrelated to Jesus' intention. No, He derives the fulfillment of the Scriptures from the facts, from the events; He does this Himself and He does it independently. He compels the facts to reveal the con-

---

1. If Christ's statement is to refer to the "literal" vinegar, then the gall is an "annoying" particular; this "gall" plays a "very subordinate role" in the cup of myrrh which Christ did not take (Matthew 27:34; see pp. 91-2) but this "gall" is lacking here in John 19:28 (just as the allusion to Psalm 69 is lacking in Matthew 27). Moreover the favor of the "gall" and "vinegar" in Psalm 69 is not intended as a favor, but is there an act of enmity. On this occasion the presentation of the vinegar was not in itself an act of enmity; only the ensuing mockery became that.

tent of the Scriptures in their fulfilled reality.[1] This is the more convincing because John indicates that Christ knew that up to this time everything had been accomplished. Up to this time: "now." That makes us ask, naturally: And what is to follow? However, our greatest objection to this interpretation arises from the fact that in this way they regard the Christ as one who Himself elicits the presentation of the vinegar in order in that way to fulfill the Scriptures. Now in its setting in Psalm 69 the presentation of the vinegar is indisputably an act of enmity; it was given with an evil intent. It represented sin and blasphemy. And can we say, then, that Christ elicits something from men in order to accomplish something which at the same moment comes to Him in the form of a sin? Even though He greatly desires to see the Scriptures fulfilled, He cannot intend on His own part to induce men to do a deed which is sinful to His spirit. It is true that He sometimes constrains men to choose what they wish to do, to take a stand on certain great questions raised in prophecy, but that is something very different from eliciting an act which is named a sin in prophecy.

Therefore we choose a third interpretation which rearranges the order of the words in the translation without doing injustice to the Greek text.[2] If we do this, two translations are possible. The first is this one: Jesus, knowing that all things were (now) accomplished, said, in order that the Scriptures might be fulfilled: I thirst. And a second, equally admissible translation would be this one: Jesus, knowing that all things were (now) accomplished (that which He had to accomplish) in order to fulfill the Scriptures, said (realizing that): I thirst.

You see the difference between these two translations. In the first the expression "in order that the Scriptures might be fulfilled" is related to the *utterance* of the fifth statement from the cross. If this translation is correct the Saviour *intended* to fulfill the Scriptures by means of His utterance. In the second transla-

1. It is true that the Greek "hina" need not always have the strong connotation of "that" or "in order that." But this word, too, must be taken in the context of the whole, a context which makes us think as indicated above (see the formulas for the references to the Old Testament; see also the discussion of the "expected" consequence, even when "hina" is used in a consecutive sense: Robertson-Grosheide, *Bekn. Gramm. op. het gr. N. T.*, Kampen, Kok, 1912, paragraph 298, 2).

2. See Blass, *Gramm. d. ntl. Gr.*, 1902, p. 297.

tion, however, the expression "in order that the Scriptures might be fulfilled" refers to the immediately preceding statement which said that Jesus had now accomplished all things. According to this Jesus would have had a clear and strong sense that He on His own part now had accomplished everything which had to be accomplished in order to fulfill the Scriptures.

Now we believe that the solution of the difficulty lies in a merging of both translations. Christ knew that He on His own part had fulfilled the Scriptures by accomplishing what had been outlined in them as the task of the Messiah. He also knew that the great examination had been passed, that the severest trial as the servant of the Lord who is faithful to the Scriptures had been fulfilled.[1] But the work of Messianic suffering had not yet been entirely completed. The act of dying still had to follow. In other words, He orientates Himself perfectly. He knows exactly what point God and His people and He have reached. And in this clear self-determination, and by virtue of the "good conscience" which He has "before God," Christ now acknowledges that there remains but one thing for Him to do: to present the sacrifice of His body. Here is His body which must be broken for many unto a forgiveness of sins. Here is His pulsing blood, which must be poured out for many unto the forgiveness of sins. Well, since this is so He must prepare Himself for that sacrifice. He must prepare Himself, He must "gather up his feet unto death," and must accommodate His flesh and blood to the altar. Certainly He is not to enter into this death without knowing of it. Death does not come upon Him unawares. The suffering does not strike Him unconscious. On the contrary, He orientates Himself to His position with a perfect sensitiveness to the very end; this had been His way throughout the day. At all times He is perfectly aware of the lay of the land of each of His domains. He knows that until this time He has lived in conformity with the Scriptures, and now He says, again intending to fulfill the Scriptures: I thirst. Accordingly we would like to give this paraphrase of the text: Jesus, knowing that He had now accomplished everything He had to do in order to fulfill the Scriptures, said (because of that knowledge and with that specific intent): I thirst.

---

1. "Already"; see p. 440.

In doing this, we have taken the letter of the second translation, but have preserved the sense of the first. This teaches us how sensitively the evangelist John indicates to us the manner of Christ's dying. A vessel of vinegar, a handful of soldiers, a sponge, a reed, and the drama has been completed. But there is another thing, the incarnate Word. John presents — quite in accordance with his purpose — that incarnate Word as it manifests itself also in the dying of Jesus. That which seems to be a "cry of nature" as weak as the bark of a thirsting dog, or as the panting of a thirsting land, now becomes a revelation of God's immeasurable strength. Why does Jesus want to drink? Why does He present a request to God and to the people, why does He appeal to them for a last little modicum of "humanity," why does He ask whether they will give Him a little water or something else to drink? Because the Scripture makes demands upon Him even in His death, just as it has throughout His life. No, He is not looking for a mechanical, for an accidental, fulfillment of the Scriptures, one which is accomplished without the spirit, when He says: I thirst. Nor is He looking for a fulfillment of the Scripture in which "the detail" of the vinegar receives the whole emphasis. In this the Scripture is being understood as broadly as it is possible to take it. No wonder, people, no wonder: for we are standing on the plane between the second and the first death. Just listen. The Christ who has struggled with all the Scriptures throughout all His days, now seizes on this main idea which He takes out of "all the Scriptures," the idea, namely, that the Messiah of the promise may not accept His death as His fate but must perform it as a deed. His death must be a gift, a priestly donation. In His last act as Priest, in His last gesture by way of preparing the Sacrifice, He must act with a free will. Certainly He has not been given back His free will for nothing. True, His thought, and in general His voluntary life, has been afflicted, has been driven into a limiting cleft by God Himself, but in His triumph, as He emerges from the depths of the terror of hell, He again keeps His rights before Him, the rights, namely, of the Priest, the Prophet, and the King.

And now, strong in His regained assurance, prepared for the complete service of God and of the people, He demands for that service what is necessary to Him in order to fulfill the last act at the altar in righteousness, He demands water or its equivalent. O God, but He is thirsty! As a hart panteth for the water brooks, so His soul pants for Thee, O God. He would drink something, for He would satisfy the thirst of all those who are to stand around the Father's throne. He wants to drink something, for He is going to sprinkle the garden of God. He holds His sacrifice in His hand — for He is His own priest, and must therefore be alert when the time for the last act of sacrifice comes. Hence by a royal command He asks for a drink. Vinegar or water, no matter, just so it strengthens for a moment. It is Israel's God who imparts strength; His are the gold and the silver and the cattle upon a thousand hills, and the vinegar in ten thousand vessels. Now He arises in a spiritual way and draws water from the rocks of the hardest of souls. He will not lose His mastery of Himself. He exerts His effort to command His last powers. Exhaustion is not to put Him to death. The last altar of sacrifice beyond the reach of the arms of nature. She is soullessly amiable, and unreasonably brutal. But today her dementia will spoil nothing. Look, He is drinking. He calls His forces back into play, clears His eye, resembles Jonathan tasting his honey — vinegar is good — in order to fight to the very last. As He does so He sings the psalms of David ("all the Scriptures") and carries the power of divination within Himself. Moreover He is true to Himself. At first He did not drink, for He did not wish a sedative.[1] Now He does drink, because He does not wish to be dulled.

Ah, angels of God, He will help Himself. In Gethsemane it happened for the last time that an angel came to sustain Him; that also happened in order to prevent exhaustion, in order that He be sustained for the burdens God would put upon Him.[2] Now He must command His own resources and must reinforce Himself. Besides, the question now is not one of a spiritual capacity, but of a concentration of His attention, a physical preparation of the body for the last act. Hence He strengthens Himself by a final drink, in order thereupon to pronounce His two last utterances greatly and sublimely and then to give up the ghost in His own strength.

Now it is not necessary to "look up the references" made to the Scriptures wherever these speak of thirst and vinegar. For the

---

1. Chapter 5, especially p. 96.
2. *Christ in His Suffering*, chapter 20, pp. 357, 358.

whole of the Scriptures bears down upon the soul of Jesus, and the whole history of Revelation is concealed behind a vessel of vinegar.

Now that we have put this emphasis in the foreground, now it strikes us that the arrangement of the events is a fulfillment of the letter. Inasmuch as Christ on His own part wishes to fulfill the Scriptures without looking for particular details about vinegar or gall, the special providence of God is by no means ashamed of details. Now the Spirit and the letter correspond. Scriptures become literally fulfilled in an unexpected way. Yes, Psalm 69 contained a lamentation about those who hated the poet, those who gave him vinegar to drink. But in the case of the poet that was a figurative way of expressing himself. "The vinegar" was the mockery, the defiance. But in Christ His figures of speech become concrete fact, become real history. Here we have a vessel filled with ordinary wine, a sour drink common among the soldiers, a mixture of water, vinegar and eggs. This they give to Jesus. One of the soldiers takes a sponge — perhaps it was used to wipe off the blood of the crucifixion, or perhaps it served to close the vessel of the soldiers — dips it in the liquid, and conveys it to Jesus' mouth on a reed of hyssop. Thus Psalm 69 was alluded to, in order immediately afterwards to be spiritually fulfilled.

Yes, also to be spiritually fulfilled. For that which the poet had in mind by his use of the figure of vinegar was the mockery. And the mockery is also heaped upon Jesus. But of that later.

I know then that I cannot unctuously and spiritually overlook that vessel of vinegar if I want to know and say something about the Christ who, through the eternal Spirit, sacrificed Himself to God blamelessly. The child lay in swaddling clothes, and was the Word of God. The Man drinks vinegar, and swallows it, and He is the Word of God. The word was made flesh and dwelt near the knapsacks of soldiers. His spirit, the Spirit of God, are absolutely present, and are also active in this manner of drinking and dying. One word still deserves our attention: namely, the word "already." Jesus knew — we read in the original — that all things had now (already) been accomplished which according to the Scriptures needed to be fulfilled. Quite justly we deduce from this that Jesus was conscious of His approaching end before He asked for the drink. And we may also deduce from it that He assumed this early conclusion to the day and to the manger-cross road as an arrangement of God which gave Him peace at heart. For it is true that the rest of death came to Him quickly. The angels said: Come, Lord Jesus, yea, come quickly. Others had been hanged on a cross who had to suffer for hours, sometimes for days. People who should know assure us that some crucified victims died not because of this brutal punishment itself but because of starvation. Certain it is that death sometimes waited long before it came to a crucified person. In death by crucifixion after all no single indispensable part of the body was directly harmed. But Christ did not have to suffer long. Everything had been accomplished "already" . . . He Himself also seems to be surprised. Is it possible that after the resurrection He Himself whispered the little word "already" to John by way of telling Him how He had sensed the approach of death? We do not know; it does not concern us. All things were accomplished already. That suffices. After He had strode through the depths of the pain of hell, He was surprised at the shortness of the distance He had to traverse. For, from the viewpoint of time, His affliction was almost past; the length of it by no means harmonized with the exceeding great eternal weight of His perdition (I Corinthians 4). O sublime majesty of the fifth utterance from the cross! He cuts straight through the Word of God in its relationships. In the temporal world it is easy to say "already." But in eternity — ah, just be quiet: you still remember that those three hours did not suffice to give expression to a single word. Time and eternity, they are two entirely different things. We would not have dared to write such an "already." But what of that — often what we do clashes with what is of God.

But we must not relate this "already" to any other word. Do we read that Jesus had already been released from the suffering and that He felt He had been released? No, the work had already been accomplished; the Father had already been satisfied. It is that which gives strength to the heart. His "already" does not betray a secret opposition to the passion. It is not intended as an Elijah-statement: May life now quickly ebb away; *komm', süsser Tod*. On the contrary, He who is here is the Offerer. Gladly He now goes on His last journey, rejoicing as a hero to walk the path of love, grateful that the *Father* can already dismiss Him in peace, according to His word. For this proves that the eyes of the Father have beheld His own salvation. Already He will enter Paradise ahead of the murderer; He will have His chance to prepare the mansion. Youth returns: because of this suppressed *"already"* He grew in grace and knowledge with God and with the angels.

We can say, therefore, that He was patient to the highest degree. He had been rejected beyond the pale of common grace. No garment, not a single ray of the sun, was His. But He had hardly returned from His abysses before He asked for His gifts of common grace, and He received a gift, a dash of vinegar. And He immediately converted this gift of common grace into a service of special grace. Yes, He is the sovereign Claimant. Do the angels persist in staying away? No matter, He has His servants, if not above the clouds, in the world of the angels, then under the clouds. Under the clouds, and among the people. He has His servants among the people, for the soldier is a Roman. A Roman hand helped to give the Son of God the last powers which were necessary to Him in presenting His sacrifice for the world. Psalm 22 ends on an international note.

But what of the vinegar of Psalm 69; what of the mockery! We must devote a thought to the mockery which made this "humane" manifestation of a friendly gift of drink a suffering for the Christ. They had heard Him crying: Eli, Eli. Naturally they knew what the word meant. The insipid pun which changes the word Eli into the name Elias could not have been inspired by the Roman soldiers who knew nothing about Elijah, but must have been the invention of the Scribes, certainly of the Jews. They, surely, were well acquainted with the significant position which Elias occupied in the Jewish expectation of the Messiah. They knew also that Elias was expected as a precursor of the Messiah. Accordingly, they knew what Christ's cry meant: Eli, Eli, my God, my God. They know Hebrew, and they know Aramaic; they know Psalm 22, and they know very well that the Hebrew name for Elias is not Eli, but Elijah, a word which has a sound very different from "Eli," or "Eloi." Consequently, no one can suppose that they did not quite understand. Nor are we to suppose that they were moved by a certain fear which, according to some interpreters, mastered these people and prompted the question whether Elias would come with fire and sword to interfere with this violence against the wonderful Nazarene. No, this again was an instance of mockery. It was a mockery which had to serve perhaps to rationalize the secret dread inspired by the darkness. But in any case it served as mockery. It was an admonition to pay attention to Elias in case he should come.

Now this was an excruciatingly painful mockery, for it was designed to break Christ's Messianic consciousness. This point had been raised[1] also in the mocking speeches they delivered a few hours before. And the lance-thrust of their words consists of the fact that they make the self-vaunted messiah summon a man who must come before the true Messiah. Elias was not to be a messiah, but a harbinger walking on the Messianic path. These mockers simply want to suggest in passing that the brain of this Nazarene is a bit confused: today He is a messiah, tomorrow He will be looking for the Messiah's precursor.

Yes, this was the gift of the vinegar. Even the soldier who was rather congenially disposed cannot avoid joining in with the others as they break into rocking laughter about the Nazarene and His unfortunate case.

Christ did not reply to the mockery. It could injure Him no longer. The mockery which was heaped upon Him before "the sixth hour" was something quite different from that which accrues to Him now after "the ninth hour." For this mockery is coming to Him after the great crisis. The first mockery, which took place before the fourth utterance from the cross, was a part of the paradoxical conflict which issued in an all-consuming "why." But now the Gospel records that Christ knew all things had already been accomplished. His super-apologetic right, His sacrosanct right, is now entirely certain to the incarnate Logos. He has regained all His certainties. Just let them mock. Unshocked, He passes on to His next statement and says: It is finished. Elias has come, and they have done to him what they wished. The Messiah has come, and they have also done to Him as they pleased. But God has fulfilled His counsel by means of their wicked counsel. It is finished.

---

1. See p. 245.

He was a man thirty-three years old, but He died a death on a plane higher than that of a patriarch. He accommodated His feet to the dying, made His announcement, and went on. For a great anxiety was in His heart; no part of His deed of sacrifice might be sluggishly done, no part of it in a slovenly way. Mark, how He strains to be alert in order that He may do everything according to the example shown Him upon the mount. Both the tabernacle and the temple thought they were altogether too nice for Him, and altogether too dignified. But never was an offer so harmoniously and purely prepared as was this one. We celebrate His Supper, and it is a cause of special gladness to us to know that He gave His flesh and poured out His blood, and that He made careful preparations for this final gift. Careful preparations! And He was faithful to His people and to His God, according to the impervious style of piety and religion.

Do you go on now, and leave me here alone. I want to look at Him long and carefully. But no, I cannot. However, do you stand aside; I want to read my Bible here. I can do that.

I read the eleventh chapter of John. I shall restrict myself to John this time, for he alone told me that Jesus suffered awful thirst and that in His thirsting He announced it with a purpose. With a purpose! He is so punctiliously Scriptural, that my neighbor in the church would shake his head about Him if He had been any other. Yes, I hear the man saying — What? So close to death and still clinging to the letter of what was written. . . . Indeed, He had a purpose when He said that He was thirsty, and I am sure that my neighbor would get a following if Jesus Christ had been a member of our church in our village. Then we would all have found it a little incredible — such extreme "objectivity" to say "I am thirsty," and to have a purpose, a purpose, mind you, — this is so terribly obvious. . . .

But away with those church members and away with me, and my neighbor. John knows what he is saying. Go away now; I must learn to read the Bible, I must learn to read it alone.

I read the passage again. I hear a cry: I am thirsty, O God and men, I am awfully thirsty, I parch with thirst. This statement was not artificial; it was the simple truth. He was moved. That is the first thing. I read: He was moved.

I read a second truth. He knew, while He was moved, that He had fulfilled all the Scriptures. And this assured knowledge was related to His crying, to His craving for drink. His spirit did not yield to silence because of the parched flesh, His piety did not become *Leidenschaft.* In all His words of emotion His spirit was one. I read a second thing: He was moved in the spirit.

Be quiet a moment longer, for I read a third thing. He has a *purpose* as He speaks. My Sister of Mercy becomes angry with me when I say that He is not natural. But did I say that? Does she know a word for it? I can find none. I know only that John says that God, the Holy Spirit, declares that Jesus Christ had a *purpose* in announcing His thirst. He still wanted to do something in conformity with the Scriptures, for, O the letter of those! Now that He desires a drink, He confesses that He desires it. He decides to speak. His voice vibrates and is an expression of sheer integrity. His voice is the voice of forthright honesty. He is moved, He is under the pressure of emotion, even though He is not exalted. His voice was deep, and it was hoarse. Nevertheless He is absolutely Himself. He moved Himself, He acted on His own initiative. How can I say all these things in a single word? I know no word, and even though I exhaust all the dictionaries and commentaries and psychologies I shall not be able to find an appropriate term for it. I can only circumscribe it as my third point and say: He exerted Himself. It was entirely forthright, and entirely purposeful. It was natural and spontaneous; intentional and conscious. It was not a fabricated thing, but it was absolutely prepared.

Dare I write this on a piece of paper now? Three points. Lord, forgive me, if the statement is very meager, and very sketchy. Three points: He was moved; He groaned in the spirit; He was troubled.

But now I recall what I read in the 11th chapter of this same gospel. When He went to the grave of Lazarus — He was on the battle-field of His powers, someone said — the same thing was written. He was moved; He groaned in the spirit; and was troubled.[1] It was John who wrote it (John 11:33). Matthew, Mark, and Luke have other things to tell us.

Thus He returned here to His former strength. He can cause strength to go out of Him. Be careful. Very soon He will cause a "loud" voice to issue from Him.

When Jesus went to the grave of Lazarus in order to battle with death, He groaned in the spirit and was troubled because of an influence which issued from Himself. In that way He conquered at that time.

Now I have peace again. Just come back now, and we will read on together. I have heard it said that when He uttered His *Eli, Eli,* He had to recall in the presence of everyone and in the presence of the crowd, that which He had spoken and spoken aloud at the grave of Lazarus.[2] That was enough for the "proud." They had understood it perfectly. But who is He internally? Who is He in the spirit? You have the answer on the tip of your tongue: internally He is the same as He was. He is just as strong as when He went out to recall Lazarus from an ugly death.

Surely, if He is just as strong and powerful and self-sufficient as when He raised Lazarus from the dead and knew that God heard Him always, then He is now back in that strength. Listen: He can save Lazarus. In very fact He can save Himself. The only question is: Does He want to? No, for He sacrifices Himself, and this He does by that same will. Hence the fact that He rescued Lazarus from death was much; but the fact that He sends Himself into death is everything. He accommodates Himself to His dying. He knows that the Father hears Him always, for He has just moved through hell. And knowing that the Father hears Him always He asks for a drop to drink. . . . Do you think I have understood it now? There was a rich Man. He was rich in

---

1. See Dr. S. Greijdanus, "Eene bladzijde uit het zielelijden van onzen Heiland," *Geref. Theol. Tijdschrift,* volume 14, number 3 (July, 1913, p. 112): "He was not passive but active in this perturbance. He was not troubled, He troubled Himself. This was not a manifestation of weakness in Him, but a manifestation of strength. . . ." p. 114: "This was not merely being affected or moved by something external, but it was a personal response to an external stimulus. *Etaraxen* (troubled) connotes shock, fright, confusion. . . ." p. 115: "John 11:33 does not . . . present a figure of speech; a reality in the Lord's emotional life is there being described. . ." In this article also the perturbance of Christ as written in John 11 is regarded as enmity against Satan, and as an organization of what was immediately before Him and the whole history of redemption, that is, "and all the Scriptures."
2. See p. 418.

mighty works; He could rescue the dead from their graves. This rich Man had been "in the pains of hell." He opened His eyes in hell, being in torments, having descended into hell. He opened His eyes, felt thirsty, and asked a drink. And Abraham came, the vinegar of a stranger was as sweet as the water of the fountains that flow in Zion. Abraham could refuse nothing to this rich Man who had opened His eyes in torments. Strange — that broad, deep gulf had suddenly disappeared.

My humanitarian sister, piety is not sentimentality here. And, my high-strung brother, piety here is not *Leidenschaft*. Not unless you want to call Jesus Christ vanity. But He has given us an example. On Golgotha you can find raw materials out of which to construct a religious thirsting, and a dialectic for honest lamentation.[1]

1. Concerning the position which this fifth utterance from the cross occupies. see chapter 21, pp. 493-96.

Christ in the Justification

CHAPTER NINETEEN

Christ in the Justification

● *When Jesus therefore had received the vinegar,
he said, it is finished.*

JOHN 19:30a.

NOW He goes on from strength to strength. His fourth utterance was an expression of weakness. In external form His fifth statement from the cross betrayed the need of help, but an infinite strength consciously expressed itself in it. Now we listen to His sixth utterance. It gives expression to a strength which is also indicated in its form.

It is very short. In this respect it resembles the fifth statement. In the Greek language it consists of a single word. It is full of heavenly realities, however. And, consequently, it is just as fully charged with earthly realities. It consists of a confession on the part of our Prophet and Priest, and is fully informed by the praise of God.[1] The incarnate Word glories in the fact that the moment of Jesus' dying does not represent a stumbling into the night, but a prolongation of the day of the Lord. It is an extension of that "day of redemption" which in the moment of Jesus' death may turn over another leaf in its journal.

"It is finished." What did the Saviour mean by that statement?

In order to answer that we must first ask ourselves to what it refers. Does Christ mean that the Scriptures and the Prophets have been fulfilled? Or is the statement simply designed to say that His cup of suffering has been emptied, and that the suffering once placed upon Him has almost passed by.

Many think that they must choose one or the other of these possibilities. As we see it no such choice is necessary. We do in-

---

1. Again it is John who is writing of this.

deed believe that the fulfillment of the Scriptures vindicated the Christ, and gave Him a free conscience; and we also believe that the completion of His life-task filled Him with an infallible and hence irresistible sense of joy. He was going home.[1] Is it necessary, then, to fix an antithesis between the one and the other? Surely no one desires that. Must we separate the one from the other? No one has need of that. If we remember that the content of the sixth utterance was in Christ's thoughts when He uttered the fifth,[2] we can better understand the meaning of the sixth. We noted in the preceding chapter that Christ knew all things had been accomplished; and we also considered the fact that He gave His full attention to the definitive and general fulfillment of the Scriptures in this awareness. Hence that was already in Christ's spirit which He now utters.

This at the same time points out to us the meaning of the sixth word. All that had definitely been given Him to do had been accomplished. In other words, He had in His historical life achieved everything that the Scriptures had indicated as His Messianic task. The eternal and the temporal, the counsel of God and the deed of Christ, are combined in this utterance of our Victor. These two have found each other, have clung to each other throughout His life on earth, and are now brought together. In the sixth utterance from the cross Christ confesses that His life from the time of His birth to the time of His death has faithfully achieved what the Father gave Him to do. The eternal did not soar over His temporal existence, but entered into it and accompanied it. Standing before the abyss of death He now knows that He is both the fulfiller and fulfilled. He is fulfiller to the extent that as a servant and as a man He has done what was demanded of Him. He is the fulfilled to the extent that as servant and man He worked not on His own authority; He did not do His own work, but the work of the Father expressing itself in the Son.

This statement of the sixth utterance was an exclamation of joy. Moreover, the joy was thoroughly human. There is an objec-

---

1. See John 3:31, 32. The word of the Baptist: He came from above; He saw and heard what was taking place in heaven. See also pp. 377-78.
2. See pp. 430-31.

tive capacity for joy in the Christ, which always remains itself. It is the deep basis, the vital source of His delight in God and of a good conscience. But the man Christ Jesus has been placed in time; He acompanies the seasons, He develops along with the ups and downs of His work. It is this which makes His joy so moving in its thorough humanness. You can notice it at once. He rejoices because He has something new to say: *It is finished.*

Yes, but just what is finished? The Messianic work? No, not that; absolutely not that. For if Christ had not arisen from the dead, had not continued to perform His service, all would have been in vain, and we would of all men be the most miserable. What is finished? The satisfaction of the justice of God? No, not that either; for He will not have satisfied the justice of God, and will not have satisfied that justice in its exacting aspect, to the extent it makes its demands in the history of Christ, until He shall have delivered up the kingdom to God, even the Father. What is finished? Being a servant? Not that. As Kurios, as exalted Saviour, Christ also remains subservient to the Father. What is finished? The humiliation? No, His sublime utterance cannot pertain to that either, for His dying presently and His burial later, will also be a part of the humiliation. What is finished? The fact that He has been appointed an offence? No, not that. For Christ is an offence in His exaltation also.[1] He is an offence also in those respects in which we cannot *see* Him but can only *believe*.

No, when we ask just what is finished a single thing serves as the answer. That which is finished is the consciously suffered humiliation in body and in spirit. Not the serving, but the being a slave in humiliation; that, observed from the active side, has now been finished. The torment of the payment, the suffering of the penalty, and both of these consciously, that is finished. The effort at compensation for the wrath of God could not be taken away from Him even if the dying and the burial had not accrued to Him. But the suffering in which Christ had to appear actively, in which He, the Second Adam, by His own effort had to surrender Himself, that is finished. True, the bearing of the humiliation, the experience of disgrace and disdain, the being a foolishness and an offence, all these will still be His in the immediate

---

1. This is opposed to Kierkegaard, Barth, Althaus, etc

future. But that which could still accrue to Him after His death by way of adding to His humiliation no longer demands His personal deed. When everything has been given in the Spirit, then the recession of life itself will no longer have to be an active deed on His part. The surrender of the spirit is the last act; thereupon death comes of itself. As for the grave, for that He has His "servants and maids." His deed will not be necessary for that.

The sixth utterance of the crucified Christ consequently is a prophetic declaration about God as well as a joyful declaration about Himself. It is full of subjective gladness. But this gladness has assumed discipline; it is an obedient joy. The speaker remains the servant of the Lord. Learn of Him now, for He speaks meekly and lowly. He does not say:[1] *I* have finished. He says: *It* is finished. He Himself is not the subject of His sublime statement. If the servant makes his own work the theme of the discussion, he does not leave the work, the name, the glory of the sender on the highest plane. But Christ, who in this respect is theocentric in His religion, does not place Himself, and His own share in the work, in the limelight, but names the whole program of work which God has done through Him. What does He say? He does not say: Eureka, I have found it. It was not His own inventive faculty, but His qualification for the service of the office, completing a task delegated to Him, which rejoices His spirit. He speaks as a servant who had an assignment to accomplish and not as the master architect. It is finished — by this statement Christ not only draws Himself but also the Satan, all the devils, and even these wicked people here, into the circle of His attention. Nor is He saying: I am free; I have escaped from the snare; I have not been unsuccessful. For — even though because of the physical pressure He could hardly breathe — He had to drink first, we remember — He prefers singing of the steadfastness of the Scriptures and of God's counsel to rejoicing in the temporal experience of the day or of the days which have just passed. Not His own "tension," not His own "suspense," but the unravelling of the seasons of God, the consummation of God's decrees, these are the

---

1. If we sometimes use the expression that Christ "did not say" this or that, we do not mean to establish a contrast between what He did say and the other possible formulations which are lacking here. The issue here is the formulation and the structure of the sentence, for this cannot be accidental.

theme of His paeans of victory. God be praised, the mandates of the Messianic life have fortunately had an end. Not the fact that His plan has succeeded, but the fact that God's plan has been finished in Him constitutes His joy. No wonder, we say again (but afterwards, of course) : no wonder, for though faith in these days may be regarded by some as an enormous risk, Christ never once regarded faith as a risk. Living according to the letter of the commandments by the Spirit — that was His primary, His sole, and His perfect security. The Scriptures took their own course, and now that the revealed will of God had been His food and His expression, it is certain that the hidden will of God must delight in His joys. His faith is not conditioned by the success of its result, but His faith postulates the effect. He is in no sense uncertain about the result; if He had been that, His entering upon death would certainly have become a risk. In other words, it would have been an act of unbelief. However, quite to the contrary, He is personally certain of God's response to His Messianic life of service. And He gives expression to a terse epitome of that certainty in this plainly and unmistakably uttered statement.

Thus Christ is justified. Both in the presence of God and in the court of His conscience He is completely vindicated. It is finished: the counsel, the Scriptures are finished. And this sublime paean of rejoicing, stating that the suffering He has undergone has accomplished the one good service, the service of God which in its own entrance upon the Sabbath takes a whole people with it into the Sabbath-joys through vindication in Christ Jesus, is now given expression in the joyous: It is finished.

Therefore we can say that not this or that detail of the Scriptures, but that all the Scriptures were present in His spirit as He uttered these last two statements. This is another reason for which we do not believe that the sixth utterance from the cross was an intentional quotation. Some wish to regard the "It is finished" as a conscious illusion to the last verse of Psalm 22. This psalm closes with the words:

A seed shall serve him; it shall be accounted to the Lord for a generation. They shall come, and shall declare his righteousness unto a people that shall be born, that he hath done this.

Now some choose to regard this last clause, "that he hath done this," as the original of the sixth utterance from the cross. They

point out that in this way the whole of Psalm 22 had its fulfillment in and dominated Golgotha: the beginning, the middle, and
also the end of the psalm. The beginning: simply recall the fourth
utterance from the cross. The middle: for the parting of the
clothes, the mockery, the disdain, the thirst — all these were motifs
derived from Psalm 22. And now the end: It is finished; it has
been done; God has done it.

Nevertheless, we raise objections to this interpretation. Psalm
22 pertains to that act of God which is being praised by the poet:
namely, the rescuing from death, the ascending line. But Christ
not only includes His deliverance from His distress, but the distress also in His vision. Not only the victory, but also the struggle, not only the powers of glorification, but also that which humiliated, was before His mind's eye. In this, Christ sees God's
counsel fulfilled and in this He sees the Scriptures and all of
prophecy brought to rest.[1]

Thus this statement of universal power and glory in all of its
genuine humanness also becomes a statement of our Lord and
God. Past the vessel of vinegar which lent physical strength to
the utterance of it, His thoughts go on and reach to the abyss of
time, to the culmination of all the eons. The Word was made
flesh, concealed itself in a crying babe, and required a sip of vinegar in order to speak. And when it spoke, it spoke of the great
deeds of God; it said that these were finished.

Yes, my Lord and my God said that up to this point it was
finished.

Three times the Word of God uses this phrase in history. The
word "finished" is clearly and ringingly heralded at the beginning
of history, in the middle of history, and at the end. At the beginning, for in Genesis 2:1 we read: "thus the heavens and the
earth were *finished,* and all the host of them." Already at this
time the eternal Word, the Logos, appeared before us: for by the
word of the Lord were the heavens made. At the end of time we
hear the same sound repeated: the Revelation of John tells us that
some day this voice will sound throughout the world: it is *done*
(Revelation 16:17). That is the call which closes the history of

---

1. We say nothing about the fact that the Septuagint apparently is not thinking
of anything that God does, but of "the people whom He hath created."

the church and of the world as it is brought to its culmination
by the Spirit of Christ. Now these two extremes, the primordial
beginning, and the accomplished end, are bound to each other by
the sixth utterance from the cross. There the Logos speaks in
the state of humiliation. There He bears the world which was
once created "by" Him into the Father's hands, surrendering it.
It is ready and ripe for the last act. The curtain may rise to it
now. The consummation of the Spirit may begin after the consummation of the work of God in the earthly tabernacle.[1] Now
that He has labored according to the Scriptures, and now that He
can neither be tried nor grieved in all eternity, now that He has
fulfilled the covenant of works which came to the Second Adam
as a proof and an examination in righteousness, and now that He
has lifted every labor of the covenant above the plane of an examination, now He also takes the Spirit in His possession, that
Spirit who ever brings to fruition what is latently potential, that
Spirit who ever consummates what the will has established in
principle, that Spirit who presently will exhaust the Christ until He
too can say: It is finished.

We have made two discoveries: the sixth utterance from the
cross proved to us to be human, and it proved to us to be divine.
Now let us permit our thoughts to return to their course. We think
back and observe that the sixth statement from the cross repre-
sents a two-fold function. In the first place, Christ as the Son of
God takes the proper position *in the divine being,* and there makes
His report. In the second place, Christ as the Son of man, as our
Mediator and Surety, takes the proper position *among His own.*

As for the first, Christ as the Son of God takes His proper
position in the divine being, and there presents His report. As
the Son of God He reports to the Holy Trinity. The word "reports" may have an irreverent connotation for some, and not
seem to be a proper expression for indicating the relationship between the three persons of God, but we shall let it stand as it is
nevertheless. We must not regard matters here in a human light,
but must take flight to God with our thoughts. If we do that, the
word we use is in place. For it is a peculiarly divine activity that
the Father, and the Son, and the Spirit report to each other about

---

1. Tabernacle, for after the resurrection the body of the Logos is temple-
"building." (II Corinthians 5).

their work. The divine life in the three persons is not merely a mutual knowedge, but it is also a reciprocal communication. The glory of the divine life, the strength of the divine life, is always announced by the one to the other in the secret language of that good pleasure of God which ever returns to God, the self-esteem of God, the self sufficient. Now the Son is entering into fellowship with the Father and with the Holy Spirit and — mark, He is rejoicing about this great day. It is finished! The song which gave expression to the divine joy of creation was not as sublimely moving as this short song of God's regenerative capacities. The Lord has introduced "something new" upon the earth and this new thing has now progressed to a certain point of ripeness and crystallization, a point at which it can be said: It is finished! It is finished! — that is an evening hymn, and also a mid-day hymn. It is an evening hymn if it is observed from the viewpoint of time; then it is the evening hymn of *Christus Moriturus,* the evening hymn of this strange Pilgrim's journey which took thirty-three years. But this evening hymn of Christ's temporal existence also becomes the mid-day hymn of God's sublime working day. God has created and regenerated; He has dug under the creation, and placed a firmer foundation under it. Now the Son comes and says: I see all that I have made, and behold, it is very good. For without the Word nothing was made that is made. By it were all things made, and without the Word nothing was regenerated that is regenerated. By it were all things brought back. Yes, "the beginning of the creation of God," the Almighty God, rejoices in His acts. In God there is a sublime pleasure in creation: He sees even before it is finished. And there is also in God a recurring joy when He sees the work after it is finished. It is finished: perfect time, *perfectum.*[1] A verb in the perfect tense has smilingly fallen from God's lips. *Perfectum beatitudinis, perfectum quiescens.* God's present tense hovers over history — hide yourself from the emanating power of a God who in His created passion is expressing Himself!

> Joyously singing,
> The mighty God
> Sings praises to His name.

---

1. (Present) perfect time; not: it is being finished, but: it is finished.

He sings praises to His name. It is finished. In a *perfectum* of perfect rest the Son announces His victory. Simply, directly, He says it to the Father and to the Spirit. He stands infinitely above the evangelizing practitioners. He makes the immanent announcement in which the Father, the Son, and the Spirit enjoy each other. And His sublime announcement of peace, of the finished act, that condition of rest which is ever there, His *perfectum* of seven blessednesses, is known only in heaven. On earth we can at best fumble with the meaning of the blessedness of such reciprocal announcement between the three persons. On earth *perfecta* are very temporary, they are constantly replaced by others, by the imperfect tense. But the *perfectum* is peculiarly heavenly; all the verbs of heaven are first conjugated in that tense.[1] It indicates the completion of the action, and all heavenly action is in its relationship to God completed. "Thou art my Son, this day have I begotten Thee." "Thou art my Father, this day have I finished it." Such is the language of heaven. Why? Well, this perfect condition of restfulness is strange to Satan, is quite unknown in hell. In hell there is only the tension, the imperfect time; there nothing is completed, and a condition of rest is an impossibility. Before it could utter a *perfectum propheticum,* hell would have to cease being hell. In hell there is an unbroken suspense, which can never be lifted. In hell there is only fearing and trembling.

But the Son arises to His rest. He also arises into His rest. His rising represents a standing, and all His standing is a sitting, a resting. Thus the Son now enters into fellowship with the Holy Trinity. The human word of Jesus the Nazarene causes a flash of the light of the divine joy in regeneration to dazzle the heavens.

Yes, the Son enters into a pure relationship with the three persons. He has finished the creative renewal and redemption of the "great Day of the Lord." Now we know that "the Day of the Lord" is divided into phases, into hours. It was evening, or it was noon, or else it was morning; but in any case there were phases, there were milestones. There were separate hours, tran-

---

1. Naturally, this is figurative language, but it is derived from the usages of the Old and New Testaments (those of the poetry and the prophecy), and from dogmatic considerations.

CHRIST CRUCIFIED

sitions. This day of creation also is divided into milestones of creative evolutions.

Listen now. Presently a voice is heard in this "Day of the Lord." My Lord and my God is speaking. He says "Finished!" Now it was morning, and it was mid-day. In this the joy which is surcharging the heart of God at once finds an outlet, an expression by means of which it can reach the earth. In that sixth utterance from the cross God's Sabbath rest is being vindicated. But because God wants men to enter into His Sabbath, there immediately takes place a reaction to His Sabbath-evolutions here below. In the sixth utterance from the cross God, my Lord and God, announces the approach of the Christian Sunday. It was finished, but finished at mid-day of the "jôm Jahwe." Hence the arduous labor, the exacting strain, and the feverish effort to arrive at the condition of rest was now completed. Completed by the Son first and completed for the people next. Hence it is part of this statement which divides the day of regeneration into segments, that now the sun which shines down upon the "jôm Jahwe" must turn. Henceforth it will not be a matter of laboring arduously in order to achieve a state of rest, but of a work whose benefits proceed to the outside. It will be this for the Son first, and for the people next. It is finished: now the Sabbath of men on earth will no longer be at the end of all their arduous effort, but at the beginning of the days and the weeks. The recreating procedure of God, the creative appointment of the new things in the kingdom of heaven changes from an appointment to an ordering, from an establishing to an elaboration, from a struggle to introduce the new things to a joyful service in ordering them, and so this procedure reaches the state of a princely and eschatological enjoyment of the established and ordained "new" works of grace. Therefore at this turning point of time the Sabbath is transferred from the last to the first day of the week, for it is the privilege of earthly realities to be a reflection of heavenly realities. The Christian Sabbath is being announced beforehand, is being legally established by this sixth utterance of Christ, and it will be proclaimed and actually instituted on the day of Christ's resurrection.

We began, when we wanted to listen to the Speaker of the sixth utterance from the cross, by paying attention to the three persons of the divine Being. In this utterance God called to God, the incarnate Word called out to the Father and to the Holy Spirit. By means of what was otherwise a genuinely human expression, God called to God. That we have observed and what else was there for us to observe? The sixth utterance from the cross placed us human beings on display as empty and very poor. A cry is passing over our heads. God is calling to God with us, about us, without us. The announcement of the Son to the Father and the Spirit echoes around us; we hear a trembling, a *vox humana*, but in the deepest essence of the call, this utterance going from God to God passes over our heads. God's announcements first of all seek Himself. Only after they have found Him and because they have, are we saved. The redemptive fact has by the power which is from above delineated its own paths upon the earth. It is finished! Looking at it this way, I detect the sovereign language of *free grace*.

Now our second consideration. In this sixth utterance from the cross Christ also proceeds to occupy the right position over-against His own. He stands erect and in His own place, in the commission of the covenant. We gave expression to this when we set down as the title of our chapter the phrase: *Christ in the Justification*. Why that strange term? Because it really is impossible to find an adequate substitute. The word "justification" is a fixed expression, suggesting vindication. By it the justifying announcement of God is indicated, by which the sinner is acquitted of the guilt of sin, and by which his right to eternal life is proclaimed to him.

Naturally justification in this strict sense was not given the Christ. He has no sin, hence it cannot be stricken from His record. If we cling to the word in its strict meaning, we must say: He does not share in the justification, but distributes it.

Nevertheless Christ — on the other hand — has been made sin, and has been made curse. He has been condemned by the justice of God, and must by that same justice be restored to favor. A punishing justice was aroused against Him. Thus, as the "Ebed Jahwe," the suffering "servant of the Lord" entered upon His shame. But now Christ is again being vindicated. He has done what was required of Him. All the obligations of the covenant of works He can cancel by adequate payment. He is righteous, also in His own conscience. As for this last remark, He knew that all the Scriptures had been relived in Him. He says as much. And now He places Himself overagainst the justice of God and glories in His justification.

The divine order of God's work is apparent in this too. We are emphatically reminded of the fact that Christ in His processes of justice first solves them within Himself, within the four walls of His own spiritual house, and only then presents the same conflicts to God and thus by means of influences proceeding from the outside, again opens the gates, and presents the issue for new discussion.[1] We can detect the same order here. For who proclaimed Christ as being righteous? Yes, the sun shone again, but that was the only thing which said anything for Him, which had a friendly voice for Him. But for the rest Christ's own spirit moved and prompted Him and He assured Himself that indeed all things were accomplished according to the word of God. And He assured Himself that the Second Adam can look upon His day with rejoicing, that now He is righteous before God. Only after He has said this to Himself, and has assured Himself of the right to the Passover does the Father intervene with an external act: then the Father rends the heavens on Sunday morning, thrusts Jesus' grave stone to one side, lets life quiveringly enter into His body, and then Himself also proclaims the justification of the Christ.

Thus the feast of the Passover had its beginning in the spirit of Christ; there He righteously arouses Himself and does not sin. The feast of the Passover had to have its beginning in Him. He must believe in His own justification. Not that it is actually anchored in His own righteousness only; it must also be embraced by His own faith, and by His own faith be proclaimed.

And this is what happened. That becomes evident to us in the statement from the cross still to follow. In the sixth He announces that all things are accomplished and the broken covenant of works can no longer lay any claims upon Him. He says to God: There is no tension in the atmosphere now; there is no need to struggle now; this matter of justice is no longer among the uncertain things; no one can charge me with guilt; the punishment is passed. This is the first element in the justification. And in the next utterance from the cross, the last one, He accepts His right

1. See pp. 305-09.

to eternal life, vindicates His eternal life as transcending His temporal death, and says: Father, into thy hands I commend my spirit. This right to eternal life is the second element in the justification.

Accordingly, we say that Christ is *in the justification*. Therefore this sixth utterance from the cross is one of the historic moments which proclaims and confirms ours.

Let us rejoice now. It is true that in the fourth statement from the cross He heard a voice saying: God repents that He made Jesus a king. But in the sixth utterance His voice declares: See my works; the rejected king certainly may be a king. He no longer hides Himself behind the vessel. Surely the king is in His justification. The prophecy is His self-defense: again He is in a state of rest. He admonishes Himself, saying: Sleep on now, and rest. It is finished: again, for Himself and for man, there is a *perfectum quietivum*.[1] The Son of man, the Second Adam, can now speak as man in a condition of perfect rest. Thus He may enjoy God. Christian dogmatics has often said of Him: He was "not *comprehensor,* but *viator.*" By that is meant: He did not go through life as one who as a calmly calculating individual was playing a carefully studied rôle, as one who with a purely intellectual insight and oversight went through life as a strange, dispassionate guest, but as a pilgrim here below who constantly experienced as a new experience that which confronted Him as a new phenomenon.

We shall not contradict this eloquent statement taken from the tradition of dogmatics. In a different form we ourselves have repeatedly stated similar things. However, we must amplify the statement. The *comprehensor,* who intellectually comprehends the relationships of things, and the *viator,* who experiences them, are never contrasted to each other in the Christ. The discrimination is not a separation.

We see that here. He is the *comprehensor*; for He says: It is finished. Yes, that much He had ever understood very well. He had never been able to think of it in any other way. He laid His stones regularly every day, and never once doubted Himself. But He is the *viator* too. That He actually is finished now is a

---

1. Perfect time: the rest-imparting thought that the work is finished.

discovery He makes in a moment of time, and it is a blessed feeling of delight to Him in this joyous moment; it suffices to make Him shout. He looks at this marvellous thing in a genuinely human way, being much moved and greatly perturbed by it.

A *comprehensor* is here. He has seen this moment beforehand in connection with all of His times. The *viator* is here. He enjoys this moment as though He understands it not at all, and as though it comes as a surprise. He is the *comprehensor*: He sees the day and the things of the day as by a bird's eye view from His sublime heights; He knows the lay of the land, and sees the various thoroughfares in their essential inter-relationship. He is the *viator*: He is as surprised as a person who suddenly turns a sharp corner and discovers an unexpected panorama of beauty. He is the *comprehensor*: He reckons in terms of time. He is the *viator*: He enjoys His moments, His seconds.

Recently they talk a great deal in the church about "the moment." By that they mean that "moment" of life in which we touch on eternity. I think I shall let them talk, for Christ suffices for me. He has His "moment." This causes an interruption, an accent, an emphasis in His rhythm. But in the last analysis it is included in that rhythm. It is a "selah," but the psalm goes on. Selah means a moment; but the psalm was the condition. He is the *viator* who experiences "His moment," but also the *comprehensor* who definitely knows that this is mid-day of the Day of the Lord.

Therefore we can say that the "mid-day" of Jahweh was enjoyed with trembling in the "moment" of Jesus. He confesses to Himself: I know that I have fulfilled all the Scriptures, and I have cried aloud in order to fulfill the Scriptures even more. I believe passionately in the Scriptures. And He puts a question to Himself: What benefit is it to me to believe all this? He knows His own answer: "That I in myself am righteous before God, and heir of eternal life." He sings His evening hymn as a man thirty-three years old but it becomes the hymn of His justification. Thus He teaches the angels the mid-day hymn of the Lord,[1] and announces the morning hymn of God.[2]

---

1. Jahwe: covenant God, regenerator; jõm jahwe, covenant of grace.
2. God; as creator of the world (before regeneration).

How rich He is, how immeasurably rich!

And yet how poor He is. Poor — in the world's reckoning. For, strictly interpreted, what does this amount to, this "It is finished." Does it give Him anything in common with "great men?" Ah, no. He did not say "I," but "it." The sixth utterance from the cross is not a conclusion written large in capital letters under an autobiography; it tells us nothing about Himself. He did not "disclose" Himself. Nor did He "characterize" Himself. He is by no means "a great man" who drew up His position on top of a conspicuous rock on the mountain of humanity, there where hardly any human being can reach Him, where He alone can carry His head in the clouds, shouting victory to the sun. God be praised, He is not one of the "great men." He is infinitely more; He is wholly different. He is the basis, the foundation, the cornerstone of human life. And hence He speaks so terribly generally now. "It is finished." All heretics can read their interpretations into it. And all exhausted little men when they die can repeat it. This is the same old song: the least of His brethren can take His utterance from the cross upon his lips.[1] It is finished: that is a word of self-concealment.

But in this self-concealment He is my Saviour now. No Caesar and no king, no philosopher and no great man, can possibly conclude his discourses as vaguely as this. They all conceive of an autobiography if they wish to leave a final typifying biography behind. But Christ has no biography, cannot bear one. As man He is entirely swallowed up of the work of God. This was "His meat," not His pose. It was His life, not His type. The zeal of God's house has consumed all biographical notice of Him. It is finished; the work is completed; the seeds have germinated. There is nothing else to say; the matter of a "biography" is quite out of place. He cannot endure the thought of a "life of Jesus."

Therefore He will die in a world which has died in giving birth to "great men." The impersonal human nature left with a statement which sounded impersonal. Men shook their heads; they beat against their breasts, when an earthquake came. They cannot be frightened by impersonal words, even though these really can be spoken by no one else and really are a miracle in Him, far

---

1. See p. 325 ff.

more miraculous, in fact, than an ordinary earthquake. The people left: He had literally said nothing particularly striking by way of further explanation or justification. *It — it* — and that was all.

But the reaction in heaven was quite different. When He ended impersonally in this way, but allowed His next to the last statement to be borne aloft by the Spirit, they in heaven said: God be praised: the first Adam has been made a living soul, and the Second Adam a life-giving spirit.

Christ Goes Out:
God Goes On

CHAPTER TWENTY

Christ Goes Out: God Goes On

● *And when Jesus had cried with a loud voice,
he said, Father into thy hands I commend my
spirit: and having said thus, he gave up the
ghost.*

LUKE 23:46.

THERE are no pauses in the kingdom of heaven. Just as the floor in God's work-room has not a single hiatus, so His labor is never interrupted. In the kingdom of heaven there is haste in everything. When one thing is finished, the next follows immediately. The one woe passes, and behold the other comes. The one benefit passes, and the other comes.

Now if this is a law of the kingdom of heaven for everyone who would breathe its atmosphere how much more must it be a law for the Great Worker of God's world labor. Has He pronounced the "finished"? Has His working program been completed so far? Then there is only one question which is still a pious question to ask: namely, *what now?* The Servant has done His work and has also reported it. The report, too, has come to an end. What can God's service require beyond this? Has He said: It is finished? If so, He is immediately caught in His own words, for He must immediately go on. There are no pauses. Lord, what next?

But He Himself knows, of course, what is pious. He stands ready for the new deed. Notice. This is what He does: He makes His departure from life the continuation of God's work. Jesus' departure becomes God's progress. He immediately makes His own evening hymn the mid-day hymn of God.[1] This struggling Hero does this, and at once both stands and speaks in the abun-

---

1. Reference to the preceding chapter, pp. 456, 462.

467

dant life. That is the life of God. No one lives in it really save God alone, God, who alone is immortal. And hence He utters the word of a created human being who stands in the midst of human life; He speaks aloud, He cries with a loud voice, He utters the word of God's faithful day-laborers, for He Himself is God's servant, who was hired "in the first hour," and who will work until the last, and who will have no complaint to make when the payment is made. He now gives expression to the word of the person who stands on the mid-day heights of life. He says: Father, into thy hands I commend my spirit.

Perhaps there is someone who wonders and who asks himself: But is this really true? We understand each other, of course. The man who wonders in this way has heard the statement standing at the head of our chapter so often, and has learned it so well out of the little book in grammar school under the caption "The seven utterances from the cross" that he immediately attaches the idea of death to this text. All you have to do, is to ask him: Just what was it that Jesus said: Into thy hands, Father, I commend my spirit? The answer will come promptly: That was Jesus' farewell speech. You can hardly expect Him to say: That was Christ's farewell speech; and even less: That was the speech uttered at Christ's continuation of the work. No, he will say: Jesus' farewell address. Jesus' last word. It is a particularly good answer, in fact, if he says: That was the last word spoken by the humiliated Christ.

And you will find that this brother will not easily relinquish his interpretation of the matter. Do not misunderstand him: he wants to exert all his effort, or rather he wants to exert no effort at all — for he finds this as natural as can be — in order to preserve his "edification." Was it not an edifying word, he asks, the word with which Jesus took leave, the *pia anima?* And the association of his thoughts immediately calls up images of other death beds, the death beds of "dear ones." He finds that it is not easy to forget the last words of a dying person, and by means of an appeal to this universally human experience he would protect this last utterance from the cross against those who would desecrate its atmosphere, its dominant tone of delicate tenderness. In other words, the man has staked off the cross by means of the death beds of dear ones. And now he asks you to pass all these dying people in order to create the proper mood for reaching the cross, and for accepting the last statement of Jesus. Now it may be that you want to protest mildly in your thoughts against this desired mood with a remark that Jesus does not die on the cross as others do on their beds. For, you add, these others all whisper, but Jesus cries out "with a loud voice." Of course, the man knows that also. He has his answer. That loud voice, he says, proves that Jesus' death is a deed; the Saviour was not yet exhausted; He could still cry with a loud voice. He was strong enough to live, you see, but He dies by a deed. The man has placed the death of Jesus under a caption, and he knows the paragraph in his book of dogmatics in which he can read about that "loud voice." Meanwhile, he has not been shocked by that loud voice, has not been frightened by it, and he has for the moment lost the other paragraphs of his dogmatics. Hence he likes to call up that series of death beds for you, in order that you may devote a consecrated and reverent attention to the word "Jesus." For our brother simply cannot be persuaded to relinquish his interpretation. All right, let that loud voice be a "strange" element in Jesus' dying, but you certainly cannot deny that His last utterance from the cross is indeed a moving farewell address; it was a word which eloquently introduced and set off the moment of death. Would it not be better for us to extinguish the lights and meditate upon it by candle glow?

No, we are not going to extinguish the lights. We are going to take up our position in the light of full day for, may we say it with your permission, brother, God's sun has also just broken through the clouds. Moreover it is not true that Jesus' last utterance spoken in humiliation was intended as a farewell statement. For Christ is not taking leave. His last word addressed to the people was a third utterance from the cross, and according to the structure present in the order of the seven utterances from the cross,[1] a farewell address directed to men at this time would profane the harmony of the series. By no means is He addressing the people here. He has sent His mother away. Yes, but surely a dying person characterizes himself by his last words. Again we must say that this is *not* "a dying person." This is *the* Dying One, and at the same time the Living One. He has no need for char-

---

1. See p. 130.

acterizing His death and His life by an epitome, for He has no characteristic words; He transcends these on the one hand; and is far below these, on the other hand.[1] In the last analysis He has no words which far transcend other words He has spoken. His last statement should not have a whit more of attention than do all those others which He spoke throughout His life. All His words are so full of the law of God, that they themselves naturally assume the character of that law. Now it happens that the law is terribly monotonous and uniform. Why? The law has not what people call an *ultimatum*. Human beings demand and ask things ten times without emphasis and without success; and then it does not help to repeat; and then, trying it an eleventh time, they speak with an ultimatum. Then, they say "they really mean it." But the law, the Word of God, never utters such an ultimatum. God uses the same will in uttering His last word that He uses in uttering His first. Hence He speaks without any real variation of inflection. It may be that He employs inflection as a pedagogue to the souls (not because His own attention fluctuates, but because the attention others give Him changes), but He Himself does not impart more worth and more strength to one word than to any other that He speaks.

Christ's speaking is similarly uninflected, similarly "monotonous." His last statement is just as "ordinary" — or extraordinary — as His next to the last statement, His mid-day utterance, His morning greeting. All of His statements carry the same weight.

Therefore we may not listen to this last utterance from the cross with a mind full of the impressions of death beds alluded to a moment ago. To do so, is to spoil our thinking. We must not explain our Great Dead in terms of the little dead. What? Do we seek the Dead One among the dead? He is not here; He has entered into Hades in His own strength. Hence His dying statement must be interpreted solely in terms of Himself. In terms of Himself — and therefore of the Scriptures.

Consequently, that last statement does not wish to punctuate or emphasize His dying. Whoever could think that would be falling into the greatest theological error. He would be saying that the moment of Christ's death is of greatest importance, even though

1. See pp. 462-63.

that is doing violence to the fulness of God's revelation. The moment of Christ's death, independent of the course He took in its coming, means nothing. Independent of that, it has no content. It must be regarded as an extension of a condition which was, and the beginning of a condition which follows. Undoubtedly Christ's dying has its own significance, but He who would emphasize the dying at the expense, for instance, of Christ's preliminary processes of suffering the pain of hell, say, His conscious surrender, his permanent grief, has not understood essentially Christ's dying and death at all. True, His death sheds His blood; but His giving His blood was also of the greatest importance. And the giving of that blood, if we set it rightly, took Him thirty-three years.

We just said that this last statement from the cross can be understood only in terms of the Scriptures which reveal Him to us. And what are we doing but following the Scriptures when we say that the last statement from the cross is not a dying utterance but a word of life. You know very well that this last statement is — to put it that way—a quotation. It is taken from Psalm 31:5, 7, 8:

> Into thy hand I commit my spirit:
> Thou hast redeemed me, O Lord God of truth.
>
> * * *
>
> I will be glad and rejoice in thy mercy:
> For thou hast considered my trouble;
> Thou hast known my soul in adversity;
> And hast not shut me up into the hand of the enemy:
> Thou hast set my feet in a large room.

Is this a "typical" *dying utterance?* Is this the kind of thing which those people whose death beds we have been asked to visit a moment ago are wont to whisper? No, you feel it at once. The person who is speaking here, is a man standing in the midst of life, who is rejoicing in the day of His deliverance. He is not a man standing in the narrow gate of death, in the cleft of the rock of His dying, for — He has just been set in a large place. But this is a new discovery, someone says, a discovery of a later time. That is not true. Even the old Jews understood it in this way. The remark has been made that these verses of Psalm 31 were prescribed in the rabbinical literature as a short evening prayer. Pupils in the schools had to pray this prayer before they went to bed, and in general every Israelite was advised to use it as an evening petition.[1]

---

1. Strack-Billerbeck, *Kommentaar zum Neuen Testament,* volume 2, 192', p. 269.

But even if the Jews had not understood it in this way, we know that Christ Himself always understands His own psalms perfectly. By this we do not mean to say that He cannot use a statement derived from the Psalms, or some other Scriptural quotation, in such a way that it surprises us or causes us to wonder for a moment. On the contrary, Christ repeatedly in His Biblical references presents an interpretation of a statement in the Old Testament which far transcends the meaning of the poet, or of some other Biblical writer, which far exceeds the meaning of what such an author consciously had in mind. Every statement which Christ quotes becomes much more eloquent in His mouth than it had been on the lips of any other. He gets everything out of such a statement that is in it; He taps the whole of its riches. But now, the other side of the matter. When Christ quotes a Scriptural passage He never cuts loose from the core, the quintessence, the elemental sense in which that quoted passage was originally employed. Christ always says more, but He never says something different than His poets and prophets of the Old Testament said. Accordingly, if we can indicate that the poet of Psalm 31 was not in a specific sense thinking of death, when he composed this prayer, but of life, then we are thereby proving that the last utterance of Christ from the cross cannot be said in the first place to refer to Jesus' approaching death. As we do this, we must keep the assumption in the foreground that the last statement from the cross in its profoundest significance must cling to the elemental reality which was the essence of the psalmist's poem. If the question of death-or-life is a subordinate one in Psalm 31, and if God's progress with His life and with His power is the predominant theme, then that must also be true of the passage cited in our text. Now it simply needs a little work to point out that such is actually the case in this Psalm. The poet of Psalm 31 is not thinking of the certainty of death. He is petitioning God, in fact, to prolong his life, to break the counsel of the enemies, and to protect him. He knows that he will certainly continue to enjoy the favor of Jahweh, and accordingly he sings a hymn of life. Now this poet says that he commits his spirit into God's hands. By this he means that through a conscious act of faith, his eye fixed on the life-work he has still to continue, standing at a milestone which encourages him to go on, he, in his inner being, in the very basis of his life, commends his spirit to his Creator for governance and direction. It is a statement uttered not at the end, but at one of a number of milestones on his way.

A moment ago we pointed to the *active deed* involved in Christ's committing his case to God.[1] Similar activity, purposiveness, and consciousness, is present in the statement of Psalm 31. The poet knows that his enemies are lying in wait to take his life. Overagainst that situation he convinces himself by an act of faith that his life is in God's hands, and that consequently all those threats cannot cause him to doubt for a moment that his life will be prolonged for further service of God. Knowing that, he turns aside from his enemies, announces that the future is by no means uncertain to him, and performs that act of faith by which he places his life in its deepest essence in God's hand.[2] In other words, he does not let himself be hampered by the enemies. They cannot really touch him. He simply goes on his way, and commends himself, looking to the life still coming, to the Father.

Hence this sense of life which is the theme of the poet of Psalm 31 must also be the theme of the last utterance from the cross. That, and all that is elementally related to it.

In the first place, then, there is the *active deed* of faith. Christ's word also is full of this thought. If we compare the several usages which the Greek has for the word "to commit" ("commit my spirit") as found in the New Testament, we will see that in every case it means a conscious, active assertion of faith, in which, with faith in God, one commends some specific desire to Him, or leaves the decisive turn of óne's life in His hands. Thus we read of committing a certain task to someone (Luke 12:48), or of committing elders of the souls of believers to the Lord (Acts 14:23; I Peter 4:19), or of commending a number of Christians to God and to the word of His grace (Acts 20:32), or, similarly, of entrusting and transmitting the content of preaching to faithful witnesses (II Timothy 2:2), or of enjoining a command (I Timothy 1:18). Christ, therefore performs an *active deed*. Yes, now we remember, He spoke in a "loud voice."

---

1. See p. 262-3.
2. The word "spirit" in Psalm 31 must be taken to mean "soul," and this word, in turn, is to be explained as "life," or the principle of life. More than that we may not try to find in it.

A second matter now demands our attention. Just as the poet of Psalm 31, by committing Himself and all his own into God's hands was virtually denying the assumed power of the enemies, and denying that they had any determinative influence on his life, so Christ also does the same. The enemies think that they have determined the course of the life of the Nazarene, but the faith of Jesus Christ says that God determines its course. He is just in every way. He has just humiliated the friends in His next to the last utterance from the cross. He spoke to God with them, above them, without them.[1] Now the enemies are humiliated. He speaks with them, beyond them, without them. Now He raises the hymn of His continuation. They say: This is the end. He does not even look up, but announces to God: At this milepost, I want to pause a moment and direct a petition to Thee, as men are wont to do at milestones. Then we will go on together: Father, the work will go on.

Now if we relate the things we have gained in the preceding paragraphs to the whole, we have the significance of the last utterance from the cross. That which echoed from the cross was not the dull sound of death, but the sonorous song of life. "Ring clearly, ring loud," hymn of life. The enemies think to have put Him to death but He who is here acts as though they did not exist. He negates them in a more sovereign way than the author of the psalm. Calmly and peacefully He says His evening prayer,[2] He falls asleep until tomorrow, Father, until the new day. He pauses for a moment, prays, and then waits the morrow. "My times are in Thy hand." This translated into the language of fulfillment means: "My Passover seasons are in Thy hand." Just as the poet of Psalm 31 at bottom simply wishes to say that he is going to continue on his way with his eyes fastened on God, so Christ calls from the cross: I shall simply go on, my eyes fixed upon God.

This last statement, therefore, is not an emphasis of His dying, but quite the contrary, an affirmation of uninterrupted life. He is not singing a song of death to Himself, but without taking His attention from His death — we noticed that He was accommodating Himself to it! — and hence without suppressing or con-

1. See p. 455.
2. See p. 471.

cealing the fact of His death, He proclaims the onward march of life. He puts the moment, the particular moment, in its proper position among all His "seasons." Very simply He goes on His way, for He has understood God. Therefore God will take care of His spirit. He does not here, in the face of an inevitable death, try to find escape in the life of God, but He publicly declares that He will assert God's life in everything which happens, and that therefore He in no sense needs "a refuge." No, brother, you who have just returned from "a" death bed, you have not grasped the central significance when you, noting His loud utterance, reverently say: His death really is a *deed*. For if only we are willing to explain the vigor of His voice in the light of the vigor of His thoughts we can paraphrase His statement thus: His *deed* in this moment is to die; and He *does* this deed. His activity is primary; the dying is secondary. This is not a taking refuge in God, because He who flees "must die." This is a *service* of God, and hence a dying, because the act of dying is scheduled for the program of this day. He is incomparably great: by faith He bears His capacity for work up to the moment of His dying and thus simply eats His daily meat. His meat is to do the will of the Father.

This, then, was Christ's last statement in the state of humiliation. Is it not a meagre manifestation, and a humble show? Michael is humiliating himself with the humble, and walks humbly before God and men. How very humble He is in his speaking. Oh yes, we know very well that the last word immediately becomes exceedingly great if we explain it according to the hermeneutics of *as-if*. For if we adopt that manner, we will treat it as if it were simply a word which He spoke, as though He spoke it first, as if it had nothing to do with an old man of the past, with the author of Psalm 31. But do you not find it to be true also that it is best in the moment of dying not to give expression to these *as-if's?* His statement simply was *not* spoken by Him the first time it was spoken; it is a statement by and for all of us. That is the truth. But not everyone likes to believe that it is. We frequently meet with gross inconsistencies. The same people who would like to conduct us past the death beds of good Christians to put us "in the mood," forget all those ordinary people the moment they think they have come close to the Christ. Once they are in the proper mood they listen to *His* dying statement, continue to look up to

Him, but then remain standing with their backs turned to those ordinary people. And they think at every word they hear Him say: that is a statement of the Messiah, the Son of God, and that, accordingly, is the sublimest, the greatest, the most edifying possible of statements. Accordingly you find them saying all kinds of eulogistic things about this last utterance from the cross. In order to explain it they labor with weighty concepts. They begin to philosophize, or to theologize about the concept "spirit," or about the notion of "committing" or "commending" the spirit. They have immediately forgotten the common people.

Now it is far from us to deny that weighty words are appropriate here. For it is true indeed that a Scriptural statement in the mouth of Christ always receives its full significance, and we are glad to acknowledge that the use of the word "spirit" was not unadvised. We admit that coming as it does from Christ's lips it means not only natural life, but everything in Him that is conscious, that has a will, that motivates Him. And we also confess, consequently, that He commends Himself to the Father with His whole conscious life, with His whole mind, and with all His motive powers and drives.

But even if we accept all this, we need subtract nothing from the contention that the man who would excite the proper emotions in us by leading us past "ordinary" dead people, before we come to this great Dead, is quite inconsistent. For as we mentioned before, the moment this person arrives at the cross, he forgets all those other dead. Just that is his mistake; he suffers loss because of his own weak point. And, on the contrary, it is we, who have *refused* to come to Jesus' cross through a proper "mood," it is we, who wanted to see the cross of Christ in its proper light, independently of all those other "cases of death," who, listening attentively to the utterance of Jesus' mouth, naturally become concerned about all those other death beds, and all the "cases of death," of the other believers. We make this beautiful discovery: Jesus' dying statement is so very common that anyone who believes in God can and must repeat it after Him. Look, now all those death beds return to our line of vision, now, that is, when we look upon them in the light of Jesus. Moreover, it is not only death beds which we see before us. Please be quiet about all your "escape" sentiment, the kind of sentiment which can excite tears only in the presence of death beds and chambers of mourning. For besides these nebulous dying chambers, all rooms of study in which faith is struggling against the arrogance of unbelief, all shops, all hospitals, all battle-fields, all rooms of prayer, in short all places in which a human spirit seeks reinforcement in God now have their place in the line of vision of the dying Saviour. All these are included in the circle drawn by Christ's last statement. He shows me those dying people, yes, but especially the living ones, and He tells me: Dying, I am one of them. For this is the miracle: Christ chooses a word which anyone can and must choose, and thus becomes one with the common man in His death. His last utterance from the cross is His last concealment.

We do well to think soberly about this. If *we* had had to choose a word which would be suitable to place on the lips of the dying Jesus, would we not have chosen a statement from Isaiah, from him who is called the eagle among the prophets? Or if not from Isaiah, certainly from messianic prophecies in general, or from a typically messianic psalm. But Christ chooses what we would call a "very ordinary psalm," one which in no respect is more, or more directly, Christological than any other text in the Old Testament. He chooses a Psalm which the theologians have not included in their lists of messianic psalms. The evening prayers of the little children of Israel and the dying cry of my Lord and my God — both these use the same text. We have found the child wrapped in swaddling clothes, and lying in a manger. We have found the man bound in the prattle of children, and kneeling beside a little Jewish boy as he prays at his cradle. Together they repeat their evening prayers. The Lord's Prayer became a child's prayer after Him, but the form of His dying statement became a children's prayer without Him. Good people, everyone can repeat what He expressed in His deepest humiliation.

There is a great difference, is there not, between this and that which He said to the Sanhedrin when He manifested Himself as the Son of man whom they should hereafter see seated upon the throne of God and coming with the clouds.[1] A great difference between this and that which He said only a few hours ago in *His last service of the Word* to the women of the city.[2] Yes, indeed,

---

1. *Christ on Trial*, p. 138 f.
2. See p. 55.

He is the Son of man, in speaking so positively and preaching so powerfully. But now He has condescended to the language of the Christian tanners of Thyatira, of the recruits of His army, of the toothless women in the hospital ward of the old people's home. For once we had better omit the capital letter: he is the son of man. In the last analysis this statement means nothing more than: man. Not, it is true, that this name, just as every "quotation"—see what was said above — has a very specific and complete content when He uses it, but whoever has learned to understand Him in the *light of that fulfillment* will see Him as He is now in His emptiness, in His *kenosis,* in His concealment. It is almost enough to make one weep, seeing the dying Jesus this way, and leaving not as much as a single word which is suitable for embroidering on a banner. He is always difficult. He always keeps us a long way from that plane of vision from which Constantine the Great could find such beautiful inscriptions for a banner; for instance: *in hoc signo vinces.* He does things so very commonly.

In terms of what we have said, we cannot agree with those who in this connection allude to John 10:18, where Christ says: "No man taketh it (my life) from me, but I lay it down of myself. I have power to lay it down, and I have power to take it again." Some say that Christ by crying aloud in committing His spirit into the Father's hand by His own act is proving to the world that He has the power to lay down His own life. We do not agree with this opinion. Naturally we admit the fact that Christ voluntarily and in virtue of His own power laid down His life and commended His spirit to the Father. But we deny that He is at this moment *saying* that to the world. For the seventh word on the cross also represents concealment. Can anyone say that the poet of Psalm 31 also had the power to lay down his life?

Do we mean that the death of Christ is not a deed? By no means; but we believe this not so much because of the letter of His dying utterance, as because of the fact that He at this time gave expression to a word of life, a word which He can use every day, and which He as a faithful interpreter of Psalm 31, and as one persisting in prayer, we may believe, *prayed and said several times.* Christ could make this statement as often as He was about to fall asleep, as often as He had to preach a sermon, perform a miracle, conduct an argument, or flee from persecutors because His hour had not yet come. How often do we not read: "His hour had not yet come." In another form, that is what Psalm 31 also says: "My times are in Thy hand." In such critical hours as those in which Christ consciously prepared for sleep or moved from one region of the country to another, passing those who cast their stones and those who drew their swords against Him, He gave Psalm 31 its normal explanation: Into Thy hands, Father, I commend my spirit. For the situation of the poet was also fulfilled in Him at such times. Again, therefore: Not the letter of the word "to commit" but the spirit in which He utters this word, the spirit and the letter together make it clear to us that He continues His deeds by the work of His death.

No, do not overlook this strong will *to conceal* in this dying utterance. Now it becomes our turn to say to the brother who spoke to us a moment ago: *Revere the attitude of this dying man.* Who can say? Perhaps Mary and John prayed precisely the same prayer that same Friday night before they went to bed. It may be that bystanders caught up that last statement and told it to the mother and the disciple. And then you need but give free reign to your fancy a moment in order to picture this situation before you: Someone tells of the last statement of Christ; a second adds that it is a text from the holy books; a third goes to look up the text and finds it; they read the psalm in John's house; he is giving fitting attention to the needs of the intimate group. They sing and pray this. Naturally all this is mere imagination; we know that. But we also know that it seeks nothing extraordinary. Psalm 31 was very suitable for the house-congregation of the scattered sheep of Jesus.

When you have understood well that Jesus' dying utterance issues from His ministration of the office for three years, you will appreciate that Christ's death is the deed, and that it seeks a prolongation of everything which has happened in that which still must happen. By this last utterance He relates His dying to the feast of the Passover. He repeated the psalm in His prayer when He assumed His office. Then He was driven of the Spirit into the wilderness — to meet the devil. Now again He repeats that prayer. Immediately He is driven of the Spirit into death — to meet the angels of God.

However, it is *only in His thoughts* that He connects Good Friday and Easter. Had it not been so, He would no longer have been in concealment. He conceals from all unbelieving people the role of the book of the pure reason of God, according to which His death has its extension in life, its continuation in the Passover. He has more Rights than anyone else, for He has fulfilled the covenant of works; nevertheless He declares Himself now to be a needy one. He is in the justification, He has the right to eternal life, right to all power in heaven and on earth. His rights are sealed in the sixth utterance on the cross: It is finished. But this sixth utterance is not followed by a demand for His wages. It is followed by a prayer for *protection*. Accordingly, He commits His spirit into God's hands. No, He does it in the manner of a child. He commends His spirit into the *Father's* hands. Now the hand of God when alluded to in the Bible is always a figure of power and strength; it is a figure of strength over which human beings have no command. Thus He comes utterly emptied and without any manifestation of sovereignty at all, to surrender Himself to the Father. He surrenders Himself according to the spirit, and that in the last analysis means that He sinks back to the beginning of creation. Now He hovers about in space. The Will, the Good Pleasure, blows Him, the created being, wherever God listeth. As He Himself sees it He is being absolutely surrendered to the highest, to the only Sovereign. For that reason He now speaks again in the imperfect tense. For the *perfectum* of the sixth utterance, He expresses the imperfect of the seventh. We pointed out a moment ago that the *perfectum*[1] — perfect time — refers to the condition of rest, that it manifests the completed task, that it designates the soul as being in a state of peace, and as being, to that extent, an image of God's own peace. It is finished — that is what He said then. But now He utters His trembling word in the imperfect tense.[2] Now He stands at the threshold of a new beginning. He must take up the thread of His life again. He assigns His spirit to the Father's hands. Hardly has the Servant done His task, before He asks a new assignment. He had reached His milestone. *Perfectum.* Now He goes on around the bend. Here a new

---

1. See p. 456.
2. In all the versions of the text.

vista is opened before Him. God, be gracious to my soul,[1] but I must go on . . . God cannot wait, not a day, not an hour.

Say now, is not this last utterance of the Christ a judgment? It is a judgment by which He condemns every biased accentuation of His dying which would do injustice to the spiritual process which has issued in His death, but without which His dying would not be a positive thing. Precisely by uttering a final word which had been in His heart also each time He reached a milestone in His onward march, He proves that His departure is God's progress. The Nazarene dies; but the Creator of heaven and of earth simply goes on. The wheel of the triumphant chariot of God moves steadily on; and God's onward marches do not pause in front of the funeral procession of the Nazarene. Where is the schedule, where the program of the continuous kingdom of heaven?

A great significance lies in the fact that Christ utters a word of life in His dying hour, for He confesses by that means that He is already in the ascendancy. He professes in this way that He is already emerging from the lowest shafts of humiliation, and that He, having arisen from "the second death," now is already ascending to heaven. On His way from hell to heaven, He must do what every pilgrim does: He strengthens Himself in His God, confesses His God, and performs the act of the moment.

The statement He uttered also contains a *judgment* for us. How often the church marvels at the "circumstances" surrounding Christ's dying, without — and this is the beginning of the error — relating the manner of Jesus' death organically to the course of Christ's life. Can it really be that after so many centuries of Christendom, after these hundreds of years of preaching, we are no farther than — a *heathen*? The heathen to whom we are referring at present is the centurion, captain of a hundred. He paid careful attention to this strange victim of the cross, he reflected sensitively on the manner of His death, and thus came to say that this was something most unusual.[2] He brought it as far as lay within his power; he had been allowed to see the dying, but the life had not given him the key by which to explain the riddle of the death. Alas, we often resemble this poor pagan. We permit ourselves to be moved by the manner of the death of Jesus and, wheth-

---

1. In the sense of Question 12, Heidelberg Catechism.
2. This will be discussed further later.

er we know all "Pieta's" or not a single one, it is often true that we look upon His *death* independently of His *life*. Then we are much perturbed. But we have no more than that pagan had. May God at such times be gracious to us all.

Yes, indeed, He *judges* us. He judges our instituting stages in the Roman Catholic Churches, and seven Lenten weeks in our Protestant churches. He does not condemn our watching and our listening to His suffering. We can never do that too much. But He condemns our attitudes. Seven times we are moved by the *dying* Saviour, but we are not moved by the living *Kurios* another seven times. It is that which He objects to in us. And if you are in dead earnest about the assurance that the last wish of a dying person is sacred to you, do what He commanded you, and repeat His words after Him. Give expression to a statement of life, to a living utterance, for that is also the way He concluded His preliminaries. As for the rest, He desires greatly the hour in which He may draw the curtain to His last act. As He mounts the throne for the Last Judgment, He will say to the Father for the last time: Father, into Thy hands I commend my created spirit.

Father, into Thy hands I commend my spirit . . . And now almost all people most naturally say: Thereupon the curtain *fell*. But *He* said: The curtain rises to the new act. The angels take up their positions to look on. Then He stood in the full light, He, the *dramatis Persona*.

Christ Passing Out and On

CHAPTER TWENTY-ONE

Christ Passing Out and On

● *And having said thus, he gave up the ghost.
And he bowed his head, and gave up the ghost.*
JOHN 19:30b; LUKE 23: 46b.

T HEN The Saviour entered into His death. He had drawn up a careful covenant with death. When His hour should sometime come, it had said, then death should take Him. When death proved unable to do this, He took Himself, and made a careful covenant with Himself. The hour had come; it was high time. He had asked His God: What next? And the answer had been: Let the body be broken, for so it is meet for Thee to fulfill all righteousness. And then: Thereupon enter in as the perfectly faithful servant; enter into the joy of Thy Lord.

Two emphases, therefore. The first is that Christ's dying was His duty; the second, that, in case He fulfilled that duty, His dying would be the entering into His glory.

Accordingly, it was a matter of *necessity* that He die. We do not wish to discuss that at great length now, inasmuch as we have formerly analyzed what place in our estimation the shedding of the blood of Christ and the disruption of the body takes in the whole of the history of revelation.[1] There are only a few things, therefore, we would still touch upon.

The first thing that strikes us is that we do not know what it means to die. Death is a riddle, and it remains a riddle even at Golgotha. Just what Jesus' death was is not definitely indicated; it is pictured to us only from one side. Twice His death is called a "giving up of the ghost." With that we must be satisfied. He surrendered Himself according to the spirit. He surrendered Him-

---

1. See especially *Christ on Trial*, pp. 410-420.

self together with what His manifestation in history determined and together with the self-revelation which this historical manifestation implied. In other words, He surrendered Himself essentially. He gave Himself up completely. In the book of Ecclesiastes dying is called the returning of the spirit to God who gave it. This is also the thing of primary importance in the death of Christ. However, there is this difference now: His returning was His own deed. He did His returning in the spirit. His spirit moved Him to return. We cannot explain this, we cannot describe it, we can suggest nothing further about it. We must simply accept it in faith, just as His having been born by His own deed is an article of faith to us.

He caused His spirit to return. By this act His task as a servant was completed. His death was determined by His own act. He allowed death, the great robber, to come upon Him, and He hated all forms of robbery. But the Father had said that it was necessary. Surely, nothing is more an act of the servant, than to give the spirit into the Father's hands without reservation. By this act, man returns to the origins of his life; he allows himself to be dissolved. As long as we have not surrendered the spirit to Him, we have not surrendered ourselves. Hence Christ completes His life as a servant by placing His spirit into the hands of the Father again. He risks it with His God; He lets Himself be led back to the elemental beginning of all things. He undergoes the great revision; His determinants may be changed. God must begin and may begin assigning these to Him anew. He risks, because he who is convinced of his innocence, knows no "risk."[1]

This surrender of the spirit, this placing oneself at the disposal of the Father once more, is a reference to His descent into hell. When He suffered the pain of hell, He was fundamentally disrupted, He was shattered within, and completely ruined without. He preserved His body, yes. But that was neither a favor, nor a victory. It was simply an obligation. That body had to keep Him as a living and working being within the bounds of time.[2] Then He tasted of death in the flesh. Then He tasted death as complete man. And then He experienced that being in the body is by no means the same as being alive.

---

1. See pp. 452-53.
2. See pp. 24, 112, 377, 399-400, 431-33.

At that time, therefore, Christ *had been dead*. He had also endured this death in His body, for His whole human existence suffered the affliction of hell. The flesh, too, had been consumed in God's anger, and forsaken. *How?* That we do not know. The things of hell are unknown to us. But now that He in His entire humanity has tasted of death as the "Second Adam" and has arisen from that death again, still aware that His body is with Him, now He also gives that body to the Father in order that in this way He may entirely submit Himself to the Judge. The ruination must be complete. First He was completely organized and united in His entirety; now He is completely scattered and disrupted. First He *tasted* of death; now struggles with it.

Accordingly, it is the time now to leave that body by surrendering the spirit. Before this it was not His privilege to do so. If Christ had desired the "first" — for Him the last — death before the "second" — for Him the first — He would have withdrawn Himself from the pain of hell, from the essence of punishment. Then such a longing to leave the body in order to escape from the affliction of hell would in principle have been the equivalent of the cry of the unwilling: mountains fall upon us; hills cover us. For such will be the cry of that man presently, to whom God does not give the instrument in which the eternal plague must be endured. But Christ did not want to surrender His spirit while suffering the pain of hell. He did not summon the robber against the will of God, the God who beat and buffetted Him. He continued to bear His flesh, even under the pangs of hell. But now that everything is finished He gives up the ghost and dies at the right time. Thus He is the perfect servant who completely puts Himself at the disposal of God. He kept His instruments together when He had to work with them. Now that the work is done, He turns them in. There are no trophies today. O Father of heroes, man does not hold his spirit in his own hands. The Father says: Now it is time to return to me who have sent you. And He simply answers: It is well. In this sense, the dying of Christ is the natural consequence of His entire death (the suffering of hell), and of His whole life of obedience. It represents a *continuation* of the task. It is the extreme form of self-humiliation. For he who has thoroughly conquered the enemy, and who then still allows that enemy to beat and buffet him before the public eye. he certainly has absolutely humiliated himself. But that is what Christ did in His death.

Nevertheless everything which Christ *does* actively is at the same time a passive surrender to the force which masters Him. The *active* obedience (disposing Himself to His death) immediately becomes converted into a passive obedience (being disposed of). Thus the death of Christ becomes a *sacrifice*. We shall not repeat here that it is impossible to look upon the death of Christ in the body as a sacrifice as long as we pay attention to His dying alone. Behind the moment of giving up the ghost lies that whole long course of His eternal death, and the whole of His pulsing, conscious life. Only in terms of that can we, and may we, speak of His dying. But after His conscious deed of surrender, and after His persistent decision to surrender Himself, a decision which He maintained overagainst every temptation and trial, the disruption of His flesh in bodily death becomes the completion of the passion, regarded now as a sacrifice. This does not mean that the surrender of His spirit in the moment of death is the whole offer or the essential part of the offer. No, we do better to regard it as the *crown* of the offer, as the last act of the sacrifice.

Now we are touching upon a problem which has great significance. What is the significance, the legal significance, of the death of our body? Is the essential part of the *punishment,* speaking generally, contained in this physical death which God exacts as a penalty for sin?

We shall do well to calmly ask ourselves: Where do you read that this is so? The question itself makes us look up Genesis 3, the chapter in which the first sin and its punishment is described. Read in that chapter about God's penalizing utterance, and then ask yourself with what the penalty of "returning to the dust" is compared. What other penalties are of equal importance? You will find, if you limit yourself to human life, that this is the case. The death of the body[1] is there named the equivalent of the travail of a mother at the birth of her child, and the anxiousness of the father in the struggle for existence (the thorns and the thistles) (Genesis 3:16, 17, 19). Now no one will say that this is the very heart and core of the punishment of sin. Look into the outer re-

---

1. This means something different from "being dead" even in the body, for that is the punishment of hell.

cesses of hell and you will at once confess that there the essence of punishment takes place. As compared with the punishment of hell, the travail of a mother, and the perspiring of a father amounts to nothing. Nevertheless, those two are made the equivalent of the death indicated by "returning to the dust." Is it not for this reason as simple as the day to remark: Surely, then, the returning to the dust cannot be the essential climax of the punishment. That is not the unique essence of the penalty. The essence, the reality of it, is *hell*. The reality of it is death in the fullest sense, the death which in general is threatened in Genesis 2:17: In the day that thou eatest thereof thou shalt surely die.

You see then that according to the Biblical trend of ideas the "separation of soul and body"[1] is not an essential part of the penalty of sin. True, the necessity of this separation exists as long as the utterance of Genesis 3:19 is in force according to God's direction. But this separation is not absolute; it is relative; it is not inherent; it is accidental; it is not a demand of punishment as such, but only of the later more specifically described manner of God's exercise of punishment. Separation of the soul and body belongs to today, but is an injunction which may be lifted tomorrow.

If we admit, nevertheless, that the threat of death indicated in Genesis 2:17 also includes the *eternal death*,[2] death in its fullest import, complete death,[3] then it follows that if this penalty had been meted out immediately, fallen men would be condemned according to soul and body, would be given up to "eternal death." Then they would have fallen, not spiritually alone but bodily also into the same affliction which hell will manifest after the final judgment.

However, something else is the case. No one can deny that after the fall the threat of complete death was not immediately realized. "An element intervened between these two by means of which this penalty was tempered and postponed."[4] Immediately after

1. We are following here the familiar expression, plain to all, which however does not lay any claim to scientific accuracy. This is not the place to insert a treatise on the concept of "the soul."

2. Dr. J. Ridderbos, "De boom des levens," *Geref. Theol. Tijdschr.*, March, 1919, p. 385.

3. Dr. H. Bavinck, *Geref. Dogm.*, volume 3, pp. 159, 160.

4. Dr. H. Bavinck, *ibid.*, p. 159.

the fall grace intervened, and this now dominates history. God is busy realizing the plan of redemption; and in order to make the fulfillment of this possible, He postpones the complete realization of His threat, until such time as the process of redemption has completed its course in the consummation of the ages. Only when that consummation has come will that condition be realized which in Genesis 2:17 is pointed out as the complete death.

Regarded in this way the announcement of the penalty before the fall takes on the character of an announcement of the one great penalty of sin, whereas all prediction of punishment after the fall must be regarded and explained in the light of the fact that God now indicates in what way He plans to accomplish His end in history. In other words, the essential punishment was indicated before the fall; the accidental punishment was indicated after the fall. Before the fall the theme; after the fall the realization of it in history. Before the fall, the penalty (complete death) was announced, nothing more. But after the fall the revelation of the postponement of the real sentence was announced and hence everything which is said after the fall must be seen in the light of and explained in terms of that postponement.[1]

This interpretation puts the statement "to dust thou shalt return" (Genesis 3:19), which is often thoughtlessly quoted, in quite a different light. The statement was made after the fall. This, too, therefore is an item on the program of the history of the world, as that history will be "in the sign" of *long suffering* and *grace*.

If the threat of death were contained in Genesis 2:17 (before sin) we should have to regard the "returning to dust," the disruption, the breaking of the body, as a real part of the quintessential punishment, the punishment in itself. Now, however, we cannot regard the destruction of the body in temporal death as anything other than an act of God which intervened later. It is a condemnation, of course, to those who are not in Christ. But for God it serves only to make it possible for that complete penalty to real-

---

1. Dr. H. Bavinck says: (volume 3, 160) "Sin deserves nothing short of the complete death. All other penalties which actually entered in, and which were announced after the fall . . . assume . . . that God still has another plan in mind for humanity and the world, and that He therefore allows these to exist in His long suffering." And: "All the penalties which enter in after sin have . . . a twofold character. They are not purely . . . penalties, . . . but also means of grace."

ize itself in the new bodily existence so many centuries after the first announcement. That will take place when history has been completed and redemption perfected. That will take place when it is possible to apply it to complete human beings. It is an act of God which opens the way for the battle of God in Christ against sin and against death; and this, in turn, is a battle which makes death an onward march to (eternal) life for those who are born again.

Surely he who can agree with the statement[1] "that Genesis 3:19 does not announce the complete realization of the threatened penalty but tempers and postpones it,"[2] cannot regard the "separation of soul and body" as anything else than a "temporal severance of the bond between soul and body which intervened for the sake of grace in Christ," necessary only in order to present all people, and these in the body, before the judgment seat of Christ simultaneously. "Dying the death" (Genesis 2) is the descent into complete punishment. "Returning to the dust" may be compared to a person's entering the reception room until such time as the judge opens the session at which the real execution of punishment will take place. This interim will have lost its purpose the moment the judge has ascended His throne, and stands ready for the final act of judgment after the ripening of the history of the world.[3] As soon as Christ will have completed His Messianic work of grace the reason for maintaining "temporal death" will be gone. Hence the people who are still alive at the last day will not die, but will be changed in an instant of time and will be transplanted to "the other world" in a moment. They will immediately be withdrawn from the "forms" of temporal existence. These will not experience the curse "death." For the real, the essential, punishment of sin is the "second death." It is the suffering of the relentless wrath of God in body and in soul, the suffering *of hell*.

Now there is one question which will not be suppressed. If the disruption of soul and body — the so-called "first death" — does

---

1. Dr. H. Bavinck, *op. cit.*, volume 3, p. 188.

2. Dr. A. Kuyper, *Locus de Peccato*, p. 97. Dr. Kuyper cannot agree with this interpretation. According to him Genesis 2:17 was immediately fulfilled by the spiritual death of Adam. Surely, however, the concept "death" in Genesis 2:17 is broader than that.

3. See my article, "De ondergang van den Antichrist," *Geref. Theol. Tijdschrift*, Vol. 21, 2.

not belong to the essential nature of punishment, why did Christ, after He had already in body and soul suffered the essential penalty and the pains of hell, still have to undergo that temporal death? Would it not have been possible for Him too, to have been transformed in a moment, and in that way have been instantly transported to the heavenly blessedness, instantly withdrawn from the earth without the preliminary breaking of the body?

Various reasons may be given to indicate that this would have been impossible. In the first place we must proceed in this matter on the assumption that the dominant idea here is the idea of the *offer*. The offer consists of two elements: first, that of the *breaking* of the body; and, second, that of the *voluntary* breaking of the body.

It is the second element which provides the explanation in this case. Plainly we cannot deduce the inevitability of Christ's dying in temporal life from the law according to which the holy sacrifice had to be broken, if we do not introduce other factors into the discussion. If seen in the proper light the suffering of the affliction of hell is in itself a living in a condition of brokenness according to the body. Even though no one can speak specifically about the suffering in hell, we can deduce from what is told us in the Bible that lost man also suffers in the body, suffers death in the body. The body of the lost creature in hell is also a basis of operation for the devastating wrath. His whole life there represents personal disruption; the wrath penetrates everything, saturates his whole life, and every single form of his existence. Hence when Christ endured the affliction of hell, in Gethsemane first and upon Golgotha later — during the three hours of darkness — He also allowed His flesh to be broken. By that we mean that then also He suffered in the flesh, was disrupted in the flesh, and offered Himself there in the flesh, with the flesh, and by means of the flesh.

However this did not suffice. The offer as a sacrifice had not yet fully realized itself in this way. For the suffering of the affliction of hell had been compulsory. Perhaps someone will say that this also holds true of the death of His body in the moment of His dying. That is quite true but for that reason we must add that the suffering of the affliction of hell came with an overwhelming coercion. Christ could not do anything about it even if He had wanted to. When God forsook Him He was oppressed by a burden which weighed more heavily than His human strength could sustain. It is for this reason that the church confesses that His divinity had to support Him. When He suffered the affliction of hell a force accrued to Him which struck deeper wounds, and which permitted severer torments to come to Him than His human knowledge could understand and assimiliate. It is for that reason that He Himself in the life of His confession becomes involved in the great impasse — witness His authentically honest "why." This was too much for Him; He could not master it. In this most terrible hour He had the courage no longer to say to Himself, and certainly not to the others: I can pray to the Father, and He will send me twelve legions of angels to support me. The affliction of hell was more than His naturally human life could master either by an act of knowledge or by an act of the will; it was more than He could bear, more than He could fathom. The coercion, the inevitability, became a consuming compulsion; an irresistible force. At this time the balance between His having to do the thing and His willing to do it was destroyed. Not in the sense, of course, that His will was opposed to it; not that in the least. But this was true in the sense that His having to do it gained the mastery over His willing and knowing it. He was being broken in these moments, but His free will had not been able to express itself with an equally great degree of activity as the force which passively had been able to express itself in devastating Him.

Nevertheless the offer must be entirely *voluntary*. The Saviour of our souls must not be taken by compulsion, by an overwhelming God, He must not be taken by surprise, but must *give* Himself to His people. His love must always be willing to take sole responsibility for the complete act of sacrifice; and this love must take that responsibility gladly, without any sense of regret, even after the sacrifice has passed. Love must delight to give the gift, before as well as after the giving.

Now it is this last consideration which explains the necessity of His physical death to us. Have we not heard the voice of Christ lamenting and crying, and demanding: I thirst? This is the last time we shall refer to that. By His "I thirst" Christ with a completely free will and with a perfect knowledge based on experience assumes the burden of the affliction of hell. Throughout His life

He had done all that the Scriptures said; the fifth utterance from the cross was saying nothing new. But there was this to add: He had now experienced what the Scriptures wanted. He had learned a terrible thing. He had never known that God could be so terrible, that God could do such a thing. That which had been mere knowledge before now became experience: namely, the affliction of hell.

Now when God wishes to try a person, He asks not once but twice: Do you wish to be obedient? Do you want what I want? He asks this the first time when the man is still facing the experience of suffering. Then man answers in the affirmative. But it might very well be that this puny human being after he has experienced how terrible and how austere his God can be, would make this confession: I did not know that it was so bad. Now that I know it, and have experienced it, now my soul shudders at it. I certainly would not make the same choice today, if I were given an opportunity to do so. And it is then that God asks a second time: Do you want what I want? Does your free will in your inclination towards your God acquiesce in the burden which He gives you to bear?

At such times there are people who resemble Abraham. They resemble not the real Abraham but the Abraham of a certain person's imagination who gives this picture of him: "Silently he arranged the wood for the fire, bound Isaac to it, and drew out the knife; thereupon he saw the ram, which God had appointed. This ram he offered, and then went on his way . . . After this day Abraham became old; he could not forget that God had made this demand of him. Isaac grew up rapidly as before, but the eye of Abraham became dimmed; he felt no joy any more."[1]

Now this image of the father of the believers is based upon unsound thinking, but even if we accepted it, we could say that Christ in no respect resembled it. When He had experienced what God can demand of a son of man, when He had felt what no one before had ever felt, when God proved to Him to be the most terrible of all in His punishing, and when He could find a ram nowhere in the bushes, He said: I thirst. And He said this in order that He

---

1. **Kierkegaard.**

might fulfill the Scriptures. He did not reject those terrible words, this terrible utterance from the Scripture, after experiencing the harshness and terribleness of God's judgment. And He did not suppress these words. He immediately appropriated them.

In that way He assumed all that the Scriptures asked of Him with a free will which had itself been enhanced by the experience of its own selection. He assumed the condition of brokenness, the state of being broken, in the *perfectum damnationis*[1] of the afflictions of hell. But that was not enough. It did not suffice for God nor for the people whom He sought in His love.

It is not enough to suffer death in the *perfectum*.[2] He must suffer death in the *aoristus*.[3] His body He had submitted to be broken, and consequently He had not cursed God; but He must also voluntarily suffer death in the immediate moment, in the second of disruption. In the case of others the brokenness comes after the disruption; the condition of complete death follows upon the moment of dying. Thus it is with those who die the natural death on earth, or with those who are transformed in an instant of time. In both cases there is a moment of immediate transition to the other world, of acute removal from the world which held us and to which we clung, and there is a sudden return to the basic forms of our existence, a basic being snatched up, vehemently, violently, catastrophically, before God, the Creator and the Judge.

And this moment of dying which precedes the condition of brokenness in all others, had to follow upon that condition in the case of Christ. We have repeatedly indicated why this was necessary for Him.[4]

Now we observe that everything is again governed by the accommodating hand and accommodating spirit of Christ Himself. The cry "I thirst," inasmuch as it assumed the burden of the Scriptures after the experience of hell, was an act of free will overagainst the condition of brokenness. And to the extent that this cry proved to be a command according to which He wished to be bruised in the body in the moment of death, it was also an act of the free will in view of this coming dying moment.

1. Completed damnation: the eternal, infinite affliction of hell. See by way of discussion of this *perfectum* as an expression of infinite worth, pp. 461-2.
2. Perfected death.
3. An abruptly impinging moment of death.
4. See pp. 24, 112, 377, 399-400, 486.

Thus He assumes the sacrifice completely. Not only the being sacrificed, but also the becoming sacrificed; for there is a distinction here to the subject who wills it. Not only the condition of death, but also the moment of death. Not only the being slain, but also the slaying. Not only what the accursed human being must suffer outside of the gates of time, but also what he must endure inside those gates. Christ passed through all our gates. He passed through the entrance by His birth; He passed through the exit by this acute dying. And there was besides that which intervened between these two: the extended human life which He lived on earth. To which we must add, again, that which was suffered as the affliction of hell quite beyond the bourne of time.

Hence we can say that the moment of dying is a natural part of the sacrifice precisely because the sacrifice is *voluntary*. It is a presentation, an offer, in the basic sense of that word. He allows Himself to be led back to His origins now. He allows Himself to be placed a captive on the chariot of God which is hurrying where God pleases. This is what is meant by dying in a moment. He had His "moment" just as each one of us must experience it. This point of time would have come sooner or later for the man of Paradise also, for, even though sin had not intervened, man would at a certain point of time have arrived at that other mode of existence in which He could live eternally, irremovably, and steadfastly before His God, and could do it without eating, without drinking, without marrying, without sexual relationships. Now this particular point of time, this moment of transference to the other world-order, to the new world-scheme — this every human being suffers in his dying hour. And those people who will still be on earth when Christ returns will also experience their "moment" in the immediate transformation which will withdraw them from this world and transplant them to the other.

In this way Christ broke His body before God in an instant of time. Nothing human was alien to Him.

How the free will of this act of sacrifice dazzles in its glory! When life could be endured again after that affliction in hell, when the burdens were diminished, when the condition of brokenness existed no longer, when light returned to caress His body, when His flesh no longer was the field of operation for the devastation of wrath — then He had to present the sacrifice, had to give the

offer. He had to disappear in natural death, He had to commit
Himself into the hand of Him who had stricken Him. He gave
Himself thus, and in this way performed the extreme act of
willingness.

How perfectly He loved God and the people! He surrendered
Himself to the one who was devastating Him. The devastation
was fundamental, elemental; His surrender is also that. His was
a radical surrender. It was the thorough-going gift. He omits
nothing, no line, no point, no hour, no minute, no circumstance,
and no incident. Ah, how He dazzles now as a sign in the center
of all epochs! If the institution of temporal death, as we observed,
was indeed punishment at bottom, but also grace, then the punishment reaches its final culmination in Him, and grace the point at
which it breaks through. For there had to be a moment of reversal in history. The moment had to come in which the vicious circle
should be cut by a vigorous life, conquering as it marched on.
Now that point of history has been reached. It is nothing if taken
out of its context, if separated from what went before and from
what follows. But it is unique in its significance also and is indispensable to its context.

Now we can go further. We can say that penalizing justice and
life-giving grace meet each other in this instant of time.

The penalizing justice makes its appearance in the moment of
time which is punctuated by Christ's physical death. For we see
Christ now as one in whom death represents complete penalty.
Elsewhere death in the last analysis is always a kind of preparation for Christ; if not for the dying person himself, in the event
that he is opposed to God, certainly it is that for the church of humanity. For it has become obvious that the temporal death must
clear the way for Christ and His spirit, in order that the curse of
eternal death should not come before its time. But He was the
One in whom death could completely and satisfactorily realize itself. The way had been cleared so that the second Adam might be
cast out of "every gate."[1] O God, but this instant of time is significant! It is very painful, for the descent into the affliction of
hell must still become a descent into Hades. He must still permit

1. See pp. 379-83.

Himself to be broken on that border-line of the world which can be seen.

Again we say that this is a penalizing justice. It demands humiliation, and this truth gives us a new subject for consideration. The necessity for humiliation makes His entrance into heaven without the moment of dying impossible. It is a part of that humiliation that the mark of shame be impressed also upon His body, upon His remains. Yes, this had taken place already when Christ suffered the pangs of hell. But no one had been a witness to that. Now that He has awakened again and been brought into the light out of those three hours of darkness, He must visibly carry the disdain of His own in the signs of His body, and be completely humiliated. He must be publicly humiliated.[1] Men must be able to see that Christ has died. His death in hell had been witnessed by none. So much the more reason for which His earthly dying must be seen by every eye.

For the dying of Christ is also *revelation*. It represents payment and compensation, yes, but it is also a revelation of the law which demanded payment. We know that revelation speaks to men in its concepts, in its forms, in its symbols, and in events which Christ sees before Him in the ordinary things of life daily. If Christ had not died as every other person dies, the terrible preaching of death as the curse of sin would not have been intelligible. After all, death is visible to men only in the form of the bodily dying. No one sees the essence of death. To be really dead means, on the one hand, to be sinner, and on the other hand, to be wholly forsaken, to be the victim of the robbery of hell. But sin is a robbery which no one sees,[2] and being forsaken in hell is also a robbery which no one living in the world today has ever seen. So we say that this disintegration of the body is the only thing that men see of death. That is another reason for which Christ had to die in the body. He had to manifest death to the world. Surely, we are taking the wrong course when we say that His dying was solely a preaching of death, that it was a naked expression of such preaching. For, as we have stated before, the dying of Christ was also necessity; it represented compensation,

---

1. *Christ on Trial*, pp. 297-300: being lifted up; also see the present volume, p. 82.
2. The essence of sin: to be distinguished from the work which sin performs.

payment. In addition to that, of course, it was also an announcement. It was an announcement of the guilt of sin. God's harsh
sermon did not correspond with the sermon on the mount, with
Christ's discourses about the fire of hell, and about that death
which consists of being a sinner. No, God struck Him down in the
presence of men; Christ had to die the death in the very body in
which men had known Him.

Having arrived at this point, our thoughts turn upwards. There
is in the instant of Christ's death also the breaking forth of
quickening grace. For now that Christ has completely finished the
course of obedience by permitting His body also to be broken,
now Paradise must receive Him in His glory.

Obediently He had permitted everything He had to be taken
away from Him, His seasons and also His moments. With all the
instruments He had, with His soul and spirit and body, He performed His service for God. Therefore the angel who guards the
gate of Paradise must stand aside when He impressively approaches. The angel draws back the guarding sword in favor of
a coursing justice headed by the second Adam; he says to himself
that this man must enter. That is the most natural thing in the
world once the covenant of works became of force. For that covenant had attached the reward of blessedness to perfect service.

Therefore Christ now surrenders His spirit. He does not give
it away indiscriminately, but gives it to the Father. He addresses
Himself to Paradise. From the fact that He gave God His spirit
we may infer His obedience and His sacrifice, His offer. But that
He could address Paradise as He did is evidence to us of His
faith; it represented the certainty of His reward. He was asking
for that reward; He was asking for the reward of the Passover.
The Passover has its beginning in Good Friday. The Saviour enters into the other world, is instantaneously withdrawn from the
bourne of time and space, enters into captivity, for all this is implied in dying. Nevertheless He moved about freely in God's
universe. He is the man who has fought His way to freedom.
The binding which accrues to Him in this instant of time really
represents an unbinding.

We do not mean to say that His possession of Paradise is already complete. His own condition, and the justice He has in mind

for His people, will constrain Him to come again. He Himself is still in the intermediary condition, the condition of the "unclothed soul"[1] who is in Paradise without his body. And intermediary conditions are never desirable in heaven to the extent precisely that they are an intermediary condition. In heaven everything is impelled in the direction of the conclusive, of the completed, of the *perfectum* of blessedness. Christ, too, is not satisfied with this intermediate position. From now on He will be constantly crying: How long, how long, O Father?[2] He thirsts for perfection, for the perfected things. Hardly has He by death obtained release from the hunger and the thirst of the earth before He begins to hunger and thirst in heaven for His own return. Thirsting can be of various kinds. The hungering and thirsting in heaven does not represent need, but a passion for life. As such it represents desire and deep yearning. Hence the intermediate condition, interim as it is, cannot represent His full peace; as far as His rights are concerned He continues to be humiliated. His name is honored in heaven, but on earth His flesh still bears the mark of shame impressed upon it by the penalty. The angels regard Him as glorious, also as glorious in His humanity; but on earth they are preparing a grave for Him. The stigma of shame still attaches to Him. For His own sake, too, He will labor hard for His Passover-victory in order that the stigma of shame attaching to His body may also be erased. Thus, as a matter of fact, He is still struggling every day in order to arrive at His last return, in order that His good name may no longer be a source of mockery in the world. However, it is not for His own sake alone, but for the sake of His people also, that He will from now on hunger to return to the earth and to arise from the dead. For He would gather His church together, draw them unto Himself, and make His power manifest in them.

This is the reason for which we called His dying the point at which God *marches* on through Him. All His struggles for obedience to God, and for the glorification of Himself, and for the exaltation of His people, now converge upon the act of His death.

Accordingly, we do not like to speak of a Jesus who has "fallen asleep." "Asleep in Jesus" — that is a word which, we hope, may appropriately pertain to us. But in reference to Him we must use

1. See II Corinthians 5.
2. See Revelation 5.

the phrase: *He gave up the spirit.* His *will* performed an action. To cry aloud with a great voice is an item hardly compatible with the gentle phrase "falling asleep." Rather than to use that, we would abandon all figurative language. The Saviour gave up the ghost, and did this by reason of a strong desire and will to march on from the manger past the cross to the hall of the Passover, the hill of ascension, the deed of Pentecost, and the last judgment.

Now be quiet, for the Saviour is dying. Be quiet, just as you must always be quiet before Him, also when He is busy at work. Is Jesus exhausted? Yes, in a certain sense He could not go any farther. However, He did not want to go any farther here below, for here the work has been finished. Hence He could not go on, and hence His heart could not go on. Is Jesus exhausted? Just say yes and no; for you will be touching on the truth only if you combine those two in a transcending unity. His strong will addressed death and said: I do not want you. And when the time had come, He said: I have summoned you. Must we again appeal to His "divinity" in order to explain this? As when we say that by an act of His omnipotence He broke His own heart? It is much simpler than that, and hence it is far more complicated. By an act of — human — *obedience* He permitted His heart to be broken, and gave it up to the Breaker.

And thus He bowed His head, and gave up the ghost. Saint Augustine said that *He bowed His head,* as though He were offering His face to us for a kiss. This is too pretty a fancy. He bowed His head because He could no longer hold it up. God Himself bent it low. No one was present to close His eyes. The angels did not look back upon His body; they had other work to do. They praised Him reverently; their voice echoed behind Abraham's chair. Heaven witnessed a miracle. For the first time heaven caught a glimpse of the Word which was made flesh. Heaven saw the second man, the second Adam, but such a one as there had never been before. Heaven *saw,* and had to *believe,* that *this* was the Head of the Church. A page of God's Book was turned over, and Adam, our father, said: He must increase here, and I simply cannot decrease; how could this come to pass, O God of miracles?

Christ as Melchizedek's Antitype Summoned Against Levi

CHAPTER TWENTY-TWO

Christ as Melchizedek's Antitype Summoned Against Levi

● *And, behold, the veil of the temple was rent in twain from the top to the bottom.*

MATTHEW 27:51.

WHEN it is very quiet in heaven you can depend upon it that a storm is in the offing. When John heard heaven maintaining a silence for "a half hour" in his vision on Patmos, he immediately also saw the seventh seal opened; the signal of a world-storm had been lifted. This was also the case on Golgotha. Heaven held its peace. It was the hour and the power of darkness. But hardly has the spirit of Christ gone on its way to the Father before the storms break loose. The catastrophes of the last judgment first realized themselves in Him in the invisible world, and heaped all their tumultous violence upon Him within the walls of His spiritual house.[1] But now these catastrophes become externally visible. Are these, however, catastrophes of the last judgment, you ask? If that were true, Christ would have suffered in vain, and the moment of His death would that very moment have been proclaimed a vanity. Well, then, are these convulsions possibly the travail accompanying the birth of unmixed *grace?* No, that cannot be; for His cross cannot gain the effects of grace without the power of the Passover and of Pentecost. Hence the catastrophes which now are made manifest are *signs,* and these signs speak a twofold language. They spell judgment against those who despise the death of Christ and refuse to take their life from His death. And they proclaim *grace* to those who are willing to come to the temple, led by this Priest. Yes, these

---

1. Page 115.

are catastrophes, but they are not the catastrophes of the curse. Nor are they the catastrophes of the blessing simply. They are signs of curse and blessing *both;* for curse and blessing both have now been released by Christ.

Brace yourself now, for God is performing greatly. He is splitting the earth, tearing the graves asunder, putting the dead on their feet again, bursting the rocks, and rending a curtain into pieces. Many centuries have been at work on this curtain, and the exhausted love of a whole nation hangs suspended in its folds. The curtain of the temple is rent in twain.

Revere this God now, for He begins at the beginning. Just as the Son who has now died did not come to "the dogs," without having first done full justice to "the children," and just as He ever took His departure from Jerusalem, so God also would begin at Jerusalem. Jerusalem *lives* in the temple. That is where the heart of the people is beating. Hence God's first utterance after Christ's separation is a temple address. God makes His majestic appearance at its portal, and He addresses His people from its front steps. It may be that an earthquake turns everything topsy-turvy for us, but the order of God is not disturbed by it. The seismographs of heaven do not indicate the slightest variation. The hour in which God rent the earth and spoke in catastrophes was *most orderly.*

The first catastrophe was the opening of the temple. The curtain of the temple was rent in twain. Do not linger too long over the many questions that arise. Many have wondered just what was meant by the curtain which was rent on this occasion. Well, we know that two well known curtains hung suspended in the temple. One of these shut off the "holy of holies." This was the inside or rearmost of the curtains. And there was another curtain which shut off the "holy place." Just how beautiful these curtains were we can learn from old books of history in which their glory has been eulogized. We shall not pause to consider that. The only significant question is: which curtain is meant?

Many maintain that the *inner* curtain is intended, the curtain which had to be drawn aside in order to enter the Holy of Holies. They base their interpretation on the thought that this curtain which occupied the last place in the public worship had the greater liturgical significance, and that it possessed more symbolically suggestive virtue than the other. The Holy of Holies was the real "dwelling place" of God. Only one person was allowed to enter it. It was the most intimate, the most special place in the temple. In opposition to this, however, others aver that the first curtain, which gave on the Holy Place, had more real significance. After all, the rearmost curtain was seen only by the priests; but the other forbade admission to the people and consequently was seen by the masses themselves. Hence this foremost curtain made a far greater impression upon the imagination of the people than the other; and thus this would be the more likely one in which to manifest a sign intended for all the people. If we accept, besides this reason, the fact that the Greek word which is used here for "temple" has reference to the temple in its broadest sense, we have good reasons for choosing the interpretation which says that the curtain which was rent in twain was the one which hung in front of the Holy Place, and not the one which shut off the Holy of Holies.

However, the question is not particularly important. The preaching of the miraculous sign which God shows here remains the same in either instance. In epitome we can say that the access to the temple, in which Levi and his priests, separated from the people, had to perform their office, is now opened to all. Levi's house now is dismissed. Now God emerges from His cleft, from His prison, leaves His exclusive dwelling place. Thus the order of Melchizedek becomes law in the house of Levi. Melchizedek returned, and was fulfilled in Christ. Well, it was not the *hand* of Christ as Melchizedek's antitype which tore Levi's curtain asunder. But observe this: the spirit, the strength of Melchizedek and his right, invade the house of Levi and throw his gates wide open to all those unfortunates who up to this time were deprived of the temple and prohibited from seeing God in His own house.

Before we go on, therefore, we must pause to adjure Jerusalem, and tell her that Jesus Christ is very *great*. They may cast Him outside of the gate, and time and again regard Him as an outcast, but He succeeds in making history nevertheless. Whether He be good or evil, Christ or Antichrist, does not matter just now. In any case He is of historical significance. After all, a torn temple curtain, a temple door thrown wide is a thing for which not only

God yearns but Satan also. The rent curtain of the temple hangs on the way of the Antichrist as well as on the way of Christ. An opening of the temple, an opening of the house of God, is the eager desire of the Antichrist. Both aim at the temple. The only question is, *Who* is to break it open, who and for what purpose? Who will tear the curtain into pieces, who, and for what purpose? The temple of the service of shadows proceeds on the assumption that there is a holy place in which the service of God is ministered officially and that outside of this lies that profane area which is not dedicated to God nor permeated by His grace. Hence the only question is on whose victorious tour will the curtain of the temple be rent, on the tour of Christ, or on that of the Antichrist, of God, or of Satan? If Satan wins the victory, he will storm into the temple from that profane area, introduce the unclean into the Holy Place through the torn curtain, and thus make the holy profane. On the other hand, God through Christ would now take the opposite course. God would now leave the temple, by going out of it from within, by stepping away from the curtain behind which He has been concealed, in order to make that which was common and profane holy also. Yes, the only question is: *Who* is to rend the veil of the temple? It will be torn in any case. But who and when? The histories of temples can never be silenced. The curtains of temples always hang in the wind. If Satan can thrust aside the curtain, and open the entrance, the whole world will enter it, swallow it up, and make everything "a world." But if God is to rend the curtain, the spirit of the temple will enter into the world, throw every obstacle aside, and then the stream of grace will overleap every boundary, and the church will be borne out into the world.

Thus we learn to see in a rent temple-veil an event of world-historical significance. The great conflict of Good Friday, and also of the *dies ater* of the Beast, is always: how does the curtain become torn? By revolution, or by reformation?

Now Good Friday gives us the answer to this question. The curtain of the temple was torn by God. In His own way and in His own strength He came from the other side of the old veil, and entered the world. The hour had come in which the statement "No admittance" could now be erased from God's murals forever.

For it was a fact that a world sorrow had attached itself to this temple veil. We pointed out before that in the time of the shadow-service the world continued to be a profane area. Revelation, the ministration of atonement, had limited itself to one people, the people of Israel; and among that people it had limited itself to one city, the city of Jerusalem; and within that city it had limited itself to one house, the temple. Behind the walls of that temple, and more particularly behind the folds of this curtain, God was hidden. There the service was administered by the hands of the priests but — pro omnibus: *one* for all. The "common man" might not approach this place; no pagan might enter it. The priesthood was a secret caste; it enjoyed privileges which were not open to the "common man." The furnishings of the temple were a delight to the eye; but they spelled out two terrible words: No admittance! The approach to God was closed. Throughout the course of many centuries this temple had passed through many revolutions; but, irrespective of how everything had changed, the protecting veil continued to occupy its place. God was separated from the people, and the children of Levi stood overagainst the children of God in the poorest relationship known to the world, the tragi-comic relationship of a hierarchical system. The famous veil served as a sign of the hierarchy, and as a vindication of it; the people did not know any better; they thought the curtain belonged there. In the days of Christ's sojourn upon earth the temple had not even been completely restored; the renovation which was begun in the year 20 B.C. was not completed until the time of Albinus in 62-64 A.D. However, whatever else it may have lacked, the curtain was hanging there a long time. That was, so to say, the first necessity. Now this whole temple really was a great fort, a bulwark. The middle court also was separated from the rest by a stone wall; placards of warning threatened the death penalty against the unqualified who came too near it. Hence this veil became a world issue. Heathendom was kept away from it, and the people of Israel too in its common ranks was prohibited from passing through it.

Now if this remains so, if the veil is not rent, Israel will remain an excluded people, having an "exclusive" God. If that curtain cannot be put aside, the sect and not the church is God's final purpose and eschatological fulness. Indeed, a solution must come. The world is waiting for it; heaven and hell keep their eyes fastened on that simple veil. As long as it remains hanging, there is a status quo; but so long also God will not be progressing, and, if seen properly, Satan either. One or the other: God must step out from behind the curtain, and stride into the open, or Satan must come from the outside, and step behind it. But in any case, of course, one or the other of these two must remove the curtain.

Who had sensed the tragedy of this veil more excruciatingly than Christ? This proud temple building was the building of His Father; but the words on the curtain "No admittance" affected Him also. For Christ was from the point of view of the world unanointed and unconsecrated. He had no priest's cloak, and was not ritually allowed to go into the Holy Place behind that curtain. His Father's house remain closed to Him. His priesthood was not acknowledged.

That is no wonder. His priesthood was of another *order*. It was a priesthood of the order of Melchizedek, and Melchizedek is the priest who without a priestly genealogy and without an inherited commission stands in the world quite alone by virtue of his own peculiar calling. Thus he ministers the office to which he is called of God. Abraham, and in him Levi, had fallen down at the feet of the Melchizedek in former days. Abraham and Levi had reverently bowed before him and as a token of his superiority had given him tithes. But when Christ came into the world and wanted to be Melchizedek's antitype, admittance to the house of Levi was denied Him. Levi did *not* bow before Melchizedek; He had forgotten how to bow.[1] Levi had *exacted* tithes of Him. The assessment levied by the temple, Christ had obediently raised. This was a topsy-turvy world,[2] for Melchizedek is not now being enriched by Levi, but must give of his riches to Levi.

Christ had died in this kind of relationship. God had given Him nothing as a loot out of the temple of Levi. On the contrary, the temple had rejected Him, and God Himself had cooperated in the rejection. Jesus' murderers sat there and prayed there, and praised God behind the curtains. God was supposed to be of their company still. Yes, the suspense is awful: something *must* happen.

---

1. *Christ on Trial*, p. 24.
2. See p. 179-82.

Yes, it had to happen. But Christ Himself had never sought to gain by the means of the revolution. He had not taken it upon Himself to raise a single finger against the beautiful veil of the temple. Not to tear that curtain apart, but to sear the placard "No admittance" with the fire of God's righteousness. That was the way He wished to gain the temple for His people, and that was the way in which He wanted to place God on the broad roads of the life of the world.

And now He had died, in order to *purchase* the right to do this Himself and for His people. Now He had gone on to fulfill the shadow; never had He forcibly rebelled against the shadow-service. But hardly had He breathed His last, before God proclaims that Christ is Melchizedek's antitype, and that He may justly open the temple wide. He carries the key in His dead hand. Heaven opens, a whirlwind so overwhelming that it cannot be heard, blows toward the temple, and sweeps all the priests aside. A hand seizes on the curtain, tears it to pieces, and God testifies that the work of the Son was perfect, that admittance is open to all who ask for God.

Thus Good Friday becomes the day of *prophecy*. The Prophet has died, but prophecy immediately goes on. No wonder; His death also was a fulfillment of the prophecy. And now when the Prophet is mute in death, God shows a sign. This is a sign designed not to accompany the prophecy of Christ, but to seal it, and also to prepare for the prophesying of the Christ which will take place in the future by the Spirit of Pentecost. God Himself accordingly is witnessing that this Nazarene has made the temple a place of fellowship and communion not by revolution but by reformation. Moreover, God is not only prophesying, but He is also beginning the new dispensation. The exclusive caste of the priesthood is deprived of all its privileges. Hereafter all those who believe and through their faith approach God, will be called priests. That which Pentecost will realize to the full has its beginning here. The temple is placed in an intermediate position between Good Friday and Pentecost. Woe to that house of God which does not regard such an intermediate condition as being very terrible.[1] The moratorium has been declared, and all the priests know that

1. Page 500.

they must hasten to repent. They have not yet been annihilated. They simply have this one thing to learn: they must be able to bear an approach to God characterized by the same righteousness as is the approach of the least of His people. On this Great Day of Atonement our High Priest did not step behind the curtain with the symbolical blood, for a higher reality is here now. This reality is not a curtain, but one who rends the curtain in order that He may enter into the Most Holy Place with His own blood.

In this we see that Christ is a Priest after the order of Melchizedek. For Melchizedek is the man who ministered the office of the priest, not because he had inherited the prerogative, because the office was traditionally handed down to him, but because a wonder which entered into and clung to him, enabled him to do the work spontaneously, *self-sufficiently.*[1] All this was fulfilled in Christ. The temple had never acknowledged Him. The plot of Levi against Melchizedek had been set in motion behind that curtain. Now that the fulfilled Melchizedek has not gone to the trouble of laying His hand on that curtain, but has calmly awaited what the God of Abraham should do for Him, now God Himself places the crown on Melchizedek's blood-stained head. Hardly has our great Melchizedek been robbed of all the treasures, of all the "tenths," and of all the "hundredths" which the earth had left Him, before God announces to the children of the house of Levi that they must pay Him their tenths ten times.

Will they refuse? Let us hope the best for them; for when we read later that a great group of priests became obedient to the faith, we may suppose that it is possible and probable that their repentance had its first preparation in the form of the tearing of the veil. Be that as it may, the children of Levi cannot blame this Melchizedek for enriching himself at their expense. In principle, after all, Melchizedek's usurpation of the temple is an act of sheer service. He did not come storming into the temple from without, but wanted to take God from inside the temple and to place Him outside. Moreover, Melchizedek Himself was consumed in this work of religious service. The zeal of the veils had eaten Him up, for the Bible points out — read Hebrews 10:20 — that this temple opening on the part of the Antitype of the old Melchizedek was

1. Naturally this is meant in a relative sense.

done at the cost of His own life. We know that He Himself was the temple of God in perfection. In Him God dwelt; God Himself was hidden behind His humiliated and broken body. God dwelt in the Nazarene; but men did not see that. Accordingly, the body of Christ is a thing which keeps God concealed. As long as the flesh of Christ, behind which God is hidden, remains unbroken, God could not reveal Himself to the world, nor share Himself with the world. Thereupon the body of Christ, which served as the veil that concealed God, was torn asunder, in order that the way from God to the people might be cleared. On Golgotha the veil of the supreme temple was rent in the form of the body of Christ. Hence the veil of the lesser temple was broken simultaneously. What could that lesser temple possibly do if the tension is at its greatest in that highest temple? The veil behind which the priests concealed themselves had merely a symbolical, a liturgical significance. But in the temple of the body of Christ the service of the reality was perfected.

It is true, is it not, priests of Levi, that you can blame Him for nothing? He supported you with His wings but was broken in the same hour. He took your tithes, but immediately gave them to God, and keeps nothing for Himself except a pitiable death.

Thus the feast of Pentecost already entered the world in its incipiency. Captivity was taken captive, God Himself stepped out into the freedom which He had gained for Himself by means of this Son. A royal people and a royal priesthood is being born on the same day. Today it is being conceived, and on the feast of Pentecost the whole host will be born. The moment of Christ's death is made actual and is sharply accentuated by God.

We know that God has made very plain to all those who are willing to hear that He is the breaker of the old curtain. We know that the curtain was rent from the top to the bottom. This means not only that the rent was a radical one, but also that this was a wonder. No human hand rent the veil; the hand came from above. It was just as anonymous as the moving hand which once frightened Belshazzar when it wrote the characters of heaven upon his palace wall. God does the writing and God does the erasing. God recalls His former statement: See that ye do it according to the pattern, according to the type, which was shown you on the mount. For the veil which was shown Moses upon the mount was conceived in heaven indeed, and thereupon revealed on an earthly mountain, on Sinai, but now that it "waxeth aged it is nigh unto vanishing away."

Thus Christ remains a living offense. This is His destiny, for He comes to His Word. The Jews hated Him first because of His cleansing of the temple when He made the profane holy once more. He found that holiness knows no aging, and can never disappear. But now the Jews will hate Him because as they see it He has defiled the temple. They blame Him from this time forth as one who has made the sacred profane. They do not know that He has made everything which was profane holy, for they do not acknowledge His priestly work.

We, therefore, would obediently follow Him to God, would approach God without an intermediary link, without a priest, without any person or any force standing in our way. Thus we would fulfill the law of the veil that was rent.[1]

---

1. The original includes a poem of Joachin Oudaen which has defied translation.

Christ Proclaimed by the Church of the Advent

CHAPTER TWENTY-THREE

Christ Proclaimed by the Church of the Advent

> ● *And the earth did quake, and the rocks rent;*
> *and the tombs were opened; and many bodies*
> *of the saints that had fallen asleep were raised;*
> *and coming forth out of the tombs after his*
> *resurrection, they entered into the holy city and*
> *appeared unto many.*
> MATTHEW 27:51b, 52 and 53.

THE sign of the rent veil had not only illuminated the temple, but had also illuminated everything which lay outside of it, and had prophesied concerning it. Nor had it merely affected the living, but it had also prophesied concerning the dead. It had prophesied about the relationship existing between the shadow-service of the past, and the future of the church. Is it any wonder, then, that this sign of the rent veil is accompanied by movements of nature, and by a prophecy which arises from the church of the advent coming up from the past, in order to establish a relationship between the past and the future, and in order to point out the Christ as the One in whom this relationship is established.

A sign is performed in nature; and a voice arises from the church of the advent. Come, see it, and hear it.

When Christ died the earth quaked. As a result of that the rocks were rent. Naturally, this last sign was limited to the vicinity of Jerusalem. For that reason we also believe that the quake was restricted to this neighborhood. We noted on a previous occasion that the Greek word which is translated "earth" here can also mean "country" or "area." Hence we accept for the reasons previously given[1] that the earthquake was also limited to this environment. By this we do not mean to deny that for the people living here the quake spoke a language of a general character.

---

1. See p. 387.

After all, every earthquake is regional. But wherever the atmosphere was tense because of expectations for the future, such a regional earthquake always was regarded as a sign of universal significance. The same holds true now. Hence the whole significance of the earthquake is not contained in the thought that it was a "gesture of mourning" on the part of nature because of the death of Christ. That does not explain the phenomenon entirely any more than the three hours of darkness sometime before can be explained completely as such a "gesture of mourning." No, again we must think of a proclamation of God, a proclamation which God is giving the people of revelation. Especially when we relate this earthquake to the destruction of the temple (to which our preceding chapter was devoted) does it take on a prophetic significance in the minds of an expectant people. God addresses the Jews in their own language. The earthquake served as a woe which heralded an advent, as a sign of the coming day of judgment, as a sign of the coming of God with eschatological intent. God took this means to say to Israel that Golgotha was not a forgotten little place in which a certain case of a certain Nazarene had been executed; but that His death is a sharply accentuated moment in the day of the Lord, and a beginning of the last judgment. An earthquake always serves as a catastrophe of the last day in all advent-prophecy. This goes to prove once more that Golgotha is indeed a place of judgment, and that it was not an exaggeration but a declaration of the truth when we chose in this book to relate the events to catastrophes of judgment. This catastrophe points out the attitude we must take. We must look here for an extreme act of judgment.

The second sign is connected with the earthquake. This second sign is a cry rising from the coming church of the dead. The graves were opened, and many bodies buried in them were laid bare. If we choose, we may regard this as a natural result of the earthquake. However, we may not take this attitude inasmuch as we are told that many of the dead were aroused to life, that they stepped out of the grave, and appeared to many in the holy city. We cannot doubt that the reference is to a definite resurrection from the dead of these people. Inasmuch as the earthquake is not a "natural" phenomenon of nature but must be regarded as a sign, we can say that this whole complex of events is to be characterized as a miracle.

Yes we see people rising from their graves. Hades opens itself and makes a statement. Christ enters into Hades. He enters into the realm of the dead, but in the same moment the mouth of Hades opens and the dead make their appearance and begin to speak.

They arise for the sake of Christ. We understand that at once. That in itself is a glorious message. Irrespective of what they wish to say or not to say, what they wish to do or not to do, the fact that human beings come for the sake of Christ at this time is already a happy message. We know that the angels do very little in the history of the passion of Christ. The angel who did come to Gethsemane was the last one. Recall the host of angels who came on Christmas eve and it strikes you as worth remarking that the angels had a very little share in the passion of Christ. But now, although the angels do not appear, men rise up to prophesy, and to point to the Christ. Plainly, this is progress. For it is good when angels speak to men, but it is better when men themselves point their finger in the direction of Christ. We know that salvation is not for the angels, but for men. A servant is much, but a son is more. The angel is the servant, but man is the son in the house of God. Yes, indeed, God has made progress. True, He has not yet reached the point He wants to reach, for the messengers of the day are but the people of Hades. And God prefers preachers who are the stalwart fishers of flesh and blood, He prefers the workaday people of Corinth to the people of Hades; for no one preaching in the busy market-place of life, can constitute a more effective proof of His power than these. Be that as it may, these are people, these sons of Hades. Inasmuch as they rise from the dead, they are the first fruits of the power of Christ. Is not this glorious? Now men refuse to be pushed off the stage. That much Christ has achieved. The angels can come later on the feast of the Passover. Our text tells us already that the announcement of the Passover by the angels presently will be *accompanied* by an announcement from men. We read that after His resurrection they appeared unto many.

Many questions can be asked in this connection which are difficult to answer. The first question probably will concern just who are meant by those who were raised from the dead. Without resorting to guesswork, or without immediately looking for "striking names," as those do who immediately think at least of Abraham, Isaac, and Jacob, of Moses and Job and others, we certainly may take it as a fact that these are people who died comparatively recently. They were still in the grave; and those graves were not very old. If they had been graves containing historical personages, these would very likely have been indicated by name. Moreover, the fact that they are designated as saints points to the truth that when they made their appearance they were immediately recognized. To this we must add the indication that they made their appearance in the holy city of Jerusalem. That also suggests that they have been dead but a comparatively short time. For this would give their appearance a more convincing character. Men must have been struck by the fact that many dead were exposed, but that only *saints,* generally acknowledged saints, were raised to life. God Himself had made the decision. The Nazarene was given a good witness by the church of the advent, a cloud of witnesses taken from the "remnant" after the election of grace, from the "remains," the best of the people. Hence it was not without reason that we spoke of the church of the advent. And if we may be allowed a guess for a moment we would ask: Were these perhaps not those members of the church of the advent who in these last trying times were looking for "the consolation of Israel"? For these had placed their own fellowship of faith overagainst the ideals of the political anticipators of the Messiah. Simeon and Anna, Zacharias and Elizabeth, are typical representatives of this "remnant of election," and the name "saints" points in the same direction. And the question concerns the problem of whether these dead, having returned to life, looked over the situation and knew what had happened to Christ. We refuse to guess, but we do want to ask: What can be said against the supposition. Even though, according to the text, their appearance[1] is to be taken as an appearance to the eye rather than as an address to the ear, the mere fact of their "appearance" indicates that they had a message. And is it conceivable that they themselves were ignorant of the content of this message? Surely they were saints whose hearts burned within them because of the messianic problem. Can it be

---

1. *Emphanizoo* means: to make apparent. This in itself, therefore, does not constitute evidence of the fact that this was an appearance of people resurrected from the dead. But the connection of this verb with the subject "bodies," not persons who had entered the holy city before, proves definitely that we must think of a public manifestation of people who have been raised from the dead.

that the spiritual world had not felt the shock caused by the death of Christ? Was their return to the life of earth not a result of a command of God, and can we, then, believe that they were silent about what He wanted? Samuel knew of Saul, and Moses and Elias knew of Christ when they had to return to the earth for a time bearing a special message. Hence it is quite possible that these delegates from Hades were also familiar with the situation. It is possible, and it is probable. The fact that they, even though it was Friday evening when they were recalled to life, made their appearance in the city on Sunday morning after Christ had arisen,[1] also suggests this conclusion.

Even though there are questions which we cannot answer, what we know suffices to build up our faith.

The *first* message which God makes known by the fact of their arising and appearing spells the word: *judgment*. The murderers of the Christ are being condemned in unmistakable language by the representatives of Hades. A sinister miracle had taken place. In general all the graves had indiscriminately been opened. But only certain graves proved after a while to be empty. When the time came to make a report it was noticeable that the graves of those who had been noted for their piety were the empty ones. That was worth some attention; that gave the sextons, and also governors of Jerusalem something to think about. And this restlessness on the part of the inhabitants of Jerusalem had been advisedly planned by God. It seemed as though God Himself was permitting Himself an unnecessary circumlocution such as Christ had once allowed Himself in order to preach His right as king.[2] Certainly the miracle was being withheld terribly long. Arisen on Friday but not appearing until Sunday — surely that is rather circumlocutive. First the city is held in suspense for a day because it cannot solve the riddle, cannot tell why the graves of the pious are the ones that are empty. And then, thereafter, as a second fact, these pious persons appear in the city by way of answering their question. Thus restlessness hovered over the city; the "atmosphere" of Endor was created. God is no longer answering His people: not by dreams because the Spirit has fled; not by visions,

---

1. See the note on page 523.
2. See *Christ in His Suffering*, pp. 101-116.

because the prophets were dumb, and the seers blind.[2] Restlessness feverishly perturbs the heart of all; the crowd had left Golgotha and gone home beating upon its breast. Just what is the meaning of all this? God has made a selection among the dead. The one was left lying, the other was called to life. And the one recalled to life was a typical example of the messianic expectation of redemption. It was a brother of that quiet congregation which had stood aloof from the program of violence sponsored by the Judases and the Barabbases. Only such pious people does God raise from the grave in the moment of Christ's death. God's selective voice is unmistakable. He has the Nazarene, that Messiah who never resorted to force, and the one who himself had also opposed Judas and Barabbas, — he has Him greeted by the covenant group of the former day. O grievous selection! God has the people who murder the Messiah contradicted by the group who expected the Messiah. This is a suggestive anticipation of the weighty chorale of Revelation 20: "Which had not worshipped the beast lived . . . and the rest of the dead lived not again." Heaven is contending with the ostentatious pretensions of Abraham's decadent people, and Hades is becoming involved in it. The saints of the last days speak for Jesus. The spirit of Samuel rises in threat above Endor-Jerusalem.

Yes, the judgment of this day is a proleptic judgment. By this selective voice of God a protest arises from the graves against the spirit which later hit upon the plan of Akeldama. Akeldama is a cemetery for "strangers." It is an insistence upon the old Jewish pride, which holds that the nation of Israel is God's only elect people.[2] Overagainst this God is pointing out that upon the cemetery of Jerusalem itself two groups are distinguishable, the sons and the strangers. There are two groups: the children of the home, who may go out to meet the Bridegroom because they have the *faith* of Abraham, and the others, who do not have that faith, and are therefore in the last analysis barbarians and aliens to God.[3]

Yes, this wonder was a judgment. It was the last judgment performed on the public stage of Israel's own life in the Old Cove-

1. See Isaiah 29:10, and *Christ on Trial*, pp. 40-44.
2. See *Christ on Trial*, p. 265 b.
3. We must remember, of course, that this does not mean that the persons have already been judged (think of the massacre of the children at Bethlehem).

nant. For this reason alone we find it strange that Christians often give so little attention to it. Peculiar to this last wonder is the fact that it took place without any human intermediary. The Prophet of Nazareth had done so many wonders "with" His hands, eyes, and voice. Now the Prophet is gone, but the wonders continue. Surely this represents a judgment. The week of the Passion began with a persecution of the Nazarene who had raised Lazarus to life. Hardly has the Nazarene died, however, before the miracle which they had attempted to stifle becomes manifest on all sides. The sign performed on Lazarus becomes multiplied. A while ago they mocked: He saved others, but now His pretensions to a miracle-working power are gone. But that miracle-working power, to all appearance has immediately returned and takes its effect this time without a human instrument. This too is prophetic. Presently this same Christ will return from the other world, through his Spirit, Himself remaining invisible the while, and thus He will effect His former influences. Herod will have a depressing week. We observed before that he very much feared those dead who still wandered about on the earth. These he regarded as a threat to himself.[1] But the fear of Herod will become very general today. Judgment is abroad. When those dead make their appearance in the city presently,[2] they will judge all the rulers of the city. These have said: Surely the Messiah has not made His appearance in Jesus, for Jesus breaks down the law of Moses. But a voice is heard issuing from Hades which says: He did not come to break down the law of Moses, but to fulfill it.

These dead stand on the border-line between the old and the new covenant, and they testify in the holy city — for that is after all the first address — of the Nazarene. They testify that He is the link between the two covenants. May Endor-Jerusalem tremble now, for it has allowed itself to be infected by the insanity of Saul, and it has bitterly fought against the fulfilled David and against Jahweh. They see gods, "supernatural beings," arising out of the earth. What do they look like? They wear the garments of prophets; the cloak of Samuel can be seen upon their

1. *Christ on Trial*, p. 389 b.
2. The words "after His resurrection" must not be related to the words "came out of the graves," but to the "went into the holy city." See Zahn *Ev. Math.*, 3rd edition, p. 715.

shoulders. God addressed the city this last time by means of a
sign which the city itself desired. Learn to tremble, thou that dost
murder the kings : the destiny of the darkling, called Saul, he who
has become your patron, hangs suspended over your luxurious
homes and over your emptied temple. Tremble, ye brothers of
"the rich man." The rich man of the parable asked for a messenger from the dead to send to his brethren. Perhaps such a one
could succeed in converting the eager heirs of his estate. Now
those messengers from the dead are here. Will the late brethren
of the Israel which boasts that it is rich and self-sufficient repent?
Tremble, ye keepers of the Sabbath, who are spotted with blood.
The last shadow-Sabbath is coming : the calm Saturday. Throughout this quiet Saturday these returned dead of the church of the
advent will be silent, and pass by your city. But hardly will the
Sunday have dawned, before the message of the Nazarene will
receive the most real of testimonies from the world of the dead.

Thus it happens that the first Sunday of the Christian church,
the first Sabbath of the New Testament, is acknowledged and
kept by the dead before it is discovered and celebrated by the living. The church of the Future sent the deputation which God appointed from Hades, and the Christian Sunday-sabbath, which
had already been fixed by Christ's sixth utterance from the cross,[1]
is proclaimed from heaven by means of Hades. Thus we can say
that the coming of the dead is an extension of the sign which preceded it : namely, the rending of the veil in the temple.

In this miracle also, however, grace goes paired with judgment.
Surely it was an instance of great grace that God still preached
the Messiah to the Jews in their own language. The Jewish rabbis
had taught that in the messianic era many righteous should arise
from the grave; these teachers had in fact asserted that the names
of certain patriarchs could be given. Now these righteous people
are here. Will the Jews believe now that they are in the messianic
era?

We do not wish to underestimate the power of this grace. Who
can say what this sign achieved by way of preparing for the feast
of Pentecost? Who knows how many among those who embraced
the word then had already felt their spirits restless in them at this

---

1. See pp. 458-59.

time because of these wonderful things? Even though the spirit of Saul may harden itself while watching the signs, God ever preserves His "remnant," his "remnant of election." David wins broken hearts for his great Son. This was an instance of grace, for these dead who have returned to life, are the first fruits of the power of Christ, the prince of the Passover. That is why they were not allowed to appear until after His resurrection. Amazed, they escort the prince of life at a distance. Thus one of Christ's utterances takes on a newer and higher form of fulfillment, the word which He once spoke about Abraham (and his communion of faith), who "rejoiced to see His (messianic) day, and who saw it, and was glad!"

In the persons of these who have been rescued from the grave at the cost of struggle, the power of grace comes to expression which is greater than that which Lazarus and those who formerly returned to life were ever able to show the world. All those others had been raised, we can say, as witnesses to the Passover in the confusion. Their arising was sporadic. In their case the rising was merely proleptic. It represented an anticipation of Christ's coming victory over death. But that victory itself was not in them. They who are here, however, arise from the dead when Christ dies, and may remain here until after His glad passover day. Thus they establish a relationship between Christ's death and resurrection, preaching the unity which exists between His state of humiliation and His state of glorification. This they do not simply as individuals, as scattered bearers of the torchlight of the Passover, but this they do as a *community*. They represent many *saints* an anthology of the church of the future.

Thus they declare that the vengeance of God is always sweet. Their resurrection from the grave is the form God's wrath takes against the bruised heel of the seed of the woman; but this execution of wrath is more than judgment; it is sweet, because grace is in it. They came out of the grave. And the Greek word for grave really means: memorial tablet, or monument. Their graves cried aloud: Remember that the church of the advent is sinking away in the dead. But today another voice issues from their monuments: remember that Christ Jesus on whom we hope is risen from the dead. Thus they become an honorable bodyguard for Christ Jesus. By means of their dumb gesture they manifest the lovely form of the defenceless priest-king of Zechariah 6 and 9, whose image the murderers had forgotten entirely through the whole trial.[1] This Christ is not making a triumphal entry in which He as the prince of the Passover rides on ahead and they pompously follow Him. No, every adornment is strange to Him. These people were never once seen in His company. It is true, of course, that overagainst "the Holy City" He glories in the fact that in Him the word of Isaiah spoken about the Messiah is fulfilled: The dead are raised. And in this glorying He repeats this message which He once gave to the Baptist (Luke 7:22). But now the situation is as it was then. Extending far beyond the claim that the dead are raised, His praise issues from the fact that the Gospel is preached to the poor (Luke 7:22; Matthew 11:5). For this reason Christ paid no attention to the bodyguard which had been sent to Him, and did not trouble Himself for a moment about them after His resurrection. He has His trophies, but He does not put them on display. His Passover heralds do enter the holy city, but without Him. As for Himself, listen, O Jerusalem. Presently He will precede the poor into Galilee, that "backwoods" province, where the poor are weaving about in a dark land. For it is those poor who are being evangelized. That is His greatest Messianic glory: through their word others will believe in Him.

The Priest-King manifests Himself here in His gentleness. The pagans conceive of mythological constructions, of heroes who die and carry others with them into their death. In pagan mythology the circle of death grows wider, ever wider. But this great Dead calls other dead *out* of the grave. In Him the area belonging to death grows smaller, ever smaller. The way of the souls maintains a living and alterable contact between "above and below." No angels are seen ascending and descending the ladder of Jacob, but the pious souls of men are crowding out the angels of God, and pointing out the place where Jacob's great son has laid His head. Presently they departed from the earthly life again. How? God alone knows. So much is certain: when they re-entered heaven everything there had changed. It was far more glorious than it had ever been. Up to this time the greatest glory of being there had been to lie in Abraham's bosom. Now the

---

1. See *Christ on Trial*, p. 429 f; *Christ in His Suffering*, pp. 121, 127, 128, and 137, 138.

greatest honor is to lie in Jesus' bosom as a beloved disciple and to sit at His holy supper as a trusted guest.

Nevertheless this glorious miracle can achieve nothing without the Word. The old law asserts itself again: a sign cannot communicate to unbelievers, but only to believers. Do not forget that even in this astonishing miracle the offense of the cross persists, and Christ remains in concealment. We said a moment ago that God multiplied the miracle of Lazarus. Then we called it very glorious, but now we must call it very grievous. Just imagine. After that Sunday people could ask: Just who of all the resurrected ones is the one great person? When the miracle becomes multiplied it becomes common. God embarrasses the disciples when He asks them to preach Christ as the resurrected one. For everyone could say: Yes, we know, but the whole city was full of such children of wonder in those days. Why should anyone ponder further about the temple-maschil? Temples that had been broken down and restored again could be found in more than one place. Are they not all Lazaruses? Are they not all Christs?

You see that this sign also requires the Word to be appropriated in faith. It represents the beginning of the Passover; it is the overture to the cantata of the Passover, but without the Word of revelation it proves nothing. The representatives of Hades cannot convert men. Yes, a large number of dead arose in order to admonish the "brothers" of the "rich man," but Abraham is right again. They have Moses and the prophets, and those must suffice for them.

The representatives of Hades cannot convert people, but shall we lament that fact? No, not that. On the mountain of transfiguration the last word was not addressed to the great of Sheol, or Hades, that is, Moses and Elias; that which transcended the miracles, and went far beyond the mystery of Hades was the clear call: Hear Him! More important than the wonder is the word! This is God's final command. And he who has heard Him through the Word, has sincerely heard Him, will not look for the dead to come back, but will hear Christ prophesying in the Word, and thus by means of the power of His word will come to the confession: That I may know Him, and the power of His resurrection and sufferings, becoming conformed unto His death. Thus he will experience a greater grace than these first fruits of the Passover feast, for in the conformity to Christ's death, herein his every-day life, which is speeding on and away from him without a single miracle, he will experience the power of Christ's resurrection. And as a regenerated creature he will himself be the evidence of it. And having entered into the graves of the church of the advent, of the Maranatha-brethren, he will make his appearance in the church of the first born. And, after his own resurrection in the great and holy city he will take up his position on the pinnacles of the pearly gates and sing the passover cantata.

Christ Apparently
Motionless

CHAPTER TWENTY-FOUR

Christ Apparently Motionless

> • *Now when the centurion saw what was done,*
> *he glorified God, saying, Certainly this was a*
> *righteous man. And all the people that came*
> *together to that sight, beholding the things*
> *which were done, smote their breasts, and re-*
> *turned. And all his acquaintance, and the*
> *women that followed him from Galilee, stood*
> *afar off, beholding these things.*
>
> LUKE 23: 47-49.

THE death of Christ, we said, was at the same time a revelation and a concealment. All of His signs were that: also
His last sign. Hence we can never understand the Christ
or His signs *without the Word*. The fact simply is that He did
not come to us without the Word.

This also became apparent in the moment in which God rent the
veil, opened the graves, gave voice to Hades, disturbed hell, and
had the heavens receive Christ.

That certainly was movement enough, tumult enough. But Jesus was silent; He said nothing: He did nothing. All was station-
ary. Every one felt embarrassed. No one could go either ahead
or backwards. All of them stood hopelessly embarrassed. Here
was one who had reflected upon the Christ, but his reflection could
not progress because it was not based on faith. There was a person who felt perturbed in his emotions; but his emotion did him
no good, because it was not based on faith. A third sensed a certain amount of devotion; but the devotion did him no good; it was
not based on faith. The Nazarene was quiet now; all was at dead
center.

Just look at Golgotha. Here was a man capable of reflection;[1] the centurion. Here was a crowd who felt strong emotions, and beat upon their breasts. And here was a group of devoted people. "Jesus' acquaintances," these were, and His ministering Marthas and Marys. But these stand afar off and look on, and cannot place the experience any better than can those who were on the way to Emmaus. The whole constitutes a pathetic spectacle, and this time it has no dramatic power. Nevertheless, we want to step nearer and observe it.

There was, first of all, the centurion, the captain of a hundred: Who is he? We do not know. His Name? Some call him Longinus. His descent? Some look upon him as a German, others as a Roman, and still others as a Syrian. The course of his life? Many count him among the converted.

But we do not know, and we may not leap to conclusions. We do not know the man, we do not know his thoughts, we do not know the kind of education he had. We know only that he was in the military service of Rome, that he had a first-hand acquaintance with the Roman world, and that on this day he was in command of those in charge of the execution.

But the man said something, and the Bible has preserved what he said. He said two things about Jesus: He called Him *righteous,* and he called Him a son of a god (Matthew 27:54; Mark 15:39).

Now we may not permit him to say more than we can actually read from the text. Much as we would like to read a confession of faith in his words stating that Jesus was the Son of the living god, we may not, for the confession is not written here. We do not deny the possibility, but we may not create the fact. In the original both the word god (the Greek language of the manuscripts has not capital letters) and the word son is used without the definite article. *A* son of *a* god,[2] that is what is written. This is a very different statement from the one Simon Peter makes to Jesus. Thou art the Son of the (our) God, the living One. (Matthew 16). There the definite article is included before the word "Son" as well as before the word "God." Hence, if we read the text care-

---

1. Reflection in the sense of pondering, of combining various phenomena and of drawing a conclusion from the comparison.
2. In general, and also in respect to this particular text, see Robertson-Grosheide, *Bekn. Gramm. op het Gr. N.T.,* Kampen, J. H. Kok, 1912, p. 136.

fully, and do not assume more about this pagan man than we actually know, we can say nothing about him except that he said: Truly, this was a son of a god. Even the paganism of that day had not completely lost the faith of former days which acknowledged the possibility of supernatural beings, children of the gods, special bearers of special qualifications. And when the old faith waned, the worship of Caesar presented the old gods in a new garb. We have only to put ourselves in the intellectual climate of the Orient, especially of the Romans, to know that these gave the same title to a Caesar, to Alexander, to Augustus, to Nero, which this centurion gave to the Saviour.[1] We have simply to recall the case of Simon Magus, Simon the "Magician," who was called the "power of God," and the whole spiritual atmosphere of the time, in order to reduce the statement of the centurion to its proper proportions. We can infer no more from the utterance of the man than that he regarded Jesus as the bearer of supernatural qualifications. It was plain that a spark of divine life had undoubtedly fallen upon the Nazarene; the man hanging on the cross was certainly a friend, if not a messenger, of the other world; and his other remark to the effect that Jesus was righteous is in harmony with this view. The man was not playing any tricks. Jesus did not deserve to die among scoundrels. He represented more than men had guessed.

Therefore we may not see a conscious confession of faith in this utterance of the centurion. Perhaps someone would still like to point out, however, that he glorified God (verse 47), but the same expression is used to characterize the reaction of a whole crowd very often. The same designation is used to indicate the response of the masses to the wonderful things which they have seen (Mark 2:12; Luke 5:26; Luke 7:16; Matthew 15:31). And certainly no one would say that the crowd at such time is making confession of faith.

Just what was it motivated this Roman military official to make this statement? If we read the text carefully, we will discover that he reflected upon the situation. His statement is the product of reflection, and not of emotion, even though we are told that the military representatives present there as a group feared greatly

---

1. Deissman, "Lich vom Osten," 1923, p. 294-295. Dr. Zwaan, "Jesus, Paulus en Rome," 1927, p. 167 f.

(Matthew 27 :54). Especially the manner in which Jesus had died captivated his attention. According to the account which Mark gives of it we learn that he was amazed by the death of Jesus. He had taken special note of "this case." There was something about the man hanging in the center of the three which fascinated him. Standing directly overagainst Jesus, he saw that He had died "so." The great calm, the mastery, the absence of all that was bitter and ugly, the triumphant trust in God, all this had caused him to reflect. Luke says that he had seen what was done. The Greek uses the singular here. In other words he had seen the thing which had been done. In the case of the crowd the plural is used. In other words, the masses had received an impression of all the miraculous signs taken together, of the earthquake, of the darkness, of Christ's calling aloud. All these things together had astonished the masses. But the centurion had been especially attracted by one thing: namely, the manner in which Jesus had died.[1] We might say that he had studied Jesus and that he could not rid himself of the impression that Jesus had not lost His life, but that He had surrendered it by an act of His will.

Now this intellectually accomplished conclusion about "Jesus" does not prove that the centurion was "in Christ." We cannot even say that it is evidence of an "historical faith." We know that an historical faith has a knowledge of the content of preaching, and unless the man goes beyond that point, he has not left the basis of an unforsaken heathendom.

Nevertheless this utterance coming from the centurion has its significance. Before the night had passed out, the sentence which Pilate imposed on the Christ was critically condemned even within the circles of the Roman soldiery. Next to the dream of Claudia we must now place this calm, reflectively attained, and sane utterance of the centurion. Both of these censure Pilate's yielding to the jealousy of the Jews. Christ is given a good testimony, not only by the realm of dreams, but also by the mind of an honest and reasonable man.

---

1. It is true that according to Matthew the centurion as well as the soldiers, were amazed by the signs—and all that was connected with them; in Matthew's account in this respect the military section of the crowd is regarded as a unit, and no further discrimination is made. The total impression of the "soldiers" was just as confused as was that of the crowd. But the centurion, perhaps a peculiarly sensitive mind, had given his attention to just that one point.

However, that is not the only thing. From the incident of this captain of a hundred, we may learn that God's lightnings are now reaching out further than they did formerly. This centurion is a representative of the pagan world. At this point we recall those oriental magi, who came to the Christmas celebration to greet the newborn King of the Jews. Just as those pagans from the Orient put Herod, his court, and the whole world of the scribes, in other words, the secular and the spiritual authorities, to shame, so these are now again put to shame by a heathen of the Occident, a man who neither through dreams nor through stars has reached his conclusion. Jerusalem no longer influences the East nor the West but is contradicted by both. The source of light is hidden from both. The pagans must do their own seeking, and they get farther than the blind of a forsaken Zion. Is it not true that God has made great progress in these thirty-three years which intervened between the two milestones? Is it not true that the history of revelation has moved apace to a higher level of the dissemination of power? Those magi first came to seek the king when a sign had appeared in heaven and only after many generations in which their learned colleges had arrived at a specific doctrine about a "king of the West." This Roman centurion, on the contrary, had not studied the stars, nor pursued the message of a Messianic preaching. He suddenly encounters this brutal spectacle of practical soldiery. Nevertheless He gives God the honor. True, the magi of the East also had to enter a very ordinary house in order to find their king, but even there they simply could not forget the dazzling sign which had conducted them to the place. The house in which they found the child was very lowly, but nevertheless heaven had been perturbed because of it. This centurion, on the other hand, has seen nothing but sheer misery. Heaven had withdrawn its light and he sees hanging before him a person whom the people call a scoundrel. Nevertheless he praises God, and believes that in this broken man powers of the world to come are at work. Thus this centurion joins the company of those Greeks who, but a short time ago, had come to see Jesus (John 12). The majesty of the man Christ captivated him so entirely that he gives the same title of honor to this tattered and abused "Jew" which his people reserve for living Caesars. "Son of a god," he calls Him.

Accordingly we can say that this is the moment of revelation in these affairs. Yes, the world of paganism reserves the title "son of god" for rulers even though they are unrighteous, are ridiculous,[1] even though they are "beasts." But now the first of these Romans comes and thinks it possible that a son of God can manifest himself in the form of a person who is robbed of all power, but who is righteous, holy, and full of spiritual majesty. Why should we say beautiful things about the magi of the East, and nothing about this centurion? Is he not a messenger of other times? Is he not a messenger of the Christian era in which there will be room among the pagans also for the preaching that the powers of God are revealed in the broken Nazarene?

If we give our attention to the centurion alone, we gain nothing. He remains an open question to us. His reflection about the Christ is nothing without the power of the Word of revelation. He wants to explain Jesus' life and nature and background on the basis of His dying, and it is necessary that he begin on the other side. Jesus' dying can only be understood by the person who has allowed himself to be instructed about His essence and His origin. Besides, the reflection of the centurion does not touch upon the issue of guilt. He did not see the conflict of sin and of the devil. He does not beat himself upon his breast. He tries to place Jesus in reference to the *ius* and the *fas,* that is, in reference to the justice of men and the justice of God; but he cannot determine his own position overagainst these two. At best only a little of the truth that Jesus' heels have been bruised will dawn on him; but the other truth that the old serpent's head has been bruised can never dawn on him. Yes, if we look upon the man as he is in himself alone, there is little that is constructive and edifying in the account. But if we place him on the broad highways of the history of revelation, we see that he has his unique significance as an index of the progress of revelation and of the world-vanquishing power of the crucified Christ.

Even on these two highways of the history of the revelation of God he has a prophetic power only as a symbol. We know nothing about him as a person. As such we need to know nothing about him any more than we need to know anything about the children of Bethlehem, in order to hear Rachel weeping in her fashion,

---

1. De Zwaan, *op. cit.,* p. 168.

and to appreciate the symbolism of that. Just so we need not know the centurion as a person in order to hear prophecy speaking in him. To us he is a sign of the change in the thinking of paganism. Everything has been put aside, his doctrine, his faith, his superstition. These can give him no satisfaction. He is in a condition of despairing confusion. The dead man hanging in the center of the crucified persons puts him in the position of dead center. Where in God's name must he go now?

The same holds true of the crowd. As compared with the centurion's reflection, they are moved by emotion. The crowd leaves the hill of Golgotha beating upon its breast. This is a sign of emotional disturbance and confusion. God's signs had confused the crowd, and conscience did the rest. They have lost their equilibrium. No longer is there any room for their haughty mockery. The depressing question simply forces itself out: Can it be that something has happened here whose significance we do not appreciate? The emotion of the crowd goes a little farther than the reflection of the centurion. The centurion does not participate in the action, but the crowd does. And their beating upon their breasts can be explained as an expression of self-accusation, or of regret, even though the cause of this may simply be the sense that they have dispatched this Nazarene too quickly.

Again, however, if you take the expression of the crowd "in itself," you will find nothing edifying in it. The faults of the centurion are repeated here. These perturbed folk also pass from the particular to the general. The circumstances of Jesus' dying make every general utterance about His life, His nature, and His origin disputable to their minds. They also want to determine the nature of Jesus' life on the basis of his death. Accordingly, their emotions can in no sense be regarded as an expression of repentance. We can even give their faith the name of "temporal faith." At best it is an acknowledgment possibly of a specific sin committed against the Nazarene and His God, but it has no room for real sorrow because of sin, because of the state of sin which keeps life under the curse of death. The crowd, too, does not do the crucified Christ justice. After all, to witness many terrors does not suffice to convert. If this were true, hell would be the most infallible means of conversion.

Nevertheless, this emotionally perturbed crowd has its significance. We look at it from the viewpoint of the history of redemption. When, a few hours ago, Jesus had been led to the knoll of the cross, only the women shed tears for Him. Now the whole crowd is disturbed. Recall for a moment the celebration of Christmas eve. How God has progressed! On Christmas the problems of the King of the Jews were dispatched and decided in private conference with the magi; the crowd had no part in the discussion. Here, however, the crowd is in principle divided against itself in its attitude towards the government. The lofty words of the exalted gentlemen mean nothing to these people any more. Thus God is preparing for the day of Pentecost, when a great crowd will ignore the seats of the judges of the Nazarene, pause before the pulpit of Galilean fishermen, and will ask in "ecstasy": What is the meaning of this? Or: What are we to do? No, the ecstasy and the emotion are not in themselves expressions of religion. It is sometimes said that great disturbances of the emotions of a crowd tend to unify the parties included in it, and to remove the differences. For confirmation, simply look at the masses gathered on a national feast day or day of mourning. But the statement is too pretty. True, such a crowd may remove the semblance of difference for a moment, but it cannot positively unite the differing parties by the power of a new community life. However, on the day of Pentecost God the Holy Spirit will unite those who are opposed to each other by the new life which is in Christ. As a preparation for that event it is good that the crowd no longer feels the differences inherent in it. Thus the spirit of Pentecost can presently give the fellowship of life to those who believe. Now the crowd is still beating upon its breast, the great and the humble, the men and the women, the people who must thank Jesus for a miracle of healing in their own family, and the others who were no more than passing acquaintances of Him. No, the seed is not being planted here, for the seed is the Word. But the ground is being cultivated for receiving the seed, which is to appear on the day of Pentecost.

Thus the crowd also reaches dead center in its despairing confusion. They are no longer in harmony with the government and are not positively opposed to the government. They simply cannot go ahead or retreat. They do not know what they do.

Then there were the women who had followed Jesus from Galilee: and besides these there were His "acquaintances." What must we say of them?

No, do not ask any further questions, and we do better to stop classifying all these people. We do not know what we are supposed to think of them. Yes, there were those among them in whom the new life had issued in works of love; but under the caption "acquaintances," there may certainly have been those who had no knowledge of Christ at all, no knowledge which comes by faith. These all are standing afar off trembling. The centurion places himself directly overagainst Jesus, but these remain at a distance. Yes, if we look at these people as they are in "themselves." everything becomes most comfortless again. Then the story ends with a question mark. There were those who loved Him, but what did they understand of the works of God? True, their love made them go farther than the reflection of the centurion and the emotion of the crowd had done. They had already to a certain extent performed works of love for Christ. And they also felt themselves involved in the problem of the day. These had caught a glimpse of the conflict being carried on by God and Satan. Theirs had not been a flighty and momentary perturbance, nor a cool and calculating "study" of the Saviour; a continuous acquaintance with Jesus had united them to Him. And yet we cannot even say of them as a group that they deserve the phrase which the church has called "true saving faith." "All His acquaintance" is too general a classification to permit us to allow them that caption.

Again, however, if we put these people in their right position, if we put them on the highway of the history of redemption, we know that God tells us something by means of them. Their standing afar off is a sign of helplessness. The family, the circle of friends, can do nothing. After all, the blood relationship of the Nazarene can do nothing against that surging stream of the spirit from below. A feeling of friendliness towards the man Jesus cannot turn the helm of the world from Christ. Now this is a sign of helplessness. This helplessness to a certain extent contains a beautiful preaching of the Spirit of God. Recall Christmas eve again. There the people, the acquaintances, have still so much to do, and the child in the manger is not yet qualified for the task. But today God's strong wind blows over the heads of the people, over the heads of "all his acquaintance," and these have nothing to do. Christ fastens His ropes to the throne of God. That had been free grace and sovereign plan which had induced Jesus to send Mary and John on their way. He could do the great deed alone. This same free grace now makes "all his acquaintance" inactive, inasmuch as not one jot or one tittle of that psalm of the cross in which the law of free grace sings, "It is finished," is removed. Again we say that God has made great progress in thirty-three years. Nevertheless, there is great sorrow in this spectacle of people who are standing "afar off." They are strayed sheep, unwitting ones, defeated ones; the travelers to Emmaus betray all their poverty-stricken misery to us after a while. They do not know where to go. Shall they work or preach, fish or evangelize, protest or acquiesce. Where to, Lord? The Sabbath is dawning, but what a Sabbath! Lord, Thy friends are at dead center. The "remnant" of Israel is at dead center. "All his acquaintance" are at dead center, and that is also the center of history.

Yes, we know it had to be this way. Thus He who is called the second Adam could achieve His effects in this same moment of time in order thus to conduct not all His acquaintances but all those whom He knew on the path of His Lordship. Yes, we can be of good courage, God is making progress; the history of redemption is going straight on. But at the time it was very grievous. Lord, where to?

Thus they all came to dead center; the company of Pilate, the crowd of Jerusalem, the circle of Jesus' acquaintances. No one feels confident any more. All that the best can do is to grope vaguely and uncertainly towards a word, towards a deed.

But this was the great glory of Christ Jesus. Up to this time He had been in constant movement. He had spoken, had pleaded, had protested. He had worked, had blessed, had condemned. He had always done something new, had kept the people busy, had incited them, provoked them to reaction, had mastered them. But hardly has He grown silent, hardly has His head nodded in death, and hardly have they supposed that now they are done with Him, before the old self-assurance is gone and all the feasts are turned into mourning. This, we said, is His glory. It proves that Christ cannot be explained and cannot be accursed without His own deed and without His own word. He apparently stood still now. This was not actually the case of course, for, as we observed, His departure spelled His progress. He was hastening Himself to the next word and the next act. But to men at least it seemed as though His action had now been thwarted. And now the psalm and the curse both were immediately stifled. People reached dead center. Reverence Him now, and learn of Him. Learn to expect Him, for He will return in order to capture psalm and curse from the world, and bring these to perfection. A Christ standing still is a pathetic manifestation, and cannot make history progress. He who deals unjustly no longer deals unjustly, but not by dealing justly. He that is filthy shamefacedly covers the filthy spots on his garment with his hand, but is not yet washed in His blood. He that is righteous stands afar off helplessly, and is not publicly justified. He that is holy takes refuge in his nocturnal haunt, and simply does not find his public manifestation among the church of the first fruits. Lord God, help us, we cannot exist and cannot even perish if Thou art so quiet.

Do not lament, O man, for this is His glory. As He stands still He drives the whole world into a blind alley; this He does by doing nothing. But be of good comfort, He is not going to stand still. He has already progressed to the next stage of God's sublime program. He has died, but He has not been put to rest. He is inactive only according to appearances. If Christ had not made His departure a progress, yes, then we would have perished. But be patient, for He is already busy with the angels and has already placed his credentials with the Father. He is hurrying Himself greatly over there behind the clouds, is finding His way to the day of Passover and to the day of Pentecost. And He is already writing the first words of the great theme of His continued program there, the words which are to be the last words of His completed Scriptures:

> He that is unjust, let him be unjust still:
> And he that is filthy, let him be filthy still:
> And he that is righteous, let him be righteous still:
> And he that is holy, let him be holy still.

God be praised. There was no such thing as a dead center in the activity of God: that was to be found only in the reaction of man. Christ merely seemed to be exhausted, but He was living as positively as He had lived throughout His days and as He lives throughout eternity. We thank Thee, Lord, for the death of Jesus; we thank Thee for the fact that it is nonsense to say to Him: Rest on now. We thank Thee that we could only frighten ourselves about a blind alley, that He at the same moment was busy preparing the great mobilization in heaven, the mobilization designed to incite the whole created world to move out of the alleys and byways, and to join in the one great struggle of Revelation 12. The centurion must give a further account of himself; he has not done with the problem yet. A further division must be made of the crowd; the differing parties have not stepped aside nor those who agree been united. The acquaintances must make their public appearance. Only those whom God has known will He give a place in His house. All those whom He has known may stand afar off, but they are irresistibly drawn to Him.

But all of these will succeed in getting off dead center. O Lord, how very hot the temperature, here, on Golgotha.

Christ Buried

CHAPTER TWENTY-FIVE

Christ Buried

● *The Jews, therefore, because it was the preparation, that the bodies should not remain upon the cross on the sabbath day, (for that sabbath day was an high day), besought Pilate that their legs might be broken, and that they might be taken away. Then came the soldiers and brake the legs of the first, and of the other which was crucified with him. But when they came to Jesus and saw that he was dead already, they brake not his legs; but one of the soldiers with a spear pierced his side and forthwith came thereout blood and water. And he that saw it bare record, and the record is true; and he knoweth that he saith true, that ye might believe. For these things were done that the Scripture should be fulfilled, A bone of him shall not be broken. And again another scripture saith, They shall look on him whom they pierced. And after this Joseph of Arimathaea, being a disciple of Jesus, but secretly for fear of the Jews, besought Pilate that he might take away the body of Jesus: and Pilate gave him leave. He came therefore and took the body of Jesus. And there came also Nicodemus, which at the first came to Jesus by night, and brought a mixture of myrrh and aloes, about an hundred pound weight. Then took they the body of Jesus, and wound it in linen clothes with the spices, as the manner of the Jews is to bury. Now in the place where he was crucified there was a garden; and in the garden a new sepulchre, wherein was never man yet laid. There laid they Jesus therefore because of the Jews' preparation day; for the sepulchre was nigh at hand.* JOHN 19:31-42.

N OW we come to the last stage in the state of Christ's humiliation. We believe in Jesus Christ, God's only begotten Son, our Lord, who suffered under Pontius Pilate, was crucified, dead, and *buried*.

Now the episode which is related in John 19:31-37, first of all, belongs to the introduction of this burial.

We are told that the Jews, that is, the leaders of the Jews, had asked Pilate to take account of the fact that according to the Jewish law it was not legitimate to leave the body of a crucified person hanging upon the cross and exposed naked on the sabbath day. We cannot ascertain definitely from the Greek text whether the Jews had asked Pilate about this beforehand, or whether they by means of a deputation had presented this request to Pilate at the last moment. In any case their meaning is plain. The law included this prescription: "And if a man have committed a sin worthy of death, and he be put to death, and thou hang him on a tree: his body shall not remain all night upon the tree, but thou shalt in any wise bury him that day; (for he that is hanged is accursed of God) that thy land be not defiled, which the Lord Thy God giveth thee for an inheritance." Now this restriction served more or less to put the Jewish authorities in conflict with Roman custom. Among the Romans it was the custom to let the body hang on the cross until it underwent disintegration of its own accord. To this, however, the Jews were opposed. To them a person hanged on the tree was an "abomination," to them a corpse was a piece of filth, a repulsive thing. A corpse might not even be allowed to hang on the tree overnight, to say nothing of a Sabbath — a whole day, a feast day. For this reason they expressly asked Pilate to make a stipulation which will permit them to circumvent this difficulty. Especially so, inasmuch as the Sabbath to follow was a feast day, was to be a Passover-Sabbath.

The Jews feel free to present their request. They ask Pilate to apply the so-called *crurifragium*. This in a few exceptional cases was the method applied in order to put someone to death quickly or in order to punish him very brutally. By means of heavy instruments the bones of the victims were then broken, probably by means of heavy hammers. Sometimes this crurifragium was applied after a crucifixion in order to put a sudden end to the suffering. At other times it served as the sole and direct means of punishment itself. The crurifragium did not always follow the crucifixion. In connection with this some suppose that the Jews by asking that this particular action be applied to the Saviour were intentionally asking the government to inflict every imaginable form of penalty upon the Nazarene. But we may not infer more than is warranted. Even though an evil passion was at work here, we know that it really was of importance to them that the crucified person should be buried before sunset even though this desire was prompted by nothing more than the outer forms of religion and the fear of a people whose temper could never be accurately guessed. The quicker everything was done the better. Now if it were historically accurate that in those days two official methods were employed for the purpose they have in mind, namely, the crurifragium, or the thrust of a lance or spear, we should indeed in brutality. But that historical accuracy is not ours in this respect. have to interpret their request for the former as a special delight

Pilate is willing to grant the request. The servants who are to carry out the brutality are quickly named. The two murderers still manifest some signs of life, and it does not take long before these are put to death by means of the brutality inflicted upon them. But when they approach Jesus, they immediately see that He has already died. In His case the brutal instrument was no longer necessary. However, they had to have official evidence to show that He actually was dead; after all, it was just possible that a breath of life still stirred in Him. Hence, in order to put an end to all uncertainty, one of the soldiers takes a spear, and thrusts it into Jesus' side.

John tells us that immediately blood and water flowed out of the wound.

A great deal has been written about this particular. Without being prompted to it by any exegetical necessity men have deduced from the text that the blood and water flowed from the wound successively, not simultaneously. And having established that, men spun out their favorite allegories and analogies. In any case they wanted to see the incident recognized as a miracle; it certainly would not do to explain the flowing of the blood and water in an "ordinary way." Why not, you wonder? Well, then the allegory would be impossible — the *allegory,* you understand that old game of masquerading in which an essential ignorance of the ideas of God contained in the redemptive events might camouflage itself. According to this allegorical interpretation the water designated baptism (water purifies), and the blood designated The Lord's Supper (blood atones) ; and, going on in this way, men concluded that "just as Eve had been formed from the side of the sleeping Adam, so from the side of Christ in His sleep of death the bride of the church was formed, that bride whose existence, strength, and significance is derived from the grace earned by the suffering of Christ on the cross, and from the ministration of the sacraments."[1] To this exegetical misunderstanding[2] we must add another according to which the coming of Christ "by blood and water" is taken to be a reference to the effects of this lance-thrust.

As we see it, however, this is not the direction we ought to take. True it is, of course, that John puts a special emphasis upon the flowing of the blood and water. He tells us that he himself saw it,[3] and that his testimony is true, and that he is emphatically stating this in order that his readers might believe. However we can ascribe the intentional emphasis[4] on the truth of the report to the fact that John, to the greatest possible extent that he can, wants to assure his readers, overagainst the heresies arising in his day, that Jesus Christ really died, that His death was not an apparent death.

Precisely for this reason the flowing of the blood and water cannot be called a miracle. If it had been something unusual, it could not have served as proof of the genuineness of Jesus' death. We know that the word "water," means a watery substance,[5] and medical men tell us that the flowing out of a fluid which is at once bloody and watery is not at all unusual if the spleen has been lacerated, and the body has not been violently shaken. The first of these conditions is likely in this case, the last one certain. For the rest then, the question how to explain the issue of blood and water is a purely medical and scientific question, with which we need not be concerned.[6] John wants to point out the fact that because of

---

1. P. G. Groenen, *op. cit.*, p. 545; Zahn, *Komm. op Joh.*, 1912, p. 663.

2. A misunderstanding, for the coming "by water" represents baptism, and the coming "by blood" represents the suffering on the cross. "The article" (in what follows of the text) "is a reference to the water of the Jordan, in which the Lord was baptized, and to the blood which He shed. It is possible that in this connection we should also refer to John 19:34, but in general the Lord's baptism and His suffering on the cross and His death are indicated by these passages." Dr. S. Greijdanus *De Brieven Van de Apostelen Petrus en Johannes en de Brief Van Judas*, Amsterdam, 1929, p. 515 f.

3. This is the interpretation of most of the commentators. According to this, John remained with Mary until the end, or if the "from that hour" (John 19:27). must be taken to mean that he left Golgotha immediately after the third utterance from the cross—by no means a necessary interpretation—he could have returned.

4. According to Th. Zahn, *Inleiding tot het N.T.* tr. by Hugenholz, Utrecht, volume 2, p. 550, the flowing out of the water and blood is a by product.

5. Zahn, *Komm. Evangelie Johannes*, 1912, p. 664.

6. Various attitudes towards the possibilities which may be considered here can be observed in Groenen, *op. cit.*, p. 542.

the thrust of the lance we can be sure that life has completely ebbed from the body.

This was to serve the world and the church as legitimate proof of the fact that Jesus of Nazareth had really died. Moses had been vindicated because everything had been done before the Sabbath, and Caesar had also been vindicated because the actual death could be recorded in the registers. Now every heart could be at rest.

But God supervised the course of prophecy. He kept the highways open for the prophetic spirit. An old prophecy was being fulfilled; and a literal fulfillment of another was being made possible.

John tells us that an old prophecy is being fulfilled; namely, that of the Old Testament according to which not a bone of . . . yes, of whom? . . . should be broken. There are two possibilities. According to Exodus 12:46 the lamb of the Passover had to be whole and unblemished, and not a bone of it should be broken. Integrity was a condition of the sacrifice (see Numbers 9:12). Now some think that John saw in the fact that Christ was spared the crurifragium the evidence to prove that God wants to point Him out as the true lamb of the Passover. Personally, we believe that the reference is not to this text, but to Psalm 34. In Psalm 34 we read:

> Many are the afflictions of the righteous:
> But the Lord delivered him out of them all.
> He keepeth all his bones:
> Not one of them is broken.[1]

---

1. We choose this interpretation for various reasons. The words of John correspond more exactly to the text of Psalm 34 in the Septuagint than with those of Exodus 12, or of Numbers 9. Besides, Exodus 16 treats of what the people must do by way of preparing the lamb of the Passover. But John is here talking about that which accrues to Jesus by means of the providence of God; there is no reference to the act of the people; in fact, the passage is emphatically in conflict with the intention and the expectation of the people. Moreover, the refusal to break the bones of the lamb of the Passover had to render it appropriate for the sacrifice; was a condition of its acceptability as an offering; but this is fully informed by the thought that Christ has already been sacrificed, that the worth of the sacrifice inheres in himself, in His wholeness and sinlessness. Now some take it as an objection to our interpretation that Psalm 34 speaks of the living favorites of God, those for whom God's providence is ever alert, so that without His will not one of their bones shall be broken, nor a single hair disturbed. But this condition supports our view of the matter. God's providence (the one element) demands our attention here (the result is different from the one we should fear), and the fact that Christ had died does not prevent Providence from giving the same anxious care to Him that it gives to God's living servants. We have observed already, for

In this psalm, in other words, the contrast is ushered in between the righteous and the wicked. The righteous shares in God's special favor. He enjoys the *providentia specialissima,* and therefore he is spared such brutality as would make him the puppet of an insane violence which could not possibly make sense. Not a bone of him shall be broken; accident, arbitrary brutality, is not to make a puppet of him.

In this sense the psalm was fulfilled by the Saviour. In the first place, He is the great Righteous One. "The righteous," that favorite type of the psalms, has its realest essence, its antitype, its reality, its justification in God's one great Righteous Man, Jesus Christ. Fulfillment! — and to go on: for Christ is no longer an exlex. He is in the justification ("the Righteous One"). God has again accepted the exlex.[1] And hence nothing more may accrue to Him now than is strictly necessary. In this the logic of Psalm 34 finds its unsought acknowledgment. Just as Christ in His burial is spared every manifestation of shame which would have no significance for the Suretyship, and just as He, therefore, is not cast among the bandits in a general grave, but in "a grave" as the Son of man,[2] so no other form of affliction is placed upon Him here save that which God regards as absolutely necessary for Him. The dying has been enough. According to His body, also, Jesus walked under the protection of special providence. After His resurrection, too, that body — and in this we already touch upon the quotation from the Old Testament — should by a special act of God's power have to retain the stigmata of His wounds. And if our theme now were the event of the Passover, we should have to say much about that. Now, however, we let the matter rest. It suffices us to notice that a special providence of God is anxiously watchful of the body of Christ. And hence God also prevented the bones of His Righteous One from being broken. His body had a future; it had a purpose, even in its wounds, in its stigmata,

---

instance, that the seventh utterance from the cross was a statement of life. The whole stress of John's text points in our direction (the contrast, the conflict between the righteous and the unrighteous and God's decision in the matter) rather than in the direction of symbolism or allegory. The offer had been finished. And the fact that the bones were not broken, although it does document the reality of death, does not prove the genuineness of the sacrifice. The integrity of the lamb in the final analysis corresponds to Christ's sinlessness.

1. See pp. 431, 460.
2. See p. 559.

for the church of the Passover. God spared the holy lamb of the sacrifice arbitrariness and accident, all meaningless suffering, all alogical humiliation.

In this way a new prophetic fulfillment in a literal sense was made possible. The text tells us that the thrust of the lance by the soldier was also an act of the special providence of God. It made possible a literal fulfillment of the prophecy of Zechariah 12:10. In this prophecy God presents Himself[1] as the gentle King of Israel, who has however been pierced in the heart as the Good Shepherd, who has been put to death and denied by His own sheep. They took the life of the servant of God, and impaled His messenger. The shepherd-king, who was pierced by the sword of Israel represents of course an anthropomorphic picture, but it was given the possibility of literal fulfillment in the incarnation of the Word, that most perfect of anthropomorphic expressions of God. Now the hatred of those in Israel who rejected God and the Good Shepherd — who was so humanly depicted in Zechariah — is given its bitterest expression in the lance thrust of the soldiers. This thrust of the lance is the last act of the murder of Christ, the last profanation of God's Good Shepherd. There was not a person who saw that this was the relationship of things, but John tells us that sometime men will understand them. The Lord announces even by means of Zechariah that men shall see Him whom they have pierced. The world shall see that, but especially the Church, after it by means of the Spirit has learned to bewail its sins. For a "remnant" who lament their evil works will arise out of the unfaithful covenant relationship (it is that which has really wounded the Shepherd). Thus prophecy becomes literally fulfilled in Christ. In Pentecost first, for there Israel's "remnant" will be gathered, then on the last day, counter-day to Pentecost.

Thus we can say that the evangelical comfort merged with a sinister threat. Not a bone will be broken . . . that is the comfort. Golgotha is surcharged with God's redeeming providence. But they shall see what was done here — that is the threat. There is no escape from this place save by lamenting their own sin. In the fact that Christ after His resurrection still bears the tokens of the wounds in His body (think of Thomas) we cannot see the natural

---

1. The text revision of Zechariah 12:10 need not be discussed here; it makes no difference to the discussion.

result of Jesus' being wounded (for the body of the resurrection has its own law of existence), but an effect of Jesus' will. God wanted this preservation of the stigmata — of the wounds — in Christ's body. They represented an intentional prolongation of the signs of the hatred of sin against God and against His Anointed. They were a confirmation of the terrible occurrence which took place at noon of the Day of the Lord, preserved in order that ing this in order that his readers might believe. However we can heart. In my hour of the "jôm Jahwe" I pierced the heart of God. Thus both enemy and friend must presently acknowledge Christ as the Good Shepherd who was put to death, yes, and sold for thirty pieces of silver, but who nevertheless is the Priest-King of Prophecy, and the perfectly Righteous One. He it is who in all His afflictions was spared the brutality which is accidental and arbitrary. History is being made here. The last act of the murderers of Christ is accentuated by the Spirit which prompts John to write, and is beset on every side with prophecies. To what end? In order that the last act by means of which the confusion of Golgotha is concluded might indeed be the culmination of the eschatological events of this day. The spikes and the hammers and the lance are all instruments of judgment, and all these instruments are driven by an electric current which is generated by the activity of all worlds and all times.

Yes, this is a world-disturbing hour. Prophecy is being fulfilled. The prophetic Spirit filled nails and hammers and lances with the energy of the day of days. And with their eyes fixed on that, a small group of dazed, orphaned, and blinded children crept towards Him whom they had loved, "to pay Him their last respects." That is the way it is often put, and that is exactly the way it was meant here. To pay respect — the last respect. The friends came together in God's name for the burial.

The scene was opened by a certain Joseph of Arimathea. It was a *certain* Joseph, for the Gospel is not a novel. The story of Christ is not a family tale. Hence there are no such things as fictive characters here. It is a part of the Gospel that figures held in reserve all of a sudden make their appearance. When this happens, people say: Well, *a certain Joseph*, a new actor in the drama. God says: I reserved him a long time for this hour; and the subordinate actors must remain in the dark a long time, for Christ alone is the *dramatis persona.* This burial is not a family matter, but a church matter. A *certain* Joseph, but be careful; this is not the last chapter of a novel. Hence the character of this certain Joseph does not affect the issue. Christ is at the center of the stage. He is buried in the cemetery of the church, and hence the *family* does not take the leading part in it. Woman, see thy Son.

A *certain* Joseph, then. This unknown friend went to Pilate before the sun's setting in order to get permission to bury Jesus. Very likely he applied to Pilate immediately, or at least very soon, after the Saviour had died. For we read that Pilate was surprised to learn that Jesus had died already. Hence the official request of the Jews to the effect that the victims be hurried to death by means of the crurifragium had not yet been entered, or had been so recently granted that Pilate could not yet expect that it had been carried out. Or, if the request for the crurifragium had already been entered, we can be sure that the report had not yet come in.

A certain Joseph of Arimathea. He was eminent; accordingly, a member of the Sanhedrin. He had had a grave hollowed out for himself in the vicinity of the city; this grave he is willing to give for the accursed Nazarene. And Pilate, glad, very likely, that he can help choose a grave for the man for whom he does not wish every last evil thing, and glad that he can annoy the Jews by means of one of them, grants the request. Moreover, it was often the custom to allow the family or acquaintances of a condemned person to have the body for burial.

Thereupon the small group, the remnant of Abraham, performed their sad duty. It did not take long, for everything had to be done before the Sabbath. Moses had to be satisfied, everything was done in a preliminary fashion. After the Sabbath day they could finish the work which was now done in haste. Thus the body of the second Adam was laid in a human grave on Friday night.

Undoubtedly this burial represented *humiliation*, and as such was a part of the work of the Messianic Suretyship.[1] Christ also

---

1. The reader will have noticed that chapters 22-25 dealing with matters which happened after the death of Christ have been treated much more briefly than those which went before. This is in harmony with the purpose of the book which wishes to put the emphasis upon the suffering and must therefore regard everything which

assumed the humiliation of the *grave.* By this, we do not mean to say that the grave is an essential part of the penalty for sin.[1] But in that day the humiliation of the grave was a part of the shame of death, and of the preaching of death. The withdrawal of the body from this world, a withdrawal which because of sin has assumed the form of devastation,[2] has its confirmation in the grave. The grave is an amen which the human being knows he must utter when death comes. The grave is a concealment; it takes away the unclean, the filthy; it is a public confession of the repulsiveness of what once in the creation of God was an adornment to us. And since the Mediator had been appointed to suffer humiliation publicly, the grave must necessarily be a part of this complex of shame and disgrace. We pointed out at several times that the crucifixion is called an exaltation, inasmuch as it indicates the public character of Christ's death.[3] In a similar sense, the burial may be regarded as an exaltation of the Christ. It is a public demonstration[4] of the fact that the Son of man is dead, is really dead. That which the thrust of the lance ascertained as a fact, the burial colored and characterized, and thus made public.

Not that the burial is completely exhausted in meaning when we say that it proves the death of Christ. This new shame, this burial of what the earth can no longer bear, of what makes life harmful, joy impossible, and taste disgusting is a separate disgrace and it was that for Christ. It was a penalty which came to Him because of our sin; because of sin the transfiguration of man from glory to glory which had once been promised had been denied

---

comes after the death as a kind of appendix. Partly for this reason we are touching on the significance of the burial but briefly. Questions related to it, which dogmatics must necessarily consider, are not even touched upon. We are saying nothing about the connection between the burial and "the descent into hell." That which was said about "the descent into hell" in the foregoing chapters, or really throughout this volume, was in accordance with the familiar interpretation of the Heidelberg catechism, willingly took over the phrase which had gained a tradition, in order to qualify the content of the Christian confession as given above by means of it, inasmuch as the term lent itself appropriately to that. But this view as outlined in the book, as well as this point, is not one subject to a strictly historical inquiry. We did not, for instance, touch upon what was originally meant by the designation "descent into hell."

   1.   We refer to chapter 21.

   2.   *Christ on Trial,* pp. 297-300, this volume, p. 81, 498.

   3.   More, therefore, than a notarized evidence of death.

   4.   We must distinguish this, both in the case of Christ and in our own case, from the grave, from the disruption; and that, in turn, is to be distinguished from the "departure" of II Timothy 4:6.

Him. Devastation took the place of transfiguration. And the grave punctuated the destruction. Yes, the grave was a penalty for Christ. It is a part of His humiliation. What holds true of Jesus' departure from the world holds true also of His grave; it must not be taken as carrying a penalty in itself, it must be placed in the entire context, and then it immediately takes on a significance and content of its own. Out of that context it may never be lifted.

We know that it is not only the being buried which constituted Christ's humiliation at this time. He is also being humiliated as effective Mediator. His own funeral-guests did not understand Him. There was none there to give a funeral oration. Every funeral is a beginning of that process by which our glamour fades, the impression which we have made upon others wanes, and our personality loses its power of self-explanation and self-revelation. We become a name, we are given the exegesis of others. We become a figure, a symbol. The burial begins with this inevitable relinquishment; it is a stripping of our power overagainst the world, a confirmation of our having departed out of time, or having lost our hold on time. Now this is more grievous in the case of Christ's burial so long at least as we look upon that burial from the outside, as indeed we should. For that is the way God is *manifesting* Him. Yes, they loved Him. Those who bury Jesus, the man who reached the age of thirty-three, love Him very much. But do they know Him? Do they know Jesus Christ the King-Priest of all ages? Have they the right exposition? Ah no, they do not understand Him as He wants to be understood. Their unbelief, their "little faith," their ignorance cannot grieve Him any more, but it can humiliate Him. And it did humiliate Him greatly. They buried Him not in the last analysis as the Son of man, but as a noble son of man. He was a man among men. His burial was an acknowledgment of His death, a confirmation of His death after the usual manner of the day. Their burying Him was not a linking of His death with the whole history of the Messianic redemption. By burying Him they simply linked His dying with the concatenation of everyday events. Never had Christ been so concealed as now, never had divinity receded so far as now, never had He become so completely unknown to the sons of His mother as now. The discrepancy between the majesty of God and the body of the man Jesus was never as great as now. This was all a part of His humiliation, but those who buried Him did not understand that. His paean of praise about the stone which should be made the "head of the corner" was a song they could not understand. Had they understood it, they either would not have buried Him, or they would have buried Him differently. This is a pathetic spectacle. The Jews, the enemies, are much perturbed about a possible resurrection. They even raise the subject to Pilate, and reckon in terms of it when they ask Pilate to appoint a guard. But Jesus' own disciples did not think about that. There is room here for a chapter on "Christ's burial and His forgotten chapter." That forgotten chapter is the priesthood.[1] And those who are forgetting it at the moment are His own. Those who are busy here are the remnant of Israel, the temple of the living God, and all the prophets have said beautiful things about it. This remnant was the great comfort of the prophets. But . . . what is this remnant worth without Him? Is that all He left behind in the world? Is this the whole of the seed of the woman? Terrible, is it not. And humiliation? Name one spiritual leader or one spiritual rebel, who was so poor as this in terms of people, of disciples, who understood. You cannot name one.

Still, the fault lay not in the instruction they had received, but in the mutual fellowship they had with each other. Think of the fact that Nicodemus suddenly puts in his appearance, and fetches his expensive accessories for the burial when Joseph summons the faithful ones to perform the last act. Obviously they must have deliberated on the matter beforehand. They knew what was going to happen. Now they are here, the two Scribes, two friends of the Nazarene, two honest lovers. And with them the small congregation. But the burial is such as can be arranged for anyone on any day. A pitiable spectacle, yes. We read of Joseph that he looked for the coming of the kingdom of God, but that, in the final analysis, means no more than that he belonged to those who looked forward to the messianic redemption. The Baptist was the greatest among them, but in spite of it all he once anxiously asked himself whether this historical Jesus was the true Messiah or probably a forerunner. Perhaps the same question has troubled all those who are today busy placing the Saviour in the grave. Remember,

---

1. *Christ on Trial*, p. 428 f.

for instance, the confession of the two men on the way to Emmaus. And in the case of Joseph we have even more reason to suppose that this is true, inasmuch as he had not been instructed by Jesus Himself, but by one of the disciples. He had caught a faint glimpse of something and this was true of the whole group.

Indeed the burial of Christ, the embalming of His dead body, the arrangement for Sunday morning, all represented a total denial of the coming resurrection. Spiritually they have all forsaken Him. It may be that Nicodemus has heard weighty words in his nocturnal conversation with Jesus, weighty words coming from Jesus' own mouth about the kingdom of heaven, and about the power of regeneration operative in it, but the great legal question as to the basis of the coming of that kingdom, and the grounds upon which the Spirit can bear fruits in it, remains an open question to him. That the death of Christ is of central significance for the "regeneration" of all things in the great legal program of God is a truth which is not clear to him.

But, someone may care to ask at this point, surely, the burial was an act of confession. Yes, it was that. But it was a confession of love rather than of faith. And it happens to be true of Christ that we cannot really love Him without a true faith, that "love" for "Jesus" without faith in "Jesus Christ" is not accepted as a good work by God. We do not deny that the seeds of regeneration have been sown here, but the fruits are still being kept from fruition because the "eyes of understanding" have not yet been "opened." This, too, represents a humiliation for Christ. From a human point of view He has not yet achieved much. We must not exaggerate the confession of these friends. It was not such an extraordinary thing, this request which Joseph presented to Pilate for the body of Jesus. In making this request, he was not becoming a martyr. After all, Pilate himself has some "sympathy" for Jesus. This act on his part did not necessarily spell an open breach with the Sanhedrin. Sympathy for Jesus as a "philanthropist" was not yet a public protest against the counsel of the Jews. It may be that any number of members of the Sanhedrin this same evening exhausted themselves in giving expression to similar manifestations of sympathy. Besides, this Joseph doubtless has a great deal for which he must make amends. In the matter of the condemnation of Christ he did not agree with the Sanhedrin. Nevertheless all the members of the Sanhedrin condemned Jesus. We must not forget that. We must conclude, therefore, that he was absent at the conclusive session. Surely, this was a kind of denial of Christ. Joseph is another Simon Peter. Can it be, then, that the zeal of this certain Joseph manifested here at the burial was a kind of compensatory reaction? Be that as it may, Joseph must make amends to the little congregation. He does his best. He even takes charge of the preparations. But people who first spoiled matters have been known to do that before. Not that we want to degrade Joseph: by no means. Our only purpose is to indicate how greatly the Saviour was humiliated. Humiliated also as a worker in the kingdom of the Spirit. Humiliation in spite of, no, because of, this expensive "distinctive" burial.

On the other hand, however, the burial of Christ represents the beginning of His glorification. Just as in the term "being lifted up on the cross" God Himself is "playing with words" and just as He by that one phrase expresses both the shame of Jesus Christ as well as His honor,[1] so a whole host of angels is here playing with Jesus' crepe of mourning, even though that heavenly host remains hidden from the sight of men. The death shroud is humiliating, but the wind which blows it up descends from the heights of God.

The burial was "expensive," was it not? Joseph was an eminent man; the grave had not yet been used; it was a grave designed for himself; the grave had been made according to prescription, and had not simply been appointed as a natural spot for burial. The grave had been prepared by means of intentional and well paid labor (it had been hewed out). It had cost a great deal of money. God did not care about that money, for it was God Himself who buried Jesus, assisted by the angels. God wanted to insist upon His rights to gold and wealth. Christ's right to requisition had been denied; it had been basically taken away from Him. But hardly has He suffered what He had to suffer according to justice, before God again lays claim to the very best that can be obtained for the Son of man. Say nothing bad about these funeral-guests; they have done a good work, we can always bury the poor, but Him we can bury but once.

---

1. See *Christ on Trial*, p. 299 f.

God makes His claims. No, he does not care for the luxurious linen which they are cutting to strips and wrapping around the limbs which they have first bathed. No, He does not care for the myrrh and aloes of Nicodemus, for these luxurious perfumes, imported from abroad, even though "appropriate" psalms can be sung about them. God wants justice done. God insists upon the justice which compels the Surety to endure no more than is necessary for the Great Payment.

That is why Christ was among the bandits, and why His lifeless physical remains were not among those of the bandits. He does not need to undergo the disgrace of a general grave into which the "class" of condemned is carelessly thrown. He does not belong to a "class." He is the Son of man, the one, the general. God does let the general disgrace of "the" grave accrue to Him; but there is no special stigma in the disgrace. God shows us that the grave is but an intermediary state, and that heaven is busy preparing for the time when this "intermediary" condition will no longer be necessary.[1] Christ receives, He accepts, the new grave in which never yet man lay. We know that in old times an altar was placed on new stones, that holy things were set on a new vehicle, that beasts which had not yet been used were employed for holy work, and that holy salt was placed in a new container. No, God was not interested in making an aristocratic display. That word is inappropriate here, but God wants such an "exaltation" of Christ as points beforehand to the feast of the Passover. Heaven is in great haste, those who listen can already hear the sound of joy in the court. He who enters the grave here is none other than the Kurios, the Lord. On the one "Day of the Lord" the transitions from the one thing to the other can never be so sharply delineated that the first suggestions of the one are not traceable in the other. Just so the real glorification of the Saviour is already being realized. The Kurios is the Chief Claimant now. He is entering into Hades, to the extent that He is "among the dead," but He is not gathered unto the fathers. This is true because of the great haste which characterized the bashful congregation. And it is also due to the fact that they did not know His forebears, and did not dare point to David as His Father. But this was due especially to the fact that God wanted to do so. He

---

1. See p. 500.

could not really be gathered unto His fathers. His congregation was too fearful. His death is but an intermediate condition. God is in great *haste*. The kingdom of David does not know Him. Why not? Well — *He* knows only the kingdom of David. And because He has borne the disgrace of father David, the disgrace of all the fathers, to the very end He does not need to enter their grave. His grave is not the grave of a given dynasty, but it is fresh and new and unused. As a matter of fact, it was not even hewn out for Him. This happened by accident; and yet it was an instance of the clearest possible prophecy of necessity. In his grave, too, He is a Prince after the order of Melchizedek. If only He enters "the" grave, the human grave, *tout court,* which makes Him share the disgrace of death together with all men as the Son of man, He may for the rest allow the luxury of what people call "aristocratic" to be selected for Him. This, in order that afterwards men may marvel that they appointed His grave with the wicked in His death, but He was nevertheless buried with the rich.[1]

We can say, then, that the line of Christ's humiliation does indeed descend to the grave, but that it there effects the strength which will exalt Him again. He was buried by people who did not understand Him. But the seeds of the Spirit had nevertheless been planted in these hearts. That which blossoms over His grave was the flower of the Old Testament. Can it be that Joseph of Arimathea kneeled next to Peter, can it be that he had to bury Jesus, because he had to go outside and weep bitterly? If so, his self-accusation has in it the essence of repentance. In this way all were converted by Him; just so the old man in them was buried with Him. And he who is buried with Him has already been glorified with Him, arisen with Him, and been placed in heaven. I asked you a moment ago to name one sage of the world who had been understood so badly as He. You will find none, I said. Name one of the world's sages, who, having been buried, buried all his

---

1. We shall not enter into the question here about whether Isaiah 53:9 is to be regarded as a prophecy which has its fulfillment now. The fact is that the New Testament does not refer to the text. Hence there is not in the New Testament a convincing explanation of this Old Testament statement. Accordingly we can freely open debate on the issue about whether the Hebrew parallelism in Isaiah 53:9 permits of a contrast such as is written in the masoretical text as it is usually interpreted, or whether the text is corrupt. Until this debate has ceased, we cannot decide.

own with him, and raised these from the dead. You cannot name one. In Jerusalem they were eating the lamb of the Passover. They thought of Egypt, and they thought of Rome, but no one had seen Satan at the feast. It is not possible to see Satan among a crowd of seething human beings, unless a person has seen the Word of God made flesh. Thus he who bruised the heel of the Son remained hidden, because the Son was hidden. But the day will come in which Satan shall be released, because the Son is preparing for the last Parousia. And every eye shall see Him, also the eye of those who pierced Him; and every spirit shall know Him, also the spirit of those who reviled Him by their words in His glory, but who mourned for Him through the Spirit of grace and of prayers after they had loved Him. He will not reject them because of their dazed and groping search for words, and He will teach them all His secrets with His own gentle voice. But the mysteries of His altar He will announce at the joy of the mysteries of the table, for the altar of atonement will have become the table of communion. After every conversation He will say: This was spoken by Jesus Christ, but it was really God who spoke it.

O God, Thou didst never yet weep, and Thou didst not weep then. Thou shalt call Him blessed, Lord, who is not offended by such a God. At least He can endure having angels as His brothers. For they grow used to God, who daily storms in His rage, and laughs. And they were much amazed by the incarnate Word, who came to paradise on Good Friday. God Himself had become oppressed, perturbed, and moved to tears in that incarnate Word, and He had worked by faith and not by sight. But God the Lord had not changed. In Him there is no change, nor shadow of turning. So the angels testified with fear and trembling. Blessed is he who sees the right relationships at the right place, for he will not be offended by such an immutable God. And the right place is here, on Golgotha — on Golgotha, near the carefully guarded tomb.

THE END.